Matthias Burghardt

Retail Investor Sentiment and Behavior

GABLER RESEARCH

Matthias Burghardt

Retail Investor Sentiment and Behavior

An Empirical Analysis

GABLER

RESEARCH

Bibliographic information published by the Deutsche Nationalbibliothek
The Deutsche Nationalbibliothek lists this publication in the Deutsche Nationalbibliografie; detailed bibliographic data are available in the Internet at http://dnb.d-nb.de.

Dissertation Karlsruhe Institute of Technology, 2010

1st Edition 2011

Editorial Office: Stefanie Brich | Anita Wilke

Gabler Verlag is a brand of Springer Fachmedien.
Springer Fachmedien is part of Springer Science+Business Media.
www.gabler.de

Cover design: KünkelLopka Medienentwicklung, Heidelberg
Printed on acid-free paper
Printed in Germany

ISBN 978-3-8349-2713-2

Acknowledgements

I am indebted to many people for their support throughout the preparation of this thesis. In particular, I am grateful to my advisor Prof. Dr. Christof Weinhardt who gave me his support and advice while granting me the freedom to explore different ways to combine academic rigor and practical relevance in interdisciplinary research.

In addition, I would like to thank Prof. Dr. Marliese Uhrig-Homburg for co-advising this thesis. My thanks also go to Prof. Dr. Ute Werner and Prof. Dr. Ingrid Ott for serving on the board of examiners.

I would like to thank my colleagues from the research group Information and Market Engineering at the Institute of Information Systems and Management (IISM) for many fruitful discussions and their valuable comments. I am grateful to Dr. Henner Gimpel who was always ready to discuss problems with me and to share his ideas how to solve them. I also thank Dr. Stefan Seifert for his advice on the direction of this work. Many thanks also go to Dr. Ryan Riordan for being my co-author on many papers and for providing me with encouragement and support. Ryan Riordan and Martin Wagener deserve special thanks for proofreading major parts of the thesis and for providing me with constructive comments.

Parts of this research have been done while I enjoyed the hospitality of London Business School. I am grateful to Prof. Bruce Weber who made this possible.

Finally, I would like to express my gratitude to Oliver Hans, Dr. Christoph Mura, and Christoph Lammersdorf for their constant support while I was a research fellow at Boerse Stuttgart. This work would not have been possible without their commitment and dedication to this project.

Matthias Burghardt

Table of Contents

Abbreviations

AAII	American Association of Individual Investors
ADV/DEC	Advances/Declines Ratio
ADV-DEC	Advances minus Declines
ASX	Australian Stock Exchange
CAUD	Consolidated Equity Audit Trail Data
CBOE	Chicago Board Options Exchange
CCI	Consumer Confidence Index
CEFA	Closed-End Funds Association
CEFD	Closed-End Funds Discount
CEFD	Closed-End Funds Discount
col.	column
DAX	Deutscher Aktienindex
DJIA	Dow Jones Industrial Average
e.g.	for example
EMH	Efficient Markets Hypothesis
et al.	et alii
EUWAX	European Warrant Exchange
G-Mind	German Market Indicator
i.e.	that is
ICE	Index of Consumer Expectations
ICS	Index of Consumer Sentiment
II	Investors' Intelligence
IPO	Initial Public Offering
ISE	International Securities Exchange
ISSM	Institute for the Study of Security Markets
LSV	Lakonishok, Shleifer, and Vishny (1992)
MSH	Morgan Stanley High-Tech Index
NASDAQ	National Association of Securities Dealers Automated Quotations
NAV	net asset value
NYSE	New York Stock Exchange
p/c	put/call ratio
REX	Rentenindex
S&P	Standard & Poor's
SMH	Signed Market Level Herding
TAQ	Trade and Quote database
TRIN	Traders Index

U.S.	United States
UBS	Union Bank of Switzerland
UMH	Unsigned Market Level Herding
VAR	Vector autoregression
VDAX	Volatility DAX
VIX	Volatility Index
VWD	volume-weighted discount index
ZEW	Zentrum für Europäische Wirtschaftsforschung

List of Figures

List of Tables

1 Introduction

"It has long been market folklore that the best time to buy stocks is when individual investors are bearish, and the best time to sell is when individual investors are bullish."

Robert Neal and Simon Wheatley (1998), p.523

This citation by Robert Neal and Simon Wheatley from their 1998 article about investor sentiment offers several insights and paves the way for this first chapter by making the following statements: First, the opinion of individual investors on the market is important. Second, they are often wrong. Third, individual investor sentiment may support market timing decisions. Fourth, none of the above is scientifically proven.

In this chapter, research about retail investor sentiment in general and the research questions addressed in this thesis in particular are motivated. In addition, the structure of the work as well as the main contributions and related publications are presented.

1.1. Motivation

The financial crisis of the year 2008 has lead retail investors to increase their trading activities. As the Financial Times reported, "US retail investors have been trading stocks and options at record levels in recent months, apparently responding to the financial crisis by taking greater control of their own investments"[1]. The reason for this increased level of trading activity is likely that retail investors want to "take more direct control of their investing, and make decisions themselves about how to rebalance their accounts".

Retail investor trading has become more and more important for financial institutions, especially during times of crisis: Retail investor orders can provide liquidity to financial institutions and represent a relatively constant source of income for order flow providers.

However, retail investors are often regarded as the "dumb money"[2], meaning that their reallocations reduce their wealth on average. The actions of retail investors often serve as contrary indicators in the sense that trading against these indicators would result in profit opportunities. In research, however, no unanimous conclusion has been reached yet. In recent years, several research articles[3] have been published indicating that certain groups of retail

---

1 Deborah Brewster, "Retail investors trading at record levels", Financial Times, November 4, 2008.

2 See e.g. Frazzini and Lamont (2008), p. 300.

3 See e.g. Jackson (2003), Dorn, Huberman, and Sengmueller (2008), Barber, Odean, and Zhu (2009a), Kaniel, Saar, and Titman (2008).

investors could be right in their trading decisions, and that their trading could serve as a positive indicator.

Apart from whether retail investors represent the "dumb money" or the "smart money", the fact that trading by retail investors is correlated is equally important. If retail investors trade in concert, their price impact on the market can be much larger than if they traded independently. Therefore, it is important for market participants to assess retail investor trading and understand their trading behavior.

Retail investor trading is largely driven by sentiment. As opposed to institutional trading which usually relies on professional analyses, tools, and expert opinions, retail investors are said to trade on noise, i.e. information that is not based on fundamental facts but on historical information, or especially attention-grabbing news. In particular, retail investors are especially prone to biases and usually make the same mistakes.

Now, the question is no longer whether retail investor sentiment is important, but rather how to measure investor sentiment correctly. In research and practice, lots of sentiment indicators have been developed or recognized as such. These indicators are usually based on different methodologies, have different underlying data sets, target different retail investors, and are used for different purposes. As of today, there is no universal measure of investor sentiment that is agreed-upon by academics and practitioners, and there is strong doubt that one indicator will establish as a generally accepted sentiment measure because all measures have distinct advantages and disadvantages.

In this work, a unique data set from the European Warrant Exchange at Boerse Stuttgart provides the opportunity to construct a new sentiment indicator and test its properties. Rather than analyzing historical time series of established sentiment indicators, it is possible to isolate the effects of certain orders, products, or brokers and therefore provide new insight on the topic while avoiding the disadvantages of other measures.

Using the sentiment indicator developed in this work, it is shown that retail investors trade in a correlated way and that their trading exhibits strong signs of herding behavior. The sentiment index, constructed from retail order flow data in leverage certificates, exhibits a large negative correlation to the market indicating that the retail investors represented by the sentiment indicator are on average contrarian investors. Finally, a trading strategy developed using the sentiment index is able to generate abnormal returns.

1.2. Research Outline

The Efficient Markets Hypothesis (EMH) has been the central theory in finance for the last 40 years (Fama 1970). Since its inception, academics have tried to challenge the EMH on many grounds. In particular, its theoretical assumptions about the behavior of individual investors are frequently called into question: First, the rationality of investors, second, the irrelevance of irrational investors, and third, perfectly working arbitrage.

The search for contradicting evidence which has started in the 1980s (e.g. Grossman and Stiglitz (1980) on the impossibility of informationally efficient markets) has consequently led to the emergence of a new field of research – behavioral finance. This field aims to integrate insights from psychology with neo-classical economic theory and rests on two major assumptions: Limited arbitrage and investor sentiment.

Investor sentiment is therefore one of the pillars of behavioral finance. It is defined as the theory of how individuals form their beliefs about the market and future securities prices. In the real world, investors make decisions not only based on simple facts and obvious information but also – and very often – on the basis of their gut-feeling, of comments and opinions of other investors, and psychological traits. Retail investors are often regarded as so-called noise traders: They trade on noise as if it were information, and thereby introduce inefficiency into the trading process. Knowing how investor sentiment is formed and what factors influence investor sentiment is important for academics as well as practitioners to assess market efficiency.

However, measurement of sentiment is difficult: In research as well as practice, many investor sentiment indicators exist that aim to accurately measure investor sentiment. There are different methods of measurement and consequently different outcomes that all have distinctive advantages and disadvantages. This leads to the first research question of this thesis:

> *Research Question 1:*
>
> How can investor sentiment be measured and how are different sentiment indicators related?

The first part of the question warrants an enumeration and a classification of existing sentiment measures in research and practice. The answer to the second part involves an analysis how sentiment measures can be evaluated and compared with each other, and how they are related to other market parameters such as returns and volatility.

As the results show, each of the sentiment measure categories has its advantages and disadvantages. Survey-based measures, on the one hand, have the disadvantage that they are costly to generate (an infrastructure is needed with a sufficient participant base which must be constantly maintained), that they can't be collected as frequent as market data based measures, and finally that people not always do what they say, and that sentiment measures therefore do not express real investor sentiment. Market data based measures, on the other hand, require a theory relating them to investor sentiment – and therefore their interpretation is more difficult.

When asked – while I was research assistant at Boerse Stuttgart – to help creating a measure of retail investor sentiment, I instantly thought of an order imbalance measure based on all retail investor orders submitted to Boerse Stuttgart, in particular to EUWAX, the market segment for securitized derivatives.

In research, measures that are based on order imbalances often have serious problems: Sometimes, measures do not distinguish between buy and sell orders because the data set they are based on does not allow a classification of investor types. Therefore, there must be a sell order for each buy order, and an order imbalance measure can only be created by distinguishing which order initiated the trade. This is often done by an algorithm which does not lead to an exact classification of orders. But there is another problem: Many existing measures do not focus on retail investors alone but include all orders executed on an exchange, such as the NYSE or NASDAQ. In order to separate retail order flow from the rest, trade size classifications or a focus on small firm stocks are used assuming that retail investors rather trade small sizes or small stocks, respectively. However, in today's times of algorithmic trading, trade sizes continue to decrease, and a separation of retail from institutional order flow becomes more and more difficult.

Imbalance measures that accurately distinguish between retail and institutional orders have other probable drawbacks: Retail investors usually do not have the possibility to sell stocks short to express negative sentiment. Due to this asymmetry of positive and negative sentiment expression, any measure based on such data would be biased.

The most recent academic literature about order imbalance measures mentions other possible problems for the interpretation of investor sentiment: A common result found in many related articles is that retail investors follow a contrarian strategy, i.e. they buy when stocks have decreased in value, and they sell when stock prices have risen. However, this negative correlation could possibly be the result of the automatic execution of stale limit orders in the order book – without retail investors' intervention. Therefore, a distinction between limit and market orders is important. Another solution to this problem – without the necessity to distinguish limit and market orders – is the use of the order submission time, regardless of whether the order is actually executed at some point in the future.

The task at Boerse Stuttgart therefore provided me with the opportunity to construct a retail sentiment index with data that has not been used by any researcher before, and at the same time to avoid known problems and shortcomings of existing sentiment measures. Consequently, the second research question involves developing the index and analyzing its properties.

Research Question 2:

Can an index be created from retail order flow data to describe investor sentiment?

This research question actually consists of two parts: First, appropriate data has to be collected and the index has to be calculated. The second part of the question warrants an analysis what properties a good sentiment index *should* have. It turns out that this is not an easy answer.

It can be argued that since investor sentiment incorporates investors' expectations and opinions about the market, sentiment measures and market returns should be correlated. In addition, a measure that is based on retail investor orders in index certificates should have a strong relation to market returns. Apart from market returns, the sentiment index should also have relations to other sentiment indexes since they may all pick up the same sentiment signals.

In the course of constructing the index, it is possible to determine the influence of certain parameters on the result, e.g. the difference between an order based measure and a volume based measure, the distinction of different product types, volume groups, order types, and option leverage. Finally, the data set allows to investigate the use of submitted orders for index construction rather than executed orders.

The data used to construct the Euwax Sentiment Index can be used to assess the behavior of retail investors. One of the most important questions in light of behavioral finance research is whether the trading of retail investors is correlated. If this is supported by the data, one of the assumptions of the EMH is seriously challenged, namely that noise traders' actions cancel each other out. However, if retail investors have the same opinion about market conditions and their trades are correlated, they may actually influence market prices.

Often, the term *herding* is used to describe a behavior that involves that retail investors buy (sell) simultaneously the same assets as others buy (sell). In research, there is no universally accepted definition of herding, and the term is used for different behaviors and different groups of investors. The first academic article about herding involves parallel trading by institutional investors (Kraus and Stoll 1972), and in the development of this strand of research, most of the work is concerned with professional behavior (e.g. the behavior of fund managers).

The availability of retail investor data and the construction of a single measure of retail investor sentiment warrant the analysis whether retail investors exhibit herding behavior which leads to the third research question.

> *Research Question 3:*
>
> Do retail investors herd?

Regardless of whether the retail investors at Boerse Stuttgart are representative of the whole population of retail investors, the analysis of their herding behavior is nevertheless interesting: Retail investors' trades are possibly correlated and their behavior is based on similar decision making activities.

Answering this research question involves two parts: First, market-wide herding must be investigated, i.e. the phenomenon that retail investors have the same opinion about the market at the same time. Second, stock-level herding is to be analyzed, i.e. the tendency of retail investors to invest in the same underlyings at the same time. This analysis can also be used to compare the findings with related herding literature.

The evidence of correlated behavior among retail investors further supports the assumption that retail investors' trades influence asset prices. As a natural consequence, the question to ask is whether a sentiment indicator reflecting retail investor sentiment is of any use for other investors.

Apart from the fact that knowing what other investors do may give individuals some affirmation regarding their own investment decisions, it has still to be established whether investors could use the sentiment indicator as a trading signal – either for imitating the other investors' trades or positioning themselves against them. This leads to the last and maybe most important research question of this thesis.

Research Question 4:

Does sentiment predict returns?

There are many attempts and methodologies that can be used to get an answer to this question. To analyze whether a sentiment indicator can be used to generate abnormal returns, a portfolio construction methodology is employed similar to those used in related literature[4]. Such a portfolio construction methodology has the advantage that historical data is used to simulate the returns of a trading strategy, and that only extreme sentiment readings are used to determine the assets that should be included in the portfolios.

The use of the Euwax data set makes it possible to disentangle effects caused by different product or order types, and investigate the use of submitted orders in index construction.

To get meaningful results, factors such as market returns, momentum, and market capitalization must be controlled for. In fact, a distinction by market capitalization of the underlying companies is necessary to control for the "small minus big" effect. In addition, the separate treatment of large and small cap firms is warranted by related behavioral finance research which indicates that noise traders have the biggest influence on stocks which are difficult to arbitrage and which most probably get their attention – both assumptions lead to small firms.

[4] See e.g. Kaniel, Saar, and Titman (2008) or Dorn, Huberman, and Sengmueller (2008).

1.3. Overview and Structure

The thesis is structured as depicted in Figure 1.1 below.

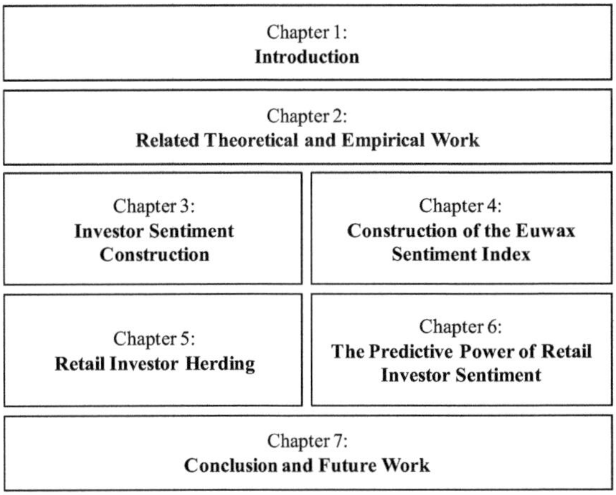

Figure 1.1: Thesis Structure

Chapter 1 motivates the research, develops the research questions, and presents an overview and the structure of the thesis as well as related publications.

Chapter 2 provides an overview of the main ideas of behavioral finance, and the most important theoretical and empirical work. The focus lies on the comparison, reconciliation, and discussion of the empirical findings.

Chapter 3 presents a classification of sentiment measures and an overview of sentiment measures used in research and practice. A particular emphasis lies on the history of the closed-end funds discount because of its importance in the financial literature. In addition, for each of the sentiment measures used in practice, a graphical presentation is shown along with related research and its main findings. Finally, the evaluation of existing sentiment indicators involves the comparison of direct and indirect measures as well as the relation of sentiment measures to market returns.

In Chapter 4, the construction of the Euwax Sentiment Index is described including the description of the unique data set used, a graphical illustration of the index, and a series of multivariate regressions analyzing the different components of retail order flow. In relation to the results of Chapter 3, the new index is compared to existing measures in research and practice.

Chapter 5 is about retail investor herding. Following an overview of herding definitions and empirical findings in the related literature, empirical results regarding retail investor herding are presented in three parts: First, evidence of market-wide herding is presented involving the examination of different market periods. Second, market-wide herding on a broker level is investigated, i.e. whether retail investors at different brokerages show the same herding behavior. Third, retail investor herding on a stock-level is analyzed to relate the findings to existing literature.

In Chapter 6, the trading strategy based on Euwax Sentiment measures is being developed. This strategy consists of buying high sentiment stocks and selling low sentiment stocks resulting in a zero-cost portfolio. The influence of product and order types is being discussed as well as the difference between using executed and submitted orders. Finally, the optimal holding period for this portfolio strategy is determined using historical data for a period of 5 years.

Chapter 7 concludes this thesis, summarizes the key contributions, and briefly outlines avenues of future research.

1.4. Related Publications

Parts of this thesis have been published and presented at various academic conferences and workshops.

At the very beginning of my research involving investor sentiment measures, I presented the general idea of creating retail investor sentiment measures for investment decision making at the Conference of Group Decision and Negotiation in Montreal, Canada (Burghardt 2007). A much more detailed extended version of this work co-authored by my colleague Ryan Riordan was presented at the Annual Conference of the Northern Finance Association (NFA) in Toronto, Canada, in fall 2007 and at the Campus for Finance Research Conference in Vallendar, Germany, in January 2008.

The retail investor sentiment construction presented in chapter 4 was presented at the 11th Symposium on Finance, Banking, and Insurance in Karlsruhe and at the FinanceCom in Paris, France (Burghardt and Riordan 2009), both held in December 2008.

Finally, a preliminary version of the herding behavior described in chapter 5 was presented at the FMA 2009 European Meeting in Turin, Italy, co-authored by our visiting research fellow Anshu Ankolekar.

The intention of this thesis is to combine this work as well as the relevant related research and present a structured and sound overview of the research involving retail investor sentiment. Furthermore, the relationship between theory and empirical results is discussed with a focus on the empirical data provided by our industry partner Boerse Stuttgart. Finally, avenues for future research are explored.

2 Related Theoretical and Empirical Work

"The assumptions of the EMH rule out the possibility of trading systems based only on information that have expected profits or returns in excess of equilibrium expected profits or returns."

Eugene F. Fama (1970), p.384

In recent years, many non-arbitrage algorithmic trading systems have been emerged that rely on the idea of trend-following as do many hedge funds. A relatively recent trend, both in financial research and industrial practice, has been the development of increasingly sophisticated automated trading strategies. Fama's statement from 1970 is obviously opposed to this development – and maybe it should be acknowledged that markets sometimes are not efficient at all.

In this chapter, an overview of the Efficient Markets Hypothesis (EMH) is given together with a summary of its theoretical assumptions. The most important theoretical and empirical challenges are presented in section 2.1 which have eventually led to the emergence of the Behavioral Finance. In section 2.2 and 2.3, related theoretical and empirical work is presented. More detailed discussions of the related work are included in the following chapters when appropriate. Finally, the focus of section 2.4 lies on the comparison, reconciliation, and discussion of the empirical findings. Section 2.5 concludes.

2.1. Introduction to Behavioral Finance

2.1.1. Are Financial Markets Efficient?

The EMH has been the central theory in finance for the last 40 years. In general terms, the theory of efficient markets is concerned with "whether prices at any point in time fully reflect available information" (Fama 1970, p. 383).

Theoretical Assumptions of the EMH

The EMH is based on three assumptions about the behavior of individual investors. First, investors are assumed to be rational and hence value securities rationally. Second, if there are investors that do not act fully rational, then the actions of these irrational investors take effect in opposite directions and therefore cancel each other out. Third, if there are actions by irrational investors that take effect in the same direction, there are enough rational arbitrageurs whose actions bring prices back to the fundamental level.

The first assumption means that all investors value each security for its fundamental value by using the net present value of its future cash flows discounted by known risk factors. When new information about future earnings emerges, investors respond to this new information by adjusting their valuation of the company and hence bidding prices up or down. These prices therefore fully reflect all relevant information which is available to all investors.

The second assumption acknowledges that there are investors that do not react rationally to new information. In this case, it is assumed that these investors trade randomly and that their trades are uncorrelated. Therefore, the trades of irrational investors cancel each other out and do not have any effect on the efficiency of the price formation process. Prices of securities remain at their fundamental values.

The third assumption concerns the situation when the trades of irrational investors are correlated and do not cancel each other out. In this case, the effect on prices could be significant and prices would not be at their fundamental values. It is then assumed that there are enough rational arbitrageurs[5] in the market that acknowledge the security's deviation from its fundamental value and bid prices up or down until the price reflects its fundamental value again. An example may clarify how arbitrage works: Suppose that the correlated trades of irrational investors have driven prices up and away from their fundamental values. Rational arbitrageurs acknowledge this situation and (short) sell the overvalued security. Since they do not want to bear any fundamental risk involved with this kind of security, they simultaneously have to buy an essentially similar security or substitute to hedge this risk. The effect of these selling activities by the arbitrageurs is to bring the overvalued security's price back to their fundamental value.

The EMH, by itself, is not a well-defined and empirically refutable hypothesis. As Lo (1997) puts it, "it is disarmingly simple to state, has far-reaching consequences for academic pursuits and business practice, and yet is surprisingly resilient to empirical proof or refutation." There is little consensus between the opinions about the EMH held in academia and industry. In academia, the EMH is widely supported and challenged at the same time. In practice, the EMH seems to be ignored by business practices such as stock-picking and technical analysis. However, the EMH is still regarded as one of the most important theories in finance for the last century.

Empirical Tests of the EMH

Empirical work on the EMH can be divided into three categories depending on the nature of the information of interest: Weak-form tests are concerned with whether historical price

[5] Arbitrage is defined as "buying an asset in one market at a lower price and selling an identical asset in another market at a higher price. This is done with no cost or risk" (Ross, Westerfield, Jaffe 2001).

sequences contain information that can be used to predict future returns. Semi-strong form tests include all obviously publicly available information while strong-form tests also include private information and test whether individuals with such information are able to use this information to their advantage.

When researchers began to test the various forms of the EMH, they broadly supported the theory. Evidence especially on the weak-form efficiency was entirely supportive. Fama (1965) finds that stock prices follow a random walk, i.e. they are as likely to rise after a previous day's increase as after a previous day's decline. Therefore, 'technical' trading strategies that incorporate buying recent winners and selling recent losers would not be profitable.

Tests of the semi-strong form of market efficiency usually use event-studies in which particular news events are studied and tested whether prices adjust to this news immediately or over a period of some days. Fama, Fisher, Jensen, and Roll (1969) present one of the first such studies to demonstrate that prices immediately adjust to new information and that there is no trending of prices after the news event. Therefore, investors cannot gain by using this information to predict returns.

The strong-form efficiency has not received such overwhelming empirical attention like the weak and the semi-strong form efficiency. Researchers seldom take the extreme position that it is not possible to make money by trading on inside information – a fact that is supported by insider traders' illegal trading activities.

2.1.2. Challenges to Efficient Markets

Theoretical Challenges to the EMH

Since its inception, academics have tried to challenge the EMH both theoretically and empirically.

One of the most cited arguments against the EMH is that people do not act fully rational and investors seldom follow the passive investment strategies expected of uninformed market participants as suggested by the EMH. There is a large body of literature that shows that investors are generally reluctant to realize their losses (Odean 1998), that they trade too much (Odean 1999), that they hold on to losing stocks and rather sell winning stocks (Shefrin and Statman 1985), and that especially retail investors actually lose money by trading (Barber, Lee, Liu, and Odean 2009).

Deviations from the expected behavior are highly systematic and even predictable. Deviations occur due to a number of reasons: First, individuals usually do not follow the concepts of the von Neumann-Morgenstern rationality theory and rather show preferences first discovered by Kahneman and Tversky (1979) in their prospect theory. For example, many people display loss aversion which means that their utility function for losses must be steeper than for their gains. Second, individuals do not follow the concepts of Bayes' rule for assessing the probability of a certain situation. For example, they put higher weight on recent events or overestimate events that somehow got their attention. The result is a biased perception of reality. Third, framing effects cause investors make different decisions depending on how a problem is presented to them. The theories of Kyle (1985) and Black (1986) rely on such behavior.

The critique of the previous paragraph is confronted with the assumption of the EMH that the actions of irrational investors take effect in the same direction and therefore cancel each other out. However, the theories by Kahneman and Tversky argue that people deviate in exactly the same way and their actions are highly correlated. Therefore, this line of defense used by the efficient markets theory could not threaten its opponents.

In addition to the rationality argument, there is the argument concerning effective arbitrage. Efficient markets proponents argue that even if individuals are not fully rational and even if their behavior is correlated, then the actions of rational arbitrageurs should bring prices back to fundamental values and markets remain efficient. However, opponents of the EMH argue that arbitrage in many cases is far from being riskless because close substitutes are often missing (Campbell and Kyle 1993). The interest of risk-averse arbitrageurs is then limited and arbitrage is therefore not as effective as assumed by the efficient markets theory.

The argument that both the irrational investors and the rational arbitrageurs face substantial risks alleviates Friedman's (1953) theory that only the irrational investors would eventually lose too much money and leave the market. Limited arbitrage can increase arbitrageurs' losses so they do not survive in the long run.

Empirical Challenges to the EMH

Empirical tests of the EMH designed to challenge its validity are plentiful. The first articles challenging the EMH empirically were written in the early 1980s but even today researchers try to find arguments against the various forms of the market efficiency hypothesis.

The weak form hypothesis has been subject of many articles trying to prove that there are ways to successfully predict security returns based on past price information. One of the first papers challenging the weak form is that of De Bondt and Thaler (1985) in which they construct stock portfolios of extreme winners and extreme losers over the past three years. They show that the loser portfolios outperform the winner portfolios for the next 5 years indicating that stock prices tend to overreact on average.

Another highly regarded finding challenging the weak form efficiency is stock price momentum. Jegadeesh and Titman (1993) find that – in contrast to the long-term trends identified by De Bondt and Thaler – stock prices tend to predict future short-term movements of up to 12 months in the same direction. In finance, stock price momentum has become a widely accepted source of risk and is now included in many risk-return models (Carhart 1997).

The semi-strong form hypothesis has been challenged by a number of empirical findings. In their seminal paper, Rozeff and Kinney (1976) find seasonal patterns in stock returns over a period of more than 70 years. They discovered the so-called 'January Effect' which states that the average monthly return for all NYSE stocks in January is 3.5% whereas other months average about 0.5%. Since small firms are overrepresented in an equal-weighted index, this effect is primarily a small firm phenomenon. Since both the month and the size of the firm are known in advance, excess returns should not occur in semi-strong form efficient markets.

Another challenge to the EMH is presented by findings that the market to book ratio of a company can predict future returns. Among others, Fama and French (1992) find that portfolios of companies with high market to book ratios ('growth firms') earn lower returns than portfolios of companies with low market to book ratios ('value firms'). Shleifer (2000) argues that this is a serious challenge to the EMH because stale information obviously helps predict returns and that excess returns are not due to higher risk as conventionally measured. Fama and French (1993), however, interpret both the size and the market to book ratio as risk factors and add them as additional factors to their Three-Factor-Model which has become a standard in the portfolio management industry. This interpretation as additional risk factors saved the validity of the EMH although this is still highly debated among researchers.

Many of the studies intended to challenge the EMH have been questioned on the grounds of data snooping, less attention to transaction costs, or an improper adjustment for risk factors as Fama criticizes. However, the search for disconfirming evidence which has begun in the 1980s as well as the theoretical doubt has eventually led to the creation of a new field of research – behavioral finance.

2.1.3. Emergence of Behavioral Finance

Behavioral Finance is the "study of human fallibility in competitive markets" (Shleifer 2000) and aims to integrate insights from psychology with neo-classical economic theory. It rests on two major assumptions, namely limited arbitrage and the presence of investor sentiment.

The first major foundation of behavioral finance is limited arbitrage. Arbitrage is defined as "the simultaneous purchase and sale of the same, or essentially similar, security in two different markets for advantageously different prices" (Sharpe and Alexander 1990). This means arbitrage is based on the valuation difference between the security and its substitute, i.e. an essentially similar security which possesses the same risk characteristics. In the real-world, however, many securities do not have close substitutes, making arbitrage more difficult if not impossible for rational investors. Moreover, even when good substitutes are available, prices often do not converge to their fundamental prices instantaneously because irrational traders continue to move prices further away. Arbitrageurs then face the risk that they have to liquidate their positions before prices converge to their fundamental values. Due to the short time horizon of arbitrageurs, arbitrage remains risky and is therefore limited resulting in inefficient prices.

The form of this inefficiency is affected by the second major foundation of behavioral finance, investor sentiment. Investor sentiment is the theory of how individuals actually form their beliefs about the market and future securities prices. In the real-world, investors make decisions not only on the basis of simple facts and obvious information but also – and very often – on the basis of their gut-feeling, comments and opinions of other investors, and many more psychological traits. Therefore, it is very important to assess which psychological biases have the greatest influence on decision-making in certain situations. The theory of investor sentiment tries to provide answers to this question.

Noise Trader Risk and Limited Arbitrage

"Noise causes markets to be somewhat inefficient, but often prevents us from taking advantage of inefficiencies." (Black 1986)

The definition of noise trading was first developed by Fischer Black in his seminal paper "Noise" from 1986 in which he refers to noise as opposed to information. Noise traders are people trading on noise as if it were information. In his definition they cannot expect to earn money from noise trading. He argues that without noise trading there would be very little trading in individual assets (this reasoning is in line with the "no trade theorem" by Milgrom and Stokey (1982)). However, with lots of noise traders in the market, it pays for those with information to trade. In Black's opinion, noise traders lose money most of the time, while information traders as a group make money.

According to Black (1986), determining whether a trader is a noise trader or an information trader is difficult: Noise trading puts noise in the prices, and information traders cannot be sure whether the information they have has already been reflected in the prices. If it has, then trading on this information is just like trading on noise. As a result, there is a lot of ambiguity on who is an information trader and who is a noise trader.

Before the discussion of the importance of noise trading and behavioral finance started in the 1980s, economists like Friedman (1953) and Fama (1965) ignored their influence on price formation because the existence of rational arbitrageurs would drive prices to fundamental values and noise traders out of the market. De Long, Shleifer, Summers, and Waldman (1990) examine these arguments and explicitly focus on the limits of arbitrage exploiting noise traders' misperceptions.

Arbitrage is a sophisticated form of risk-free speculation. Arbitrageurs – in the presence of noise traders – do bring prices to the fundamental values in line with the Friedman/Fama argument. However, this kind of arbitrage is not riskless: There is the risk that noise traders' beliefs will not revert to their mean for a long time and might in the meantime become even more extreme. De Long et al. (1990) call this source of risk noise trader risk. If noise traders are, for example, pessimistic about a security, they sell it and therefore drive its price down and below its fundamental value. Rational arbitrageurs buy the security and hope that its price recovers soon. If, however, more noise traders come into the market and continue selling the asset, arbitrageurs may be forced to liquidate their position in order to limit their losses. The fear of this loss limits their original arbitrage position in the first place.

The two main assumptions of limited arbitrage are that arbitrageurs are risk-averse and have reasonably short horizons. Assuming that arbitrageurs are rather risk-averse is intuitive since arbitrage is commonly defined as a riskless transaction. The second assumption about the short horizons of arbitrageurs can be justified by agency arguments: Since most arbitrageurs are assumed to manage not their own money but money from other investors, they are required to report positive results in relatively short periods of time. If a mispricing they have identified takes longer to vanish they may be forced by their investors to liquidate their positions at a loss. Interest payments on borrowed money even increase this problem.

Investor Sentiment

Investor sentiment is the theory of how investors form their beliefs. Barberis, Shleifer, and Vishny (1998) present a formal model which takes both the available empirical evidence as well as the known psychological theories of belief formation into account.

Their theory is based on the empirical observation of both overreaction and underreaction of investors inconsistent with the weak-form and the semi-strong form of the EMH. On the one hand, the underreaction evidence shows that security prices tend to underreact to news announcements: After good news, prices show an upwards trend after the initial price reaction, and after bad news, prices trend downwards indicating that they have not fully adjusted to the news. This phenomenon is also called momentum, i.e. the nature of prices to trend expressed by the positive autocorrelation of returns over relatively short horizons. The overreaction evidence, on the other hand, shows that over longer horizons security prices overreact, especially if there is a longer pattern of the same type of news. The study by De Bondt and Thaler (1985) as mentioned in section 2.1.1 is an example of overreaction: Investors overreact to a series of either good or bad news, and as a result, winners underperform and losers outperform in the following years. Eventually, prices revert to the mean after a period of exaggeration.

The model of Barberis, Shleifer, and Vishny (1998) is based on two main observations in psychology: conservatism and the representativeness heuristic. Conservatism is a phenomenon identified by Edwards (1968) that states that individuals are slow to change their beliefs in the face of new evidence. In particular, their beliefs are changed in the right direction as suggested by the Bayes Theorem but the change is too small in magnitude so that an underreaction to the new evidence is perceived. The second phenomenon is the representativeness heuristic discovered by Tversky and Kahneman (1974). People subject to this heuristic think that they see patterns in truly random sequences. They evaluate the probability of an event by the degree to which it is similar to other e.g. past events although past events may not be representative of future ones. For example, investors affected by this bias might conclude that firms with a consistent history of earning growth rates over the past several years continue to grow at the rate suggested by past earnings. As a consequence, investors disregard the possibility that earnings do not grow into the sky and eventually reverse.

2.2. Theoretical Work

In this section, five models involving noise trading or investor sentiment are presented. The purpose of this chapter is therefore to give an overview of the motivation, the structure, and the basic results of the theoretical work that shaped the behavioral finance.

Noise Trader Risk in Financial Markets

The model of De Long et al. (1990) was one of the first models that included noise traders in the calculation of market prices. They introduced the concept of the noise trader risk which has to be borne by arbitrageurs with a short time horizon.

The model is a simple overlapping generations model with two groups of agents: On the one hand, there are risk averse sophisticated investors with rational expectations, and on the other hand, there are noise traders with incorrect beliefs and irrational misperceptions. Agents have the choice between a safe asset with a fixed dividend and perfectly elastic supply, and an unsafe asset with the same fixed dividend but without elastic supply – it is in fixed and unchangeable quantity. Agents live two time periods. They choose their portfolios in the first period to maximize the perceived expected utility given their own beliefs about the mean of the distribution of the price in the second time period. The representative sophisticated investor accurately perceives the distribution of returns from holding the risky asset, and so maximizes expected utility given that distribution. The representative noise trader misperceives the expected price of the risky asset.

Noise traders in the model create an additional risk for all agents. The price of the risky asset depends on the direction and intensity of the next noise trader generation's misperception. The time horizon for the liquidation of the assets is very short since all agents have to sell their assets to the next generation in the second period.

One of the main contributions of the De Long et al. (1990) model is the interpretation of the rational arbitrageurs' decisions as a reaction to existing noise traders. In the model, it is rational to take future noise traders' sentiment into account when deciding about the own portfolio. Eventually, rational arbitrageurs trade not only on fundamental data but also on noise.

A Model of Investor Sentiment

Barberis, Shleifer, and Vishny (1998) present a model of investor sentiment[6] which explains phenomena of underreaction to new information as well as overreaction to either good or bad news because people tend to see familiar patterns.

The model incorporates one risk-neutral representative investor and one asset. The beliefs of this representative investor should be regarded as 'consensus beliefs' even when real investors' opinions are different. The investor's beliefs affect prices and returns.

The earnings of the asset follow a random walk. However, the representative investor believes that the behavior of earnings moves between two states (or regimes): In the first state, earnings are mean-reverting. That means e.g. upward price movements are followed by price declines with a high probability. In the second state, earnings trend, i.e. earnings tend to rise further after an increase and to decline after a drop. The probabilities for the change between two states, i.e. the transition probabilities, are fixed in the investor's mind. In any given period, the investor thinks that the firm's earnings are more likely to stay in the state they are in than to change to the other state. The investor then observes earnings and updates his beliefs according to the Bayes' model. In particular, he raises the likelihood that he is in the trending state if earnings increase in subsequent periods. On the other hand, the likelihood for the mean-reverting state is increased if good and bad earnings alternate.

The model describes an investor who does not know the true state of the world. His decision only depends on the observed results of the very last period. Conservatism leads to a slow reaction to new information. Overreaction to information is caused by the representativeness heuristic when this information follows a series of news with the same sign.

Investor Psychology and Security Market Under- and Overreaction

The model by Daniel, Hirshleifer, and Subrahmanyam (1998) presents a theory of an under- and overreaction of securities markets. It is based on investor overconfidence about the precision of private information on the one hand, and the underestimation of public signals.

In their model, each member of a continuous mass of agents is overconfident in the sense that if he receives a signal, he overestimates its precision. Not all agents, however, receive a signal in each time period. Those agents receiving a signal belong to the group of the informed whereas those who do not receive a signal belong to the group of the uninformed agents. Informed agents are risk neutral and uninformed agents are risk averse.

[6] This model has already been briefly mentioned in section 2.1.3.

Each agent is endowed with a securities portfolio at the beginning of the first period (there are three periods in total). At date 0, individuals begin with their endowments and identical prior beliefs. They trade solely for the purpose of optimal risk transfer. At date 1, the group of informed agents receives a noisy private signal about the underlying security value and trades with the uninformed. The informed agents underestimate the variance of the signal. The uninformed agents know that some agents have received a signal, and estimate the variance of this signal correctly. At date 2, a noisy public signal arrives and trading continues. This time, the signal variance is estimated correctly by the informed as well as the uninformed agents. Finally, at date 3, conclusive public information arrives, the security pays a liquidating dividend, and consumption occurs.

The central aspect of the model is that overconfidence regarding the private signal leads to an overreaction of the security's price to new information. In the long run, this overreaction is partially corrected so a long term price reversal can be explained. Furthermore, overconfidence of the agents leads to higher volatility, especially in period 1 in which the noisy private signal is perceived. In addition, price movements as a result of public information are positively correlated with future price movements.

To incorporate momentum in their model, Daniel, Hirshleifer, and Subrahmanyam (1998) expand their basic model by linking the agents' confidence to the success of their previous actions. A public signal confirms their choice if it points into the same direction. For example, if an agent buys an asset and later a positive signal confirms his choice, his confidence is strengthened. Therefore, overreaction can occur in periods 1 and 2 and a momentum effect can be observed.

A Unified Theory of Underreaction, Momentum Trading, and Overreaction in Asset Markets

Hong and Stein (1999) present a model in which two types of bounded rational traders – momentum traders and news watchers – interact. Effects involving under- and overreaction are not explained by phenomena from psychology but are solely a result of this interaction.

In their basic model, a risky asset is traded in each time period with a fixed dividend in the final time period. News watchers are bounded rational because they can observe only a part of the available information at one point in time. In addition, it is not possible for them to conclude any price information from each other's actions. Information regarding the final dividend is distributed in independent and non-overlapping parts such that the full information is distributed over several time periods. In contrast to the news watchers, momentum traders have a finite time horizon. They trade with the news watchers who act as competing market makers. Momentum traders follow a positive feedback strategy and solely trade on historic price information. Due to their bounded rationality, they are not capable to obtain a better prediction of the price by more sophisticated models.

The model has the following core contributions: First, the piece-wise distribution of information to the news watchers leads to an initial underreaction to incoming information. Momentum traders who want to profit from this underreaction and follow a positive feedback strategy, thereby cause the momentum effect and as a result an overreaction of the prices. Both under- and overreaction are therefore caused by the slow information diffusion. The model explains an underreaction of market prices in the short run and an overreaction in the long run. Eventually, the overreaction is reversed by the actions of the momentum traders and a correction can be observed.

Hong and Stein (1999) enhance their model by expanding the strategies of the momentum traders to increase the degree of rationality. They are now able to act not only as momentum traders but as contrarians. In addition, they can choose a better model to predict prices and base their decision on several past periods. However, it is shown that the results from the basic model still hold. Even with the addition of a third group of traders – the smart money – Hong and Stein (1999) still explain underreaction, the momentum effect and the resulting overreaction. Only if the smart money accepts infinite risks do prices follow a random walk.

Distinguishing between Rationales for Short-Horizon Predictability of Stock Returns

The model by Subrahmanyam (2005) is primarily concerned with short-horizon return reversals. He identifies two possible explanations in the literature: Some authors take the position that market microstructure phenomena (e.g. risk-aversion-related inventory effects or the bid-ask bounce) are the causes of these reversals. Other authors suggest that market overreaction and correction (belief reversion) drive the predictability of monthly returns.

Subrahmanyam (2005) presents an equilibrium model that incorporates both risk-aversion-related inventory phenomena as well as behavioral effects. In his model, risk averse agents absorb order flow from outside investors. A risky security is traded at dates 1 and 2, and pays off a random amount at date 3. There is a continuum of risk averse agents who absorb liquidity shocks that appear in the market. At date 2, each agent receives a signal. Part of the agents misassesses the variance of the signal as too low. This captures overreaction and correction in the model. A demand shock arrives at the market on date 2, and risk averse agents demand a premium to absorb it. Therefore, the security price has two components: The liquidity premium and the conditional expectation of the asset's value.

By capturing agents' beliefs as well as risk aversion, the model allows to obtain implications for the relation between current returns, past returns, and past order flows. The model indicates that risk-aversion-related inventory effects are accompanied by a relation between current returns and past order flows. However, no such relation can be found with respect to belief reversion. Subrahmanyam (2005) concludes – as other research indicates – that inventory effects do not appear to completely account for the return reversal usually found at a monthly horizon. His results accord with the notion that monthly reversals are caused, in substantial part, by reversals in beliefs of financial market agents.

2.3. Empirical Work

This section presents related empirical work regarding noise trading, investor sentiment, individual investors, and correlated trading. The purpose of this section is to give an overview of the important literature along these research fields. A more detailed review of the relevant work can be found in the literature sections of the respective chapters when appropriate.

2.3.1. Noise Traders

Since De Long et al. (1990) have researches tried to measure noise trading activity and investigate its impact on market quality. Often, market sentiment plays an important role in this research.

Brown (1999) argues that if noise traders affect prices and the resulting noise can be interpreted as sentiment causing systematic risk, i.e. additional volatility, then sentiment should be correlated with volatility. Sentiment is measured directly using the AAII Sentiment Survey, and the resulting risk is measured by the volatility of closed-end investment funds. Brown finds that unusual levels of investor sentiment are in fact associated with greater volatility of closed-end investment funds.

Beaumont et al. (2005) propose an integrated framework that jointly tests for the effects of individual as well as institutional sentiment on return and volatility. They use weekly direct measures of sentiment and relate them to stock returns and volatility. They find that individual investor sentiment is a market wide risk factor that does not only affect small cap stocks.

Berkman and Koch (2008) empirically study the influence of noise trading on market liquidity. They use the dispersion in daily net initiated order flow across brokers as a proxy for the level of noise trading in stocks traded at the Australian Stock Exchange (ASX). They find that market liquidity increases with the level of noise trading (i.e. greater trading volume, market depth, higher arrival rate of uninformed investors, lower spreads) and that the sensitivity of stock prices to net initiated order flow decreases in the level of noise trading.

Barber, Odean, and Zhu (2009b) investigate individual investor trading at two large brokers and measure the tendency to buy or sell the same set of stocks. They conclude that the buying and selling behavior of individual investors is systematic and individual investors therefore do have the potential to affect asset prices.

2.3.2. Investor Sentiment

There is a large body of literature that tries to relate measures of investor sentiment to volatility and returns in an attempt to analyze the impact of investor sentiment on asset prices. Most of them use direct measures of sentiment (see Chapter 3 for a more detailed overview).

Lee, Jiang, and Indro (2002) use the Investors' Intelligence sentiment to test the impact of noise trader risk on the formation of conditional volatility and expected returns. They explicitly jointly test the four behavioral effects as introduced in De Long et al. (1990) and find that shifts in sentiment are negatively correlated with market volatility.

Brown and Cliff (2004) explore the relation between investor sentiment and near-term stock returns in a vector autoregression framework. Although sentiment levels and changes are strongly correlated with contemporaneous market returns, they find that sentiment has little predictive power for near-term future stock returns. In a later article, Brown and Cliff (2005) use the Investors' Intelligence sentiment to test two hypotheses: First, excessive optimism leads to periods of market overvaluation. Second, high sentiment is followed by low cumulative long-run returns as prices revert to their fundamental level. Both hypotheses are supported by the results, and so Brown and Cliff (2005) – in contrast to their earlier paper – conclude that asset values are affected by investor sentiment.

Wang, Keswani, and Taylor (2006) investigate the relationships between sentiment, returns, and volatility. They explicitly test whether sentiment is useful for volatility forecasting purposes. By using different sentiment indicators (e.g. the put/call ratio, the ARMS index and survey measures), they find that most of these measures are caused by returns and volatility rather than vice versa.

Related research is not restricted to stock markets but extends to the futures and options markets as well: Han (2008) uses three sentiment proxies and examines whether they affect prices of the S&P 500 options. He presents evidence that investor sentiment helps explain both the shape of the S&P 500 option volatility smile, and the risk-neutral skewness of the index return extracted from the index option prices. Kurov (2008) uses the AAII and II sentiment measures and relates them to trading in the S&P 500 and Nasdaq E-mini futures markets. They show that index futures traders use positive feedback trading strategies, and that there is a positive relation between investor sentiment and the intensity of positive feedback trading.

2.3.3. Individual Investors

Research on the behavior of individual investors has started in the 1990s with the importance of individual investor trading on asset prices established by the noise trader theories of Black, Kyle, and De Long et al. De Bondt (1998) draws a portrait of the individual investor and reviews prior research.

Recent studies about individual investor behavior include Griffin, Harris, and Topaloglu (2003) who explore the dynamics of institutional and individual trading by classifying trading data for Nasdaq securities as originating from individuals, institutionals, and market makers. Coval, Hirshleifer, and Shumway (2005) analyze the transactions of individual investors at a large discount brokerage and evaluate the investors' trading performance. They provide evidence that some individual investors are able to persistently beat the market. Dorn and Huberman (2005) link individual investor performance to survey results and find a relation between self-reported risk-aversion and actual portfolio volatility.

Barber, Lee, Liu, and Odean (2005) draw a less positive portrait of the individual investor: Using day trading data from Taiwan they find that the profits of day traders are not sufficient to cover their transaction costs. Only a relatively small group of day traders are actually able to earn consistently strong returns. In a later paper involving the same data set from Taiwan, Barber, Lee, Liu, and Odean (2008) find that virtually all individual trading losses can be traced to their use of aggressive orders.

2.3.4. Correlated Trading

Since the discovery of individual investors in the context of noise trading, researchers have tried to empirically measure the behavior of individual investors. In particular, they have tried to show that individual investors buy and sell stocks in concert and that this behavior has a significant impact on asset prices.

One of the most straightforward methods to measure the behavior of individual investors is the creation of order imbalance measures. Order imbalance measures put the buying and selling of individual investors into proportion and aggregate it to a single ratio which can then be compared to other key indicators such as stock returns or volatility. In particular, order imbalances can signal excessive investor interest in a stock, and if this interest is autocorrelated, then order imbalances could be related to future returns. However, order imbalance measures only work if it is possible to separate a subgroup of investors and measure the order imbalance of this subgroup. Otherwise, there would be the "for every buyer, there's a seller" argument which would make it impossible to calculate imbalance measures.

Traditionally, volume has provided the link between trading activity and returns in the literature. Chordia, Roll, and Subrahmanyam (2002) (and subsequently Chordia and Subrahmanyam (2004)) are among the first to explore an order imbalance measure and analyze long-term order imbalances on a comprehensive cross-sectional sample of NYSE stocks. Jackson (2003) focuses on retail transactions and creates an order imbalance measure for individual investors in Australia. Kumar and Lee (2006) develop a buy-sell-imbalance measure using retail investor transactions. They are among the first to empirically support a role for investor sentiment in the formation of returns.

Pan and Poteshman (2006) analyze options trading data and construct a put/call ratio from option volume initiated by buyers to open new positions. Their work is unique in that they empirically transfer the concept of information trading in the options market. Andrade, Chang, and Seasholes (2008) examine changes in margin holdings by individual investors on the Taiwan Stock Exchange. They find that weekly changes in margin holdings correlate positively with contemporaneous returns and negatively with returns over subsequent weeks.

More recently, there are several papers analyzing individual investors' trading behavior by creating order imbalance measures: Dorn, Huberman, and Sengmueller (2008) use the data set of a large German discount broker to construct a herding measure which shows that retail investors tend to be on the same side of the market in a given stock. Schmitz, Glaser, and Weber (2007) also use data of a German discount broker and construct an imbalance measure for warrant investors. Using exchange data on individual investors, Kaniel, Saar, and Titman (2008), Barber, Odean, and Zhu (2009a), and Hvidkjaer (2008) – in contemporaneous research – construct imbalance measures and analyze the dynamic relation between net individual investor trading and short-horizon stock returns. Subrahmanyam (2008) provides a longer-term perspective on lagged order flows and returns by studying a large sample of NYSE stocks and relates it primarily to inventory effects. Boehmer and Wu (2008) use a unique data set from the New York Stock Exchange which enables them to differentiate between order imbalances of institutions, market makers, and individuals.

2.4. Discussion

2.4.1. Behavioral Finance

Behavioral finance as a new research field is as intensely debated as its counterpart, the theory of efficient markets. There are at least as many opponents to the emergence of the behavioral finance as there are critics of the EMH.

Behavioral finance emerged because traditional finance appears to play a limited role in understanding questions especially regarding individual investors, such as a) why individual investors trade, b) how they form their expectations, or c) how they perform. In the consequence, behavioral finance literature has addressed questions such as a) what mistakes to avoid when trading or b) how to develop strategies that generate superior returns (Subrahmanyam 2007).

In general, opponents of the behavioral finance usually offer the same objections: First, behavioral finance is said to create ad-hoc models explaining specific stylized facts and thereby failing to provide a general theory. Second, behavioral finance research is said to be subject to data mining because researchers are focused on finding deviations from traditional finance models. Third, it is claimed that behavioral finance does not present a unified theory (e.g. utility maximization using rational beliefs).

The main reason why the behavioral finance fails to satisfy the requirements of traditional finance researchers is that it is a "positive" theory, i.e. a theory that explains how people behave rather than how people should behave. In contrast, "normative" theories are based on rational economics and concepts whose empirical support appears to be limited. Subrahmanyam (2007) concludes that "the evidence in favor of inefficient financial markets is far more compelling than that in favor of efficient ones" (p. 18).

In contrast, Fama (1998) argues that "market efficiency survives the challenge from the literature on long-term anomalies" (p. 283). He bases his arguments on two observations: First, many of the studies on long-term returns that suggest market inefficiency establish underreaction or overreaction. Fama (1998), however, argues that these anomalies are consistent with market efficiency if they are split randomly between under- and overreaction. In other words, underreaction will be as frequent as overreaction in an efficient market. Second, he finds that the long-term anomalies described in the literature are sensitive to methodology. In particular, they may completely disappear when different statistical approaches are used to measure them or when other models for expected returns are taken into consideration.

Fama (1998) also criticizes that the studies challenging market efficiency rarely test a specific alternative to market efficiency. Rather than presenting an alternative theory that can be tested they merely dispute market efficiency. Market efficiency could only be replaced by a better model of price formation that itself would then be potentially rejectable by empirical tests. Fama explicitly acknowledges the work of Barberis, Shleifer, and Vishny (1998) and that of Daniel, Hirshleifer, and Subrahmanyam (1997) because both present rejectable hypotheses. He concludes, however, that the models do well on the anomalies they are designed to explain. But their prediction of long-term reversal would not capture the long-term results observed in the literature. Fama predicts that "we will soon see a menu of behavioral models that can be mixed and matched to explain specific anomalies" (p. 291).

2.4.2. Correlated Trading

Section 2.3 has shown that there is a growing amount of literature about individual investors, their behavior, and especially their correlated trading. Retail investors obviously have an ability to forecast future returns, although the explanation for this finding is still to be explored. Most scholars admit that "some individuals behave foolishly all the time and all individuals behave foolishly some of the time" (Chordia, Roll, Subrahmanyam 2005, p. 272).

Table 2.1: Overview of Empirical Work on Trading Imbalances

This table summarizes recent empirical papers about correlated trading and trading imbalances. Data sources, periods, and frequency are shown in columns 2 to 4, Signing in column 5 refers to how buy and sell orders are separated, Measure in column 6 shows the measures developed in the respective papers, Target group in column 7 compares different investor groups as indentified in the papers, and Order type in the last column indicates whether different order types are distinguished.

Article	Data source	Period	Frequency	Signing	Measure	Target group	Order type
Andrade, Chang, and Seasholes (2008)	Taiwan Stock Exchange	1994-2002	weekly	exact	change in shares held in margin accounts	individual investors	all order types
Barber, Lee, Liu, and Odean (2005)	Taiwan Stock Exchange	1995-1999	daily	exact	trading volume	individual investors, day traders	passive and aggressive orders
Barber, Lee, Liu, and Odean (2008)	Taiwan Stock Exchange	1995-1999	daily	exact	trading volume	individual investors	passive and aggressive orders
Barber, Odean, and Zhu (2009a)	NYSE, Amex, Nasdaq (ISSM, TAQ)	1983-2001	monthly, weekly	Lee and Ready	number of small buyer-initiated trades	small orders	market orders only
Barber, Odean, and Zhu (2009b)	two large U.S. discount and retail brokers	1991-1999	monthly	exact	number of trades	individual investors	all order types
Berkman and Koch (2008)	ASX	1991-1994	daily	n/a	trading volume	all investors	market orders only
Boehmer and Wu (2008)	NYSE (CAUD)	2000-2004	daily	exact	number of transactions, shares, and dollars	six account types	all order types
Chordia and Subrahmanyam (2004)	NYSE (ISSM, TAQ)	1988-1998	daily	Lee and Ready	volume and number of transactions	all investors	market orders only
Chordia, Roll, and Subrahmanyam (2002)	NYSE (ISSM, TAQ)	1988-1998	daily	Lee and Ready	number of transactions, shares, and dollars	all investors	market orders only
Dorn, Huberman, and Sengmueller (2008)	German Discount Broker	1998-2000	daily	exact	number of shares traded	individual investors	market and limit orders
Griffin, Harris, and Topaloglu (2003)	Nasdaq 100	2000-2001	daily	exact	trading volume	retail, institutional, market maker	all order types
Hvidkjaer (2008)	NYSE, Amex, Nasdaq (ISSM, TAQ)	1983-2005	monthly	Lee and Ready	signed small trade turnover (SSTT)	small trades by size proxy	market orders only
Jackson (2003)	ASX (56 brokers)	1991-2002	weekly	exact	trading volume	individual investors	all order types
Kaniel, Saar, and Titman (2008)	NYSE (CAUD)	2000-2003	daily, weekly	exact	trading volume	individual investors	all order types
Kumar and Lee (2006)	U.S. discount brokerage firm	1991-1996	monthly	exact	trading volume	individual investors	all order types
Pan and Poteshman (2006)	CBOE	1990-2001	daily	exact	trading volume	four investor classes	all order types
Schmitz, Glaser, and Weber (2007)	German Discount Broker	1997-2001	daily	exact	buyers ratio	individual investors	all order types
Subrahmanyam (2008)	NYSE (ISSM, TAQ)	1988-2002	monthly	Lee and Ready	trading volume	all investors	market orders only

This section presents an overview of the empirical research about correlated trading and identifies differences among the respective papers while trying to summarize and reconcile them. Table 2.1 presents an overview of the individual papers and provides summaries of data sources, periods, data frequency, and details how the order imbalance measures are constructed and what kind of data is used for that. There are some crucial differences among the papers concerning the source of the data, its frequency and period, regional focus, target group, and the construction of the imbalance measure.

Data Sources

There are several kinds of data sources that are used for individual investor research: First, researchers use proprietary data sets from brokers that reveal customer transactions as well as customer holdings on an anonymous account level. These data sets allow for the analysis of customer profitability, holding periods, and imbalance measures on the basis of individual investors. In particular, imbalance measures such as the percentage of investors that are net buyers (buyers ratio) can be calculated.

Second, proprietary stock exchange data is used including transactions from several different brokers but seldom on an account level. Therefore, measures such as the buyer ratio cannot be calculated. There are exceptions such as the Taiwan Stock Exchange whose data reveals transactions on an individual investor level. For this reason, researchers such as Andrade, Chang, and Seasholes (2008) and Barber, Lee, Liu, and Odean (2009) have made extensive studies in this market. Boehmer and Wu (2008) and Kaniel, Saar, and Titman (2008) both use the proprietary Consolidated Equity Audit Trail Data (CAUD) provided by the New York Stock Exchange that includes information whether the order originates from an institution or an individual.

Third, publicly available exchange data can be used to infer order imbalance measures. This methodology is the least reliable methodology but is used by several authors due to the availability of the data. It has some drawbacks: The sign of the trade has to be inferred in order to distinguish aggressive from passive orders. Usually, the Lee and Ready (1991) algorithm is used to sign transactions. In addition, if the target is the individual investor, trades have to be sorted by trade size to distinguish the different investor groups such as individual investors and institutionals.

Signing

Five of the articles mentioned in Table 2.1 use the Lee and Ready (1991) algorithm to identify the side of the trade. Rather than distinguishing orders by order type or investor group, order imbalances are defined in terms of order aggressiveness. Based on this algorithm, a trade executed at a price higher than the prevailing quote midpoint is classified as buyer-initiated. If the transaction price equals the quote midpoint, it is classified as buyer-initiated if the transaction price is above the previous transaction price. Seller-initiated orders are defined analogously.

This signing procedure seeks to identify the active side of the trade which is willing to pay a premium over the quote midpoint. In practice, aggressive orders are likely to be market orders or marketable limit orders whereas passive orders are usually limit orders or market maker orders. Order imbalances based on this algorithm count only the initiating side of the trade and, therefore, provide a measure of the relative impatience of buyers and sellers.

The correctness of the Lee and Ready (1991) algorithm, however, is controversial: Lee and Radhakrishna (2000) show that 40% of NYSE trades cannot be classified at all, and 7% of the remaining trades are not classified correctly. On the other hand, Barber, Odean, and Zhu (2009a) find that order imbalance measures based on buyer- and seller-initiated small trades from the TAQ/ISSM data base correlate well with order imbalance measures based on trades of individual investors from proprietary brokerage data. They conclude that small trades signed by the Lee and Ready (1991) algorithm are reasonable proxies for the trades of individual investors.

Whether the signing algorithm leads to a reasonable measure of order imbalance or whether an exact classification should be preferred – fact is that these different methodologies probably lead to different results which have to be interpreted as such.

Regional Differences

There are certainly differences among the behaviors of individual investors in different parts of the world. For example, individual investors in Taiwan may show a totally different behavior than investors in Germany or the USA. Therefore, inferences about the behavior of individual investors must always be made in light of the investment culture of the country or region where the data is collected from.

Period and Frequency

Data period and frequency differs throughout the related research. In most of the papers a daily frequency is used though some authors present results on a monthly basis. This is not only due to the availability of the data but also to the specific research focus, i.e. whether long-term or short-term anomalies are to be investigated.

It is therefore important to judge any differences in the conclusions in light of the data frequency. For example, both Barber, Odean, and Zhu (2009a) and Hvidkjaer (2008) use the same data and a similar imbalance measure but come to different conclusions regarding short-term return predictability. In a reconciliation, however, Barber, Hvidkjaer, Odean, and Zhu (2006) show that their short-term results are not necessarily contradictory when the data frequency is harmonized.

Order Types

Another important difference among previous research is the differentiation between market and limit orders. All papers using the Lee and Ready (1991) algorithm only include market orders by assumption whereas all other papers may include limit orders as well.

Dorn, Huberman, and Sengmueller (2008) are among the first to distinguish market and limit orders and get different results depending on the order type. Their data set from the discount broker allows them to determine the order type exactly and differentiate even further between speculative and non-speculative orders. Barber, Lee, Liu, and Odean (2009) differentiate between passive and aggressive orders due to their unique data set from the Taiwan Stock Exchange. Investors in Taiwan are not allowed to submit market orders, so an executed limit order must be identified as marketable or non-marketable.

In recent research, Linnainmaa (2009) finds that trading patterns such as the disposition effect or contrarian behavior can be explained in large part by investors' use of limit orders. He argues that these pattern arise mechanically because limit orders are price-contingent and suffer from adverse selection. Besides, the differentiation between market and limit orders has not received a lot of attention in the related literature although Dorn, Huberman, and Sengmueller (2008) show that this differentiation is important. In addition, research on submitted rather than executed orders is missing – a gap that we would like to fill with our work.

Order Imbalance Measure Calculation

Although an order imbalance measure is being developed in all papers, authors have done it in different ways: Some researchers report trading volume imbalance, some report imbalances based on the number of trades or the number of stocks traded. In some papers, an imbalance measure based on the number of buyers as opposed to all traders is calculated.

Given the many differences among all empirical papers, there is no doubt that their results and conclusions differ as well. The main questions are whether order imbalance measures are correlated with contemporaneous and future return data.

2.4.3. Return Correlation

Contemporaneous Returns

Empirical results regarding a contemporaneous correlation of order imbalances and stock returns are mixed. Among the papers that report a positive contemporaneous correlation are Chordia, Roll, and Subrahmanyam (2002), Chordia and Subrahmanyam (2004), Dorn, Huberman, and Sengmueller (2008), Andrade, Chang, and Seasholes (2008), Hvidkjaer (2008), and Barber, Odean, and Zhu (2009a). In general, their work suggests that periods of intense buying correlates with rising stock prices, i.e. investors are positive feedback traders and buy when prices go up.

In contrast, Griffin, Harris, and Topaloglu (2003), Jackson (2003), Kumar and Lee (2006), Kaniel, Saar, and Titman (2008), and Boehmer and Wu (2008) report a strong negative correlation between order imbalances and stock returns. Their work suggests that individuals are negative feedback traders and buy when prices decline and sell when prices go up. Table 2.2 summarizes the findings regarding contemporaneous and subsequent correlation of order imbalances and returns.

Table 2.2: Evidence of Return Correlation Found in Empirical Work

This table presents a summary of findings on return correlation found in recent empirical work. *Frequency* is reported to explain differences in subsequent columns. The column *Contemporaneous correlation* shows whether returns and order imbalance measures are negatively or positively (or not at all) correlated. The column *Forecasting power* indicates whether the authors have found any return forecasting ability of their measures. The last column (*Duration*) reports the duration of return predictability.

Article	Frequency	Contemporaneous correlation	Forecasting power	Duration
Boehmer and Wu (2008)	daily	negative (individuals); positive (institutions)	positive	up to 4 days
Chordia and Subrahmanyam (2004)	daily	positive	positive	one day
Chordia, Roll, and Subrahmanyam (2002)	daily	positive	negative	
Dorn, Huberman, and Sengmueller (2008)	daily	positive	positive	up to 2 days
Griffin, Harris, and Topaloglu (2003)	daily	negative (individuals); positive (institutions)	none	--
Pan and Poteshman (2006)	daily	--	positive	up to 3 weeks
Schmitz, Glaser, and Weber (2007)	daily	--	positive	up to 2 days
Jackson (2003)	weekly	negative	positive	up to 2 weeks
Kaniel, Saar, and Titman (2008)	weekly	negative	positive	up to 4 weeks
Andrade, Chang, and Seasholes (2008)	weekly	positive	negative	up to 10 weeks
Barber, Odean, and Zhu (2009a)	weekly	positive	positive	up to 4 weeks
Hvidkjaer (2008)	monthly	positive	negative	up to 2 years
Kumar and Lee (2006)	monthly	negative	positive	one month
Subrahmanyam (2008)	monthly	--	negative	up to 2 months

It is not straightforward to reconcile the results. Boehmer and Wu (2008) as well as Griffin, Harris, and Topaloglu (2003) find that order flow and prices have a high contemporaneous correlation but that signs differ for individuals and institutions. According to their results, order flow of individuals is negatively correlated to stock returns whereas order flow of institutions is positively correlated to stock returns suggesting that individuals provide liquidity to actively investing institutions. This reasoning complements the results in Kaniel, Saar, and Titman (2008) as well as Jackson (2003) whose results support the existence of very strong negative feedback trading at the individual stock level by small investors.

On the contrary, both Chordia, Roll, and Subrahmanyam (2002), and Chordia and Subrahmanyam (2004) report a positive contemporaneous correlation, i.e. excess buy orders drive up prices and excess sell orders drive down prices. However, they do not differentiate between individual and institutional investors – an omission that could very well lead to these results.

The remaining papers summarized in Table 2.2 also report a positive correlation but a missing differentiation between individual and institutional investors cannot be found because all of them focus on individual investors' data. However, their methods defining individual investors' trades differ: Barber, Odean, and Zhu (2009a) and Hvidkjaer (2008) use small trades as proxies for small individual investors' trades. It is possible that their measure includes different trades than e.g. Boehmer and Wu's (2008) measure that provides an exact differentiation between all investor groups.

Andrade, Chang, and Seasholes (2008) acknowledge that their results differ from those reported in Kaniel, Saar, and Titman (2008). They argue that the results reported by Kaniel, Saar, and Titman (2008) are possibly driven by the execution of stale limit orders (on average) which causes the U.S. investors to trade against price movements whereas the data used in their study, by contrast, are placed by active Taiwanese investors who demand liquidity. Therefore, differences between investor behaviors across countries could explain the results.

Dorn, Huberman, and Sengmueller (2008) report a positive contemporaneous correlation. They argue that the negative correlations between limit order imbalances and contemporaneous returns found by other researchers are due to the strong mechanical relation between price movements and limit order execution. They do things differently, in that they only use speculative market orders by individual investors. Order imbalances on these orders are positively correlated to contemporaneous returns which they explain with serially correlated price pressure.

Subsequent Returns

In the case of subsequent return correlations, the related work is apparently not consistent either. Four papers find that order imbalances are negatively related to future returns, i.e. periods of intense buying are followed by subsequent returns reversals suggesting that retail investors' behavior is suboptimal. One paper does not find a significant correlation of order imbalances and future stock returns. All others, i.e. the majority of the related literature in Table 2.2, find a significant positive correlation of order imbalance and subsequent stock returns differing in the observation frequency and the duration of the observed effect.

It is easier to reconcile the seemingly contrarian results, especially after the work by Barber, Odean, Zhu, and Hvidkjaer (2006) who find that their earlier contrarian findings are easily reconciled when using the same data frequency. They find that both papers document strong reversals at long horizons (e.g. one year) and strong continuations at short horizons (e.g. one week). In this light, the negative correlations documented by Hvidkjaer (2008) as well as Subrahmanyam (2008) are due to their monthly frequency. When changing the frequency from monthly to weekly, results in Hvidkjaer (2008) equal those of Barber, Odean, and Zhu (2009a) which is likely to be the case with the data in Subrahmanyam (2008) as well.

Griffin, Harris, and Topaloglu (2003) do not find any forecasting power in their data. This might be due to their relatively short data set, and the missing differentiation concerning market capitalization or order type.

The results by Chordia, Roll, and Subrahmanyam (2002) suggest a negative correlation as well. In their later paper (Chordia and Subrahmanyam 2004) they find the opposite pattern regarding future returns. However, they explain the difference by the focus on market-wide order imbalances on the one hand, and order imbalances at the individual stock level on the other hand.

The negative correlation found by Andrade, Chang, and Seasholes (2008) does not seem to fit among all other results. Again, maybe the Taiwanese investors show a very different behavior than those in Europe, Australia, and the United States. Lee, Liu, Roll, and Subrahmanyam (2004) support this reasoning and find that all trader classes act as market makers and that they are quite successful in doing it. This suggests that the behavior of individual investors in Taiwan can be quite different from other markets in which market makers or designated sponsors provide liquidity.

2.4.4. Market Efficiency

Does the evidence presented in the last section pose a threat to market efficiency? In general, almost all empirical studies show that future returns are to some extent predictable by order imbalances. Order imbalance measures may differ according to frequency, inclusion of order types, order size, market capitalization, target group, etc. but overall they point into the same direction: Today's order imbalances can be used to successfully predict tomorrow's returns.

According to the semi-strong form of the EMH, it is not possible to earn excess returns by trading on past information. However, many investors still follow technical trading strategies that appear to generate little revenue and considerable cost. Such strategies have long been the object of derision by Finance professors. But the recent evidence of return predictability (under assumptions) presents the EMH in a new light, and a discussion is evolving whether these excess returns can be explained by existing or additional risk factors (such as the risk factors suggested by Fama and French 1993) or whether retail order imbalance is such a risk factor itself.

Chordia, Roll, and Subrahmanyam (2005) argue that traders act collectively to push prices to market efficiency, and that this process cannot happen instantaneously. The goal of their paper is to present evidence of the speed of conversion to market efficiency. They find that even weak-form efficiency is not attained immediately and that order imbalances predict future returns over very short horizons. However, their data is from 1996 to 2002 – a time in which algorithmic trading was still evolving with levels far below those experienced today. The same studies with more recent data could lead to very different results.

2.5. Conclusion

Over the last 30 years, the growing evidence against the assumptions on which the EMH is based has lead to the creation of a new research field in finance: Behavioral Finance. Behavioral Finance is the "study of human fallibility in competitive markets" and primarily concerned with questions regarding the behavior of individual investors, such as why individual investors trade or how they form their expectations.

The Behavioral Finance presents many challenges to the EMH, both theoretically and empirically. In an attempt to provide the theoretical foundation for the Behavioral Finance, several models have been developed in related research of which five are summarized in section 2.2. In general, none of the models discussed in this chapter develops a general theory that explains all anomalies found in empirical research. Rather, ad-hoc models have been created to address certain aspects of empirical findings. This can be regarded as its major weakness. However, the understanding of certain phenomena, such as noise trader risk or the momentum effect, has improved substantially by developing theoretical models parallel to recording empirical findings.

The most important empirical work is presented in section 2.3. All related studies are divided into four categories: noise traders, investor sentiment, individual investor behavior, and correlated trading.

Finally, section 2.4 briefly discusses the relation of Behavioral Finance and the EMH. The main part of it is concerned with the relation of order imbalance measures and contemporaneous stock returns on the one hand, and the relation of order imbalance measures and future returns on the other hand. First, 18 of the most important empirical papers in this context are analyzed and compared with respect to data source, period, frequency, signing, measure, target group and inclusion of order types. Second, 14 of the papers that relate order imbalances to stock returns are analyzed with respect to their findings on whether order imbalance measures are positively or negatively correlated to contemporaneous stock returns, and whether order imbalance measures positively or negatively predict returns.

The reconciliation of the different research findings is not straightforward, and has to take the different aspects of the data sets into account. The main finding from the literature is that retail investor net trades (i.e. generally measured by order imbalances) are negatively correlated to stock returns[7]. In addition, and more importantly, it is found that retail investor net trades (order imbalances) positively predict stock returns[8] and that the forecasting power lasts for a period of a couple of days to up to 4 weeks. After all, more and more recent empirical evidence supports the theory that retail sentiment as measured by retail investor order imbalance accurately and positively predicts returns. This is contrary to the commonly expressed opinion that retail investors acting as "noise traders" are always wrong and lose money on average by trading.

The overall conclusion of this chapter is that there is much more empirical evidence on noise trading, investor sentiment, and individual investor behavior than there are theoretical models. Moreover, there is no general theory that is able to explain all phenomena at once – a fact the field of Behavioral Finance is still suffering from.

7 Boehmer and Wu (2008), Jackson (2003), Kaniel, Saar, and Titman (2008), and Kumar and Lee (2006).

8 Boehmer and Wu (2008), Dorn, Huberman, and Sengmueller (2008), Jackson (2003), Barber, Odean, and Zhu (2009a).

3 Investor Sentiment Construction

"Now, the question is no longer, as it was a few decades ago, whether investor sentiment affects stock prices, but rather how to measure investor sentiment and quantify its effects."

Malcolm Baker and Jeffrey Wurgler (2007), p.130

What is a good measure of investor sentiment? Several attempts have been made to quantify investor sentiment and evaluate existing sentiment measures.

In this chapter, different measures of investor sentiment as suggested and discussed in research as well as used in practice are presented. Different measures can be categorized into direct measures and indirect measures of investor sentiment.

In an attempt to evaluate different measures of investor sentiment and validate them against each other, pairwise correlations are computed and compared. This evaluation is based on the assumption that the measures should somehow move in concert if they are to rest on the same underlying factor – namely investor sentiment.

This chapter is structured as follows: In section 3.1, related work regarding the classification of different sentiment measures is presented together with a discussion of their advantages and disadvantages. Section 3.2 commences with an overview of the most-discussed sentiment indicator in research, the closed-end funds discount, and also presents recent research measures. In section 3.3, the most important sentiment measures used in practice are presented, along with a graphical representation and related findings from research when available. Section 0 finally compares all measures and discusses how sentiment measures should be evaluated. Section 3.5 concludes.

3.1. Classification of Sentiment Measures

3.1.1. Related Work

According to Robert J. Shiller, one of the first researchers to study investor expectations and behavior, most data on investor sentiment refer to simple expectations for price change or indicators of these expectations (Shiller 2000, p. 49). The problem is that most people do not have precise expectations for future changes over specific horizons.

Shiller distinguishes two kinds of market sentiment measures: those that are derived from prices or quantities in markets under a theory relating them to sentiment, and those that are based on polling of investors. The first group of sentiment indices includes the put/call ratio, the short interest ratio, and the closed-end funds discount (CEFD). In the second group of indexes, he mentions the survey of the American Association of Individual Investors (AAII), the University of Michigan Consumer Sentiment Index, and the Investors' Intelligence (II) index predicting a correction in market prices.

Brown and Cliff (2004) also identify two basic types of sentiment measures: direct and indirect sentiment measures. Direct sentiment measures, on the one hand, are created from surveys that directly measure the sentiment of market participants. They also use the AAII and the II sentiment measures in their study. Indirect sentiment measures, on the other hand, are created from financial data and can be categorized, according to Brown and Cliff, into four groups: indicators based on recent market performance, indicators that relate to particular types of trading activity, indicators that relate especially to derivatives variables, and other sentiment proxies that do not fall within one of the above three categories.

Qiu and Welch (2006) also distinguish two measures: Financial measures that are based on financial data, and survey measures that are based on the polling of investors. In particular, they examine the closed-end funds discount and the consumer confidence index as two different proxies for investor sentiment.

Bandopadhyaya and Jones (2006) survey studies that use investor sentiment measures and classify them into five categories: 1. optimism/pessimism about the economy, 2. optimism/ pessimism about the stock market, 3. riskiness of the stock market, 4. riskiness of an individual stock, and 5. risk aversion. Their focus is not on how the sentiment measures are gathered but rather which attitudes are expressed through them.

Beaumont et al. (2005) classify sentiment measures as implicit and explicit, with implicit measures being constructed from objectively observable financial data and explicit, survey-based measures that try to capture the mood of the market directly. In addition, they consider another type of sentiment measure: The combined direct and indirect measure of sentiment which includes the combination of different indicators and techniques such as those used by Brown and Cliff (2004) and Baker and Wurgler (2006). They conclude that the integration of several measures of sentiment has proven a fruitful approach to exploring the relationship of investor sentiment and stock returns.

In addition to the already mentioned two categories of sentiment (and combinations thereof), however, there is a third type of measure that is neither based on pure market data nor investor surveys. This type is referred to as meta-measure. Typically, these measures are based on an amalgam of opinions.

Recent innovative non-standard methods for sentiment extraction fall into this third category: Ciccone (2003) uses analyst opinions as a human-level measure of investor sentiment. Antweiler and Frank (2004) study messages in internet chat rooms focused on stocks and characterize the content of the messages as buy, sell, or hold recommendations. They find evidence of relationships between message activity and trading volume and message activity and return volatility. Das, Martínez-Jerez, and Tufano (2005) examine the information flow for stocks to trace the relationship between online discussion, news activity, and stock price movements. Applying language-processing routines to message board postings and news, they create sentiment and disagreement measures which they call "eInformation". Das and Chen (2007) use statistical and natural language processing techniques to extract the emotive content of a message posted by stock message board users about a specific stock. Using principal components analysis, Tetlock (2007) constructs a simple measure of media pessimism from the content of a *Wall Street Journal* column and estimates intertemporal links between this measure of sentiment and stock prices.

3.1.2. Advantages and Disadvantages

All categories of sentiment measures have advantages and disadvantages and neither can be said to be the best. This section presents advantages and disadvantages of each category.

Direct Measures

Direct measures of investor sentiment have one big advantage: Surveys measure sentiment directly by asking people about their expectations of the market, thereby producing a very precise indicator.

However, surveys have many possible sources of errors, e.g. the interviewer, the questionnaire or the respondent (e.g. Groves 1989). There are often problems related to inaccurate responses, non-response and self-selecting biases that can influence the results. In particular, investor sentiment surveys assume that people actually do what they say, i.e. invest in the market when they consider themselves bullish. However, investors do not always do what they say, and when it comes to investing real money, many of them might change their opinion. Some surveys have already reacted to that and ask their participants to what degree they have invested in the market, i.e. their relative bullishness.

Another important disadvantage of survey measures is the low-frequency sampling period: A weekly frequency has established as the most common sampling frequency for individual investors (e.g. Sentix, Cognitrend, AAII), though there are many more surveys conducted on a monthly basis. These surveys are not suited to infer short term sentiment and relate it to trading days, even intraday events. In addition, surveys give respondents some time for their answer resulting in incoming responses over the course of days or even weeks. Therefore, it cannot be guaranteed that all respondents answer at the same time.

Indirect Measures

Indirect sentiment measures refer to financial variables and require a theory relating them to sentiment. The weakness of the indirect measures lies in the necessity of building up this theory and their respective interpretation. Furthermore, the definite link between theory and empiricism is missing.

However, the use of indirect measures of investor sentiment is wide-spread in the academic literature because they are easily constructed and based on simple market data. Indirect measures offer the opportunity to extract high-frequency sentiment and relate it to events, high-frequency returns time series, or other high-frequency data such as volatility.

The right choice of market data is equally important as filtering methods in order to ensure a high degree of expressiveness. For example, if an indirect measure of retail investor sentiment is to be constructed, it is important to either include only retail data or filter the data accordingly (e.g. by trade size or instruments). Applying filters and other modifications of the original data, however, always bears the risk of data mining, i.e. researchers modifying the data until they get significant results. In order to prevent this, modification of the data and inclusion of other variables usually have to be backed on theory and decided upon in advance.

Meta-Measures

Meta-measures, as termed in the previous section, have the advantage that they are based on innovative methods that enable the researcher to look beyond established extraction methodologies and investigate the relationship between investor sentiment and the expression thereof found in next generation internet applications.

The most difficult task when constructing meta-measures for research lies in establishing its relation to theory. As for the indirect sentiment measures, the meta-measures must be linked to theory to draw conclusions about investor sentiment.

However, meta-measures seem to be a promising approach to create new sentiment extraction methods that are more flexible in terms of frequency, more targeted towards a specific group of investors, and well-suited to keep up with technological developments.

3.2. Sentiment Measures in Research

3.2.1. The Closed-End Funds Discount

One of the first and also the best known academic study of investor sentiment using market data is the closed-end funds discount (CEFD) authored by Lee, Shleifer, and Thaler (1991), and has been the source of much debate. The basic premise of the study is that since retail investors are known to disproportionately hold closed-end funds, the CEFD can be interpreted as a measure of investor sentiment.

Closed-end funds are collective investment schemes with a limited number of shares. New shares are rarely issued after the launch but investors are able to buy existing shares from other investors on the secondary market. The price of a share is determined partially by the value of the investments in the fund, and partially by the premium or discount placed on it on the market. The per share net asset value (NAV) of the fund, i.e. the total value of all the securities in the fund divided by the total number of shares, minus its per share market value constitutes the discount or premium. If the fund trades at a price above the per share NAV it is said to be trading at a premium; if it trades below, at a discount.

The Closed-End Funds Discount Puzzle

The closed-end funds discount puzzle is the empirical finding that closed-end fund shares typically sell at prices not equal to the per share market value of assets the fund holds. Discounts of 10 to 20 percent have been the norm.

Lee, Shleifer, and Thaler (1991) mention four parts of the closed-end funds discount puzzle: First, newly opened closed-end funds usually start out at a premium of about 10 percent of their NAV. Second, closed-end funds move to an average discount of about 10 percent within the initial 120 days of trading. Discounts remain substantial thereafter. Third, discounts do not represent a constant fraction of the NAV but even fluctuate over time. Fourth, when closed-end funds are terminated, the fund share prices rise and discounts disappear.

Several studies have attempted to solve the puzzle by explaining that the methods used to value the securities in the fund might overstate their true value. Standard explanations include agency costs, illiquidity of assets, and tax liabilities. First, agency costs could result in discounts if fund management fees are too high or future portfolio management is expected to be too expensive. However, agency costs could explain the presence of the discount but would not serve as explanation for the initial premium, or the fluctuation during the lifetime of the fund since agency costs would rather be a constant fraction of the NAV. Second, illiquidity of assets could serve as an explanation for discounts if the closed-end fund held a substantial amount of restricted stock, i.e. stock for which public trading is restricted and which usually trades at a lower price. This argument, however, can be ruled out for the largest U.S. closed-end funds which only hold liquid, publicly traded securities. Third, the reported NAV of a closed-end fund does not incorporate the capital gains tax that must be paid by the fund if the assets in the fund are sold, and therefore overstates its true value. It has been demonstrated, however, that this theory can only explain up to 6 percent of the observed discount. To summarize, none of the theories mentioned can fully explain all parts of the closed-end funds discount puzzle.

Lee, Shleifer, and Thaler (1991) conjecture that the discount movements reflect the differential sentiment of individual investors since closed-end funds in the United States are primarily owned and traded by individual investors. However, this does not mean that individual investors are, on average, pessimistic about the funds or its holdings. The average underpricing of the fund, i.e. the discount, can be explained by noise trader risk, i.e. the fact that holding the fund is riskier than holding its portfolio. According to Lee, Shleifer, and Thaler (1991), the existence of noise traders also explains the other three parts of the puzzle.

The Closed-End Funds Discount as a Sentiment Indicator

Lee, Shleifer, and Thaler (1991) collect closed-end funds data and calculate a value-weighted index of discounts of a total of 20 stock funds. They find that both the levels of discounts and the changes of discounts are highly correlated among funds. Average pairwise correlation of year-end discounts amounts to 0.497 and the average pairwise correlation of changes in discounts is 0.389. They argue that these high correlations justify the construction of the value-weighted discount. They conclude that the positive correlations are consistent with the hypothesis that discounts on different funds are driven by the same investor sentiment. They do not find, however, that discount levels or changes are closely related to levels of stock market prices or the returns thereof.

Lee, Shleifer, and Thaler (1991) compare the changes in their value-weighted discount index (VWD) with returns of portfolios of stocks with different market capitalization. They find that the lowest market capitalization stocks do well when discounts shrink, and that the largest market capitalization stocks do poorly when discounts widen. In other words, when individual investors become optimistic, smaller stocks do well and CEFDs narrow. This empirical finding relates a measure of investor sentiment with the returns of small stocks that may have nothing to do with the funds themselves.

Their work suggests that as the discount increases, retail investor sentiment decreases. Figure 3.1 displays the discount history for one of the best-known closed-end funds, Tri-Continental Corporation[9]. This corporation has already received attention in the early works of Lee, Shleifer, and Thaler (1991). The graph confirms that there were still large CEFDs during the last 10 years amounting to 13.5% on average. From January 2006 to July 2007, however, discounts decreased by over 10 percentage points indicating that investors were becoming more and more pessimistic.

[9] The closed-end funds discounts presented here are calculated and published by the Closed-End Fund Association (CEFA) at http://www.cefa.com/.

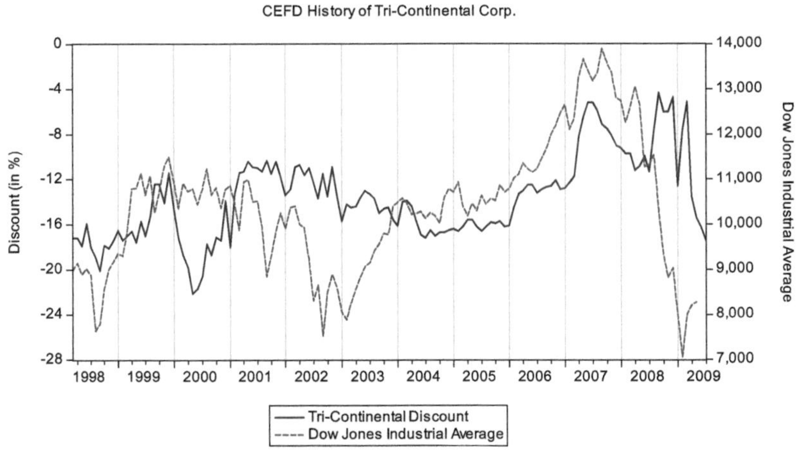

Figure 3.1: CEFD History of Tri-Continental Corp.

This shows the monthly discount history of the closed-end fund Tri-Continental Corp. (left axis, solid line) along with the monthly Dow Jones Industrial Average close prices (right axis, dashed line).

Lee, Shleifer, and Thaler (1991) concede that several factors are likely to influence the CEFD, for example agency costs. Ross (2002) explores these factors in more detail and argues that transaction costs play a much larger role than Lee, Sleifer, and Thaler originally assumed. Qiu and Welch (2006) criticize that they primarily base their validation on the correlation of the CEFD with the small firm return and that this method would validate one financial measure (the CEFD) with another (decile stock returns). They suspect that it is more likely that both measures are driven by financial markets phenomena that are not yet fully understood.

3.2.2. Meta-Measures

Composite Sentiment by Brown and Cliff

Brown and Cliff (2004) demonstrate that surveys measuring investor sentiment are related to other popular measures of investor sentiment and recent stock market returns. They extract the common component(s) of the different sentiment measures and hope that it represents a cleaner measure of investor sentiment. In order to exploit as much information as possible and efficiently include all of the information about the 'true unobservable sentiment', they combine the various sentiment measures and use two well-established methods to extract common features of the data: the Kalman filter and principal component analysis.

They are able to isolate common features of these indicators for a long monthly time period and a shorter weekly time period. In the weekly sample, they have generated two separate measures that are meant to represent institutional and individual investor sentiment. For all of the aggregate sentiment measures, they find strong evidence of co-movement with the market but little evidence of short-run predictability in returns.

Composite Sentiment by Baker and Wurgler

Baker and Wurgler (2006) form a composite index of sentiment[10] that is based on the common variation in six underlying proxies for sentiment: the CEFD, NYSE share turnover, the number and average first-day returns on IPOs, the equity share in new issues, and the dividend premium. Because each sentiment proxy is likely to include a sentiment component as well as idiosyncratic, non-sentiment-related components, they use principal components analysis to isolate the common sentiment component. In addition, they acknowledge the fact that some variables take longer to reveal the same sentiment than others.

Baker and Wurgler (2006) therefore choose either the current or the lagged values to include in their composite sentiment index depending on which one better correlates with the first-stage index consisting of all the proxies with both the current and the lagged values. As a result, the composite sentiment index consists of the current values of the CEFD, the number of IPOs, and the new issues sentiment, as well as the one period lagged values of NYSE share turnover, the lagged IPO return, and the dividend premium. Furthermore, each component enters the resulting sentiment index with the expected sign.

Figure 3.2 displays the composite sentiment index created by Baker and Wurgler (2006) along with the Dow Jones Industrial Average as benchmark. For an eyeball test, they argue that "perhaps the best evidence that the index generally succeeds in capturing sentiment is simply that it lines up fairly well with the anecdotal accounts of bubbles and crashes" (Baker and Wurgler 2007, p. 141). Further analysis reveals that the correlation between an equal-weighted market index and composite sentiment changes is a highly significant 0.43.

[10] Their data is available at http://pages.stern.nyu.edu/~jwurgler.

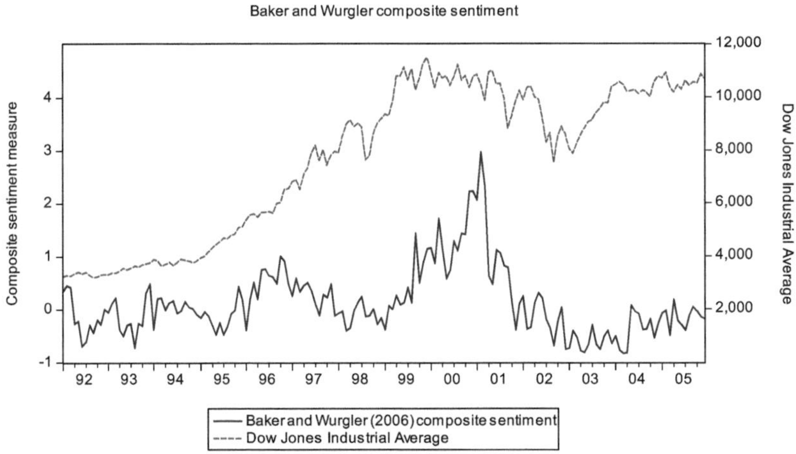

Figure 3.2: Baker and Wurgler (2006) Composite Sentiment

This figure shows the monthly composite sentiment measure (left axis, solid line) by Baker and Wurgler (2006) along with the monthly Dow Jones Industrial Average close prices (right axis, dashed line).

Baker and Wurgler (2007) also investigate their composite sentiment's predictability on the cross-sectional as well as the aggregate level. For a cross-section of stocks they find that sentiment has a larger influence on stocks that are hard to arbitrage. In particular, when sentiment is low, the average future returns of speculative stocks exceed those of bond-like stocks. When sentiment is high, the average future returns of speculative stocks are lower than the returns of bond-like stocks. On the aggregate level, high sentiment is followed by low subsequent market returns. They admit, however, that the statistical significance of their results is modest.

Sentiment Extraction from Online Investment Forums

Das and Chen (2007) investigate a methodology to analyze messages in stock message boards driven by providers like Yahoo!. In their paper, "sentiment" takes on a specific meaning, i.e. the net of positive and negative opinion expressed about a stock on its message board. They use statistical and natural language processing techniques to extract the emotive content of a message classifying the author as bearish, bullish or neutral. A sentiment index is created based on the stocks included in the Morgan Stanley High-Tech Index (MSH). The MSH and the sentiment index show a strong correlation. At the individual stock level, however, the relationship is weaker. They conclude that the aggregation of sentiment reduces some of the noise from individual stock board postings.

3.3. Sentiment Measures in Practice

In this section an overview of existing sentiment measures is presented along with the relevant work in the literature that refers to them. Charts of the time series and relevant market indices as benchmarks are plotted where appropriate. This selection of sentiment measures is not meant to be exhaustive but rather to provide a good overview of different methods employed in practice.

3.3.1. Survey-Based Measures

Sentix

The Sentix index has been published weekly since February 2001. Meanwhile, about 2600 investors took part in the survey. Individual and institutional investors are interviewed separately. The respondent has to assess the future trend of the DAX, TecDAX, EuroStoxx50, S&P500, NASDAQ Composite and the Nikkei225. Either the respondents are bullish, bearish or neutral regarding their opinion for the next month (short-term) and the next six months (mid-term). For every market, time horizon, and type of investor (institutional as well as individual investors) an index is constructed according to the following formula:

$$Sentix = \frac{\sum bullish - \sum bearish}{\sum all\ votes} \tag{3.1}$$

Figure 3.3 illustrates the Sentix for individual investors using both time horizons (short-term and mid-term expectations). For the purpose of illustration, the 20-day moving averages of both the short-term and the mid-term Sentix measure are plotted along with the weekly DAX close prices.

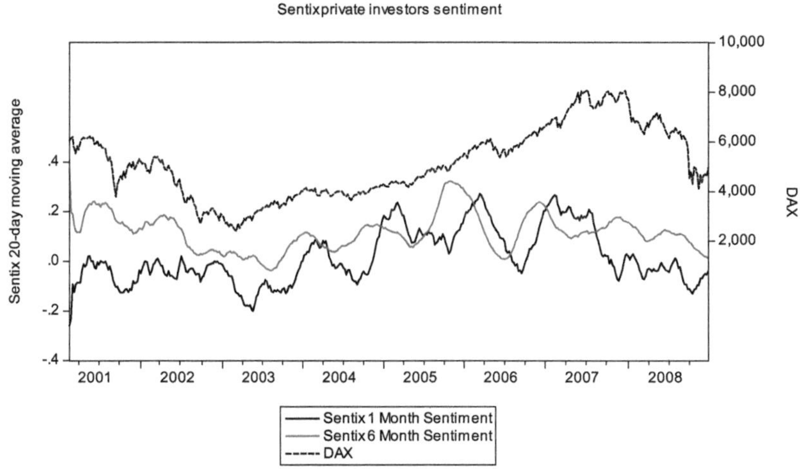

Figure 3.3: Sentix Private Investors Sentiment

This figure shows 20-day moving averages of the 1-month (solid black line) and the 6-month (solid grey line) Sentix private investors sentiment (both left axis) along with the weekly DAX close prices (right axis, dashed line).

There are a couple of academic papers about the Sentix. Among them, Beaumont et al. (2005) find that the individual Sentix is a proxy for individual sentiment which influences both the return and the conditional volatility of large and small cap stocks. Schmeling (2007) finds that institutional sentiment as measured by the Sentix forecasts stock market returns correctly whereas individuals have wrong expectations. Zwergel and Klein (2006) come to the same conclusion.

Cognitrend Bull Bear Index

The Bull Bear Index is constructed for the DAX as well as the TecDAX and is mainly composed of institutional investors' opinions. Since 2002 Cognitrend, a German financial consultancy with a focus on behavioral finance, has asked some 170 medium-term institutional investors at Deutsche Börse, with trading horizons between 3 weeks and 12 months, for their market opinions. Fund and asset managers in the DAX and TecDAX, as well as notable private investors in the case of the latter, are asked on a weekly basis if the index will find itself higher, lower or at the same price in one month time.

By limiting the survey to market participants who carry risk in equity indices, the developers of the Bull Bear Index "attempt to gage the psychological as well as the material commitments to underlying positions. That is, someone who is invested will hardly ever give a negative forecast about ones holdings. In the same way, one who has just squared a position is unlikely to express positive prospects for the former strategy."[11]

Figure 3.4 displays the DAX Bull Bear Index, the TecDAX Bull Bear Index along with the DAX for the entire period since the start of the survey.

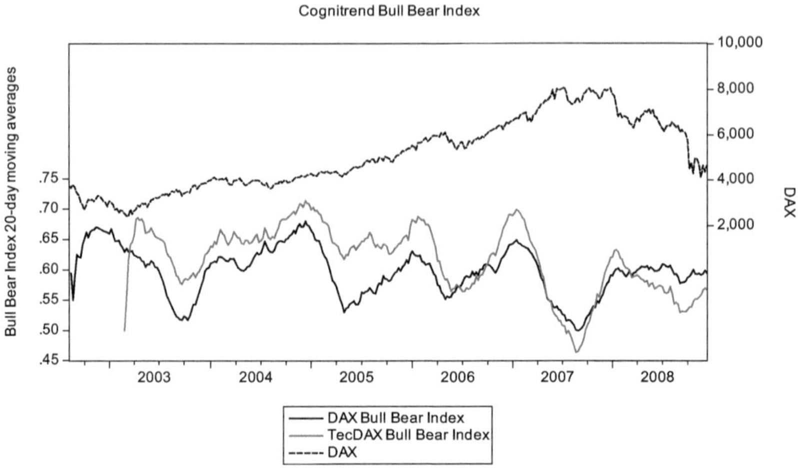

Figure 3.4: Cognitrend Bull Bear Index

This figure shows 20-day moving averages of the DAX Bull Bear Index (solid black line) and the TecDAX Bull Bear Index (solid grey line, both left axis) along with the weekly DAX close prices (right axis, dashed line).

The developers of the index claim that they have accurately predicted the long-term bear market from 2000 to 2003, and equally, the subsequent recovery. However, there are no academic papers that confirm these findings.

American Association of Individual Investors Survey

The American Association of Individual Investors[12] (AAII) polls a random sample of their members weekly since 1987. The sample size of the survey has been at least 300 since 1993, and the average number of respondents in the study's 1993-94 sample period was 167[13]. The respondents are asked whether they are bullish, bearish or neutral about the stock markets in the next six months. Only subscribers who are typically individual investors are allowed to vote. Figure 3.5 displays the AAII sentiment as the "bull ratio" i.e. the percentage of bullish investors over the sum of the percentages of bullish and bearish investors.

[11] Source: http://www.cognitrend.de/de/english/sentiment.php.

[12] http://www.aaii.com/.

[13] Brown (1999), p.85.

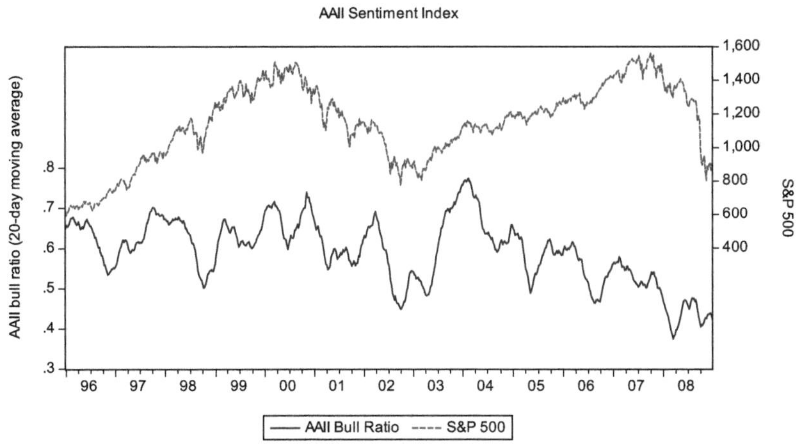

Figure 3.5: AAII Sentiment Index

This figure shows the 20-day moving average of the AAII bull ratio (left axis, solid line), i.e. the percentage of bullish investors over the sum of the percentages of bullish and bearish investors, along with S&P 500 close prices (right axis, dashed line).

Brown (1999) uses the AAII data to construct a sentiment index equal to the percentage of bullish respondents plus the percentage of neutral respondents. He then calculates a new index designed to capture abnormally bullish or bearish sentiment by taking absolute deviations from the mean of the sentiment index. He then tests whether this direct measure of sentiment is associated with the volatility of closed-end funds. His work provides strong evidence that individual investor sentiment is related to increased volatility in closed-end funds.

Fisher and Statman (2000) use the percentage of bullish investors from the AAII survey as a proxy for individual investor sentiment. They find a significantly negative relationship between their sentiment measure and future (next-month) S&P 500 returns. Their results suggest that the sentiment of individual investors as measured by the AAII sentiment survey is a reliable contrary indicator for S&P 500 returns.

Fisher and Statman (2003) construct an AAII sentiment index as the ratio of bullish investors to the sum of bullish and bearish investors. They find a positive and statistically significant relationship between changes in consumer confidence and changes in the sentiment of individual investors as measured by the AAII sentiment index.

Wang, Keswani, and Taylor (2006) use the ratio of the bearish percentage to the bullish percentage as a measure of investor sentiment in their paper. They test for Granger-causality between sentiment and returns by estimating bivariate VAR models. They find that sentiment does not cause returns but rather returns cause sentiment.

Michigan Consumer Sentiment Index

The Michigan Consumer Sentiment Index (ICS) is based on a nationally representative survey of about 500 U.S. households, which has been conducted monthly by telephone interviews since 1978. It consists of 50 core questions, of which only five questions are used to calculate the ICS. The respondents are asked to assess their financial situation in the next year and the economic situation in the next as well as in the next five years. Further they are asked about their present conditions, which include questions regarding their financial situation today compared to the situation in the previous year as well as their readiness to buy major household items. Additionally, the Index of Consumer Expectations (ICE) is calculated. Only three questions about the consumer expectations flow into the ICE. Figure 3.6 illustrates the two indices as well as the S&P 500 index for comparison.

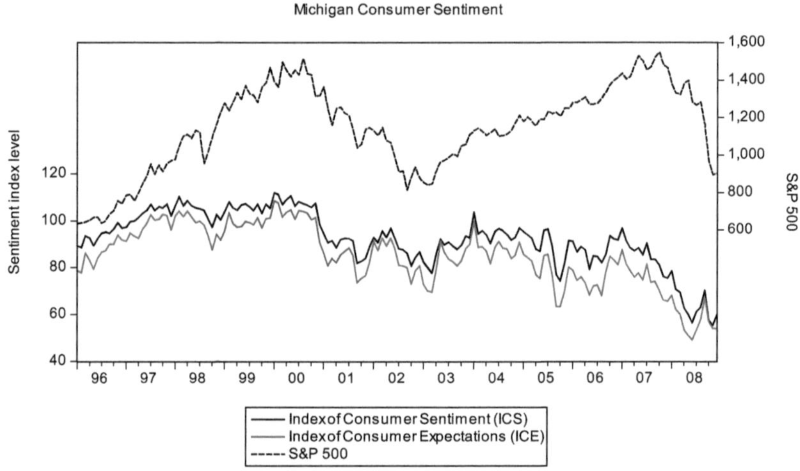

Figure 3.6: Michigan Consumer Sentiment

This figure shows the Index of Consumer Sentiment (solid black line) and the Index of Consumer Expectations (solid grey line, both left axis) along with monthly S&P 500 close prices (dashed line, right axis).

Consumer Confidence Survey

The Consumer Confidence Survey[14] has been conducted as a nationally representative survey monthly since 1977. The questionnaires are mailed to a sample of 5,000 U.S. households of which approximately 3,500 respond. The Consumer Confidence Index (CCI) is based on five questions of the survey. Three questions are on the expectations regarding business conditions, employment conditions and family income in the next six months. The present condition component comprises the current business and employment conditions. The CCI is

[14] http://www.conference-board.org/economics/indicators.cfm.

very similar to the ICS. However, the ICS focuses more on the financial situation whereas the CCI is influenced more by macroeconomic conditions.

Many studies deal with both confidence indices. Fisher and Statman (2003) find a negative correlation between consumer confidence and returns in the next month, and the next six months and the next twelve months, which, however, is not always statistically significant. Otoo (1999) documents a strong contemporaneous relationship between the ICS and stock prices. Charoenrook (2003) state that sentiment measured by the ICS can predict excess stock returns. Lemmon and Portniaguina (2006) reveal that changes in the ICS correlate especially well with small stocks and stocks held disproportionately by retail investors. Figure 3.7 illustrates movements of the index for the last 10 years. A comparison with the S&P 500 index suggests that the two indexes are positively correlated.

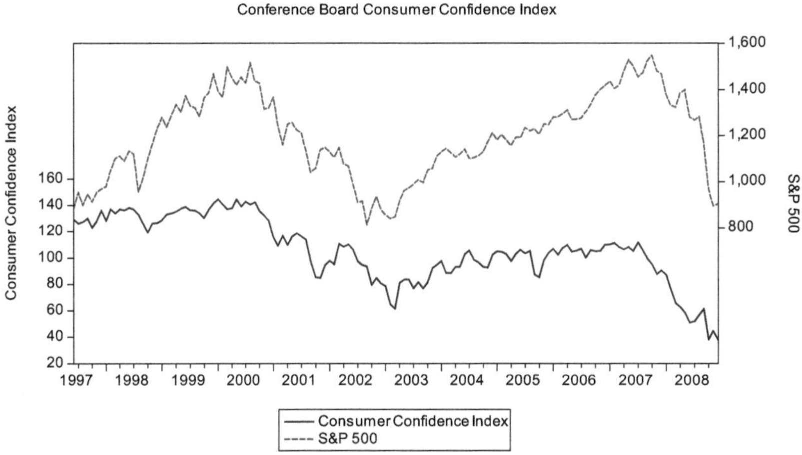

Figure 3.7: Consumer Confidence Index

This figure shows the Consumer Confidence Index (solid line, left axis) along with monthly S&P 500 close prices (dashed line, right axis).

UBS/Gallup Index of Investor Optimism

The UBS/Gallup Index of Investor Optimism is based on a representative and carefully sampled survey of investors. The index is constructed from surveys of randomly chosen wealthy investors. During the first two weeks of every month, UBS/Gallup conducts 1,000 interviews of investors. It reports the results on the last Monday of the month.

UBS/Gallup is especially careful to retain the same investor profile every month although they are not able to sample the same individuals every month. This is a major difference to the Consumer Confidence Index (CCI). However, Qiu and Welch (2006) find a strong relationship between Consumer Confidence and the UBS/Gallup sentiment survey. In particular, they document a positive correlation between changes in consumer confidence and changes in the UBS/Gallup investor sentiment series of 55.2%. Figure 3.8 shows the UBS/Gallup Index for the period from 1996 to 2007 (it has been published monthly since 1999 – before that, numbers are available only on a quarterly basis).

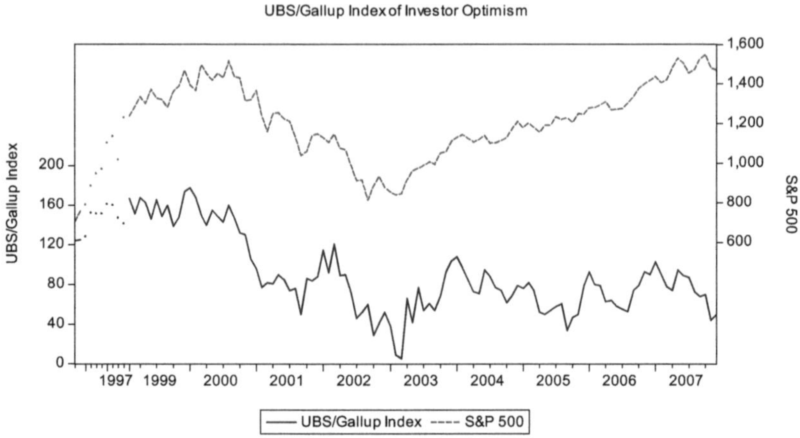

Figure 3.8: UBS/Gallup Index of Investor Optimism

This figure shows the Index of Investor Optimism as surveyed by UBS/Gallup (solid line, left axis) along with monthly S&P 500 close prices (dashed line, right axis). Until February 1999, surveys were conducted on a quarterly basis. Afterwards, monthly surveys were conducted.

G-Mind

The German Market Indicator (G-Mind) is published by the Centre for European Economic Research (ZEW). It is a monthly survey which provides an indication of the level of bearish- or bullishness among a selected sample of German investors. The survey among 350 financial analysts and institutional investors is the basis for the indicators used. The resulting sentiment index can take on values between minus ten and plus ten, the latter representing optimism or bullishness and the former representing pessimism or bearishness. Figure 3.9 displays the G-Mind along with the German DAX index.

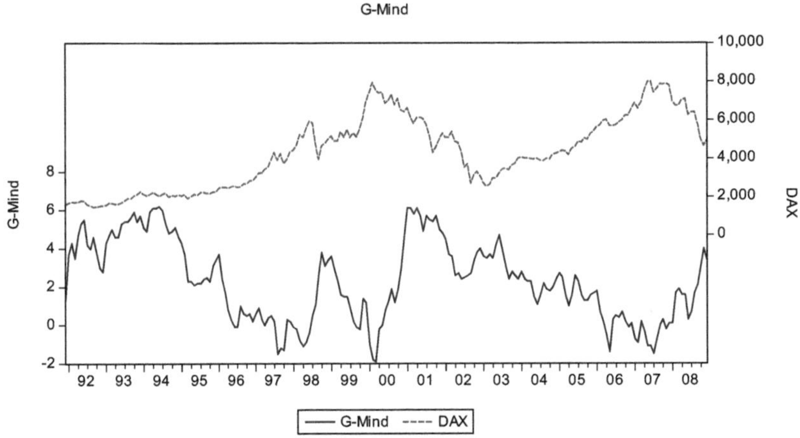

Figure 3.9: G-Mind

This figure shows the G-Mind (solid line, left axis) along with monthly DAX close prices (dashed line, right axis).

Honcoop and Lehnert (2007) investigate whether sentiment based on the G-Mind can be predicted to have cross-sectional effects. They find that when investors are bullish, next period returns are relatively high for growth stocks, small cap stocks, highly leveraged firms, low volatility stocks and profitable stocks.

3.3.2. Market-Data-Based Measures

Put/Call Ratio

Several stock exchanges compute a put/call ratio. The most widely-used p/c ratio in the literature is calculated by the Chicago Board Options Exchange (CBOE). Half-hourly, the CBOE collects data on put and call options traded on equities and indices. Hence it publishes three put/call ratios: the equity p/c, the index p/c and the total p/c ratio (see Figure 3.10). The CBOE estimates the ratios according to the following formula: volume of put options contracts divided by the volume of call options contracts. A high ratio suggests a negative market sentiment. Simon and Wiggins (2001) find that the p/c ratio can predict S&P futures returns. Martikainen and Puttonen (1996) come to the conclusion that option volumes can predict stock returns. In contrast, Wang, Keswani, and Taylor (2006) only document a limited forecasting power for returns and volatility.

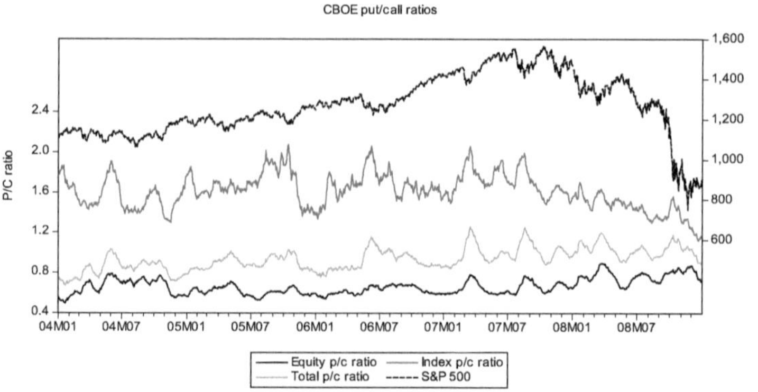

Figure 3.10: CBOE Put/Call Ratios

This figure shows the 20-day moving averages of the CBOE put/call ratios for equity (solid black line), index (solid dark grey line), and total (solid light grey line, all left axis) along with the daily S&P 500 close prices (black dashed line, right axis).

VDAX

The VDAX is an index based on the implied volatility of options. Option pricing models can be inverted to calculate the implied volatility as a function of option prices. The VDAX illustrates the 45-day market's expectation of the DAX volatility included in the prices of at-the-money DAX options traded on the Eurex. The VDAX has been replaced by the VDAX-New which uses the square root of implied variance across at- and out-of-the-money options of a given time to expiration. A graph of the VDAX-New is shown in Figure 3.11.

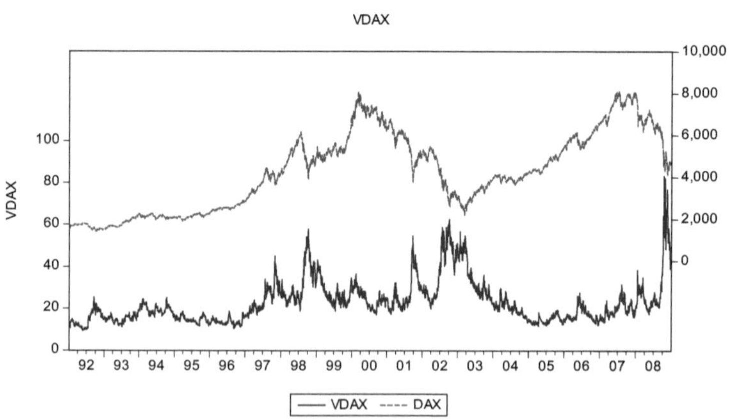

Figure 3.11: VDAX-New

This figure shows daily levels of the VDAX-New (solid line, left axis) along with daily DAX close prices (dashed line, right axis).

The American cousin of the VDAX is the VIX which is a measure for the 30-day market's expectation of S&P 500 volatility included in the prices of near-term S&P 500 options traded on the CBOE. A predictive power for S&P futures returns has been found by Simon and Wiggins (2001). Bandopadhyaya and Jones (2008) find that the CBOE p/c ratio is a better measure for sentiment than the VIX.

ISEE Sentiment Index

The ISEE Sentiment Index is computed by the International Securities Exchange (ISE). The ISE only examines opening long call and opening long put options purchased by customers. Market makers and firm trades are excluded. The index is calculated as follows: (opening long calls / opening put calls) x 100. A value above 100 implies bullish sentiment; a value above 100 implies bearish sentiment. Figure 3.12 displays the 20-day moving average of the ISEE Sentiment Index along with the S&P 500.

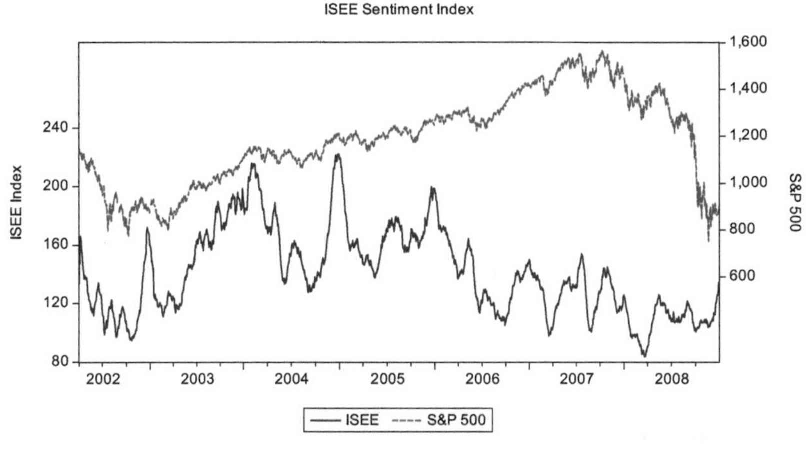

Figure 3.12: ISEE Sentiment Index

This figure shows 20-day moving average levels of the ISEE Sentiment Index on all underlyings (solid line, left axis) along with daily S&P 500 close prices (dashed line, right axis).

The ISEE Sentiment Index calculation is based on the idea of the work of Pan and Poteshman (2006). They use options trading data from the CBOE. One of the key features of their data set is that the options trading data is signed, i.e. it distinguishes whether option traders opened a new position or closed an existing one. In their analysis, they find that the information contained in "open buy" volume, i.e. volume of trades initiated by a buyer to open a new position, has predictability for underlying stock returns and that it takes several weeks for the returns to fully adjust to the information embedded in the option volume.

The ISEE Sentiment Index is calculated for all underlyings as well as for the group of all single equity options (ISEE Equity) and all index options (ISEE Index) separately. In addition, sentiment values are calculated for single underlyings so investors can access sentiment values on every contract traded on the exchange. This also allows for the comparison of single ISEE values on large exchange traded funds (e.g. QQQQ for the NASDAQ 100 or SPY for the S&P 500) and the comparison with market returns.

Advance Decline Ratios

According to Brown and Cliff (2004), one of the most common technical indicators is the ratio of the number of advancing stocks to declining stocks (ADV/DEC). They calculate this measure in their work for NYSE stocks but it can be calculated for other groups of stocks as well. For the purposes of this study, a DAX advance decline ratio is calculated for German stocks in order to compare it to German market sentiment surveys. An alternative measure is calculated as the difference between the number of advancing and declining stocks (ADV-DEC).

Another modification is the trading index typically called TRIN. This index is often called the ARMS index because it has been popularized by Richard Arms in 1967. The TRIN is equal to the number of advancing stocks scaled by the trading volume of advancing stocks divided by the number of declining stocks scaled by the trading volume of declining issues. Daily TRIN values are available for both NYSE and NASDAQ stocks. According to Simon and Wiggins (2001), high levels of the TRIN are viewed as indicative of market bottoms because the relatively low number of advancing issues on low volume compared with the high number of declining issues on high volume may indicate that sellers are finished selling.

Simon and Wiggins (2001) find that he TRIN has a significantly negative correlation with lagged S&P returns and a significantly positive correlation with the VIX and the put/call ratio.

3.3.3. Meta-Measures

Investors' Intelligence Bearish Sentiment Index

Each week, Investors' Intelligence[15] collects data from independent market newsletters like the *Zweig Forecast*, the *Cabot Market Letter* and the *Todd Market Timer* and assesses each author's approach to the market. About 150 newsletter writers are categorized as bullish, bearish or neutral regarding their expectation of future markets. Investors' Intelligence has collected the data since 1963 biweekly; afterwards in 1969 it became weekly. Figure 3.13 presents a historical chart of the index along with the DJIA close prices (The chart is taken from Solt and Statman (1988) since the data is not publicly available).

[15] http://www.investorsintelligence.com/.

The sentiment index is the percentage of bullish authors relative to the sum of bullish and bearish authors. Hence, a high index value indicates positive and a low value negative sentiment. Solt and Statman (1988) are among the first academics who examine the effectiveness of the index. They conclude that it is useless as a forecasting tool. Ten years later, Clarke and Statman (1998) do not find any forecasting power for stock returns either. In contrast, Brown and Cliff (2005) conclude that sentiment measured by Investors' Intelligence has predictive power regarding long-term stock returns.

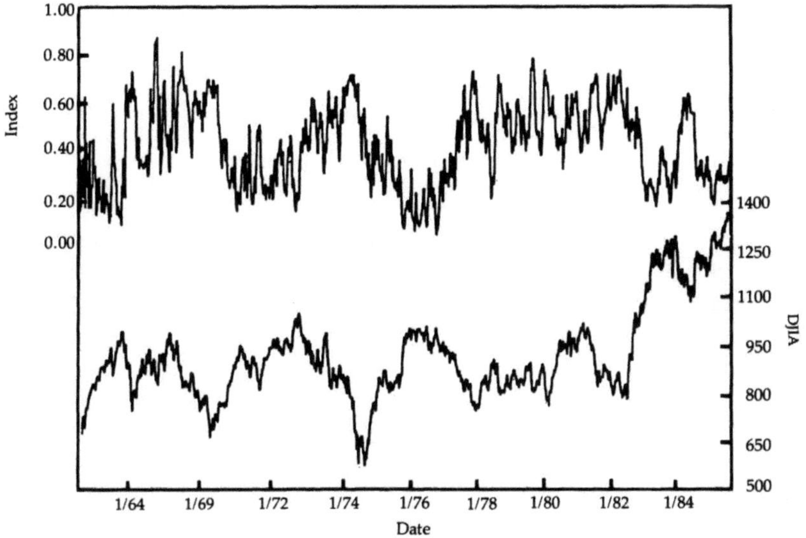

Figure 3.13: Investors' Intelligence Bearish Sentiment Index

This figure (taken from Solt and Statman (1988)) shows Investors' Intelligence Bearish Sentiment Index (left axis) along with the Dow Jones Industrial Average (right axis).

3.3.4. Summary Statistics

Before a more detailed analysis of all the sentiment measures presented in this chapter is carried out, summary statistics of all of the measures are presented in Table 3.1 below. All measures are available until December 2008 with the exception of the UBS/Gallup survey and the CEFD measure collected by Wurgler.

Table 3.1: Summary Statistics of Sentiment Measures

This table presents summary statistics of the sentiment measures discussed in previous sections of this chapter. The data is grouped into daily, weekly, and monthly sentiment measures. Daily measures are indirect, and weekly and monthly measures are direct. Start and End indicate the duration of time series used in this and subsequent chapters. The number of observations, mean, median, minimum, and maximum are presented.

	Start	End	No. obs.	Mean	Median	Minimum	Maximum
Panel A: Daily Sentiment Measures							
ADV-DEC DAX	01/2004	12/2008	1250	0.437	2.000	-30.000	30.000
ADV-DEC DJIA	04/2005	12/2008	921	0.396	0.000	-30.000	30.000
Put/Call Total	10/1995	12/2008	3336	0.785	0.769	0.300	1.704
Put/Call Equity	10/2003	12/2008	1311	0.663	0.644	0.351	1.345
Put/Call Index	10/2003	12/2008	1311	1.604	1.549	0.242	3.894
TRIN NYSE	06/2003	12/2008	1384	1.688	1.020	0.120	673.890
TRIN NASDAQ	06/2003	12/2008	1390	1.061	0.890	0.020	7.050
VDAX	01/1992	12/2008	4281	22.950	20.408	9.350	83.226
VIX	01/1990	12/2008	4788	19.697	18.260	9.310	80.860
ISEE All	04/2002	12/2008	1703	141.133	137.000	0.000	415.000
ISEE Equity	01/2006	12/2008	755	170.176	167.000	66.000	280.000
ISEE Index	01/2006	12/2008	755	55.993	48.000	13.000	312.000
Panel B: Weekly Sentiment Measures							
Sentix 1M/P	02/2001	12/2008	403	0.022	0.019	-0.516	0.597
Sentix 1M/I	02/2001	12/2008	403	0.081	0.105	-0.511	0.717
Sentix 6M/P	02/2001	12/2008	403	0.112	0.099	-0.188	0.433
Sentix 6M/I	02/2001	12/2008	403	0.128	0.143	-0.226	0.476
Bull Bear DAX	08/2002	12/2008	330	0.597	0.600	0.394	0.778
Bull Bear TecDAX	03/2003	12/2008	302	0.616	0.621	0.321	0.843
AAII Bull Ratio	07/1987	12/2008	1119	0.567	0.576	0.163	0.917
Panel C: Monthly Sentiment Measures							
G-Mind	12/1991	12/2008	205	2.294	2.300	-1.900	6.200
G-Mind Stocks	12/1991	12/2008	205	5.668	6.100	0.700	9.100
G-Mind Bonds	12/1991	12/2008	205	-2.664	-3.800	-8.500	7.500
Michigan ICS	01/1978	12/2008	372	87.221	90.650	51.700	112.000
Michigan ICE	01/1978	12/2008	372	79.555	81.750	44.200	108.600
Conference Board CCI	06/1997	12/2008	139	105.960	105.600	38.000	144.700
UBS/Gallup	10/1996	12/2007	117	93.385	84.000	5.000	178.000
CEFD	01/1995	12/2005	132	7.828	8.346	1.132	15.189

3.4. Evaluation of Sentiment Measures

In this section, direct and indirect sentiment measures are being compared. Firstly, pairwise correlations between sentiment measures within one group are calculated to evaluate whether they measure the same sentiment. Secondly, correlations are calculated between groups, i.e. pairwise correlations of direct and indirect sentiment measures are analyzed to evaluate whether the different methodologies (survey-based, market data based) deliver the same results. Finally, sentiment measures are related to market returns, i.e. different stock market index returns in particular. Since investor sentiment incorporates investors' expectations and opinions about the market, sentiment measures and market returns should be correlated.

3.4.1. Direct Sentiment Measures

Table 3.2 presents correlation coefficients among all weekly surveys (Panel A), among monthly surveys (Panel B), and between weekly and monthly surveys (Panel C). Statistical significance is indicated by the superscripts ***, **, and *.

Among the weekly surveys, correlation is relatively high and significant: Sentix, Bull Bear Sentiment, and AAII are positively correlated with the lowest correlation coefficients found between the German sentiment measures and the American AAII. The highest correlation is found between the Sentix measures for institutional and private investors in the short term: A high 82.1% correlation means that in the short run, institutional and private investors have similar expectations. In the longer run, however, correlation is not as high. A 32.2% correlation indicates that both investor groups disagree to a greater extent. However, correlation is still positive and significant.

The comparison of the correlation among the monthly sentiment surveys reveals that sentiment measured in the U.S. may be contrary to that measured in Germany: The G-Mind is significantly negatively correlated to all monthly U.S. sentiment measures: ICS, ICE, CCI, and UBS/Gallup. Interestingly, correlation among those is high and significantly positive meaning that these indicators measure similar sentiment although questions, methodologies, exact time period of surveys, etc. are different.

Panel C of Table 3.2 compares weekly and monthly surveys. In order to calculate correlations between time series of different frequencies, average values are computed for the higher-frequency time series (weeks) and correlations are calculated using the 4-week averages afterwards.[16]

There are a couple of interesting facts to note: First, the G-Mind for stocks has a positive and significant correlation with the AAII, the Bull Bear Indices as well as the Sentix 6-month institutional and private investor indices. Second, the U.S. sentiment indicators correlate well:

[16] Robustness checks (not reported) reveal that the results remain the same when using first/last observations per month.

AAII and ICS, ICE, CCI, and UBS/Gallup are positively correlated. This shows that the general direction of the sentiment measured over a few weeks is the same as of sentiment measured during the course of a whole month.

Table 3.2: Correlation of Weekly and Monthly Sentiment Measures

This table presents correlation coefficients among direct sentiment measures. Panel A shows correlation coefficients among weekly surveys, Panel B among monthly surveys, and Panel C between weekly and monthly surveys. The superscripts ***, **, and * denote statistical significance at the 1%, 5%, and 10% level, respectively.

Panel A: Weekly surveys

	Sentix 1M/P	Sentix 1M/I	Sentix 6M/P	Sentix 6M/I	Bull Bear DAX	Bull Bear TecDAX
Sentix 1M/I	0.821***					
Sentix 6M/P	0.109**	-0.024				
Sentix 6M/I	0.015	0.032	0.322***			
Bull Bear DAX	0.312***	0.376***	0.073	0.008		
Bull Bear TecDAX	0.429***	0.410***	0.126**	0.106*	0.716***	
AAII Bull Ratio	0.230***	0.154***	0.187***	0.171***	0.077	0.321***

Panel B: Monthly surveys

	G-Mind	G-Mind Stocks	G-Mind Bonds	Michigan ICS	Michigan ICE	Conference Board CCI
G-Mind Stocks	0.573***					
G-Mind Bonds	0.715***	0.127*				
Michigan ICS	-0.297***	0.263***	-0.310***			
Michigan ICE	-0.279***	0.239***	-0.280***	0.978***		
Conference Board CCI	-0.322***	0.236***	-0.025	0.910***	0.865***	
UBS/Gallup	-0.307***	0.019	0.176*	0.897***	0.874***	0.888***

Panel C: Weekly and monthly surveys

	Sentix 1M/P	Sentix 1M/I	Sentix 6M/P	Sentix 6M/I	Bull Bear DAX	Bull Bear TecDAX	AAII Bull Ratio
G-Mind	-0.296***	-0.038	-0.026	-0.155	0.196*	0.310***	-0.104
G-Mind Stocks	0.044	0.197*	0.231**	0.382***	0.207*	0.482***	0.273***
G-Mind Bonds	-0.352***	-0.195*	-0.088	-0.517***	0.084	-0.169	-0.203***
Michigan ICS	0.170	0.166	0.125	0.390***	-0.017	0.312***	0.515***
Michigan ICE	0.083	0.139	0.045	0.297***	0.032	0.335***	0.555***
Conference Board CCI	0.253**	0.156	0.329***	0.244**	-0.109	0.132	0.417***
UBS/Gallup	0.207*	0.021	0.135	-0.245**	-0.109	0.017	0.427***

3.4.2. Indirect Sentiment Measures

Table 3.3 shows the correlation coefficients among daily indirect sentiment measures. For the volatility indicators, first differences (denoted by Δ) are calculated in order to detect any correlation between changes of volatility (rather than levels) and other sentiment indicators.

Volatility changes (Δ VDAX as well as Δ VIX) are negatively correlated to the advance-decline measures. In addition, there are especially high positive correlations between the VDAX/VIX and the equity Put/Call ratio indicating that high volatility is usually related to increased put volume. Furthermore, the equity Put/Call ratio is negatively correlated to the ISEE Equity measure due to its similar construction methodology (the ISEE is a modified Call/Put ratio, i.e. the sign differs).

Interestingly, the TRIN measures do not have much in common: TRIN NYSE and TRIN NASDAQ are uncorrelated, and while the TRIN NASDAQ correlates well with other indicators, the TRIN NYSE does not seem to relate to any other measure. However, the TRIN NASDAQ seems to be a contrary indicator since it is positively correlated to the equity Put/Call ratio and negatively correlated to the ISEE equity measure.

Table 3.3: Correlation of Daily Indirect Sentiment Measures

This table presents correlation coefficients among daily indirect sentiment measures. First differences are denoted by Δ. The superscripts ***, **, and * denote statistical significance at the 1%, 5%, and 10% level, respectively.

	ADV-DEC DAX	ADV-DEC DJIA	Put/Call Total	Put/Call Equity	Put/Call Index	TRIN NYSE	TRIN NASDAQ	VDAX	Δ VDAX	VIX	Δ VIX	ISEE All	ISEE Equity
ADV-DEC DJIA	0.158***												
Put/Call Total	-0.371***	-0.113***											
Put/Call Equity	-0.335***	-0.129***	0.740***										
Put/Call Index	-0.208***	-0.125***	0.541***	0.059**									
TRIN NYSE	0.044	-0.035	0.001	0.014	-0.034								
TRIN NASDAQ	-0.276***	-0.111***	0.282***	0.324***	0.088***	-0.015							
VDAX	-0.107***	-0.046	0.031*	0.425***	-0.179***	0.114***	0.204***						
Δ VDAX	-0.548***	-0.162***	0.215***	0.265***	0.182***	-0.044	0.201***	0.073***					
VIX	-0.113***	-0.065**	0.038**	0.448***	-0.179***	0.099***	0.268***	0.868***	0.077***				
Δ VIX	-0.318***	-0.087***	0.207***	0.222***	0.186***	-0.210***	0.496***	0.006	0.450***	0.095***			
ISEE All	0.046	-0.023	-0.371***	-0.440***	0.012	-0.039	-0.080***	-0.314***	0.037	-0.363***	0.009		
ISEE Equity	0.150***	0.098***	-0.436***	-0.650***	0.128***	-0.041	-0.242***	-0.458***	-0.086**	-0.481***	-0.068*	0.773***	
ISEE Index	-0.049	-0.066*	0.036	0.234***	-0.236***	-0.004	0.162***	0.387***	0.006	0.418***	0.015	0.246***	-0.282***

3.4.3. Direct vs. Indirect Sentiment Measures

Table 3.4 and Table 3.5 show correlations between direct measures on the one hand and indirect sentiment measures on the other hand. A strong correlation implies that indirect sentiment measures contain the expectations of market participants as measured by direct sentiment.

Brown and Cliff (2004) compare direct and indirect sentiment measures and document strong relations between many disparate measures of investor sentiment. They use direct sentiment measures such as the AAII and the II surveys, and indirect measures such as the ARMS index, odd lot sales, put/call ratio, and the CEFD. They find that many commonly cited indirect measures of sentiment are related to direct measures (surveys) of investor sentiment.

Qiu and Welch (2006) investigate the CEFD measure, the Consumer Confidence survey, and the UBS/Gallup survey and validate them against each other. They compare an indirect sentiment measure with a direct measure, as well as two direct measures of consumer confidence and investor sentiment, respectively. They find that the CEFD has no correlation with the UBS/Gallup survey, while the consumer confidence index does. Regardless of the specific correlation results, it seems plausible to compare different kind of sentiment measures and the correlations among and between them.

Table 3.4: Correlation between Indirect and Direct Weekly Sentiment Measures

This table presents correlation coefficients between indirect (vertical axis) and direct (horizontal axis) weekly sentiment measures. Indirect measures have been converted from daily to weekly frequency using daily averages. The superscripts ***, **, and * denote statistical significance at the 1%, 5%, and 10% level, respectively.

	Sentix 1M/P	Sentix 1M/I	Sentix 6M/P	Sentix 6M/I	Bull Bear DAX	Bull Bear TecDAX	AAII Bull Ratio
ADV-DEC DAX	0.682***	0.629***	0.047	0.073	0.247***	0.387***	0.164***
ADV-DEC DJIA	0.105	0.107	-0.039	0.044	0.052	0.064	-0.056
TRIN NYSE	-0.035	0.006	-0.024	-0.077	-0.003	-0.017	-0.017
TRIN NASDAQ	-0.432***	-0.327***	-0.129**	-0.161***	-0.093	-0.213***	-0.251***
VDAX	-0.323***	-0.053	-0.385***	-0.058	0.112**	-0.119**	-0.226***
Δ VDAX	-0.232***	-0.191***	-0.020	0.001	-0.106*	-0.239***	-0.230***
VIX	-0.302***	-0.108**	-0.297***	-0.290***	0.075	-0.156***	-0.336***
Δ VIX	-0.285***	-0.239***	-0.002	0.035	-0.099*	-0.244***	-0.228***
Put/Call Total	-0.316***	-0.350***	-0.029	-0.012	-0.209***	-0.422***	-0.502***
Put/Call Equity	-0.619***	-0.482***	-0.213***	-0.300***	-0.110*	-0.318***	-0.510***
Put/Call Index	-0.135**	-0.130**	0.181***	0.290***	-0.196***	-0.135**	0.025
ISEE All	0.263***	0.145***	0.100*	0.196***	0.002	0.286***	0.637***
ISEE Equity	0.519***	0.368***	0.145*	0.441***	-0.087	0.155*	0.537***
ISEE Index	-0.180**	-0.022	-0.341***	-0.487***	0.148*	-0.025	-0.326***

Table 3.4 presents correlations between indirect and direct weekly sentiment measures. The indirect measures (with the exception of the ADV-DEC DAX measure) are transformed to the weekly frequency using daily averages. The ADV-DEC DAX measure is an exact measure of the advances and declines per week.

There is ample of evidence that weekly survey measures are related to sentiment measures based on market data: The German private investor survey Sentix (short-term) is positively correlated to the DAX Advance-Decline measure, negatively to the equity put/call ratio and the VDAX, and positively to the ISEE Equity Index. All correlations have the direction as expected in advance: high ADV-DEC measures and high ISEE values mean positive investor sentiment whereas high put/call ratios and high VDAX levels stand for negative sentiment. Therefore, since the Sentix measure is expected to express positive sentiment, correlation coefficients differ by sign but indicate the same relationship. The institutional version of the Sentix (short-term) – due to the high correlation of 82.3% – has similar properties as the private investor version.

The AAII survey and the ISEE Index are positively correlated whereas the correlation with the put/call ratio is negative. Instead of the VDAX, the AAII measure is compared to the VIX, the U.S. volatility measure. The correlation between the AAII and the VIX is negative. The different sentiment measures express sentiment levels as expected.

The monthly direct and indirect sentiment measures are presented in Table 3.5. As for the weekly transformation, daily indirect sentiment measures have been transformed to a monthly frequency by calculating the daily averages (with the exception of the ADV-DEC DAX measure which is computed exactly as well as the CEFD for which monthly data is available).

Table 3.5: Correlation between Indirect and Direct Monthly Sentiment Measures

This table presents correlation coefficients between indirect (vertical axis) and direct (horizontal axis) monthly sentiment measures. Indirect measures have been converted from daily to monthly frequency using daily averages. The superscripts ***, **, and * denote statistical significance at the 1%, 5%, and 10% level, respectively.

	G-Mind	G-Mind Stocks	G-Mind Bonds	Michigan ICS	Δ Michigan ICS	Michigan ICE	Δ Michigan ICE	Conference Board CCI	Δ Conference Board CCI	UBS/Gallup	Δ UBS/Gallup
ADV-DEC DAX	0.029	0.333***	-0.224*	0.337***	0.255**	0.268**	0.195	0.373***	0.337***	0.010	0.364**
ADV-DEC DJIA	-0.421***	-0.091	-0.128	0.278*	-0.055	0.249*	-0.120	0.362**	0.024	0.175	-0.147
TRIN NYSE	0.176	-0.150	0.309**	-0.271**	-0.316***	-0.182	-0.236*	-0.350***	-0.429***	0.018	-0.176
TRIN NASDAQ	0.251**	-0.346***	0.580***	-0.500***	-0.150	-0.392***	-0.121	-0.570***	-0.371***	0.100	-0.249*
VDAX	0.070	-0.011	-0.062	-0.055	-0.129*	0.032	-0.119*	-0.271***	-0.242***	-0.119	-0.060
Δ VDAX	-0.044	-0.090	0.012	-0.122*	-0.348***	-0.100	-0.300***	-0.071	-0.446***	-0.097	-0.354***
VIX	0.016	-0.114	0.003	-0.106	-0.172**	-0.002	-0.164**	-0.217**	-0.305***	0.130	-0.163*
Δ VIX	-0.080	-0.129*	-0.022	-0.105	-0.323***	-0.074	-0.270***	-0.090	-0.406***	-0.058	-0.401***
Put/Call Total	-0.056	-0.327***	-0.211***	-0.761***	-0.204***	-0.789***	-0.179**	-0.688***	-0.227***	-0.729***	-0.139
Put/Call Equity	0.132	-0.460***	0.603***	-0.625***	-0.244*	-0.542***	-0.217*	-0.637***	-0.351***	-0.208	-0.349**
Put/Call Index	-0.538***	0.071	-0.475***	0.385***	-0.244*	0.268**	-0.184	0.632***	-0.039	-0.158	-0.178
ISEE All	0.186*	0.526***	-0.554***	0.565***	0.211*	0.551***	0.159	0.302***	0.319***	0.331***	0.211*
ISEE Equity	-0.617***	0.327*	-0.707***	0.698***	0.079	0.642***	0.045	0.719***	0.323*	0.413**	0.243
ISEE Index	0.716***	-0.335**	0.713***	-0.788***	0.047	-0.743***	-0.015	-0.839***	-0.166	-0.511**	-0.271
CEFD	-0.640***	-0.451***	0.044	0.519***	0.054	0.436***	0.063	0.655***	0.064	0.660***	-0.005

The monthly G-Mind Stocks measure is negatively correlated to the equity put/call ratio and positively to the ISEE equity index as well as the DAX ADV-DEC measure. Interestingly, the G-Mind Bonds is also correlated but in the opposite direction: There is a positive correlation to the equity put/call ratio and a negative correlation to the ISEE equity index. The reason is the opposite expectation of investors towards the asset classes stocks and bonds: When investor sentiment towards stocks is rather negative, investors tend to buy bonds, and vice versa. Therefore, correlation coefficients have different signs.

The monthly U.S. confidence and sentiment surveys have a lot in common: They all correlate well with the CEFD and the total put/call ratio, though the direction differs: Correlation with CEFD is large and positive indicating that all measure a common source of sentiment. However, correlation with the total put/call ratio is large and negative which confirms that the put/call ratio typically is a contrary indicator. With the exception of the CCI, all other surveys are also positively correlated to the ISEE total index.

The results presented in this section confirm Qiu and Welch's (2006) finding that the UBS/Gallup measure and the Michigan ICS are positively correlated (89.7%) and that they are indeed likely to pick up the same underlying factor – investor sentiment. In contrast to their original study, however, the results of this section show that the UBS/Gallup measure and the CEFD as reported by Baker and Wurgler (2006)[17] are also positively correlated: A large and highly significant 66% correlation suggests that the CEFD may also pick up the same investor sentiment.

3.4.4. Sentiment Measures vs. Market Returns

Brown and Cliff (2004) investigate the correlation of sentiment and market returns and find that changes in the survey and their composite measures of investor sentiment are highly correlated with contemporaneous market returns.

The contemporaneous correlations between all sentiment indices and market returns are presented in Table 3.6. Panel A shows correlations between market returns and daily sentiment measures, Panel B weekly sentiment measures, and Panel C monthly sentiment measures.

[17] Jeffrey Wurgler makes the CEFD data available on his website (http://pages.stern.nyu.edu/~jwurgler/). They take the value-weighted average discount on closed-end stock funds for 1962 through 1993 from Neal and Wheatley (1998), for 1994 through 1998 from CDA/Wiesenberger, and for 1999 through 2001 from turn-of-the-year issues of the Wall Street Journal.

Table 3.6: Correlation of Sentiment Measures and Market Returns

This table presents correlation coefficients between sentiment measures and market logreturns as proxied by several international stock market indexes. Panel A presents coefficients for daily, Panel B for weekly, and Panel C for monthly sentiment measures. The superscripts ***, **, and * denote statistical significance at the 1%, 5%, and 10% level, respectively.

	Logreturns							
	DAX	TecDAX	ESX50	S&P 500	Nasdaq 100	DJIA	Russel 2000	REX
Panel A: Daily sentiment measures								
ADV-DEC DAX	0.785***	0.673***	0.760***	0.369***	0.355***	0.370***	0.368***	-0.153***
ADV-DEC DJIA	0.132***	0.142***	0.147***	0.120***	0.116***	0.124***	0.101***	-0.022
Put/Call Total	-0.264***	-0.257***	-0.272***	-0.257***	-0.228***	-0.240***	-0.276***	0.097***
Put/Call Equity	-0.372***	-0.361***	-0.354***	-0.290***	-0.283***	-0.279***	-0.297***	0.113***
Put/Call Index	-0.185***	-0.163***	-0.194***	-0.195***	-0.197***	-0.194***	-0.219***	0.024
TRIN NYSE	0.206***	0.183***	0.200***	0.209***	0.195***	0.217***	0.131***	-0.200***
TRIN NASDAQ	-0.372***	-0.349***	-0.344***	-0.634***	-0.746***	-0.604***	-0.608***	0.081***
VDAX	-0.099***	-0.076***	-0.086***	-0.041***	-0.014	-0.040**	-0.053***	0.053***
Δ VDAX	-0.649***	-0.577***	-0.712***	-0.346***	-0.258***	-0.334***	-0.341***	0.120***
VIX	-0.120***	-0.127***	-0.117***	-0.128***	-0.074***	-0.120***	-0.139***	0.064***
Δ VIX	-0.437***	-0.416***	-0.486***	-0.784***	-0.548***	-0.751***	-0.693***	0.137***
ISEE All	-0.026	0.006	-0.043*	-0.012	-0.045*	-0.016	0.007	0.007
ISEE Equity	0.153***	0.173***	0.131***	0.114***	0.130***	0.108***	0.109***	-0.077**
ISEE Index	-0.086**	-0.084**	-0.092**	-0.068*	-0.090**	-0.067*	-0.053	0.049
Panel B: Weeky sentiment measures								
Sentix 1M/P	0.542***	0.500***	0.512***	0.469***	0.485***	0.451***	0.461***	-0.283***
Sentix 1M/I	0.490***	0.446***	0.474***	0.411***	0.432***	0.406***	0.413***	-0.233***
Sentix 6M/P	0.042	0.070	0.047	0.019	0.049	0.011	0.036	-0.078
Sentix 6M/I	-0.002	0.066	0.029	0.038	0.089*	0.010	0.043	-0.051
Bull Bear DAX	0.174***	0.128**	0.180***	0.168***	0.189***	0.172***	0.179***	-0.034
Bull Bear TecDAX	0.328***	0.321***	0.319***	0.268***	0.266***	0.245***	0.271***	-0.070
AAII Bull Ratio	0.193***	0.188***	0.170***	0.148***	0.103**	0.137***	0.183***	-0.138***
Panel C: Monthly sentiment measures								
Δ G-Mind	0.082	-0.041	0.078	0.045	0.022	0.071	-0.023	0.235**
Δ G-Mind Stocks	0.068	-0.024	0.088	0.043	0.030	0.072	-0.005	-0.014
Δ G-Mind Bonds	0.000	-0.040	-0.029	-0.069	-0.006	-0.083	-0.114	0.360***
Δ Michigan ICS	0.209***	0.172*	0.211**	0.165**	0.052	0.166**	0.230***	-0.121
Δ Michigan ICE	0.176**	0.161*	0.185**	0.126*	0.040	0.127*	0.191***	-0.107
Δ Conference Board CCI	0.297***	0.143	0.292***	0.245***	0.117	0.252***	0.302***	-0.227**
Δ UBS/Gallup	0.316***	0.254**	0.281***	0.245**	0.245**	0.200**	0.345***	-0.216**

As a proxy for market returns, we use several indices: the DAX for the German market, the EuroStoxx50 for the European market, the S&P500, the NASDAQ100, and the broader Russell 2000 for the American market. Also, we have included the REX index, the German Index for government bonds, to detect correlations between this index and the German G-Mind Bonds measure.

The following findings can be noted for the daily measures: The advance/decline measure for the DAX is positively correlated to contemporaneous DAX returns which is not surprising since DAX returns are positive when there are more advancing stocks than declining. The relationship is not linear, however, due to the different weights of the member stocks. The equity put/call ratio and equity market returns are negatively correlated. This means that market rises are accompanied by large call volumes and market declines by large put volumes. In other words, the put/call ratio measured at the CBOE moves with the market and supports market movements.

High negative correlations exist between the TRIN NASDAQ measure and contemporaneous market returns, especially of the NASDAQ 100. One usually sees high TRIN readings near market lows and extended periods of low readings near market peaks. This means that the TRIN can be used as a contrary indicator.

Changes of the VIX are negatively correlated to S&P 500 returns and other American market index returns. This finding is in line with related research about volatility and returns (e.g. Whaley 2000). If expected market volatility increases, investors demand higher rates on returns on stocks, and so stock prices fall. The same relationship applies to the German volatility measure, the VDAX, and the DAX returns.

The ISEE Sentiment, although its construction suggests that its behavior is contrary to that of the put/call ratios, does not correlate to such a large extent with market returns. Correlation of the ISEE equity index and market returns is significantly positive but economically small.

The weekly short-term surveys show a positive correlation with market returns, especially the DAX. The Sentix private investor survey's correlation amounts to 54.2% and the Sentix institutional investor survey's correlation to 49.0%. The medium-term surveys, however, do not correlate with contemporaneous market returns. The Bull Bear ratios and the AAII survey are significantly positively correlated to market returns, though correlation is not very high.

Changes in the monthly surveys show a medium positive correlation with market returns, especially the DAX. Survey levels do not exhibit any correlation (and are therefore not presented in Table 3.6). Correlation coefficients of the G-Mind are low and not significant with the exception of the G-Mind Bonds Index and the REX. They correlate significantly with a correlation coefficient of 36.0%.

3.4.5. Review of Results

The purpose of section 3.3.4 was to investigate three main questions: First, do direct or indirect investor sentiment measures pick up the same signals and therefore correlate within each group? Second, are direct and indirect measures correlated and can they be validated against each other? Third, are investor sentiment measures correlated to market returns and therefore explain part of the movements of the market?

Firstly, an overall high correlation among survey measures can be documented although they generally have a different set of respondents (e.g. Sentix and Bull Bear TecDAX have a 40% correlation). Furthermore, correlations among surveys conducted in different countries are correlated (e.g. Sentix in Germany and AAII in the U.S. have a 23.0% correlation) with the exception of the G-Mind. Although survey frequencies may be different (e.g. the weekly AAII survey and the monthly G-Mind survey), high correlations of up to 51.7% are documented.

Secondly, most direct and indirect measures can be successfully validated against each other: Correlations between weekly and monthly surveys on the one hand and indirect measures on the other hand are generally very high and have the expected direction. The high-to-low frequency conversion, however, could possibly disguise a higher correlation at the monthly levels.

Thirdly, the majority of all sentiment indicators (or their first differences) is correlated to market returns, higher correlations for high-frequency measures and lower correlations for lower-frequency measures are documented. The direction of the correlation, however, is not unanimous: Most survey measures have a positive correlation with stock market returns whereas the results for the indirect daily measures are mixed. Especially changes in the VDAX/VIX and the NASDAQ Traders Index (TRIN) are negatively correlated with market returns.

3.5. Conclusion

In this chapter, different classifications of investor sentiment measures are presented as suggested by related research and sentiment measures in practice. Direct sentiment measures are surveys in which investors are asked directly about their attitude towards the economic situation or the stock market in particular. Indirect sentiment measures refer to financial variables and require a theory relating them to sentiment. Meta-measures are sentiment measures that are neither based on surveys nor pure financial data but involve meta-information about investor sentiment.

In research, the closed-end funds discount has received a great deal of attention in the 1990s. Today, researchers still cannot explain the existence of a CEFD and its variance. Many other studies have tried and are still trying to create composite or meta-measures to extract investor sentiment that is useful for explaining investor behavior and/or market returns.

In practice, there are many investor sentiment measures whose usefulness is widely debated in the media. Many of the measures involve the polling of investors, the collection of financial data and the construction of technical indicators.

The evaluation of sentiment measures is difficult and not straightforward. Qiu and Welch (2006) state that "we have what we believe to be the best available empirical direct proxy for investor sentiment" and measure the quality of a sentiment index according to its correlation with their direct measure of sentiment. In general, most of the measures, regardless of whether they are indirect or direct, have a high pairwise correlation indicating that they indeed pick up the same sentiment signal. Therefore, correlation with other sentiment measures could serve as an indicator for sentiment quality, but not as a necessary or sufficient condition.

Another evaluation method of sentiment measures is the comparison with market returns. Since investor sentiment incorporates investors' expectations and opinion about the market, sentiment measures and market returns should be correlated. We confirm this reasoning and find that most of the sentiment indicators correlate well with market returns, with high-frequency indirect measures having the highest correlation and lower-frequency indirect measures a lower correlation with the market.

To sum up, there are many different measures of investor sentiment in research and practice but their evaluation remains difficult. A high correlation among each other and with market returns is a good indication that they react to the same underlying factor. Future research, however, is needed to identify this factor which will make it easier to construct new measures and evaluate existing ones.

4 Construction of the Euwax Sentiment Index

Using a unique data set consisting of more than 36.5 million submitted retail investor orders over the course of 5 years, the Euwax Sentiment Index is being developed. It is based on retail investor orders submitted to the European Warrant Exchange, the market segment for securitized derivatives at Boerse Stuttgart. What makes this data unique is the fact that it consists of retail orders only, retail buy and sell orders can be determined exactly due to the market maker model, expression of negative sentiment is possible by buying puts, and not the data includes executed as well as submitted orders.

This chapter is structured as follows: Section 4.1 presents an introduction of structured products in general and trading at EUWAX in particular and summarizes key facts. The data set is described in 4.2. The basic index calculation is shown in section 4.3, followed by multivariate regressions that determine the influence of certain parameters on the index in section 4.4. Finally, section 4.5 compares the Euwax Sentiment Index with other direct and indirect sentiment measures found in practice. Section 4.6 concludes this chapter.

4.1. Introduction

4.1.1. Securitized Derivatives

History of Securitized Derivatives

The history of securitized derivatives started in the 1980s with the creation of covered warrant markets in Switzerland and Germany (a detailed history of covered warrants can be found in McHattie 2002). Since then, covered warrants have been established in many European countries, among them France, Italy, and the United Kingdom. Covered warrants are securities issued by banks or financial institutions representing the right for the investor to buy or sell an asset at a fixed price, on or before a specified future date.

In particular, covered warrants may give rights over single stocks, a basket of stocks, an index, a currency, a commodity, or any other financial asset. Investors thereby gain exposure to the performance of an asset for a fraction of a price. This is called gearing. The name 'covered' warrant was coined when these financial products held the right to purchase a physical stock at the end of their term. The issuer of the warrant commonly held the stock in order to be able to satisfy the right when the warrant reached maturity. Therefore, the warrant was covered by the underlying security. Today, issuers use dynamic hedging techniques to cover their financial exposure.

Today, covered warrants make up only a fraction of all traded securitized derivatives. Issuers have continually advanced their products to meet growing investors' demands. Knock-out certificates (also known as mini-futures) have been invented as well as investment certificates. In general, a distinction between leverage products (i.e. products with a gearing) and investment products (i.e. usually 100% participation with no gearing) can be made.

Types and Terms

The term "warrant" is very broad and stands for a highly flexible instrument which can be transformed to match a wide range of demands. However, there are several types and terms all these instruments have in common.

Calls and Puts: With securitized derivatives, investors can benefit from both rising and falling markets by choosing call products or put products. Like in the traditional options market, call products give a right to buy an underlying asset whereas put products entitle the holder to sell the underlying asset at a predetermined price. Most investors are by nature optimistic, and a falling market is usually an opportunity for them to find the bottom. However, in recent years investors have gained more and more experience with the opportunity to speculate on falling markets, so that put products have become popular instruments for retail investors.

Exercise Style: The exercise terms of plain-vanilla warrants are usually described by the terms 'European style' and 'American style'. European exercise style means that the warrants can only be exercised on a specific date whereas American exercise style means that they can be exercised at any point in time to maturity. Exercising a warrant means that investors make use of their right to buy or sell the underlying asset at the predetermined price. Therefore, issuers prefer the European style because exercise occurs infrequently, and investors may prefer the American style since it offers more flexibility. In practice, however, this difference does not matter much since most investors never exercise their warrants and rather sell them before maturity.

Strike Prices: For leverage products, the strike price is the primary determinant of leverage and associated risk. The strike price is the specified price at which the warrant may be exercised, i.e. the price at which call option buyers can buy the underlying and at which put option buyers can sell the underlying. In practice, the ratio of the strike price to the underlying spot price determines the risk of the product. The difference of the strike and the spot price is the intrinsic value of the warrant.

Pricing and Trading

Prices of securitized derivatives are not driven by supply and demand like in traditional order-driven markets for equities and traditional listed warrants. The issuer is usually the sole market-maker who is obliged to make a two-way price throughout the trading day. Quotes are commonly derived from underlying prices in their respective liquid order-driven markets.

Computers automatically calculate quotes and distribute them to exchanges, order flow providers, and financial web portals.

A single-market-maker-model is common in the established markets for securitized derivatives. However, competition is far from absent: Competition simply occurs across products rather than within a particular security. On popular underlyings, several issuers offer products with similar terms, i.e. similar strike prices and maturity. In addition, issuer reputation plays an important role in competition: If an issuer makes prices to the detriment for the investor, such as widening the spread during times of financial stress, investors will quickly become aware of that and the issuer will lose business. These two forces – inter-product competition and reputation – usually ensure a fair and orderly market.

Fair prices are calculated taking a number of different factors and assumptions into account which may vary from issuer to issuer. These factors are the underlying asset price, the volatility of the underlying, the time to expiry, dividend yields, and the interest rate of a risk-free asset. Basically, the well-known options pricing model of Black and Scholes (1973) is based on these factors, but issuers may arrive at different prices due to different assumptions about volatility or interest rate development. However, the inter-product competition leads to a general convergence of market-maker quotes for popular underlyings.

Advantages

There are many advantages for retail investors when investing in securitized derivatives. Securitized derivatives, especially warrants and knock-outs, provide retail investors with gearing and leverage. Gearing is defined as the degree of additional exposure gained by buying a warrant. It is calculated by dividing the asset price by the warrant price. Leverage measures how much more a warrant will move in percentage terms against the underlying asset. It is calculated by multiplying the gearing with the delta which represents the change expected in the price of a warrant for a given change in the underlying instrument.

Gearing is an obvious advantage for investors because it is a way to achieve a large equity exposure from a relatively small amount of money. Sometimes, gearing-up and gearing-down are differentiated but the concept is essentially the same. Gearing-up means that e.g. a warrant investment of 5.000 € can lead to a much higher exposure of 25.000 €. Gearing-down means the investor's aim is to gain an equity exposure of 5.000 € and therefore invest only 1.000 € in warrants.

Another advantage of warrants for investors is the fact that warrants (and other securitized derivatives) are securities as opposed to contracts in futures and options markets. Securities have the property that their value can never be smaller than zero, so that investors' losses are limited by their initial investment. In futures markets, investors face the possibility to lose more than their initial investment. Therefore, warrant investors have the chance to unlimited gains while their losses are limited.

In contrast to equity markets, retail investors have opportunities in both Bull and Bear markets. While short-selling of stocks is usually not possible for retail investors, put warrants and other short products provide the opportunity to speculate on falling markets.

Securitized derivatives in general also provide the retail investor with the ability to invest in assets otherwise unavailable to them. For example, they can be based on currencies, baskets of stocks or commodities, foreign indices or stocks which are not traded in their home market. In addition, in most of the cases, securitized derivatives are a low transaction cost alternative to investing in the underlying stocks directly.

Disadvantages

Credit Risk must be mentioned as one of the disadvantages of securitized derivatives, especially since the financial market crisis when the investment bank and issuer Lehman Brothers went into bankruptcy and many retail investors suffered losses because they held investment certificates issued by this bank. However, credit risk has received a lot of attention lately, and the majority of retail investors now know the possible dangers linked to issuer default risk. Transparency has been increased and credit risk has become an integral part of the decision process of retail investors.

Complexity can be mentioned as another disadvantage when considering securitized derivatives. One driver is the higher complexity of derivative products in contrast to stocks – prices are derived and their calculation can be complex because many factors such as interest rates, volatility, etc. determine prices. Another driver is the amount of products available to retail investors: More than 380.000 products securitized derivatives were listed at the end of October 2009 in the EUWAX segment at Boerse Stuttgart. However, the large amount of products is due to different issuers, different strike prices, and different underlyings. If retail investors know their preferred issuer, underlying, and strike price (i.e. risk) in advance, there are several finders on the internet that help retail investors find the product that fits their needs best.

Usually, securitized derivatives do not rank for any income, i.e. they do not qualify for dividend payments on underlyings because these payments are usually used by the issuer to finance the specific structure. There are exceptions like DAX certificates that incorporate dividends because the DAX is a so-called performance-index that includes dividend payments of the stock index members. In addition, and common to all securitized derivatives, holders have no voting rights and do not receive annual or interim reports as they are not directly linked to that company. Usually, this disadvantage is not important for retail investors because most of them usually do not make use of their voting rights.

4.1.2. European Warrant Exchange

EUWAX is the trading segment for securitized derivatives at Boerse Stuttgart. It is Europe's largest trading platform for securitized derivatives in terms of turnover and number of trades. Securitized derivatives comprise a wide range of securities, e.g. covered warrants (bank-issued options), knock-out certificates (bank-issued barrier options), and investment certificates. They all have in common that their value depends on another financial instrument such as stocks, indices, commodities or fixed income products. Securitized derivatives are usually issued by banks which are obliged to continuously calculate and publish bid and ask prices for their products.

Executed order volume in securitized derivatives accounts for about 3.5 billion Euros per month totaling 211.7 billion Euros for the period of January 2004 to December 2008). At the end of the sample period, more than 150,000 leverage products and more than 180,000 investment products were listed. As a retail investor exchange, Boerse Stuttgart tailors its products and services offered to retail investors. The design of the issued securities is such that they are largely unattractive to institutional investors, but all the more appealing to retail investors. Products are not standardized and strike prices, duration, underlyings, payoff profile, and multiplier all vary from product to product. They are constructed in order to attract retail investors that value variability, dynamic combinations of underlyings, and optically low prices. These characteristics actively dissuade institutional investors that typically value standard and therefore easily hedged products, low counterparty risk, liquidity, and volume. These market characteristics and general acceptance that large investors avoid these types of markets obviate the need to control for institutional investors' influence in the data set.

4.1.3. Key Facts

Quote-Driven Market

Trading at the EUWAX takes place in a quote-driven market where market-makers continuously publish quotes. There are two kinds of trading participants in this context: Firstly, there are the market-makers (usually the product issuers) who publish bid and ask quotes for their products. Secondly, there are order flow providers (usually banks or brokerages) who route client orders to the exchange. Thirdly, there are quality liquidity providers acting on behalf of the exchange who assist in the matching procedure by providing quality and liquidity. They also continuously check the order book for executable orders and start the matching procedure.

This type of market model allows a distinction of retail orders and market maker orders. Our main assumption is that retail investors express their expectations about the market by buying and selling derivatives whereas issuers do not express any opinion because they have an obligation to trade. A retail investor's order can therefore be matched either against an issuer's order which will be the usual case, or against another retail investor's order from the order book.

Risk

The derivative products listed at EUWAX can be categorized as either leverage or investment products. Leverage products comprise covered warrants and knock-out certificates whereas investment products comprise all types of investment certificates.

Derivative products can be further categorized according to the risk inherent in their structure. Leverage products are usually regarded as riskier than investment products because investors face the risk of losing their whole investment in a relatively short time period. Knock-outs, for example, are worthless when the price of the underlying falls below (down and out) or goes above (up and out) a specific price. Investment certificates, on the other hand, usually exhibit some security features so that the investor is partially protected against a total loss.

Positive and Negative Sentiment

For each product category there are two basic option types: calls and puts. The purchase of a call option can be interpreted as a positive sentiment about the future return of the underlying whereas the purchase of a put option can be interpreted as a negative sentiment about the future value of the underlying. Although the terms call and put are typically used in the options market, this distinction can also be made in the securitized derivatives market.

The possibility of buying puts is a clear advantage of the data set since investors have the opportunity to express negative sentiment without the need for short sales. On most retail investor exchanges, short selling is constrained to professional investors.

4.2. Data Set

The data set contains order data from the EUWAX trading segment at Boerse Stuttgart for the period of January 2004 to December 2008. This data set contains 24,348,822 executed orders from retail investors. Market maker orders are not taken into account. The whole set of orders account for a volume of about 211.7 billion Euros. Table 4.1 reports summary statistics of the number of executed orders during the whole sample period. Statistics are grouped along four dimensions: product group (horizontal axis), option type (Panel A), order type (Panel B), and underlying type (Panel C).

Summary statistics of the volume of executed orders as well as the number of submitted orders are similar to these reported in Table 4.1 and can be found in Appendix A.

Table 4.1: Summary Statistics

This table reports summary statistics about the number of executed orders by derivative product group (warrants, knock-outs, and investment certificates). Panel A groups the orders by option type and trade direction, Panel B by order type, and Panel C by underlying type. The percentages in brackets provide information about the relative frequency of the different order classes within each product group.

Panel A: Executed orders by option type

		Warrants		Knock-outs		Investment certificates		Total	
Call	Buy	3,553,189	(43.5%)	3,727,704	(34.1%)	2,703,625	(51.6%)	9,984,518	(41.0%)
	Sell	2,791,118	(34.1%)	3,468,948	(31.7%)	2,416,436	(46.1%)	8,676,502	(35.6%)
Put	Buy	1,003,689	(12.3%)	1,885,706	(17.3%)	67,266	(1.3%)	2,956,661	(12.1%)
	Sell	829,584	(10.1%)	1,845,794	(16.9%)	55,763	(1.1%)	2,731,141	(11.2%)
Total		8,177,580		10,928,152		5,243,090		24,348,822	

Panel B: Executed orders by order type

	Warrants		Knock-outs		Investment certificates		Total	
Market Orders	4,727,776	(57.8%)	5,813,977	(53.2%)	4,172,416	(79.6%)	14,714,169	(60.4%)
Limit Orders	2,901,586	(35.5%)	3,008,653	(27.5%)	899,047	(17.1%)	6,809,286	(28.0%)
Stop Orders	548,218	(6.7%)	2,105,522	(19.3%)	171,627	(3.3%)	2,825,367	(11.6%)
Total	8,177,580		10,928,152		5,243,090		24,348,822	

Panel C: Executed orders by underlying type

	Warrants		Knock-outs		Investment certificates		Total	
Stocks	4,537,798	(55.5%)	2,234,376	(20.4%)	2,241,935	(42.8%)	9,014,109	(37.0%)
Indices	2,739,865	(33.5%)	6,702,157	(61.3%)	2,432,471	(46.4%)	11,874,493	(48.8%)
Fixed Income	55,212	(0.7%)	174,622	(1.6%)	80,236	(1.5%)	310,070	(1.3%)
Currencies	445,337	(5.4%)	502,380	(4.6%)	8,649	(0.2%)	956,366	(3.9%)
Commodities	391,975	(4.8%)	1,032,518	(9.4%)	428,691	(8.2%)	1,853,184	(7.6%)
Other	7,393	(0.1%)	282,099	(2.6%)	51,108	(1.0%)	340,600	(1.4%)
Total	8,177,580		10,928,152		5,243,090		24,348,822	

As can be expected from a retail investor exchange, call products account for more than 76% of the total number of orders whereas puts for only 24%. This is mostly due to the fact that most retail investors neither have the knowledge nor the willingness to trade put products. Due to the short-term nature of leverage products, there are more executed put orders in leverage products (warrants and knock-outs) than in investment products. The ratio of puts in leverage products amounts to more than 29%.

Retail investors at Boerse Stuttgart have a choice of the following order types: They can submit market orders without specifying a price, limit orders with a limit price, and stop orders with a stop limit. Due to the market-maker model, market orders are always executed against the market-maker quote, so retail investors do not face the risk of being executed at an inferior price than quoted. Investors submitting limit orders may want to save the spread that they pay when submitting market orders. Stop orders are activated when the market-maker quote reaches the stop limit. An activated stop order becomes a market order and is executed immediately.

For the purposes of this study, all orders are sorted according to their order type into three groups: The first group, market orders, contains market orders as well as marketable limit orders and marketable stop orders. Orders are defined as marketable if they are submitted with a (stop) limit and executed within 60 seconds of submission. The rationale behind this classification is that market orders without a limit and limit orders with a very aggressive limit should be treated the same since investors often use them interchangeably. The second and third groups are limit orders and stop orders with a limit that prevents orders from being executed immediately. These orders should be treated separately. Panel B of Table 4.1 shows the number of executed orders by order type.

The use of the different order types differs across instruments. Market orders are used more frequently when trading investment products than leverage products. One reason for that is that investors have longer horizons and do not care about the spread they have to pay by using market orders. Stop orders are used most often when trading knock-out certificates due to their higher risk level. Overall, retail investors prefer market orders over other order types.

Panel C of Table 4.1 presents the number of executed orders and their relative distribution by underlying type of the traded products. Each derivative product's underlying can be categorized into different underlying categories such as stocks, indices, commodities, currencies, or fixed income products. Indices and individual stocks are the most used underlyings for securitized derivatives and account for more than 85% of the number of executed orders. Among the most traded equity underlyings are Allianz, Daimler, Deutsche Bank, Deutsche Telekom, Siemens, SAP, and Munich Re. The most traded index underlyings are the DAX, EuroStoxx, and Nikkei equity indices. Commodities include Brent Crude Oil, Gold, and Silver futures. Volume in Fixed Income underlyings is highest for Euribor and Bund Futures.

4.3. Basic Index Calculation

Intuitively, positive investor sentiment should be expressed by a high index level, and negative investor sentiment by a low index level. The intuition of the index level is the following: Bullish investors buy calls or sell puts whereas bearish investors sell calls or buy puts. Therefore, order volume is categorized as driven by positive and negative sentiment and the ratio of the net order volume to the overall order volume is calculated.

As a requirement for the index design, the index should be invariant to a rise or drop in overall order volume, i.e. the index values should not depend on the absolute order volume but rather on the relative proportion of buy and sell order volumes. Therefore, investor sentiment values are not influenced by an overall rise in market volume.

The sentiment index is calculated for a given time period t as follows

$$vol\_sentiment_t = \frac{\sum_i (v_i \cdot o_i \cdot t_i)}{\sum_i v_i} \tag{4.1}$$

$$trd\_sentiment_t = \frac{\sum_i (o_i \cdot t_i)}{\sum_i 1} \tag{4.2}$$

where

v_i ... transaction volume of order i (trade price × trade size)

o_i ... option type of the instrument traded through order i ($o_i = 1$ call option, $o_i = -1$ put option)

t_i ... trade direction of order i ($t_i = 1$ buy order, $t_i = -1$ sell order)

Sentiment can be calculated using either the aggregate order volume (see formula 4.1) or the number of executed orders (see formula 4.2). Time periods used for calculation can be daily, weekly, or monthly. The higher the frequency, the noisier becomes the index. On the other hand, when choosing a lower frequency, e.g. monthly, the resulting index has less granularity and less overall descriptiveness.

Instead of choosing different calculation periods, a moving average of the daily index calculation can be introduced in order to reduce noise. A backward-looking moving average of the daily index calculation seems to be the most appropriate because noise is reduced, trends can be recognized, and a new index value is calculated every day. A disadvantage, however, is that sudden changes in the investor sentiment are not represented immediately as a delay is introduced as an artifact of the backward-looking moving average.

Before a more detailed analysis of different aspects of sentiment construction is performed, Figure 4.1 plots the 20-day moving average of the daily sentiment index based on the number of all executed orders in derivative products.

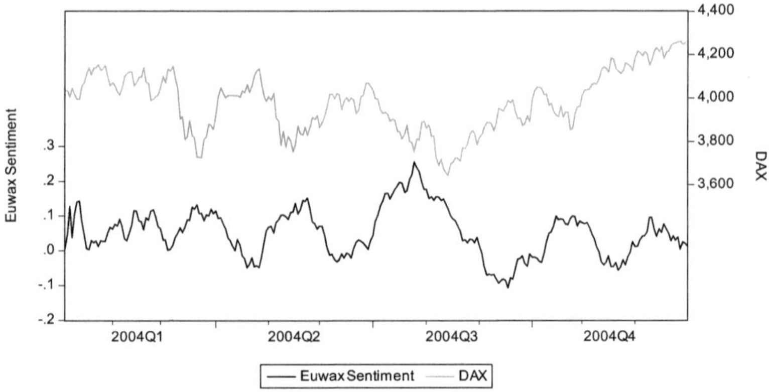

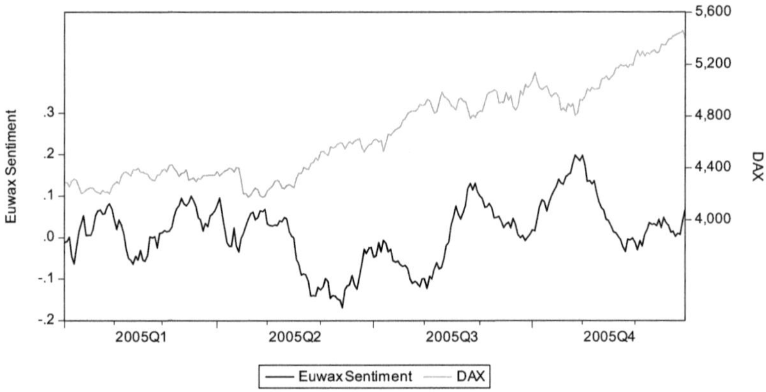

Figure 4.1: Euwax Sentiment Index (2004 - 2008)

These figures (above and next page) show the 20-day moving averages of the Euwax Sentiment Index based on the number of executed orders in all derivative products (investment products and leverage products) along with the daily DAX close prices.

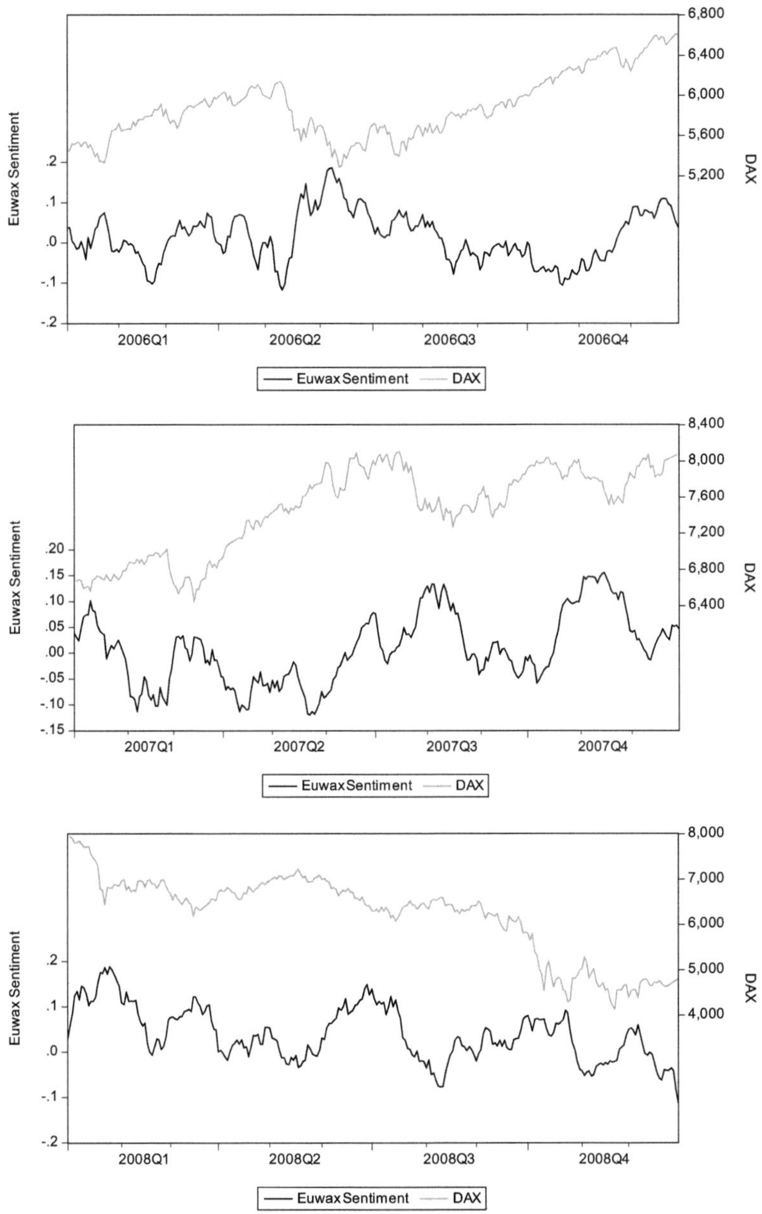

Figure 4.1: Euwax Sentiment Index (2004 - 2008) - cont'd

4.4. Sentiment Analysis

The purpose of this section is to further understand the influence of certain aspects of the raw order flow on the sentiment index construction and relate it to contemporaneous market returns. The sentiment measure and its different order flow components are compared to market returns because if sentiment is a driver of equity prices, correlations should be found between its measurement and market returns.

Multivariate regressions are used that test how different sentiment measures influence market returns and how much of the variance in the market returns can be explained by investor sentiment.

4.4.1. Number- vs. Volume-Based Measures

Different components of the order flow can be distinguished: buy call volume, sell call volume, buy put volume, and sell put volume. In order to be invariant from an overall rise or fall of absolute order volume, the ratio of all order flow subgroups to the sum of the order flow is calculated for each order flow component as follows:

$$buy\_call\_ratio = \frac{buy\_call\_volume}{total\_volume} \tag{4.3}$$

$$sell\_call\_ratio = \frac{sell\_call\_volume}{total\_volume} \tag{4.4}$$

$$buy\_put\_ratio = \frac{buy\_put\_volume}{total\_volume} \tag{4.5}$$

$$sell\_put\_ratio = \frac{sell\_put\_volume}{total\_volume} \tag{4.6}$$

where *total_volume* is the sum of buy call, sell call, buy put, and sell put volume in a certain time period. Order flow ratios are calculated for all product categories and two sub categories, namely leverage products (i.e. warrants and knock-out certificates) and investment certificates. In addition, ratios are calculated using the number of executed orders instead of the executed order volume.

A multivariate linear regression (see equation 4.7) is performed with the DAX logreturns as the dependent variable and the order flow ratios as independent variables. Newey-West standard errors are used that are robust to heteroskedasticity.

$$dax\_logreturns = \beta_1\, buy\_call\_ratio + \beta_2\, sell\_call\_ratio + \beta_3\, buy\_put\_ratio + \beta_4\, sell\_put\_ratio \tag{4.7}$$

Regression results are presented in Table 4.2 and Table 4.3. The first table shows the results for sentiment measures that are based on the volume of executed orders whereas the second table is based on the number of executed orders. For each table, results are presented for ratios based on different input parameters: Panel A presents results differentiated by product type,

Panel B by option type, and Panel C by volume group. Panel D provides results for submitted orders.

The adjusted R^2 values indicate the amount of variance explained by the model. The adjusted R^2 value of 0.5626 (Table 4.3) can be interpreted in a way that 56% of the variance of the DAX logreturns can be explained by the sentiment measure based on the number of executed orders. The model that uses sentiment ratios based on the volume of executed orders (Table 4.2) receives an R^2 value of 0.4752 which is lower than the number based model.

Table 4.2: Multivariate Regression Results for Order Volume

This table presents regression results for the multivariate linear regression as presented in formula 4.7. Executed order volume is used to construct the ratios. Panel A presents results for ratios based on the volume of executed orders by product type. Panel B differentiates executed orders by order type and Panel C by order volume group. Panel D provides information about regression results using submitted order volume instead of executed order volume. The superscripts ***, **, and * denote statistical significance at the 1%, 5%, and 10% level, respectively.

	Buy Call Ratio	Sell Call Ratio	Buy Put Ratio	Sell Put Ratio	adj. R^2
Panel A: Executed order volume by product type					
all products	-0.0053 ***	0.0064 ***	0.0497 ***	-0.0554 ***	0.4752
leverage products	-0.0050 ***	0.0062 ***	0.0498 ***	-0.0594 ***	0.5221
investment products	-0.0003	0.0009	0.0038 ***	-0.0147 ***	0.0958
Panel B: Executed order volume by order type					
All Products					
market orders	-0.0034 ***	0.0046 ***	0.0305 ***	-0.0378 ***	0.2899
limit orders	-0.0055 **	0.0106 ***	0.0568 ***	-0.0682 ***	0.5348
Leverage Products					
market orders	-0.0036 ***	0.0047 ***	0.0286 ***	-0.0376 ***	0.3474
limit orders	-0.0105 ***	0.0120 ***	0.0614 ***	-0.0688 ***	0.5593
Investment Products					
market orders	0.0006	-0.0005	0.0035	-0.0080 **	0.0505
limit orders	-0.0002	0.0021	0.0045	-0.0158 ***	0.1192
Panel C: Executed order volume by volume group					
0 - 1,000€	-0.0517 ***	0.0945 ***	0.0219 ***	-0.0297 ***	0.5974
1,000€ - 10,000€	-0.0115	0.0277 **	0.0544 ***	-0.0877 ***	0.5506
10,000€ - 100,000€	-0.0053 *	0.0128 **	0.0526 ***	-0.0651 ***	0.4546
> 100,000€	-0.0010 ***	0.0013 ***	0.0061 ***	-0.0084 ***	0.2252
Panel D: Submitted order volume by product type					
All Products	0.0000	0.0000	-0.0005 ***	0.0000	0.0142
Leverage Products	0.0000	0.0000	-0.0002 ***	0.0000	0.0145
Investment Products	-0.0002	0.0000	-0.0008	-0.0001	-0.0012

The difference can be explained by possible outliers caused by extremely high volume orders that belong to a few wealthy individuals. In this case, retail investor sentiment is not based on the majority of individuals but rather the majority of the capital invested – and therefore does not represent the overall opinion of the market participants.

Taking this finding into account, further analyses focus on the number of executed or submitted orders instead of their order volume.

Table 4.3: Multivariate Regression Results for Order Number

This table presents regression results for the multivariate linear regression as presented in formula 4.7. The number of executed orders is used to construct the ratios. Panel A presents results for ratios based on the number of executed orders by product type. Panel B differentiates executed orders by order type and Panel C by order volume group. Panel D provides information about regression results using submitted orders instead of executed orders. The superscripts ***, **, and * denote statistical significance at the 1%, 5%, and 10% level, respectively.

	Buy Call Ratio	Sell Call Ratio	Buy Put Ratio	Sell Put Ratio	adj. R^2
Panel A: Executed order by product type					
all products	-0.0161 *	0.0294	0.0572 ***	-0.0894 ***	0.5626
leverage products	-0.0316 ***	0.0593 ***	0.0335 ***	-0.0621 ***	0.5805
investment products	-0.0022	0.0010	0.0051 ***	-0.0303 ***	0.1235
Panel B: Executed orders by order type					
All Products					
market orders	-0.0121 *	0.0113	0.0584 ***	-0.0744 ***	0.4560
limit orders	-0.0319 ***	0.0643 ***	0.0433 ***	-0.0875 ***	0.5959
Leverage Products					
market orders	-0.0293 ***	0.0477 ***	0.0327 ***	-0.0502 ***	0.4928
limit orders	-0.0361 ***	0.0684 ***	0.0389 ***	-0.0776 ***	0.5907
Investment Products					
market orders	0.0008	-0.0017	0.0130 **	-0.0192 ***	0.0615
limit orders	-0.0134 ***	0.0103	0.0431 ***	-0.0405 ***	0.2729
Panel C: Executed order by volume group					
0 - 1,000€	-0.0527 ***	0.0824 ***	0.0253 ***	-0.0231 **	0.5862
1,000€ - 10,000€	-0.0194 ***	0.0382 ***	0.0455 ***	-0.0765 ***	0.5520
10,000€ - 100,000€	-0.0067 *	0.0150 **	0.0589 ***	-0.0737 ***	0.4853
> 100,000€	-0.0018	0.0039 **	0.0125 ***	-0.0158 ***	0.2570
Panel D: Submitted orders by product type					
All Products	-0.0172 ***	0.0103 ***	0.0113 ***	-0.0049 ***	0.3816
Leverage Products	-0.0132 ***	0.0081 ***	0.0081 ***	-0.0039 ***	0.4109
Investment Products	0.0008	-0.0021	0.0213 ***	-0.0229 ***	0.0710

4.4.2. Product Types

Panel A of Table 4.3 presents different regression results by product type. The ratios based on leverage products have much higher regression coefficients than the ratios based on investment products leading to an overall higher R^2 and a better fit of the model. The adjusted R^2 value is even higher when using leverage products than using all product types.

This result is due to the nature of the different financial products and the use thereof by retail investors. Leverage products are products that are traded much more frequently and actively than investment products and therefore their trades must have a much higher correlation with the overall market. Investors who trade leverage products monitor the market very closely and react to market movements immediately. In contrast, investment products are bought and usually stay in the investors' account for a longer amount of time.

4.4.3. Order Types

The different use of order types also has an influence on the multivariate regression results. Due to the nature of limit orders, covariance with market returns should be extremely high since limit sell orders are being executed when market returns are positive, and limit buy orders are being executed when market returns are negative. Therefore, the coefficients of *buy_call_ratio* and *sell_put_ratio* should be negative, and the coefficients of *sell_call_ratio* and *buy_put_ratio* should be positive, leading to an overall high adjusted R^2.

The results in Panel B of Table 4.3 confirm this hypothesis. A high ratio of call buy orders (and put sell orders) is related to lower market returns (negative coefficient), whereas a high ratio of call sell orders (and put buy orders) is related to higher market returns (positive coefficient).

Adjusted R^2 values are highest when using sentiment values based on limit orders alone. This is due to the automatic execution of limit orders that are in the order book for a longer period of time and get executed because the market is moving below (above) their buy (sell) limit price.

4.4.4. Order Volume Groups

The difference in the correlation between sentiment measures based on order volume and those based on the number of executed orders could arise from a few orders with a high volume that somehow distort the overall sentiment. Orders above 100,000 € could originate from few wealthy individuals or semi-professional traders that are still regarded as retail investors but distort the overall retail investor sentiment measure.

To investigate this issue, orders are sorted into four categories according to their Euro volume: orders below 1,000 €, orders between 1,000 € and 10,000 €, orders between 10,000 €

and 100,000 €, and orders above 100,000 €. Panels C of Table 4.2 and Table 4.3 present the regression results.

Results for orders below 100,000 € have high R^2 values whereas results for orders above 100,000 € only lead to R^2 values of about 0.257.

This result has two important implications: First, sentiment measures including large orders may be distorted because few large orders have a comparatively high influence on the measure. Second, creating the sentiment index using the number of executed orders is much less susceptible to distortions by large orders. A very large order would be counted as just one order regardless of its volume.

4.4.5. Submitted Orders

The measurement of executed orders is a natural candidate for a sentiment index since executed orders indicate that retail investors are willing to trade and invest real money depending on their expectation of the market. However, as the analysis of executed limit orders shows, order executions may happen based on orders that have been submitted a long time ago, and therefore sentiment is not measured accurately.

One idea to improve the sentiment measurement is to distinguish market and limit orders and base the sentiment measurement solely on market orders. This method has the advantage that real transactions are included and that these transactions express the actual market sentiment without delay. Another idea to overcome the time-of-submission and time-of-execution gap is to use the time-of-submission timestamp in the sentiment measurement.

This demands that all submitted orders have to be included in the index since it is unknown at the time of submission whether the order will be executed at some point in time in the future. Furthermore, if the sentiment index is based on the volume of submitted orders, the order volume is calculated using different methods depending on the order type: For market orders, submitted order volume is equal to the executed order volume determined by the execution price since it is assumed that market orders are executed shortly after order submission. For limit orders, order volume is equal to the product of the order limit times the size of the order. It is possible that the submitted order is not equal to the executed order volume since the execution price may differ from the order limit. It is also possible that the order will never be executed and that the execution volume is therefore zero.

Summary statistics of submitted orders can be found in Appendix A. Panel D of Table 4.3 shows regression results for sentiment ratios based on the number of submitted orders. Regression results for the volume of submitted orders can be found in Panel D of Table 4.2.

The following observations can be made: First, submitted orders in leverage products lead to high R^2 values, i.e. correlate with the market returns almost as good as executed market orders in leverage products. Second, sentiment based on submitted orders in investment products does not correlate well with market returns and thus the model has a low R^2 value. Third, coefficients based on submitted order volume are almost all statistically insignificant and models have generally low R^2 values.

The first conclusion is that sentiment measures based on submitted orders in leverage products are almost similar in quality than sentiment measures based on executed market orders in leverage products. This result is intuitive since both measures express the sentiment that retail investors have at the moment of order submission – in contrast to executed limit orders which may just be executed due to market movements.

The second conclusion is that leverage products are a much better instrument to capture actual short-term investor sentiment. Investment products are often submitted without reference to the market, and therefore are relatively independent from market movements.

Lastly, a measure based on submitted order volume is not a good indicator of investor sentiment since order volumes that are measured may not reflect the true values that investors were willing to risk since limits could be far from the current market prices and an execution therefore highly unlikely.

4.4.6. Leverage

The separation of the different product categories makes it possible to look at the influence of risk on sentiment. In particular, the delta for each warrant can be calculated, and all executed orders can be sorted according to their delta[18]. The delta of a stock option is defined as the rate of change of the option price with respect to the price of the underlying asset (Hull 2006, p.344). The delta is often regarded as a measure of the sensitivity of the option price and therefore a proxy for risk of the derivative.

The delta for call options is always between 0 and 1 whereas the delta for put options ranges between 0 and -1. Delta values are calculated using the standard Black-Scholes formula and warrants' implicit volatilities which are calculated using the transaction price and the value of the underlying index level.

All trades are sorted according to their delta into 10 categories using absolute delta values (0.1, 0.2, 0.3, etc.) as break points. The percentages in Table 4.4 illustrate that most of the executed warrant orders have an absolute delta value between 0.2 and 0.4. That means retail investors neither prefer low-delta warrants (i.e. deep out of the money options) nor high-delta warrants (i.e. deep in the money options). Instead, they choose near-the-money warrants which makes intuitively sense because this is the delta-region where warrants are cheapest. This finding is also further confirmation that EUWAX investors are generally uninformed investors who prefer the liquidity and cost advantages of near-the-money warrants over the

[18] For the delta calculation a subsample of the data set is used that contains all executed warrant orders from January 2004 to March 2008 because of missing data for the rest of the sample period.

leverage advantages of out-of-the-money warrants as would informed investors do (Jayaraman, Frye, and Sabherwal 2001).

Table 4.4 reports the number of executed orders for call and put warrants by absolute delta (left column). The relative values do not change substantially when distinguishing between buy and sell orders (not reported).

Table 4.4: Leverage

This table presents statistics and results on the influence of leverage on the regression. The left part of the table shows the number of orders in call and put warrants in absolute as well as relative terms. The right part of the table presents regression results for the different delta groups. All regression coefficients are statistically significant below the 1% level (***).

	number of call orders		number of put orders		Buy Call Ratio	Sell Call Ratio	Buy Put Ratio	Sell Put Ratio	adj. R^2
Executed orders by absolute delta values									
0.1	97,991	(10.4%)	108,405	(14.2%)	-0.0297	0.0291	0.0181	-0.0139	0.3938
0.2	125,300	(13.3%)	131,452	(17.3%)	-0.0286	0.0399	0.0159	-0.0201	0.5440
0.3	132,916	(14.1%)	157,963	(20.7%)	-0.0301	0.0421	0.0149	-0.0214	0.5458
0.4	135,809	(14.4%)	148,128	(19.5%)	-0.0292	0.0391	0.0144	-0.0204	0.5412
0.5	143,375	(15.2%)	102,471	(13.5%)	-0.0200	0.0275	0.0183	-0.0268	0.4960
0.6	129,124	(13.7%)	50,490	(6.6%)	-0.0159	0.0202	0.0239	-0.0286	0.4611
0.7	83,791	(8.9%)	30,987	(4.1%)	-0.0125	0.0154	0.0203	-0.0284	0.3721
0.8	43,208	(4.6%)	19,211	(2.5%)	-0.0126	0.0116	0.0202	-0.0234	0.2973
0.9	28,405	(3.0%)	9,122	(1.2%)	-0.0095	0.0091	0.0170	-0.0181	0.2357
1	22,261	(2.4%)	3,174	(0.4%)	-0.0067	0.0066	0.0125	-0.0165	0.1455

When combining put and call options according to delta group, separate order ratios for each delta group can be calculated and the multivariate regression can be performed. The right part of Table 4.4 shows the results.

The highest adjusted R^2 value of 0.5458 is reached by using only trades including warrants that had an absolute delta value between 0.2 and 0.3, i.e. out of the money options. Generally, warrants with an absolute delta in the range from 0.1 to 0.4 all have similarly high R^2 values meaning that trades in these instruments correlate best with market returns. The reason for this is that retail investors who trade near-the-money warrants closely monitor market movements and react very quickly when the market is moving in either direction.

4.5. Comparison with Other Sentiment Measures

As part of the evaluation of the sentiment index, index levels and first differences (Δ) are being compared to the sentiment measures reported in Chapter 3 which can be distinguished into direct and indirect sentiment measures. In general, as reported in Chapter 3, an overall high correlation among these indicators can be observed, although a high-to-low frequency conversion may possibly disguise higher correlations.

However, as already argued in Chapter 3, high correlation with other sentiment indicators is an indicator for sentiment quality, but not a necessary or sufficient condition. Findings in this section should therefore be valued with caution.

A total of 9 different sentiment measures developed in this chapter are used in the respective tables: Sentiment measures based on all executed orders (col. 1), all executed limit orders (col. 2), all executed market orders (col. 3), executed orders in investment products (col. 4), executed orders in leverage products (col. 5), executed market orders in leverage products (col. 6), all submitted orders (col. 7), submitted orders in investment products (col. 8), and submitted orders in leverage products (col. 9). For reasons of simplicity, all sentiment measures developed in this chapter will be referred to as "Euwax Sentiment measures".

Correlation coefficients are calculated on the levels of sentiment measures (exceptions, when first differences are used, are marked with a Δ). Statistical significance is indicated by *** ($p<0.01$), ** ($p<0.05$), and * ($p<0.1$).

4.5.1. Indirect Sentiment Measures

Daily Measures

Table 4.5 presents correlations between daily indirect measures of sentiment and the Euwax Sentiment measures. Generally speaking, there is a high correlation between the sentiment measures developed in this chapter and the daily direct sentiment measures used in practice.

The Advance-Decline measure (ADV-DEC DAX) and the Euwax Sentiment measures are negatively correlated to a very high extent: The correlation coefficient amounts to a highly significant -74.4% (using market orders in leverage products). This finding is consistent with the negative correlation to market returns documented in this chapter because the ADV-DEC DAX measure must be positively correlated to DAX returns by construction. The advance-decline measure for the Dow Jones Industrial Average Index is also negatively correlated but to a much lower extent.

The construction of the Euwax Sentiment Index based on puts and calls should lead to a high correlation with regular put/call ratios from futures and options exchanges. We document a large and positive correlation coefficient, especially when using the total put/call ratio and all Euwax orders in leverage products (31.7%). Since a high put/call ratio expresses negative sentiment and a high Euwax Sentiment Index positive sentiment, the positive correlation coefficient means that the two indicators measure contrarian opinions: The put/call ratio is usually regarded as the institutional sentiment indicator whereas the Euwax Sentiment Index is constructed to represent retail investor sentiment. This relation suggests that retail investor sentiment may be contrary to that of institutional investors.

Table 4.5: Daily Sentiment Correlation

This table presents correlations between daily indirect measures of sentiment (vertical axis) and the Euwax Sentiment measures represented by nine measures based on executed and submitted orders. A Δ in front of a sentiment measure means that first differences are used. The superscripts ***, **, and * denote statistical significance at the 1%, 5%, and 10% level, respectively.

	Executed Orders by Order Type			Executed Orders by Product Type			Submitted Orders		
	All	Limit	Market	Investment	Leverage	Leverage Market	All	Investment	Leverage
ADV-DEC DAX	-0.801***	-0.807***	-0.719***	-0.225***	-0.809***	-0.744***	-0.546***	-0.061**	-0.569***
ADV-DEC DJIA	-0.148***	-0.153***	-0.131***	-0.014	-0.154***	-0.145***	-0.135***	-0.030	-0.138***
Put/Call Total	0.308***	0.329***	0.241***	-0.001	0.317***	0.264***	0.169***	-0.031	0.208***
Put/Call Equity	0.285***	0.312***	0.213***	0.032	0.295***	0.241***	0.246***	0.041	0.269***
Put/Call Index	0.202***	0.207***	0.179***	0.096***	0.201***	0.180***	0.089***	-0.008	0.099***
TRIN NYSE	-0.008	-0.017	0.006	-0.016	-0.009	0.004	0.027	0.001	0.026
TRIN NASDAQ	0.258***	0.320***	0.174***	-0.030	0.274***	0.206***	0.145***	-0.093***	0.165***
VDAX	0.044	0.093***	-0.031	-0.329***	0.079***	0.037	0.078***	-0.238***	0.108***
Δ VDAX	0.401***	0.419***	0.346***	0.062**	0.416***	0.381***	0.257***	-0.046	0.287***
VIX	0.037	0.089***	-0.041	-0.391***	0.075***	0.032	0.040	-0.259***	0.080***
Δ VIX	0.261***	0.335***	0.177***	0.018	0.275***	0.203***	0.118***	-0.055*	0.135***
ISEE All	0.026	0.005	0.068**	0.130***	0.024	0.063**	0.035	0.103***	-0.002
ISEE Equity	-0.081**	-0.126***	-0.002	0.090**	-0.097***	-0.039	-0.166***	-0.016	-0.179***
ISEE Index	0.053	0.074**	0.002	-0.194***	0.070*	0.040	0.033	-0.142***	0.056

Correlation between Euwax Sentiment and the TRIN Nasdaq measure is positive: Correlation coefficients of 27.4% are documented for the leverage product measure. Annual correlations reveal that in some years, coefficients may be as high as 38% (not reported). At first sight, the TRIN NYSE measure is not related to Euwax Sentiment, although annual correlations reveal that the correlation coefficient can be as high as 43.1% (in the year 2006 – not reported).

Regarding the relation to volatility, Euwax Sentiment measures are found to be positively correlated to changes (first differences) in the VDAX: The correlation coefficient between the Euwax Sentiment and changes in the VDAX amount to a highly significant 38.1%. This result is especially driven by orders in leverage products because investors are more likely to buy leverage products when volatility increases because option prices are lower. In addition, sentiment measures on orders in investment products are negatively correlated to VDAX levels (-32.9%). This can be interpreted that retail investors buying investment certificates are more likely to buy when volatility is on a low level. A further interpretation, however, would be more than speculative.

Although it is based on a similar idea, there is no obvious relation between the ISEE Sentiment Index and the Euwax Sentiment Index. Coefficients are generally very low and mostly insignificant.

4.5.2. Direct Sentiment Measures

In order to assess the correlation among levels as well as changes of sentiment measures, Euwax Sentiment levels are compared to survey levels, and Euwax Sentiment changes are compared to changes of survey measures. Table 4.6 reports correlation coefficients for levels (Panel A) as well as changes (Panel B) of the Euwax Sentiment measures.

Table 4.6: Weekly Sentiment Correlation

This table presents correlations between weekly direct measures of sentiment (vertical axis) and the Euwax Sentiment measures represented by nine measures based on executed and submitted orders. For Panel A, sentiment levels are used for the correlation analysis. For Panel B, first differences are used. The superscripts ***, **, and * denote statistical significance at the 1%, 5%, and 10% level, respectively.

Panel A: Levels

	Executed Orders by Order Type			Executed Orders by Product Type			Submitted Orders		
	All	Limit	Market	Investment	Leverage	Leverage Market	All	Investment	Leverage
Sentix 1M/P	-0.587***	-0.194***	-0.110*	-0.035	-0.158**	-0.512***	-0.495***	-0.086	-0.487***
Sentix 1M/I	-0.568***	-0.082	-0.043	-0.021	-0.058	-0.509***	-0.489***	-0.101	-0.477***
Sentix 6M/P	0.071	-0.113*	0.035	0.203***	-0.069	0.088	0.039	0.161***	0.040
Sentix 6M/I	0.076	-0.063	0.070	0.275***	-0.023	0.112*	-0.010	0.120*	-0.001
Bull Bear DAX	-0.197***	0.157**	0.180***	0.212***	0.160**	-0.167***	-0.094	0.112*	-0.102
Bull Bear TecDAX	-0.259***	-0.019	0.018	0.215***	-0.020	-0.207***	-0.104*	0.158**	-0.143**
AAII Bull Ratio	0.056	-0.085	0.034	0.151**	-0.050	0.107*	0.187***	0.107*	0.135**

Panel B: Differences

	Executed Orders by Order Type			Executed Orders by Product Type			Submitted Orders		
	All	Limit	Market	Investment	Leverage	Leverage Market	All	Investment	Leverage
Δ Sentix 1M/P	-0.756***	0.257***	0.261***	0.223***	0.272***	-0.730***	-0.535***	0.088	-0.528***
Δ Sentix 1M/I	-0.695***	0.297***	0.310***	0.260***	0.316***	-0.682***	-0.484***	0.125**	-0.482***
Δ Sentix 6M/P	0.247***	-0.158**	-0.125**	-0.058	-0.141**	0.229***	0.147**	-0.021	0.141**
Δ Sentix 6M/I	0.201***	-0.051	-0.041	-0.046	-0.051	0.203***	0.162***	-0.044	0.160***
Δ Bull Bear DAX	-0.407***	0.259***	0.234***	0.212***	0.243***	-0.384***	-0.288***	0.104*	-0.292***
Δ Bull Bear TecDAX	-0.375***	0.140**	0.078	0.075	0.109*	-0.337***	-0.248***	0.022	-0.270***
Δ AAII Bull Ratio	0.076	0.093	0.075	-0.088	0.071	0.070	0.107*	-0.123**	0.120*

Weekly Measures

Euwax Sentiment measures are negatively correlated to Sentix survey measures: Levels between the measures show correlation coefficients of up to -58.7%, and differences show correlation coefficients of up to -75.6%. Results for private and institutional investors, as distinguished by the Sentix survey, are almost identical.

The Bull Bear Index on the DAX shows a similar picture: Changes in survey values and changes in the Euwax Sentiment Index are negatively correlated (-40.7% for all orders/products and -38.4% for market orders in leverage products). Both the Sentix and the Bull Bear Survey therefore seem to have the same relation to sentiment picked up by the Euwax Sentiment measure.

Changes in the six-month Sentix survey are positively related to Euwax Sentiment measures: The 24.7% (20.1%) correlation between Euwax Sentiment and the private (institutional) investor survey differences could possibly indicate that moods as picked up by the Euwax Sentiment are similar to those expressed by the 6-month survey.

Lastly, there is no apparent relation between Euwax Sentiment measures and the U.S. AAII survey among private investors.

Table 4.7: Monthly Sentiment Correlation

This table presents correlations between monthly direct measures of sentiment (vertical axis) and the Euwax Sentiment measures represented by nine measures based on executed and submitted orders. For Panel A, sentiment levels are used for the correlation analysis. In Panel B, first differences are used. The superscripts ***, **, and * denote statistical significance at the 1%, 5%, and 10% level, respectively.

Panel A: Levels

	Executed Orders by Order Type			Executed Orders by Product Type			Submitted Orders		
	All	Limit	Market	Investment	Leverage	Leverage Market	All	Investment	Leverage
G-Mind	-0.088	-0.002	-0.162	-0.140	0.001	-0.007	0.279**	0.005	0.319**
G-Mind Stocks	-0.028	-0.127	0.103	0.481***	-0.070	0.045	0.208	0.313**	0.150
G-Mind Bonds	-0.083	0.066	-0.248*	-0.547***	0.004	-0.117	-0.038	-0.409***	0.081
Michigan ICS	0.000	-0.119	0.163	0.497***	-0.068	0.058	0.100	0.262**	-0.001
Michigan ICE	0.023	-0.066	0.152	0.467***	-0.026	0.081	0.190	0.260**	0.093
CCI	-0.017	-0.169	0.175	0.463***	-0.116	0.013	-0.138	0.177	-0.219*
UBS/Gallup	0.029	0.017	0.039	0.178	0.018	0.024	0.271*	-0.011	0.230

Panel B: Differences

	Executed Orders by Order Type			Executed Orders by Product Type			Submitted Orders		
	All	Limit	Market	Investment	Leverage	Leverage Market	All	Investment	Leverage
Δ G-Mind	-0.259**	-0.285**	-0.219*	0.016	-0.272**	-0.241*	-0.023	-0.013	-0.009
Δ G-Mind Stocks	-0.210	-0.228*	-0.188	0.109	-0.234*	-0.231*	-0.039	0.017	-0.029
Δ G-Mind Bonds	0.059	0.051	0.086	-0.049	0.073	0.112	0.078	-0.018	0.089
Δ Michigan ICS	-0.037	-0.053	-0.015	-0.025	-0.040	-0.016	-0.076	-0.053	-0.096
Δ Michigan ICE	0.028	0.008	0.052	0.028	0.026	0.052	-0.047	-0.017	-0.067
Δ CCI	0.044	-0.004	0.091	0.060	0.006	0.031	-0.028	-0.045	-0.059
Δ UBS/Gallup	0.075	0.004	0.145	0.104	0.061	0.123	-0.018	-0.026	-0.037

Monthly Measures

Correlation of Euwax Sentiment measures (calculated on a monthly frequency, i.e. using monthly periods instead of daily) and monthly surveys is rather poor: Table 4.7 presents correlation coefficients for levels (Panel A) as well as changes (Panel B) in sentiment survey measures.

There is no clear picture of a correlation between Euwax Sentiment and the G-Mind measures: Differences seem to be negatively correlated but the Euwax Sentiment from submitted orders seem to have a positive relation to the G-Mind.

However, Euwax Sentiment measures based on investment products do correlate with most of the monthly surveys: Investment products sentiment is positively correlated to the G-Mind

Stocks Index and the Michigan and CCI sentiment surveys, and negatively related to the G-Mind Bonds Index. The submitted order data leads to the same results.

These findings indicate that retail sentiment expressed by buy and sell orders on investment certificates correlates well with the monthly consumer sentiment surveys in Germany (G-Mind) and the U.S. (ICS, ICE, CCI). Due to their lower frequency, these surveys rather represent a medium-term to long-term sentiment on general market conditions which obviously correlates well with the views of retail investors in investment certificates on the DAX.

4.5.3. Review of Results

In this section, other sentiment time series have been compared to the Euwax Sentiment measures. The results can be grouped into two categories: Comparison with indirect daily sentiment measures on the one hand, and direct weekly and monthly sentiment measures on the other hand.

The indirect sentiment measures show a generally high correlation with the Euwax Sentiment because the Euwax Sentiment measures are also indirect indicators based on market data. The reasons for the high correlation, though, differ throughout all the examples: First, the negative correlation with the advance-decline measures stems from Euwax investors acting as contrarians. Second, the positive correlation with put/call ratios expresses the difference between retail and institutional sentiment. Third, the positive correlation between the TRIN measure and the Euwax measure means that both indicators measure a similar sentiment. Fourth, the positive correlation with the volatility changes in VDAX/VIX is largely due to option pricing considerations.

The comparison with direct sentiment measures reveals that there are highly significant correlations between survey measures and the Euwax Sentiment measures, and that the results differ between weekly and monthly indicators. Correlations are larger for higher-frequency measures and lower, or insignificant, for lower-frequency measures. Changes of Euwax Sentiment and the German weekly survey measures are highly negatively correlated. This may suggest that investors react to the same signal, i.e. at the same time, but in a contrary way. Related research about the Sentix, however, concludes that the private investor surveys have to be regarded as a contrary indicator for investment decisions. Therefore, if Euwax investors act contrary to the Sentix investors, chances are that the Euwax investors are actually right in their investment decision.

To sum up, significant correlations between the Euwax Sentiment measures and existing indicators can be observed though the respective reasons may differ and results should be interpreted accordingly. However, it is shown that most of the sentiment measures have common sources or react to the same signals. A further investigation regarding causality, interdependencies, and sensitivities remains to be subject to future research.

4.6. Conclusion

In this chapter, the development of the Euwax Sentiment Index, a measure of retail investor sentiment at the European Warrant Exchange, is presented.

A unique data set consisting of more than 36.5 million retail investor orders provides a history of 5 years. The data set has several key advantages over comparable order data sets and is especially suited for sentiment extraction: First, it consists exclusively of retail investor orders. Second, the trade direction is determined exactly and does not have to be inferred from the data. Third, investors are able to express negative sentiment. Fourth, the differentiation of order types is possible. Fifth, not only does it consist of executed orders but also includes submitted orders.

The historical order data is used to run multivariate regression models to assess the impact of the various components of the retail investor order flow on market returns: First, leverage products explain more of the return variance than investment products. Second, the number of executed orders has higher explanatory power than the volume of executed orders. Third, executed limit orders show the expected behavior, i.e. are negatively correlated to market returns. An important result is, however, that market orders in leverage products are also negatively correlated. Fourth, a sentiment measure based on submitted orders in leverage products leads to similar results as executed market orders. As a guideline for sentiment index development based on retail investor orders, it is therefore recommended to include only executed market orders in leverage products on the DAX to get the highest possible explanatory power.

The comparison of the developed sentiment measures with existing sentiment indicators used in practice shows that in the majority of cases there is a significant correlation between measures although the exact causality for this correlation cannot be determined. It is likely that a large correlation points to similar underlying factors that finally determine sentiment even though the sign of the correlation may differ. A further investigation is subject to future research.

5 Retail Investor Herding

„Institutions are herding animals. We watch the same indicators and listen to the same prognostications. Like lemmings, we tend to move in the same direction at the same time. And that, naturally, exacerbates price movements."

Wall Street Journal, October 17, 1989

Investor herding plays an important role in behavioral finance models. The quotation above is taken from Lakonishok, Shleifer, and Vishny (1992, p. 25). It exemplifies that the effect of herding on price discovery can be large when several large investors attempt to buy or sell a given stock at the same time. The herding behavior of institutional investors has seen a lot of attention in the last twenty years. Individual herding behavior, however, has been neglected.

Using the data set on retail investor orders to the European Warrant Exchange at Boerse Stuttgart, a measure of retail investor herding on an aggregated market level is being constructed. The level of herding differs in bearish and bullish market conditions, and retail investors are more prone to herding when they are optimistic than when they are pessimistic. High levels of herding can be found even on an individual broker level although there are differences between different types of brokers. In addition to market-wide herding, retail investors also herd into and out of single underlyings: Excess herding in those is substantial and significant.

This chapter is organized as follows: Section 5.1 gives an introduction to herding behavior in financial markets and relates it to the EMH. Section 5.2 presents definitions of herding, found in related research, and discusses empirical findings. In section 5.3, the herding measures are introduced and evidence of market-wide herding is presented. Section 5.4 extends the analysis by distinguishing different broker types. Finally, section 5.5 presents evidence of stock-level herding and compares the results to findings in the empirical herding literature. Section 5.6 concludes.

5.1. Introduction

The EMH holds that at any given time an asset's price fully reflects all available relevant information about the asset and the wider market conditions in which it exists (Fama 1970). Investors are assumed to be rational and trade based on fundamental information. Any mispricing due to those who trade on other factors, such as noise or behavioral biases, will only be transitory because at an aggregate level the irrational trades will cancel each other out.

In case they do not, arbitrage will bring asset prices back in line with their true values. In other words, the EMH rests on two assumptions: uncorrelated trades and unlimited arbitrage opportunities. While much empirical support has been found for EMH, there is a growing body of evidence that trades are not uncorrelated. Ample evidence has been found that investor trades tend to cluster and investors tend to move in and out of securities in tandem with one another. If these correlated trades represent the collective reaction of market participants to a relevant information signal the outcome would in fact be efficient and cause swift price adjustment. However, trades that are correlated due to other factors, such as psychological biases, feedback trading or fads, may cause and exacerbate mispricing. Limits to arbitrage, in the form of high transaction costs and/or lack of liquidity, may prevent this mispricing from being corrected resulting in volatility and instability over time.

Past studies have found mixed evidence of herding among different investor classes, usually either institutional or retail investors. While some evidence has been found that investors tend to follow each other in and out of stocks, few studies have been able to measure whether this herding survives aggregation to the market level. This chapter examines retail investor herding at the aggregate as well as the cross-sectional level and aims to find out whether herding is more prevalent in certain market conditions, i.e. bullish and bearish periods, and whether there is a higher degree of herding when investors are optimistic or when they are pessimistic.

5.2. Related Work

5.2.1. Definitions of Herding

Herding defined in its most simple terms refers to a group of investors trading on the same side of the market at a certain time. Lakonishok, Shleifer and Vishny (1992) define herding as "buying (selling) simultaneously the same stocks as others buy (sell)". Other definitions refer to herding as "the extent to which the group either predominantly buys or predominantly sells the same stock at the same time" (Grinblatt, Titman, and Wermers 1995) or identify investors as herding when "following each other into (or out of) the same securities over some period of time" (Sias 2004).

The literature is rich in theoretical models outlining the rationale behind herding and culminates in two main hypotheses about who herds and why. The information asymmetry hypothesis proposes that the costs (both time and monetary) of gathering information makes it prudent and perhaps even rational for traders to assume that the crowd knows more than they do and as a result they base their trading decisions on the actions of the majority. Under this hypothesis, individual investors are expected to exhibit a greater tendency to herd than institutional investors as the latter have access to better information and superior methods of processing it, eliminating the need to mimic their supposedly better informed peers. Psychological biases such as conformity may amplify existing herding among individuals.

An alternative perspective is that herding is likely to be more prevalent among institutions, such as mutual funds, rather than individual investors due to the following reasons: Firstly, institutional investors' trades are more visible to their peers, thus there is more scope for mimicking among this class of investors. Since individual investors do not have to disclose their holding positions like institutional investors do, it might be more difficult for individuals to observe each others' trades. Secondly, certain institutional investors such as fund managers are evaluated based on their performance relative to other fund managers. In such a case it pays to stay with the crowd as individual funds are less conspicuous when wrong in the crowd than wrong alone.

These two seemingly contrasting lines of reasoning however are not irreconcilable. It is possible that both types of investors herd to a considerable extent but that herding is more detectable in the case of institutional investors due to the large volume of their trades and better availability of data. Data on individual trading flows is typically more difficult to access and individual investors' actions may not have as great an impact on the market as the large trades of institutional investors, thus even if they herd it may be difficult to observe it empirically.

Regardless of which type of investor has a greater tendency to herd, empirically measuring the degree of herding in a market or among a particular group of investors presents considerable methodological challenges. Investigating herding on a large scale in equity markets is difficult because the "buyer for every seller argument" leads to a net trade equal to zero. In addition, while herding by definition would manifest in some form of correlated trading, it remains a challenge to isolate the effect of intentional herding. It is only possible to infer investors' motives from their trades, and these trades could be influenced by a variety of factors including common information. A test of intentional herding would require factoring out these information effects. As such, evidence of intentional herding could be hidden in the results of general correlated trading.

Despite the challenges, much progress has been made to broaden our understanding of this phenomenon. The next section outlines a selection of the major works investigating herding among different market participants.

5.2.2. Empirical Findings

Early research sought evidence of herding in the trades of institutional investors, as this class of investors tends to make large trades that 'move the market' and consequently has the greatest potential to destabilize prices if herding based on factors other than common information is indeed prevalent. One of the earliest works is that of Kraus and Stoll (1972) which seeks evidence of what was initially termed 'parallel trading' among institutional investors such as mutual funds and banks. Operating under the definition of herding as the state in which a large number of investors are predominantly on the same side of the market in a security at a given time, Kraus and Stoll measure herding as an order imbalance by netting the purchases and sales of each stock in their sample every month. They create two order imbalance measures: the absolute value of the net dollar imbalance for each stock-month, and the absolute percentage net imbalance which is the former measure expressed as a percentage of gross trading volume in that stock-month. Both these measures are unsigned, that is to say they do not consider the direction of herding – whether it is predominantly buy herding or sell herding – only its magnitude. Kraus and Stoll then subtract from their herding measures the level of order imbalance that can be attributed to chance, calculated by means of simulations. They find that the two figures do not differ significantly and conclude that institutional investors in their sample do not tend to trade in parallel with one another.

Lakonishok, Shleifer and Vishny (1992) – henceforth LSV – adapt the standard order imbalance measure to construct a herding measure that expresses the order imbalance for a given stock during a certain quarter relative to a certain baseline expected herding level which is calculated based on the number of purchasing institutional investors relative to the number active in that period. Unlike Kraus and Stoll, LSV's herding measure is based on the number of buyers and sellers active during a given quarter rather than the monetary value of their trades. One could argue that using the number of traders creates a more appropriate measure of herding as institutional investors' trades tend to be large in volume telling little about whether an instance of particular herding is due to a large number of traders or simply a single large trade. LSV calculate herding measures for each stock-quarter in their sample of 769 equity funds and then take the mean herding measure over all stock-quarters as their herding measure. They find low herding measures for their overall sample as well as across subsamples based on past performance and industry type and only partial evidence of herding in smaller stocks. The corresponding lack of impact on stock prices leads them to conclude that institutional investors are heterogeneous and follow distinct trading strategies the results of which cancel each other out and leave stock prices in equilibrium.

One limitation of the LSV herding measure is that it considers correlated trading in one time period only and does not allow for observation of herding patterns over time. As such, it does not measure whether herding in one stock persists and whether there is a cascading effect in that increased interest in one stock causes more and more investors to flock to it. Nevertheless it is arguably the most popular herding measure and has been reproduced in several studies at both the institutional and individual investor level, most notably Grinblatt, Titman and Wermers (1995), Dorn, Huberman and Sengmueller (2008), and Barber, Odean and Zhu (2009b).

Grinblatt, Titman and Wermers analyze the methods by which institutional investors pick stocks for their portfolios. They consider whether the managers of mutual funds choose stocks based on the stocks' past performance (momentum trading) and/or whether they choose the same stocks their peers tend to favor (herding). They modify LSV's herding measure to create a signed measure that takes into account the type of herding – buy or sell – and measures the extent to which a mutual fund's trading behavior is with or against the majority in a certain period. This measure is then combined with the fund's rebalancing activity every period resulting in a measure of how the fund rebalances its portfolio based on the excess buying/selling of all funds in the sample during that period. Their results indicate that herding is prevalent among mutual fund managers.

While Grinblatt, Titman and Wermers provide new insights into the decision-making process of institutional investors, their measure too is a static measure of correlated trading that does not isolate intentional herding. Using a different approach, Sias (2004) explores whether an institutional investor's tendency to purchase a stock in one quarter persists in subsequent quarters. He defines a measure that distinguishes between spurious herding and intentional herding, and asserts that one is unlikely to find evidence of herding unless herding is measured across periods. In contrast to LSV's static herding measure, Sias computes a dynamic measure of herding intensity in a stock over time by regressing his herding measure, based on order imbalance, against its lagged values thereby getting a sense of whether herding persists over time. He finds evidence of herding and then deepens his analysis by distinguishing between herding investors who follow each other's trades and those who follow their own trades.

Overall, the evidence of herding – both intentional and unintentional – is sporadic at the institutional level. As mentioned previously, herding at the individual level has been seldom considered because early research assumed that herding at the institutional level would have a greater impact on prices. While this may be true, it is important to consider the effects individual investors can have at the aggregate level. Previous research has outlined the extent to which noise traders can potentially push prices away from fundamentals due to their correlated trading and the limited presence of arbitrage as a force to counter such mispricing (De Long et al. 1990).

While there has been much debate about the tendency of individual investors to herd and their reasons for doing so (Shiller (1984), Shleifer and Summers (1990), Shleifer and Vishny (1997)), Jackson (2003) is among the first who specifically tests for individual herding. He uses an order imbalance measure based on net flows into or out of the equity market to explore the patterns in the trades of Australian investors trading through different types of brokers. By calculating weekly net order flows first on an aggregate market level and then at a cross-sectional level for each stock in his sample and then regressing these imbalance measures against their lagged values, past stock returns and past volatility as explanatory variables, he finds systematic correlations in the trades of individual investors at both levels.

He further finds that these correlations hold for both the number of trades and the volume of trades and the relationship is consistent over his observation period.

In a similar vein, Kumar and Lee (2006) investigate the correlation among individual investor trades in the U.S. market and relate the effects of herding to the movement of market returns. Like Jackson, Kumar and Lee proxy herding with an order imbalance measure and focus purely on correlated trades without adjusting for any expected level of herding. They use data from a large U.S. discount broker which contains information on the stock trades and portfolio positions of over 60,000 individual investors and define the buy-sell imbalance as the difference in a stock's daily bought and sold volume as a fraction of the total buying and selling activity for that stock on that day. This daily sentiment figure is aggregated over a month, yielding a measure of whether investors were net buyers or net sellers of that stock in that particular month. This measure is used to construct equally-weighted stock portfolios, allowing Kumar and Lee to detect shifts in sentiment over groups of stocks. After randomly forming portfolios of various sizes over the sample period and determining the correlations between them, Kumar and Lee find that the average correlation between such portfolios is positive. This result even holds when the same test is reproduced for subsets of investors instead of portfolios of stocks. In other words, there is strong evidence of systematic correlation in the trading activities of individual investors. They further find that their herding metric has a positive relationship with future returns; when investors are bullish the stocks have higher returns and vice versa.

Dorn, Huberman and Sengmueller (2008) shed light on the influence of order types in their analysis of the correlated trades of German retail investors. They apply the LSV herding measure at daily, weekly, monthly and quarterly time horizons to retail investors trading through a large German discount broker. Their results vary considerably from LSV and other studies of herding in that their herding measure is considerably higher than those found in prior studies. They find the strength of the correlated trading increases as the time horizon increases. What sets their study apart from others is that their data allows them to distinguish between market orders and limit orders to control for the possibility that automatically executed limit orders distort the results by inflating their herding measure.

5.2.3. Discussion

The studies reviewed so far provide mixed evidence of herding. The main gaps in the literature are the lack of focus on aggregate herding. The study presented in this chapter sheds light on herding in the market for securitized derivatives – an area that has seen scant attention in the literature[19]. The focus of this work lies on retail investors in the German

[19] Schmitz, Glaser and Weber (2007) also study retail investor trades in bank-issued warrants in Germany and construct an indicator of the relative degree of bullishness/bearishness over time and analyze the relationship between their indicator and stock returns.

securitized derivatives market which is among the largest retail markets in the world in terms of traded volume and number of orders. The data allows combining the advantages of the work of Jackson (2003) and Dorn, Huberman and Sengmueller (2008) by addressing a number of the methodological limitations in the current literature on herding at the individual level.

Firstly, the clear focus on the securitized derivatives market permits the exclusive study of retail investors. Secondly, due to the nature of the data set, executed market orders and limit orders can be separated exactly. This allows for addressing the effect of automatically executed limit orders due to price changes, giving a more accurate assessment of herding. Finally, since the focus of this study is the market for securitized derivatives where the majority of trades are between retail investors and market makers, the argument that aggregate trades sum to zero can be bypassed and herding can be explored at the wider market level. In addition, a unique view on optimistic and pessimistic herding is provided by including call as well as put options in the herding measure – in addition to buys and sells.

In addition, the understanding of herding in the literature is extended from the individual stock level to the market level: Measures such as the LSV herding measure do not capture market-wide herding, i.e. herding behavior of the population across all stocks (see Oehler 1988 for a similar discussion with respect to investment funds). Detecting herding in single stocks does not answer the question whether individual investors tend to have the same opinion about the market as a whole and therefore move into or out of the market at the same time. The LSV type of herding can be described as "stock-picking" or "excess" herding whereas the latter approach can be described as "market-wide" herding. In this chapter, market-wide herding is investigated in sections 5.3 and 5.4 and stock-level herding in section 5.5.

The data, however, does not include order flow that can be traced to individual investors' accounts which makes it impossible to distinguish between intentional herding and spurious herding. In light of the empirical challenges outlined in the previous section and the various definitions of herding in the literature, herding is regarded as the tendency of retail investors to simultaneously move into or out of the market at the same time. Whether this behavior is intended or solely at random cannot be empirically explored with the available data. However, a high level of herding among retail investors stresses the importance of retail investors in the price formation process. Rather than a wide dispersion of retail orders (and hence retail orders cancelling each other out), a highly correlated behavior would have high impact on the market.

5.3. Evidence of Market-Wide Herding

The analysis begins by searching for evidence of herding at the market level. As described in Section 5.2, the vast majority of studies test whether certain subgroups of investors tend to herd in and out of a group of stocks. Few studies consider whether the evidence of this correlated trading aggregates to the market level. It is reasonable to expect that if noise traders can potentially have a significant impact on prices their trades would be correlated to an extent large enough to be detectable at the aggregate level. The data used by previous studies limits the ability to test for aggregate herding because the main focus on equity and bond markets, where investors trade amongst each other, results in the situation where for every buyer there is a seller and aggregate trades will sum to zero. The focus on the securitized derivatives market and its specific market model allows for test of herding at the aggregate level because in this market trades are predominantly between investors and issuers making the market in their respective products.

5.3.1. Data

To measure market-wide herding, all orders in securitized derivatives which derive their value from the DAX, the German market benchmark, are taken into account. Many retail investors use products like these to invest in the whole market without having to buy single stocks. Since more than 90% of the trading volume in index derivatives comprises products on the DAX, this index is chosen to test for market-wide herding.

Since the data set used in this chapter equals the data set from Chapter 4, no additional summary statistics are presented in this section.

5.3.2. Herding Measure Construction

The basis of the herding measure is the entirety of all executed retail investor orders as described in chapter 4. Each trade can be categorized as optimistic or as pessimistic. In contrast to other studies, there is not only a buy/sell component but also a put/call component in the herding measure which is a clear advantage of the measure. Optimistic trades are executed buy orders in call products and sell orders in put products. Pessimistic trades, on the other hand, are executed sell orders in call products and buy orders in put products.

Herding is expressed as the imbalance of optimistic and pessimistic transactions during a predefined herding period, e.g. one day or one week. This imbalance can be measured either on the basis of the number of trades in each category or on the basis of the Euro denominated order volume.

Furthermore, two different herding measures are constructed to analyze different effects on herding: signed vs. unsigned herding. Unsigned herding captures the total level of herding independent of whether investors exhibited optimistic or pessimistic herding behavior. Signed herding allows for distinguishing between optimistic and pessimistic herding but cannot be used when calculating averages to determine the overall level of herding. The signed (SMH) and unsigned (UMH) market level herding measures for herding period t are as follows:

$$\mathrm{SMH_t} = r_t^{opt} - \mathrm{E}\left(r_t^{opt}\right) \quad (5.1)$$

$$\mathrm{UMH_t} = \mathrm{abs}(\mathrm{SMH_t}) \quad (5.2)$$

$$r_t^{opt} = \frac{b^C + s^P}{b^C + s^C + b^P + s^P} \quad (5.3)$$

where r_t^{opt} is the ratio of optimistic investors as measured in formula 5.3: In it, b^C represents all buy orders in call products, s^P all sell orders in put products, s^C all sell orders in call products, and b^P all buy orders in put products in period t. As already noted, t can be daily, weekly, or monthly, though longer herding periods usually lead to lower herding measures. The investor ratio can be measured in two ways: a) order volume in Euro and b) number of executed orders in that period.

The SMH measures the ratio of optimistic investors to all investors minus the expected ratio which is set to 50% following the consideration that optimistic and pessimistic investors should be equally represented in case of no herding. The UMH is simply the absolute value of the SMH.

UMH and SMH are distinguished analogously to Grinblatt, Titman, and Wermers (1995) who also distinguish between an unsigned and a signed herding measure which separates buy and sell herding. The major difference is, though, that Grinblatt, Titman, and Wermers (1995) calculate one measure for each stock which indicates whether a fund is following a crowd or trading against the crowd. Therefore, the average proportion of buyers and sellers in a given stock is subtracted to determine the relation to the other funds. However, since the herding measure is not based on different stocks but the whole market, the average or expected level of herding does not need to be adjusted for.

In other words, following the discussion in section 5.2.3, the focus of this section is to determine the average level of herding among retail investors in certain periods, and relate it to optimistic and pessimistic behavior.

5.3.3. Results

Influence of Order Types on the Herding Measure

Summary statistics of market-wide herding using DAX securitized derivatives are presented in Table 5.1. Panel A presents statistics for the herding measure based on the number of executed orders, panel B based on the volume of executed orders. The columns show means and medians for the unsigned market herding measure (UMH), the signed market herding measure (SMH), and the signed herding measure for both optimistic and pessimistic trades.

Results for all order types, market as well as limit orders are presented by different rows. Herding period is daily, comprising all executed orders from January 2004 to December 2008.

Table 5.1: Signed and Unsigned Market Herding Measures

This table presents summary statistics on the unsigned market herding measure (UMH) and the signed market herding measure (SMH). Numbers in Panel A are calculated using the number of executed orders, whereas numbers in Panel B are calculated using executed order volume. For the signed market herding measure, optimistic and pessimistic herding are distinguished. Herding period is daily, comprising all executed orders from January 2004 to December 2008.

	UMH		SMH					
	all		all		optimistic		pessimistic	
	mean	median	mean	median	mean	median	mean	median
Panel A: Number of executed orders								
all order types	10.3%	9.1%	1.2%	1.3%	10.8%	9.5%	-9.9%	-8.7%
market orders	7.6%	6.2%	1.9%	2.2%	8.2%	7.1%	-6.9%	-5.5%
limit orders	16.8%	15.3%	-0.1%	-0.1%	16.8%	15.2%	-16.8%	-15.5%
Panel B: Volume of executed orders								
all order types	9.7%	8.3%	2.9%	2.9%	10.5%	9.3%	-8.6%	-6.9%
market orders	8.6%	7.3%	3.9%	4.2%	9.5%	8.1%	-7.0%	-5.5%
limit orders	15.6%	13.9%	0.2%	0.0%	15.8%	13.8%	-15.4%	-14.1%

A substantial level of market-wide herding can be observed: The average UMH which captures the level of herding disregarding optimistic and pessimistic herding is 10.3% for the number based measure and 9.7% for the volume based measure. This value can be interpreted as follows: Under the assumption that the benchmark is virtually the equal distribution, i.e. on average roughly 50% of all trades (transaction volume) are optimistic and 50% are pessimistic, a UMH value of 10.3% means that on average 60.3% of all trades (transaction volume) are on the same side of the market (either optimistic or pessimistic) in the observed herding periods.

The SMH indicates that daily optimistic and pessimistic herding almost level out when averaging over the whole period of five years: The average number based SMH is 1.2% and the average volume based SMH is 2.9%.

It is worthwhile to pay respect to the use of different order types when analyzing the level and the sign of herding. As Dorn, Huberman and Sengmueller (2008) note, the execution of stale limit orders in the order book could possibly lead to biased results and a wrong level of herding. For this purpose, market orders (and marketable limit orders as explained in section 4.2) and limit orders that are not executed immediately are distinguished and reported separately in Table 5.1. There is a much higher level of unsigned herding in limit orders than in market orders which is a result of optimistic (pessimistic) limit orders being executed when the market moves downward (upward). This is in line with the observations by Dorn,

Huberman, and Sengmueller. However, the herding level for all order types is still substantial although a part of the market order herding vanishes because of stale limit orders. The reason why the UMH value for "all order types" is lower than either the value for "market orders" or "limit orders" is that market and limit orders usually work in different directions and the aggregate effect on the herding measure is lowered.

As noted in the preceding section, optimistic and pessimistic herding are distinguished to analyze whether herding is a result of optimistic investors or pessimistic investors being on the same side of the market in a given period. The last four columns of Table 5.1 present mean and median optimistic and pessimistic SMH values. Absolute herding levels are not significantly different when distinguishing between optimistic and pessimistic investors. The only significant difference can be observed in the herding level of market orders: Investors using market orders herd to a much greater extent when they are optimistic than when they are pessimistic.

Influence of Bullish and Bearish Market Periods on the Herding Measure

The first half of this section highlights the differences between herding measures, the use of order types, and the behavior of optimistic and pessimistic investors. In the second part it is analyzed whether the level of herding can be explained by the overall market situation, i.e. by bullish and bearish market periods.

In the absence of a generally accepted method of classifying bull and bear markets, the approach of Fabozzi and Francis (1977) is adopted who propose two methods: Up and Down Markets (UD) and Substantial Up and Down Months (SUD). Under the UD method, months in which the monthly market return is positive are classified as bull markets and those experiencing negative returns are taken as bear markets. The drawback of this method is that all months under observation will be classified as either bull or bear months even if the magnitude of returns is small. The second method, SUD, addresses this issue by classifying a month as a bullish period if the absolute value of the market return in that month is greater than one half of the standard deviation of returns over the sample period.

The latter criterion is applied as it better reflects the general definition of bullish/bearish periods as being characterized by substantial up/down trends in market return rather than merely up/down trends as with the first criterion. Although the authors concede that the choice of half a standard deviation is arbitrary, the method incorporates a simple rule-of-thumb that helps us exclude months with small returns and consider only months with substantial movements.

In contrast to Fabozzi and Francis, the method is applied to weeks instead of months[20] and all weeks in the sample are characterized as bullish, neutral, and bearish. A weekly classification of market sentiment better captures the relatively high volatility in the sample. In addition, the weekly frequency is a better match for the daily herding measure calculation.

Having decomposed the sample into bullish, bearish, and neutral periods, the question is how the herding levels differ under these market environments. Table 5.2 provides a summary of the mean and median unsigned and signed daily herding measures under different subsamples. As in the analysis before, results are presented for different order types to explore the effect of automatically executed limit orders.[21]

Table 5.2: Signed and Unsigned Market Herding Measures by Market Period

This table presents means and medians of the unsigned and signed market herding measures, differentiated by order type and market period, i.e. bullish, neutral, or bearish. Results for the SMH are further broken down into optimistic and pessimistic herding. The calculation is based on the number of executed orders.

	UMH		SMH					
	all		all		optimistic		pessimistic	
	mean	median	mean	median	mean	median	mean	median
all order types								
bull	10.4%	8.6%	-6.5%	-6.5%	6.7%	5.7%	-11.9%	-11.1%
neutral	9.8%	8.7%	2.0%	2.4%	10.4%	9.0%	-9.0%	-8.2%
bear	11.6%	11.2%	9.0%	10.0%	13.4%	13.3%	-5.6%	-4.5%
market orders								
bull	7.3%	5.8%	-3.7%	-3.5%	5.3%	4.4%	-8.4%	-6.7%
neutral	7.2%	5.9%	2.7%	2.7%	8.1%	6.7%	-5.9%	-4.5%
bear	8.9%	8.1%	7.2%	8.0%	9.8%	9.6%	-4.7%	-4.8%
limit orders								
bull	17.3%	15.9%	-11.7%	-12.5%	10.9%	8.8%	-19.5%	-19.6%
neutral	15.8%	14.6%	0.7%	1.3%	15.9%	14.5%	-15.6%	-14.7%
bear	18.5%	17.6%	12.5%	14.3%	20.6%	20.6%	-12.0%	-11.0%

Looking first at the UMH, it is clear from the results that there is a higher level of herding during bearish periods than in bullish periods. This result is robust across both market and limit orders. Retail investor trades seem to cluster more when the market is facing a downturn. There are two possible explanations for this observation. First, investors may trade in the same direction due to panic. In such a case more selling in general might be observed

[20] As a robustness check, the method is also applied to months and each month is classified as bullish or bearish as proposed by Fabozzi and Francis (1977). The results are qualitatively similar though herding values are a bit smaller.

[21] Since the number based measure and the volume based measure seem to deliver the same results, from now the number based herding measure is calculated only.

than buying. Alternatively, the general decline in the market index could be seen as an opportunity for bargain hunting. Such investors would be following a contrarian strategy.

The SMH sheds more light on these explanations. It indicates whether the order imbalance tilts towards optimistic herding or pessimistic herding. The positive sign of the overall SMH during bearish periods indicates that optimistic trades dominated these periods. As with the UMH, the results are robust across both order types. It appears from the results that investors are contrarian.

The last four columns of Table 5.2 provide further insights into the motivation of retail investor trades by classifying trades into optimistic and pessimistic and presenting average and median SMH values for the different subsamples. In all three subsamples – all order types, market orders, and limit orders – pessimistic herding is higher in bull markets than in bear markets, and optimistic herding is higher in bear markets than in bull markets. This result holds for the mean as well as the median herding measure. For limit orders, this result is expected since limit orders are executed automatically. It is interesting to observe, however, that this result holds for market orders as well. Retail investors indeed act as contrarians and exhibit a higher tendency towards positive herding in bear markets and negative herding in bull markets.

5.3.4. Review of Results

A high level of market-wide herding in stock market index certificates can be observed. In order to assess the influence of optimistic vs. pessimistic investors, market vs. limit orders, and bull vs. bear markets on herding levels, the sample is divided in different subsamples. The main results are that herding levels are substantially higher in bear than in bull markets, and that a contrarian behavior leads to generally higher herding levels.

5.4. Market-Wide Herding on a Broker Level

The preceding section has shown that substantial market-wide herding can be found in instruments on a market index. It is worthwhile to break the order flow data further down on a broker level to investigate whether herding is a market-wide phenomenon that is only observable on an aggregate basis or a phenomenon that can be observed for order flows coming from different brokers. In addition, it can be analyzed whether the flows of different types of brokers are correlated or whether there are substantial differences. These differences could be due to different clienteles that show distinct trading patterns.

5.4.1. Data

Sample data with a broker ID for each order reaches from January 2007 to December 2008. This sub sample includes the 22 brokers with the largest order volume in the sample period.

The goal is to calculate a herding measure for each single broker. Table 5.3 shows descriptive statistics of daily herding measures for each of the 22 brokers in the sample.

Table 5.3: Daily Herding Measures on a Broker Level

This table presents means and medians for the unsigned and signed market herding measures separately for each of the 22 brokers in the sample. Additionally, the far right column reports the number of orders submitted by each broker in the sample.

		UMH		SMH				
Broker Type	Broker #	mean	median	mean	median	min	max	# of orders
online	1	4.6%	3.6%	-0.6%	-0.5%	-20.3%	16.7%	228,620
	2	4.8%	4.0%	-0.7%	-0.2%	-27.7%	17.0%	277,554
	3	5.8%	4.7%	-0.6%	-0.4%	-26.8%	27.7%	643,622
	4	6.0%	4.9%	-1.4%	-1.3%	-25.5%	19.4%	122,872
	5	7.3%	6.3%	-0.1%	0.1%	-29.5%	20.1%	236,972
private	6	6.1%	5.0%	0.6%	1.0%	-22.7%	24.7%	149,124
	7	6.8%	5.9%	-0.2%	0.1%	-30.8%	27.5%	167,570
	8	7.3%	6.2%	0.1%	0.8%	-33.8%	25.1%	224,666
	9	7.4%	6.3%	-0.4%	0.2%	-29.4%	24.1%	160,230
	10	7.9%	6.9%	0.3%	0.5%	-35.4%	26.2%	238,776
	11	9.2%	8.1%	0.0%	0.0%	-32.1%	27.5%	168,704
public	12	7.9%	7.3%	1.3%	1.8%	-33.5%	24.6%	315,860
	13	8.0%	7.1%	1.2%	1.4%	-34.6%	25.7%	166,446
	14	8.5%	7.4%	1.6%	2.3%	-28.2%	28.3%	168,260
	15	9.3%	8.0%	0.1%	0.6%	-32.1%	32.6%	67,812
	16	9.4%	8.3%	1.2%	2.2%	-35.6%	30.2%	312,446
	17	9.4%	8.2%	1.0%	1.6%	-40.3%	31.5%	59,624
	18	10.0%	8.7%	-0.3%	0.0%	-32.5%	35.2%	21,492
	19	10.6%	9.8%	1.5%	1.6%	-31.5%	33.2%	133,772
prop	20	6.6%	5.3%	-0.4%	0.0%	-31.4%	26.2%	77,656
	21	7.8%	6.4%	-1.5%	-1.2%	-38.9%	23.3%	28,368
	22	10.0%	7.7%	0.2%	0.0%	-41.9%	50.0%	23,062

Substantial herding can be detected in the order flows of all brokers though herding levels differ across brokers. Average UMH values vary from 4.6% to 10.6%. Herding levels have almost the same range as the values in section 5.3 where aggregate order flow is investigated. The total number of executed orders for each broker is reported to acknowledge the fact that there are brokers of different size in our sample.

5.4.2. Results

All brokers in the sub sample are sorted into 4 categories: The first category ("online") comprises all brokers that only have online customers and no branches. The second category ("private") includes all private banks with branches. It is unknown, however, how much of their order flow is generated online or in branches but it is assumed that the majority of the flow is generated through investment advisors offline. The third category ("public") comprises banks that belong to the cooperative and the savings bank sector. These institutions have a long tradition in Germany and are assumed to have rather conservative clients. The last category ("prop") comprises brokers with mostly semi-professional, proprietary traders. These traders are considered to be retail clients although their trading behavior differs from those of the other investors in that they also use arbitrage trading strategies.

Table 5.4 presents descriptive statistics for order flows categorized by broker type. The level of herding, expressed by the UMH mean and median, differs across broker types. The level of herding is lowest for proprietary brokers and highest for public brokers. Prop traders obviously follow very different trading strategies than individual investors – such as the customers of a savings bank – leading to a much lower herding measure.

Table 5.4: Daily Herding Measures by Broker Type

This table presents means and medians for the unsigned and signed market herding measures separately for the four broker types. Measures are calculated using the number of executed orders.

	UMH		SMH			
Broker Type	Mean	Median	Mean	Median	Min	Max
online	5.4%	4.3%	-0.6%	-0.1%	-23.6%	17.9%
private	6.8%	5.7%	0.2%	0.4%	-29.8%	25.5%
public	8.3%	7.3%	1.2%	1.8%	-32.4%	26.2%
prop	5.2%	4.5%	-0.3%	0.4%	-23.6%	20.4%

To test the correlation of herding measures across brokers the pairwise correlations between the daily SMH time series of all brokers are calculated and presented as a heat map of correlation coefficients in Figure 5.1. All correlations are statistically significant at the 5% level. UMH correlation is not presented because the UMH time series of two different brokers could have a high correlation although clients trade in different directions. Using the SMH allows for an examination of the degree to which investors from different brokers move together in and out of the market at the same time.

In the heat map, all brokers are sorted into the four categories and within each category according to their time series' average correlation coefficient with those of the other brokers.

		public								private						online					prop		
	Broker #	16	12	14	13	17	15	19	18	8	11	9	10	7	6	5	3	2	1	4	21	22	20
public	16		0.9	0.9	0.9	0.8	0.8	0.8	0.8	0.9	0.9	0.9	0.9	0.9	0.8	0.9	0.9	0.7	0.6	0.5	0.4	0.2	0.2
	12	0.9		0.9	0.9	0.8	0.8	0.8	0.7	0.9	0.9	0.8	0.9	0.9	0.8	0.9	0.8	0.7	0.6	0.4	0.4	0.2	0.2
	14	0.9	0.9		0.9	0.8	0.8	0.8	0.7	0.9	0.9	0.9	0.9	0.8	0.8	0.9	0.8	0.7	0.6	0.4	0.4	0.2	0.2
	13	0.9	0.9	0.9		0.8	0.8	0.8	0.8	0.9	0.9	0.8	0.9	0.8	0.7	0.8	0.8	0.7	0.6	0.4	0.4	0.2	0.2
	17	0.8	0.8	0.8	0.8		0.7	0.7	0.6	0.8	0.8	0.8	0.8	0.8	0.7	0.8	0.8	0.7	0.7	0.5	0.4	0.2	0.2
	15	0.8	0.8	0.8	0.8	0.7		0.7	0.7	0.8	0.8	0.7	0.7	0.8	0.7	0.7	0.7	0.6	0.5	0.3	0.3	0.2	0.2
	19	0.8	0.8	0.8	0.8	0.7	0.7		0.6	0.7	0.8	0.7	0.7	0.7	0.6	0.7	0.7	0.6	0.5	0.3	0.3	0.2	0.1
	18	0.8	0.7	0.7	0.8	0.6	0.7	0.6		0.7	0.7	0.7	0.7	0.7	0.6	0.7	0.7	0.6	0.5	0.4	0.4	0.2	0.1
private	8	0.9	0.9	0.9	0.9	0.8	0.8	0.7	0.7		0.9	0.9	0.9	0.9	0.8	0.9	0.9	0.8	0.7	0.5	0.5	0.2	0.2
	11	0.9	0.9	0.9	0.9	0.8	0.8	0.8	0.7	0.9		0.9	0.9	0.9	0.8	0.9	0.8	0.7	0.6	0.5	0.4	0.2	0.2
	9	0.9	0.8	0.9	0.8	0.8	0.7	0.7	0.7	0.9	0.9		0.8	0.8	0.7	0.9	0.9	0.8	0.7	0.5	0.5	0.2	0.2
	10	0.9	0.9	0.9	0.9	0.8	0.7	0.7	0.7	0.9	0.9	0.8		0.8	0.7	0.8	0.8	0.7	0.6	0.5	0.4	0.2	0.2
	7	0.9	0.9	0.8	0.8	0.8	0.8	0.7	0.7	0.9	0.9	0.8	0.8		0.7	0.8	0.8	0.7	0.6	0.5	0.5	0.2	0.2
	6	0.8	0.8	0.8	0.7	0.7	0.7	0.6	0.6	0.8	0.8	0.7	0.7	0.7		0.8	0.7	0.7	0.6	0.5	0.4	0.2	0.2
online	5	0.9	0.9	0.9	0.8	0.8	0.7	0.7	0.7	0.9	0.9	0.9	0.8	0.8	0.8		0.9	0.8	0.8	0.6	0.5	0.3	0.2
	3	0.9	0.8	0.8	0.8	0.8	0.7	0.7	0.7	0.9	0.8	0.9	0.8	0.8	0.7	0.9		0.8	0.7	0.6	0.5	0.2	0.2
	2	0.7	0.7	0.7	0.7	0.7	0.6	0.6	0.6	0.8	0.7	0.8	0.7	0.7	0.7	0.8	0.8		0.8	0.6	0.6	0.2	0.3
	1	0.6	0.6	0.6	0.6	0.7	0.5	0.5	0.5	0.7	0.6	0.7	0.6	0.6	0.6	0.8	0.7	0.8		0.6	0.5	0.2	0.2
	4	0.5	0.4	0.4	0.4	0.5	0.3	0.3	0.4	0.5	0.5	0.5	0.5	0.5	0.5	0.6	0.6	0.6	0.6		0.5	0.2	0.2
prop	21	0.4	0.4	0.4	0.4	0.4	0.3	0.3	0.4	0.5	0.4	0.5	0.4	0.5	0.4	0.5	0.5	0.6	0.5	0.5		0.2	0.2
	22	0.2	0.2	0.2	0.2	0.2	0.2	0.2	0.2	0.2	0.2	0.2	0.2	0.2	0.2	0.3	0.2	0.2	0.2	0.2	0.2		0.1
	20	0.2	0.2	0.2	0.2	0.2	0.2	0.1	0.1	0.2	0.2	0.2	0.2	0.2	0.2	0.2	0.2	0.3	0.2	0.2	0.2	0.1	

Figure 5.1: Pairwise Broker Correlation

This figure shows a heat map of pairwise broker correlation coefficients. Within each broker category, single brokers are sorted by average correlation, i.e. the brokers with the highest average correlation are ranked first.

It is important to note that the level of correlation is generally very high: The average of the pairwise correlation coefficients across all broker types is 0.64. This value is mostly driven by the high correlation between public and private brokers' order flow. Order flow of proprietary brokers generally does not correlate well with the flow of any of the other broker types.

Panel A of Table 5.5 shows the average pairwise correlation between signed market herding measure time series within and between each broker type. All single correlations are statistically different from zero on a 1% significance level (using t-tests).

Table 5.5: Correlation between Broker Types

This table presents correlation coefficients between SMH time series of the four broker types. Correlations are performed on the signed market herding measures using the number of executed orders. Panel A reports average pairwise correlation coefficients within and between brokers of different types. Panel B reports correlation coefficients between aggregate signed market herding measures of different broker types. All correlation coefficients are statistically significant on a 1% level.

Panel A: Average pairwise broker correlation

Broker type	public	private	online	prop
public	0.80			
private	0.80	0.82		
online	0.64	0.71	0.73	
prop	0.25	0.28	0.32	0.16

Panel B: Correlation between aggregated broker types

Broker type	public	private	online	prop
public	1.00			
private	0.96	1.00		
online	0.84	0.89	1.00	
prop	0.32	0.37	0.44	1.00

For public, private, and online brokers, the average pairwise correlation of signed herding measures within their broker type is higher than the average pairwise correlation of herding measures of different broker types. For proprietary brokers the opposite pattern can be observed: Their herding measure time series have a higher correlation with those of other brokers than among themselves but are well below the measures from the other broker types. This supports the assumption that semi-professional traders follow different trading strategies that are not even correlated within their own category.

When aggregating all order flow within each broker type, time series correlation coefficients of signed herding measures for each broker type can be calculated. Panel B of Table 5.5 shows the results. Again, SMH time series of private and public brokers show the highest correlation whereas the time series of the proprietary brokers exhibit a substantially lower correlation with the other broker types' time series.

5.4.3. Review of Results

This section analyzes the flows of 22 different brokers in four distinct categories and calculated the herding measures for each of them. Across all brokers a substantial herding of retail investors can be observed though differing in the level of herding: The level is highest among public brokers with a rather conservative clientele and lowest among online brokers that neither give investment advice nor operate any branches. Proprietary brokers do not seem to fit into the same schema as they exhibit very different trading patterns.

5.5. Stock-Level Herding

The preceding sections have shown that there is a substantial level of retail investor herding on the market as well as the broker level. Subject of investigation are all orders in DAX products. Trading on a well-known financial instrument like the DAX may lead to a higher degree of herding because of its higher visibility and stronger correlated reactions by retail investors.

To analyze whether there is retail investor herding in single stock underlyings, herding measures introduced in section 5.3.2 are calculated using all orders in securitized derivatives based on a sample of 244 stocks. Results are presented for different order types, different product types, and different market capitalizations of the underlying companies. Finally, findings of this section are compared with the findings of Lakonishok, Shleifer and Vishny (1992) and other related work.

5.5.1. Data

In the data base, 37% of all customer orders comprise securitized derivatives with individual stocks as underlying value (see Table 4.1 on page 75, Panel C). The underlying stocks include companies from different European countries, from the U.S and Asian countries. Table 5.6 presents summary statistics by the underlying companies' geographical origin. Both executed and submitted orders are considered. The sample includes orders in the period of January 2004 to December 2008.

The calculation of an order flow herding measure demands that there is a minimum amount of trading in related instruments otherwise such a measure cannot be calculated. Therefore, all underlying stocks are filtered by employing the following methodology: All underlyings are sorted according to the average number of executed orders per month. As a rule of thumb, an average trading amount of 3 executed orders per day is demanded resulting in 60 executed orders per month (assuming 20 trading days per month). This filter is applied to all underlyings and results in 244 stocks comprising about 97% of all executed trades on stocks in the data base.

Table 5.6: Summary Statistics by Geographical Origin of Company

This table presents summary statistics on the number of underlying sample stocks and the number of executed and submitted orders by geographical origin of the company. German stocks are excluded from the category *Europe*. Panel A presents statistics on executed orders. Panel B presents statistics on submitted orders. Sample period is from January 2004 to December 2008.

	Origin of company					
	Germany	Europe	N. America	Asia	S. America	Total
No. companies	121	71	42	9	1	244
Panel A: Number of executed orders						
all trades						
all products	6,851,733	778,066	393,834	60,411	4,771	8,088,815
leverage	5,296,019	546,333	374,460	57,969	4,732	6,279,513
investment	1,533,550	230,132	19,332	2,442	39	1,785,495
market orders						
all products	4,367,022	492,990	233,516	40,187	2,415	5,136,130
leverage	3,040,019	301,483	218,883	38,267	2,380	3,601,032
investment	1,313,821	190,514	14,606	1,920	35	1,520,896
limit orders						
all products	1,956,916	228,205	122,878	15,989	1,798	2,325,786
leverage	1,754,813	191,997	118,890	15,561	1,797	2,083,058
investment	194,881	35,688	3,978	428	1	234,976
stop orders						
all products	527,795	56,871	37,440	4,235	558	626,899
leverage	501,187	52,853	36,687	4,141	555	595,423
investment	24,848	3,930	748	94	3	29,623
Panel B: Number of submitted orders						
all trades						
all products	12,077,191	1,390,663	757,281	99,268	9,541	14,333,944
leverage	9,958,261	1,072,730	728,041	95,213	9,469	11,863,714
investment	2,082,735	315,285	29,145	4,055	72	2,431,292

Market Capitalization

The 244 stocks in the sample are chosen regardless of market capitalization. However, summary statistics for the stocks by market capitalization are provided to show that the sample is not tilted towards companies with either high or low market capitalizations.

Barber, Odean and Zhu (2009a) identify small, medium, and large firms using NYSE breakpoints. NYSE breakpoints are percentiles of all NYSE listed firm's market capitalizations and therefore are a good representation of the whole market. Small firms are those in their sample below the 30th percentile of NYSE market cap, while large firms are those above the 70th percentile.

Kaniel, Saar, and Titman (2008) define small, medium, and large capitalization stocks as stocks below the 40th percentile, between the 40th and the 70th percentiles, and above the 70th percentile, respectively. In contrast to Barber, Odean, and Zhu, they do not use an external source such as the NYSE breakpoints to validate their classification.

For the purpose of this study, the market capitalization of each stock in the sample is calculated at the beginning of each year (2004 to 2009), and the respective averages of the whole 5-year-period are computed. As breakpoints, 2 billion and 20 billion Euros are used. Small firms are defined as firms with an average market capitalization below 2 billion Euros, medium firms between 2 billion and 20 billion Euros, and large firms above 20 billion Euros. Table 5.7 shows median and mean values for market capitalizations in the respective categories. The classification almost divides the sample into three equally-sized groups of about 80 stocks.

Table 5.7: Summary Statistics on Market Capitalization

This table presents the breakpoints for the market cap classification as well as the number of companies in the sample assigned to each group. The two columns on the right report the median and the mean market capitalization for each group.

	Market capitalization (in million €)	No. companies in sample	Median	Mean
Small cap	< 2,000	80	710	827
Medium cap	2,000 - 20,000	81	6,682	8,385
Large cap	> 20,000	83	50,072	66,625

Market capitalization statistics are used to test whether there are any differences in retail investor herding between small capitalization stocks and large capitalization stocks.

5.5.2. Herding Measure

The herding measure used in this section is very similar to the one used in Lakonishok, Shleifer, and Vishny (1992). The LSV measure, H_{LSV}, is defined as

$$H_{LSV} = \frac{1}{\sum_{t=1}^{T} N_t} \sum_t \sum_j (|br_{jt} - br_t^{LSV}| - E_t[|br_{jt} - br_t^{LSV}|]) \tag{5.3}$$

where N_t is the number of stocks traded during period t, the buyers ratio br_{jt} is the number of net buyers of stock j during period t divided by the number of active traders of j during t, and the period-average buyers ratio br_t^{LSV} is the number of net buyers aggregated across all stocks during period t divided by the number of all active traders during t.

Subtracting the term br_t^{LSV} controls for general shifts into or out of stocks that affects all stocks alike – for example due to an economic crisis or a stock market boom. The term $E_t[|br_{jt} - br_t^{LSV}|]$ is an adjustment factor that accounts for the statistical fact that the absolute value of $br_{jt} - br_t^{LSV}$ is greater than zero even if there is no herding at all. For this reason, LSV calculate the expected value of $|br_{jt} - br_t^{LSV}|$ using the binomial distribution and subtract this term from the empirically determined term $br_{jt} - br_t^{LSV}$. For any stock, however, the adjustment factor declines as the number of active traders in that stock rises.

The message of the LSV measure can be illustrated by an example as follows: Suppose there are 100 active traders of a stock during a certain period, and 60 of them are net buyers, i.e. during the period they buy more than they sell. As a result, the buyers ratio for this stock is 0.6. For all stocks traded in the same period, there are 1000 traders dividing into 500 net buyers and 500 net sellers resulting in a period-average buyers ratio of 0.5. The LSV measure for stock j in period t is then |0.6-0.5|=0.1 which means that 10% of all traders more than indicated by the period average are on the same side of the market.

The concept of the LSV measure cannot directly be transferred to this work's data set because there is a major difference in the data: Since all orders are anonymous, i.e. it is not possible to determine whether two orders have originated from the same individual (though it is possible to determine the broker), a measure that is based on the number of individuals cannot be computed. Instead, the modified measure is based on the number of orders rather than the number of investors. Therefore, the measures should be equal if every order for each instrument is submitted by a different investor. Since this is not realistic there will be differences between the measures. However, the greater the dispersion of orders among retail investors, the smaller is the expected difference. In addition, there is no need for an adjustment factor in our measure due to the different calculation basis.

The herding measure used in this section is calculated as follows:

$$H'_{LSV} = \frac{1}{\sum_{t=1}^{T} N_t} \sum_t \sum_j \left| r_{jt}^{opt} - \overline{r_t^{opt}} \right| \tag{5.4}$$

$$\overline{r_t^{opt}} = \frac{\sum_j \left(r_j^{opt} \cdot n_j \right)}{\sum_j n_j} \tag{5.5}$$

where N_t is the number of stocks with at least 5 executed orders in period t. This restriction on the minimum number of transactions per stock and time period ensures that a meaningful herding measure can be calculated. r_{jt}^{opt} is the ratio of optimistic investors as defined in section 5.3.2 for stock j and period t. $\overline{r_t^{opt}}$ is the average optimistic investor ratio based on all stocks with the minimum number of orders in period t. It is weighted by the number of orders.

5.5.3. Results

The herding measure H'_{LSV} is calculated for different time periods (daily, weekly, monthly, and quarterly), different product types (all product types, leverage products, investment products), and different order types (all order types, market orders, limit orders). Table 5.8 presents the results.

Table 5.8: Modified LSV Herding Measure by Product and Order Type

This table presents summary statistics for the H'_{LSV} measure. Statistics are reported for different time periods, different product types, and different order types.

	All Order Types			Market Orders			Limit Orders		
	all	leverage	investment	all	leverage	investment	all	leverage	investment
Daily									
Mean	17.0%	17.5%	17.5%	16.9%	17.5%	17.2%	21.8%	22.1%	20.5%
Median	14.3%	14.8%	14.6%	14.0%	14.7%	14.3%	19.2%	19.6%	16.9%
Std. Dev.	12.9%	13.1%	13.7%	13.1%	13.3%	13.6%	15.4%	15.5%	15.6%
Observations	147,591	131,798	56,882	118,854	100,531	51,134	79,978	74,481	13,472
Weekly									
Mean	14.1%	14.3%	17.6%	14.5%	14.7%	17.6%	17.9%	18.1%	19.1%
Median	11.4%	11.7%	14.7%	11.6%	11.8%	14.7%	15.5%	15.7%	16.1%
Std. Dev.	11.2%	11.3%	13.9%	11.7%	11.8%	13.9%	13.0%	13.1%	14.6%
Observations	46,377	44,311	24,699	42,809	39,535	22,491	35,938	33,981	10,274
Monthly									
Mean	11.0%	10.7%	16.9%	11.6%	11.4%	17.1%	13.6%	13.6%	17.7%
Median	8.5%	8.3%	14.1%	8.9%	8.7%	14.0%	11.2%	11.3%	15.0%
Std. Dev.	9.3%	9.2%	13.5%	10.0%	10.0%	13.7%	10.6%	10.7%	13.6%
Observations	11,796	11,689	8,597	11,599	11,397	8,098	11,190	10,961	5,304
Quarterly									
Mean	8.7%	8.0%	15.3%	9.3%	8.5%	15.8%	10.3%	10.3%	16.1%
Median	6.6%	6.0%	12.6%	7.2%	6.2%	12.9%	8.2%	8.2%	13.2%
Std. Dev.	7.8%	7.5%	12.4%	8.4%	8.2%	12.9%	8.7%	8.7%	12.8%
Observations	4,023	3,998	3,393	4,000	3,973	3,289	3,954	3,930	2,648

Results include the mean, the median, the standard deviation and the number of observations. Note that the number of observations is a measure of the number of stock-period-measures r_{jt}^{opt} with at least 5 trades in the respective underlying. For this reason, numbers of sub categories do not add up to 100%.

The average daily herding measure on a stock level is 17% which means that on average 17% of all trades more than expected are on the same side of the market every day. This means that there is substantial herding also on the stock level.

Herding measures are lower for longer time periods: For example, the average quarterly herding measure on a stock level is 8.7% indicating that the longer time period smoothes the higher daily herding values and brings them back to a more moderate level. For a given quarter, trades on different days and on different sides are more likely to cancel each other out so the quarterly herding measure is not affected.

Herding in investment products is higher than in leverage products: In each quarter, of all trades in investment products, 15.3% more than the average are on the same side of the market whereas the value is 8.0% for leverage products. This is a result of different time horizons of the products: Leverage products are flow products that are bought and sold within days whereas investment products are instruments that are likely to be held for months or even years.

Herding measured by limit orders is higher than by market orders. This is due to the automatic execution of limit orders as a result of market movements. The interesting part of the comparison, however, is the finding that herding measured by market orders is substantial and almost as high as the herding measured by limit orders: The average daily herding measure using market orders is 17.5% and the average quarterly herding measure equals 8.5%. These results prove that the herding found in the data is not only an artifact of the execution of stale limit orders.

Table 5.9 provides another view on the data. As a robustness check, herding measures are presented not only by product type but also by size of the underlying company. Market capitalization of each stock is determined at the beginning of each year (2004 to 2009) and the respective averages of the whole 5-year-period are computed. 2 billion and 20 billion Euros are used as the size breakpoints as explained in section 5.5.1.

Table 5.9: Modified LSV Herding Measure by Firm Size

This table presents summary statistics for the H'_{LSV} measure. Statistics are reported for different time periods, different product types, and different firm sizes.

	Small Caps			Mid Caps			Large Caps		
	all	leverage	investment	all	leverage	investment	all	leverage	investment
Daily									
Mean	18.2%	18.8%	21.8%	16.4%	16.9%	18.5%	16.9%	17.3%	15.7%
Median	15.6%	16.2%	19.9%	13.8%	14.3%	16.0%	13.9%	14.3%	12.6%
Std. Dev.	13.4%	13.6%	14.9%	12.4%	12.6%	13.7%	13.1%	13.3%	13.0%
Observations	37,597	34,376	6,389	54,938	51,078	22,673	55,056	46,344	27,820
Weekly									
Mean	14.7%	15.0%	20.1%	13.2%	13.4%	17.6%	14.4%	14.6%	16.3%
Median	12.1%	12.6%	17.7%	10.8%	11.0%	15.0%	11.5%	11.7%	13.1%
Std. Dev.	11.4%	11.6%	14.5%	10.6%	10.6%	13.7%	11.5%	11.7%	13.5%
Observations	12,348	11,922	5,447	15,949	15,555	9,371	18,080	16,834	9,881
Monthly									
Mean	11.1%	11.2%	18.8%	10.3%	10.0%	16.3%	11.4%	11.0%	16.2%
Median	8.7%	8.9%	15.8%	7.9%	7.7%	13.7%	9.0%	8.7%	13.1%
Std. Dev.	9.5%	9.5%	14.0%	9.0%	8.8%	13.0%	9.4%	9.3%	13.3%
Observations	3,161	3,123	2,354	4,040	4,023	2,951	4,595	4,543	3,292
Quarterly									
Mean	8.8%	8.6%	16.4%	8.1%	7.4%	15.0%	9.2%	8.0%	14.7%
Median	6.7%	6.6%	14.1%	6.1%	5.6%	12.3%	7.0%	6.0%	11.8%
Std. Dev.	8.1%	8.2%	12.4%	7.4%	7.1%	12.4%	8.0%	7.2%	12.4%
Observations	1,088	1,079	945	1,372	1,370	1,124	1,563	1,549	1,324

On a daily basis, average herding in small stocks is higher than average herding in large stocks. This difference is statistically significant as a t-test on the time series means involving all instruments shows (p-value < 0.0001). On a weekly basis, herding in smaller stocks is still higher than herding in large stocks though not as significant. The t-test on the weekly time series averages shows that the time series are different with a p-value of 0.048, i.e. at the 5% level. When looking at longer periods, this difference reverses: For monthly and quarterly time series, herding is higher in large stocks than in small stocks. However, differences in the weekly and quarterly time series are not statistically significant.

On a quarterly level, this result is seemingly contrary to the result reported in Lakonishok, Shleifer, and Vishny (1992): They find greater herding in small stocks and argue that intentional herding should indeed be higher in small stocks since institutionals follow each other's actions more closely when public information is not widely available.

On a daily level, however, the significant difference between the small and large cap time series can be explained similarly: Since small capitalization stocks usually receive less attention than large capitalization stocks, investors are more likely to react similarly and simultaneously to the same news and price movements. On a daily basis, this behavior leads to a higher herding measure. For large capitalization stocks, information is widely available and opinions of retail investors are more likely to be different and so trades can cancel each other out.

5.5.4. Review of Results

Overall, the magnitudes of our modified herding measure values are similar to those reported by other recent studies (see Table 5.10 for a comparison):

Grinblatt, Titman, and Wermers (1995) find an overall fund herding measure of 0.84 meaning that a fund that traded 10 percent of its portfolio each quarter bought stocks that had about 8.4 percent excessive buying by all funds, or sold stocks that had about 8.4 percent excessive selling. This is equivalent to the value found in quarterly herding (8.7%) in the Euwax data set.

Dorn, Huberman, and Sengmueller (2008) calculate LSV measures for a German discount broker, and their monthly results come very close to those for the discount broker in the study by Barber, Odean, and Zhu (2009b). They do find, however, that herding in the more liquid stocks of the DAX30 is almost twice as high as herding in all stocks taken together – a finding that cannot be confirmed. However, the herding levels found for large cap stocks in the Euwax data set closely match the findings of Dorn, Huberman, and Sengmueller: Both studies show an 11.4% herding level. This close match confirms the findings for large cap stocks.

Barber, Odean and Zhu (2009b) calculate monthly LSV herding measures and find that they are reliably positive for both their datasets (a retail broker and a discount broker). They find that herding measure values at the retail brokerage are more than double of those at the discount brokerage. Their values (6.8% and 12.8%, respectively) are similar to the monthly Euwax herding measure (11%) considering that the data incorporates discount brokers as well as traditional retail brokerages. Barber, Odean and Zhu also differentiate firms of different sizes but do not find a consistent difference in the results when distinguishing firms by market capitalization. This finding is in line with the monthly results reported in this section.

Table 5.10: Comparison of LSV Measures across Studies

In this table, average monthly herding measures found in different studies are compared to each other. The bottom line reports average monthly UHM values based on the number of executed orders.

Study	all sizes	small	medium	large
Barber, Odean, and Zhu (2009b)				
Discount Broker	6.8%	7.6%	6.6%	5.4%
Retail Broker	12.8%	11.4%	13.1%	12.5%
Dorn, Huberman, and Sengmueller (2008)	6.4%	n/a	n/a	n/a
DAX30 stocks				11.4%
Grinblatt, Titman, and Wermers (1995)	8.4%	n/a	n/a	n/a
this study	11.0%	11.1%	10.3%	11.4%

To sum up, herding in single underlyings by retail investors is high and substantial. In addition, although there are methodological differences, the herding measure developed in this section is comparable to other herding measures in the relevant literature, and they are similar in value. The magnitude of herding does not change when controlling for firm size (market capitalization). Herding is higher for limit orders than for market orders due to the automatic execution of limit orders.

5.6. Conclusion

In this chapter, retail investor herding in securitized derivatives is examined using order data from the European Warrant Exchange. A herding measure is constructed that allows for the detection of retail investor herding on a market-wide level as well as a stock-level.

The results show that substantial retail investor herding exists on the market level and that the degree of herding is closely related to the use of limit and market orders as well as overall market conditions. Bearish periods are characterized by an overall injection of capital by retail investors. The level of herding in bear markets is generally higher than in bull markets. This result holds for limit as well as market orders. Pessimistic herding is higher in bull markets than in bear markets, and optimistic herding is higher in bear markets than in bull markets.

Together, these results support the hypothesis that retail investors are contrarian. Mechanical execution of limit orders alone cannot explain this phenomenon.

By measuring herding on a broker level, the question is answered whether herding is an aggregate phenomenon or whether it can be observed for the order flows of individual brokers. Substantial herding of retail investors is observed across all brokers: The level is highest among public brokers with a rather conservative clientele and lowest among online brokers that neither give investment advice nor operate any branches. Proprietary brokers do not seem to fit into the same schema as they exhibit very different trading patterns.

In addition to market-wide herding, the results show that retail investors also herd into and out of single underlyings: Excess herding is substantial and significant, meaning that retail investors choose the same underlying securities with a probability that is higher than expected by chance. This result is neither fully explained by the use of limit orders, nor by retail investors' focus on small firms. On a daily basis, however, herding is higher in small firms than in large firms meaning that small firms tend get the attention of retail investors at the same time.

To put these results into the larger context of retail investor behavior and price formation, it has to be concluded that retail investor trading is highly correlated and as a whole, retail investors may have the potential to actually affect stock prices.

6 The Predictive Power of Retail Investor Sentiment

"In general, the contrarian behavior we document of individual investors on the NYSE seems important for understanding short-horizon return predictability."

Kaniel, Saar, and Titman (2008), p. 306

The contrarian behavior of individual investors, as documented in the previous chapter, may present a link to stock return predictability as suggested by Kaniel, Saar, and Titman. They find that individual investors are contrarians implicitly providing liquidity to other market participants and that their behavior may predict returns.

The central goal of this chapter is to determine whether it is possible to successfully use sentiment data – the Euwax Sentiment measures in particular – in trading strategies to generate abnormal returns, i.e. returns in excess of known risk factors and above market returns. In this chapter, a trading strategy involving single underlyings is being developed that consists of buying high sentiment stocks and selling low sentiment stocks resulting in a zero-cost portfolio. In the course of the chapter, the influence of product and order types is being discussed as well as the difference between using executed and submitted orders.

The results show that the returns of the zero-cost portfolio are significantly positive even after controlling for market returns and momentum. Controlling for firm size reveals that sentiment only predicts returns for small firms whereas there is no predictive quality for medium and large capitalization firms. This is in line with theoretical results of small investor research.

The chapter is structured as follows: In section 6.1, related work with respect to order imbalance measures is presented and discussed in detail. Section 6.2 provides an overview of the data set. Section 6.3 is the main section of this chapter. It contains the description of the methodology, the results as well as the description of control variables. Section 0 adds some robustness checks. Section 6.5 concludes this chapter.

6.1. Related Work

There is a growing body of literature that examines the dynamic relationship between investor sentiment and contemporaneous as well as future stock returns. These studies typically use indirect sentiment measures such as order flow data, put/call ratios, and buy/sell imbalances, and relate them to stock returns.

Jackson (2003) analyzes a unique dataset of individual investor trades in Australia and examines whether the investment decisions of individual investors aggregate in a systematic way. He finds that the aggregation assumption holds across 56 unrelated brokerage firms, across sub-periods, and across subsets of stocks. Regarding the relationship between individual investor trading and future stock returns, he finds that net trades (buy minus sell volume) of full-service brokerage clients positively and significantly forecast future short-term market and cross-sectional returns. Similar to Jackson (2003), Barber, Odean, and Zhu (2009b) show that the trading of individual investors at a large discount brokerage and a large retail brokerage is systematically correlated. Using another brokerage data set from the U.S., Kumar and Lee (2006) show that retail investor trades are systematically correlated and retail investors buy and sell stocks in concert. Moreover, they find that monthly changes in retail sentiment induce co-movement in stock returns.

Baker and Stein (2004) use trading volume as a measure of liquidity which can also be interpreted as a measure of investor sentiment. They identify short-selling as a problem and assume that investors generally only invest when they are optimistic and thereby assume that investors reduce liquidity as they become more pessimistic. In their data, they find a negative relation between annual turnover and subsequent annual stock returns suggesting that irrational investors overreact and cause stock prices to revert.

Pan and Poteshman (2006) analyze option trading data and construct open-buy put-call ratios from option volume initiated by buyers to open new positions. When comparing the predictability of the other option volume types (open sell, close buy, close sell) they find that they do predict the correct direction but to a much lower extent than the open buy volume. Using this non-publicly available put-call ratio and publicly observable option volume, Pan and Poteshman examine the predictability of option trading for future stock price movements. They find that the open-buy put-call ratio positively predicts future stock prices on a weekly horizon.

Kaniel, Saar, and Titman (2008) examine individual investors' trading behavior using a unique dataset from the New York Stock Exchange that contains the aggregate volume of executed buy and sell orders of individual investors over four years. Very similar to the methodology applied in this work, they define individual investors' net trading as the difference between buy and sell volume. They find that the trades of individual investors can indeed be used to systematically forecast stock returns and show that statistically significant positive payoffs can be realized using this information.

In a similar study, Barber, Odean, and Zhu (2009a) use TAQ/ISSM data to investigate the effect of order imbalance of individual investors. Like several previous studies, they document strong herding by individual investors. Over shorter periods, they find that stocks heavily bought by individual investors in one week earn strong returns in the subsequent week, while stocks heavily sold in one week perform poorly in the subsequent week. Over longer periods, however, Barber, Odean, and Zhu document that stocks with small-trade selling pressures outperform those with buying pressures, indicating a negative relationship between investor sentiment and stock returns at longer horizons.

Using the same data set, Hvidkjaer (2008) shows that stocks with intense sell-initiated small-trade volume, measured over several months, outperform stocks with intense buy-initiated small-trade volume. His findings support the role of retail investor sentiment as a contrary indicator for long-term stock price movements and positively relate to those of Barber, Odean, and Zhu. In a paper similar in spirit, Frazzini and Lamont (2008) study the effect of mutual fund flows on stock returns and find that stocks favored by retail investors tend to underperform in subsequent years.

Using the dataset of a large German discount broker, Dorn, Huberman, and Sengmueller (2008) show that retail investors tend to be on the same side of the market in a given stock. They argue that aggregated market orders lead returns whereas aggregated limit orders appear to be negative feedback trades. They point out that the distinction between market and limit orders is crucial for understanding the relation between individual investor trading and returns.

Schmitz, Glaser, and Weber (2007) identify warrant trades as an effective measure of sentiment. Their data is collected from a German discount broker and includes the portfolio data of a large number of investors. They calculate a simple sentiment measure using investors' warrants holdings. Investors that only hold calls (puts) are classified as optimistic (pessimistic), and investors that hold both are classified as neutral.

Discussion

The evidence on the relationship between individual investor trading seems to differ depending on three dimensions that distinguish the different studies: (i) the horizon of the relationship, (ii) the underlying data set (trades, transactions, instruments, etc.), and (iii) the method of aggregating the data.

Concerning the horizon, all of the studies above document a positive relation of individual investor sentiment and future stock returns on a daily or weekly level, whereas many of the studies find a negative relation on much longer horizons, i.e. months and years. Of course, the availability of high-frequency data has improved considerably in the last couple of years so that short-horizon relations were difficult to detect in earlier studies.

The underlying data sets also differ in a couple of important dimensions: First, there are two major sources for transaction data: exchange data with executed transactions for a whole market, and brokerage data with trades and portfolio information on an individual account level. The brokerage data has the advantage that trading decisions can be traced to individual accounts, and individual portfolios can be reconstructed. The exchange data usually does not contain information about individuals but contains trades from multiple brokerages and therefore allows for the distinction of different order flows. A second dimension is the differentiation of trade direction: Some of the papers rely on algorithms such as the one proposed by Lee and Ready (1991) to infer buyer- or seller-initiated trades, others use unique data sets where the trade direction is part of the data. The third dimension is the problem of disentanglement. Disentanglement is the act of separating institutional transactions from retail investor transactions. Some studies use retail brokerage data sets where all trades are supposed to come from retail investors, others rely on the small-trade volume or low-market-capitalization stocks. Fourth, the country of origin may be of importance since investors in Taiwan may act differently from those in the U.S. or in Germany. A fifth aspect concerns whether it is possible for retail investors to express negative sentiment. A retail investor has two practical alternatives in the equity market when trying to express a negative investor sentiment. They have the option to sell stock currently held, or if they already hold nothing they can decide not to buy. The option to sell stock short is practically impossible due to margin requirements, short-sell restrictions, and levels of investor knowledge. This severely limits a retail investor's ability to express a negative sentiment, and so an important part of the whole picture may be missing.

The aggregation methodology across the literature has similarities but differs in certain aspects: Studies based on market data usually use order flow data of executed transactions and aggregate them creating measures of imbalance for buy and sell decisions, put and call volumes, small trades and large trades, etc. There are many possible ways to construct a sentiment measure out of order flow data, and many of them are highly correlated.

In this chapter, most of the weaknesses mentioned above are addressed and avoided by using a data set that (i) consists of retail investor orders only, (ii) captures orders from different brokerages, (iii) includes the explicit trade direction due to the market model and (iv) allows for the expression of negative sentiment through put options.

6.2. Data and Methodology

In addition to market-wide retail investor sentiment as explored in chapter 4 there is the possibility to calculate retail investor sentiment individually for single stocks. A large number of covered warrants and investment certificates is based on single stocks as underlyings. Sentiment measures for individual stocks have the advantage that they can be compared across all stocks and thereby sorted by value. At one point in time, it is possible to sort all stocks according to their sentiment value. This methodology has the advantage that only extreme values with unambiguous interpretation are used whereas values with no clear conclusion can be omitted.

6.2.1. Data Set

In the data base, 37% of all customer orders comprise securitized derivatives with individual stocks as underlying value (see Table 4.1 on page 75, Panel C). The underlying stocks comprise global companies with a focus on European and especially German companies. This is not surprising since EUWAX and most of its customers are based in Germany. Trading intensity and frequency vary across all instruments. While there are on average more than 10,000 executed orders per month on underlyings such as Allianz, Daimler, and Deutsche Telekom, there are also stocks that do not receive such a high attention. There are stocks in the data base with less than 10 executed orders in related derivative instruments during the whole time period of five years.

The calculation of a sentiment measure based on executed or submitted orders demands that there is a minimum amount of trading in related instruments otherwise such a measure cannot be calculated. Therefore, all underlying stocks are filtered by employing the following methodology[22]: All underlyings are sorted according to the average number of executed orders per month. As a rule of thumb, an average trading amount of 3 executed orders per day is demanded resulting in 60 executed orders per month (assuming 20 trading days per month). This filter is applied to all underlyings and results in 244 stocks comprising about 97% of all executed trades on stocks in the data base.

Summary statistics on the number of executed and submitted orders are presented in Table 5.6 on page 111. About half of the stocks that serve as underlyings for the derivatives in the sample are German stocks, almost 30% are other European stocks, and the rest is from North and South America as well as Asia. In addition, the number of all executed as well as submitted orders by geographical region as well as product and order type is shown. The overall relation of executed to submitted orders by product type is shown in Table A.2 in the appendix (Panel C).

The 244 stocks in the sample are chosen regardless of market capitalization. Summary statistics by market capitalization are provided in Table 5.7 on page 111 to show that the sample is not tilted towards companies with either high or low market capitalizations. As explained in section 5.5.1, small firms are defined as firms with an average market capitalization below 2 billion Euros, medium firms between 2 billion and 20 billion Euros, and large firms above 20 billion Euros. The classification divides the sample in three almost equally-sized groups of about 80 stocks.

Market capitalization statistics are used later in this chapter to test whether there are any differences between small capitalization stocks and large capitalization stocks in how retail investor sentiment predicts returns.

---

[22] The same methodology as in section 5.5.1 is used.

6.2.2. Methodology

In this section a portfolio trading strategy[23] is implemented that consists of buying stocks when their respective sentiment measures are high and selling stocks when sentiment measures are low. The idea behind this portfolio methodology is to focus on stocks with extreme (positive and negative) sentiment values and disregard the stocks with sentiment values in between.

Two portfolios are constructed: One portfolio, the high sentiment portfolio, includes the highest decile of stocks that have the highest sentiment values on the portfolio formation day. The other portfolio, the low sentiment portfolio, includes the lowest decile of stocks with the lowest sentiment values. Throughout this section, sentiment values based on the number of executed orders are used for portfolio construction (instead of the volume based sentiment values) as Chapter 4 has shown that this measures yields better results. Robustness checks later in this chapter come to the same conclusion.

The returns of a long-short strategy that involves buying the high sentiment portfolio and selling the low sentiment portfolio are calculated, henceforth referred to as the high-low sentiment portfolio.

Two periods in general are differentiated: the portfolio formation period and the portfolio holding period. The portfolio formation period comprises all trading days over which sentiment values are being aggregated. For example, a portfolio formation period of one means that sentiment values are calculated based on the last trading day whereas a portfolio formation period of five means that sentiment values are derived from all trades in the last five trading days. The portfolio holding period determines how long the respective portfolios are being held. Returns are then cumulated using the sum of logarithmic returns of the single holding days after portfolio formation.

Day t=0 is regarded as the last day of the portfolio formation period which means that t=1 would be the first day of the portfolio holding period. Returns for day 1 would be calculated using the end-of-day logreturns from day 0 to day 1. To illustrate this, consider the following example for a one-day portfolio formation and a one-day portfolio holding period: On Monday (t=0), shortly before the end of the trading day, sentiment values for all stocks are being calculated and sorted, and high and low sentiment portfolios are being formed. All stocks are being bought just before the end of trading and held for exactly one day and finally sold on Tuesday (t=1) right before the end of trading. The return of the portfolio is expressed as the average of all logreturns calculated using the respective closing prices of all stocks in the portfolio.

[23] Jackson (2003), Pan and Poteshman (2006), Kaniel, Saar, and Titman (2008), Dorn, Huberman, and Sengmueller (2008), and Barber, Odean, and Zhu (2009a) use similar portfolio construction methodologies.

Not all stocks in the sample are being considered for inclusion in the portfolios. To be eligible for the portfolio formation procedure, underlying instruments must have at least 3 executed orders per day during the portfolio formation period on average. This prevents stocks from getting high sentiment ranks when there are only 1 or 2 orders per day.[24]

6.3. Results

This section presents the results of the cross-sectional portfolio formation analysis. Sentiment deciles are used to capture only extreme sentiment. Sentiment measures based on the number of executed orders are chosen to be invariant against extremely high volumes, outliers, and potential errors in the data set. In addition, the following sections use a one-day portfolio formation period (i.e. portfolios are formed on day t=0). Variations of this are considered in additional robustness checks.

Other parameters, such as product type or order type, are varied throughout the rest of this section to investigate the different effects of these parameters on the results. Additional robustness checks are reported in section 0.

6.3.1. Pre- and Post-Portfolio-Formation Returns

Product Type

Table 6.1 shows daily average portfolio logreturns for five days before and five days after the portfolio formation day. As explained in the previous section, portfolios are formed according to sentiment values in t=0, and their returns are observed for days t=-5 to t=5. Returns are expressed in basis points.

Using all product types, i.e. sentiment values based on leverage and investment products, average low sentiment portfolio returns are negative for days t=1 to t=5 whereas high sentiment portfolio returns are positive for the first five trading days after portfolio formation. Taken together, the high-low sentiment portfolio excess returns that are the result of a long-short strategy using these two portfolios yield statistically and economically significantly positive returns for at least the first five trading days after portfolio formation. p-values indicate that the excess returns are significantly different from zero.

[24] Additional robustness checks (not reported) have shown that setting the minimum number of orders to 5 or 10 does not change the portfolio formation significantly.

Table 6.1: Return Statistics by Product Type

This table presents average portfolio logreturns for a 5-day pre- and post-portfolio-formation period. The low sentiment portfolio includes stocks with the lowest sentiment values on the day of portfolio formation (t=0). The high sentiment portfolio includes stocks with the highest sentiment on the day of portfolio formation. The high-low excess portfolio is constructed by selling the low sentiment portfolio and buying the high sentiment portfolio. The p-values in brackets show the statistical significance of a t-test that tests whether the excess returns are different from zero. Results are shown for sentiment based on different product types.

	Return Day										
	-5	-4	-3	-2	-1	0	1	2	3	4	5
All products											
Low Sentiment Portfolio Returns	12.4	14.6	14.0	19.1	29.8	56.9	-6.4	-6.3	-2.9	-3.8	-1.7
High Sentiment Portfolio Returns	-17.9	-17.6	-18.8	-25.8	-35.5	-55.9	3.8	2.5	0.9	4.8	1.8
High-Low Portfolio Excess Returns	-30.3	-32.2	-32.8	-44.8	-65.4	-112.7	10.2	8.8	3.7	8.7	3.5
p-value	(0.000)	(0.000)	(0.000)	(0.000)	(0.000)	(0.000)	(0.000)	(0.000)	(0.088)	(0.001)	(0.086)
Leverage products											
Low Sentiment Portfolio Returns	11.8	13.6	16.5	21.8	33.6	64.3	-6.8	-6.7	-5.4	-4.8	-1.9
High Sentiment Portfolio Returns	-20.5	-20.5	-22.8	-27.8	-40.1	-63.5	3.2	1.7	-2.2	1.8	2.1
High-Low Portfolio Excess Returns	-32.3	-34.1	-39.3	-49.6	-73.7	-127.8	10.0	8.4	3.2	6.6	4.0
p-value	(0.000)	(0.000)	(0.000)	(0.000)	(0.000)	(0.000)	(0.001)	(0.001)	(0.125)	(0.012)	(0.077)
Investment products											
Low Sentiment Portfolio Returns	5.5	9.5	8.8	10.0	17.8	23.4	-1.5	-5.1	-1.5	-2.3	-1.4
High Sentiment Portfolio Returns	-8.9	-13.4	-15.3	-12.0	-19.1	-31.6	-1.2	1.7	-1.9	0.3	-3.8
High-Low Portfolio Excess Returns	-14.4	-22.9	-24.1	-22.0	-36.9	-55.1	0.3	6.8	-0.3	2.6	-2.5
p-value	(0.000)	(0.000)	(0.000)	(0.000)	(0.000)	(0.000)	(0.463)	(0.039)	(0.466)	(0.253)	(0.231)

The results suggest that on the day of portfolio formation (t=0) investors on average act as contrarian traders being pessimistic about stocks that experience high returns and being optimistic about stocks that experience low returns. In the case of the leverage products sentiment portfolios, stocks in the low sentiment portfolio experience an average daily return of 64.3 basis points whereas stocks in the high sentiment portfolio yield a loss of about the same amount (-63.5 basis points).

One possible explanation for these results is the automatic execution of stale limit orders that are in the order book for a long period and wait for their execution. Finally, when the market experiences a down- or an upturn, they are being executed automatically without any action by investors. It is therefore questionable to regard any extremely positive or negative sentiment values as real and especially timely investor sentiment (Linnainmaa (2009) elaborates on this).

Dorn, Huberman, and Sengmueller (2008) caution that "a failure to separate market and limit orders would lead us to classify retail investors as contrarian" and that "the mechanical correlation between limit order execution and returns masks the previously undocumented relations between speculative trading and returns" (p. 888). In order to determine whether the contrarian behavior is purely a result of limit order execution, the differentiation between order types is investigated in detail, i.e. the differentiation between limit and market orders.

Order Type

For this purpose, each order is classified into two order types: limit orders which are not executed immediately, and market orders which also comprise marketable limit orders that are executed within 60 seconds of order submission (see section 4.2). There are two reasons why this rule is applied to distinguish limit orders from marketable limit orders: First, the data set does not include intraday reference prices that indicate whether a limit order was executable at the time of submission. Second, due to the market model at Boerse Stuttgart, even market orders may not be executed immediately but rather wait some seconds before the quality liquidity provider starts the execution process.

As in the previous section, results are shown for sentiment portfolios based on the different product types. Furthermore, Table 6.2 distinguishes between limit and market orders. Panel A shows the portfolio returns for sentiment portfolios based on sentiment that is constructed using limit orders only. The influence of limit orders can thereby be isolated.

The portfolio construction based on limit orders shows the expected results: On the day of portfolio formation, returns are positive for low sentiment stocks and negative for high sentiment stocks. Low sentiment stocks experience an average increase of 162 basis points, i.e. 1.62% on a single day whereas high sentiment stocks decline in value by 130.1 basis points on average. This phenomenon can be observed across product types although sentiment portfolios based on investment products alone exhibit lower absolute return values. This can be explained by the different investment horizons of leverage and investment products. Obviously, leverage product investors are more sensitive to contemporary price changes than investors seeking a longer term investment.

The results in panel A of Table 6.2 show that the influence of limit orders on sentiment values makes retail investors look as if they indeed behaved as contrarians. However, the same pattern can be observed in panel B of Table 6.2 when using sentiment portfolios constructed from market orders: Investors tend to submit market buy orders when stocks are declining in value on the same day and market sell orders when stock prices are rising. This behavior is contrarian, and it is not due to the automatic execution of limit orders.

Although portfolio returns on day t=0 suggest a contrarian behavior for market as well as limit orders, there are two important differences. Firstly, portfolio returns based on market order sentiment are not as high as portfolio returns based on limit order sentiment. Secondly, and more importantly, returns on day t=1 are different. Using limit orders for sentiment construction, portfolio returns for the low as well as the high sentiment portfolio are both negative (-0.6 and -6.3 basis points for leverage products), whereas portfolio returns for the high sentiment portfolio are positive (7.8 bp for leverage products) when using market orders for sentiment construction.

Table 6.2: Return Statistics by Order and Product Type

This table presents average portfolio logreturns for a 5-day pre- and post-portfolio-formation period. The low sentiment portfolio includes stocks with the lowest sentiment values on the day of portfolio formation (t=0). The high sentiment portfolio includes stocks with the highest sentiment on the day of portfolio formation. The high-low excess portfolio is constructed by selling the low sentiment portfolio and buying the high sentiment portfolio. The p-values in brackets show the statistical significance of a t-test that tests whether the excess returns are different from zero. Panel A presents results based on sentiment created only from limit orders. Panel B presents results based on sentiment created from market orders.

Panel A: Limit Orders						Return Day					
	-5	-4	-3	-2	-1	0	1	2	3	4	5
All products											
Low Sentiment Portfolio Returns	10.9	14.4	15.2	22.2	58.4	162.0	-0.7	-6.4	-4.5	-3.3	-2.8
High Sentiment Portfolio Returns	-13.0	-12.4	-13.2	-19.3	-48.1	-130.1	-6.1	5.7	1.1	-0.8	-1.0
High-Low Portfolio Excess Returns	-23.9	-26.8	-28.4	-41.6	-106.5	-292.1	-5.4	12.2	5.6	2.5	1.8
p-value	(0.000)	(0.000)	(0.000)	(0.000)	(0.000)	(0.000)	(0.053)	(0.000)	(0.038)	(0.218)	(0.288)
Leverage products											
Low Sentiment Portfolio Returns	10.1	13.3	14.8	22.8	58.7	165.4	-0.6	-8.0	-3.6	-3.9	-2.6
High Sentiment Portfolio Returns	-16.2	-12.5	-13.2	-20.8	-51.0	-131.6	-6.9	4.5	-1.6	-1.7	-0.1
High-Low Portfolio Excess Returns	-26.3	-25.8	-28.0	-43.6	-109.7	-297.0	-6.3	12.5	2.0	2.1	2.4
p-value	(0.000)	(0.000)	(0.000)	(0.000)	(0.000)	(0.000)	(0.032)	(0.000)	(0.279)	(0.257)	(0.233)
Investment products											
Low Sentiment Portfolio Returns	5.5	7.2	12.7	13.8	40.4	92.5	2.2	-4.9	-9.5	-5.5	-5.0
High Sentiment Portfolio Returns	-12.7	-17.4	-15.8	-14.3	-38.0	-102.2	-1.5	5.2	-4.7	-5.9	5.6
High-Low Portfolio Excess Returns	-18.2	-24.6	-28.5	-28.1	-78.4	-194.7	-3.7	10.1	4.8	-0.5	10.6
p-value	(0.004)	(0.000)	(0.000)	(0.000)	(0.000)	(0.000)	(0.294)	(0.051)	(0.196)	(0.459)	(0.020)

Panel B: Market orders						Return Day					
	-5	-4	-3	-2	-1	0	1	2	3	4	5
All products											
Low Sentiment Portfolio Returns	8.9	10.4	12.1	15.3	21.4	30.3	-10.4	-5.4	-2.3	-4.3	0.0
High Sentiment Portfolio Returns	-13.5	-13.3	-15.6	-20.7	-26.5	-36.5	4.4	0.5	-0.5	2.2	0.4
High-Low Portfolio Excess Returns	-22.4	-23.7	-27.7	-36.0	-47.8	-66.8	14.9	5.9	1.8	6.5	0.3
p-value	(0.000)	(0.000)	(0.000)	(0.000)	(0.000)	(0.000)	(0.000)	(0.017)	(0.255)	(0.012)	(0.450)
Leverage products											
Low Sentiment Portfolio Returns	9.6	9.6	11.0	19.3	24.0	36.2	-11.0	-6.9	-3.6	-6.2	-1.8
High Sentiment Portfolio Returns	-14.0	-14.9	-18.7	-22.4	-30.1	-45.0	7.8	-1.6	-3.7	1.1	0.9
High-Low Portfolio Excess Returns	-23.5	-24.5	-29.7	-41.8	-54.1	-81.2	18.8	5.3	-0.1	7.3	2.7
p-value	(0.000)	(0.000)	(0.000)	(0.000)	(0.000)	(0.000)	(0.000)	(0.032)	(0.491)	(0.006)	(0.188)
Investment products											
Low Sentiment Portfolio Returns	7.1	9.8	6.1	8.7	15.8	16.0	0.7	-5.5	0.5	-0.9	-1.1
High Sentiment Portfolio Returns	-11.6	-11.9	-13.7	-15.8	-17.0	-15.7	-0.8	5.0	-2.6	2.3	-1.9
High-Low Portfolio Excess Returns	-18.6	-21.7	-19.8	-24.5	-32.8	-31.8	-1.5	10.5	-3.1	3.2	-0.8
p-value	(0.000)	(0.000)	(0.000)	(0.000)	(0.000)	(0.000)	(0.344)	(0.002)	(0.174)	(0.195)	(0.410)

The long-short strategy based on sentiment constructed from market orders in leverage products would yield 18.8 basis points on the first day after portfolio formation (t=1) and 5.3 basis points on the second. Both are statistically significant.

Executed vs. Submitted Orders

Since the automatic execution of limit orders is an important factor in the sentiment construction and obviously influences the relation between sentiment and returns, the difference between submitted orders and executed orders is investigated. Submitted orders include all orders that have been submitted or changed and resubmitted, separately by product type but regardless of order type. The distinction between different order types is not necessary because the number of submitted market orders should equal the number of executed market orders already analyzed. In addition, the date of submission should equal the date of execution. Therefore, no distinction regarding the order type is made. Table 6.3 shows the results by product type.

Table 6.3: Return Statistics for Submitted Orders

This table presents average portfolio logreturns for a 5-day pre- and post-portfolio-formation period. Sentiment values used for portfolio formation are based on the number of submitted orders. The p-values in brackets show the statistical significance of a t-test that tests whether the excess returns are different from zero. Results are shown for sentiment based on different product types.

Submitted Orders	Return Day										
	-5	-4	-3	-2	-1	0	1	2	3	4	5
All products											
Low Sentiment Portfolio Returns	12.5	11.8	15.3	18.4	22.9	9.8	-8.3	-4.0	-3.1	-0.9	1.7
High Sentiment Portfolio Returns	-19.4	-22.5	-21.5	-26.9	-30.6	-17.7	7.2	3.6	2.3	3.8	0.1
High-Low Portfolio Excess Returns	-32.0	-34.3	-36.9	-45.3	-53.6	-27.5	15.6	7.5	5.4	4.7	-1.6
p-value	(0.000)	(0.000)	(0.000)	(0.000)	(0.000)	(0.000)	(0.000)	(0.001)	(0.013)	(0.030)	(0.254)
Leverage products											
Low Sentiment Portfolio Returns	12.1	13.2	14.7	19.3	24.4	10.7	-9.3	-4.4	-5.6	-2.6	-0.1
High Sentiment Portfolio Returns	-21.5	-23.3	-22.5	-28.1	-34.9	-21.8	6.4	3.0	0.8	2.4	1.6
High-Low Portfolio Excess Returns	-33.6	-36.4	-37.3	-47.4	-59.3	-32.4	15.6	7.4	6.4	5.0	1.7
p-value	(0.000)	(0.000)	(0.000)	(0.000)	(0.000)	(0.000)	(0.000)	(0.002)	(0.006)	(0.027)	(0.253)
Investment products											
Low Sentiment Portfolio Returns	1.7	6.0	9.3	9.7	8.2	0.0	-2.5	-3.7	-2.5	-1.7	-2.9
High Sentiment Portfolio Returns	-12.7	-12.8	-15.0	-13.8	-13.1	-7.7	2.4	2.2	-0.6	-2.4	-4.7
High-Low Portfolio Excess Returns	-14.4	-18.8	-24.2	-23.4	-21.4	-7.7	4.9	5.8	1.9	-0.7	-1.8
p-value	(0.000)	(0.000)	(0.000)	(0.000)	(0.000)	(0.029)	(0.068)	(0.050)	(0.278)	(0.423)	(0.295)

The most notable findings are the following: First, contrarian behavior can be observed on day t=0 with sentiment data on submitted orders as well. Low sentiment portfolios experience relatively high returns whereas high sentiment portfolios experience relatively low returns. Second, in contrast to the results based on executed orders, absolute returns on the day of portfolio formation are lower than on the day before portfolio formation. Third, and most importantly, on the first four days after portfolio formation, the high-low sentiment portfolio yields statistically and economically significantly positive returns: On the first day, it yields 15.6 basis points, followed by 7.5 bp, 5.4 bp, and 4.7 bp. This result is primarily driven by leverage products: Portfolio returns based on leverage product sentiment are even higher, yielding 15.6 bp, 7.4 bp, 6.4 bp, and 5.0 bp, all statistically significant at the 5% level.

To summarize, a portfolio of stocks that retail investors are optimistic about develops well during the next four trading days, whereas a portfolio of stocks that retail investors are pessimistic about experiences negative returns on the days after order submission.

6.3.2. Control Variables

In order to attribute any portfolio returns to retail investor sentiment, known effects have to be controlled for and thereby excluded. For example, results have to be invariant against a generally rising or declining market, known momentum effects, or effects resulting from different market capitalizations.

Market Returns

Market returns are controlled for by subtracting proxies for market returns from the high-low sentiment portfolio returns. On each trading day in the sample, we calculate the equal-weighted average return of all stocks in the sample and use this as the first benchmark. The second benchmark is simply the German market index DAX which represents the returns of Germany's blue chip stocks. While this benchmark is suited for the sample as a control variable due to the high percentage of German stocks, the first benchmark – the average sample returns – better accommodates the fact that about 50% of all stocks in the sample are international.

Table 6.4 presents the high-low portfolio returns using sentiment values based on market orders in leverage products as well as the excess returns after subtracting the equally-weighted average sample returns (line 2) and the DAX returns (line 3). Results for executed market as well as submitted orders are shown.

Even after controlling for market returns, there are still statistically and economically significantly positive excess returns: The portfolio excess returns based on executed market orders are even higher when subtracting the average sample returns. Controlling for DAX returns yields a smaller excess return which is still statistically and economically significant.

Table 6.4: Controlling for Market Returns

This table presents portfolio return statistics as a result of controlling for market returns. Statistics are restricted to sentiment based on leverage products. Panel A shows portfolio returns formed on the basis of executed market orders in leverage products. Panel B shows portfolio returns formed on the basis of submitted orders in leverage products. The average sample excess returns are calculated by subtracting the average sample returns from the high-low portfolio returns. DAX excess returns are calculated similarly. The p-values in brackets show the statistical significance of a t-test that tests whether the excess returns are different from zero.

Leverage Products	Return Day										
	-5	-4	-3	-2	-1	0	1	2	3	4	5
Panel A: Executed market orders											
High-low portfolio returns	-23.5	-24.5	-29.7	-41.8	-54.1	-81.2	18.8	5.3	-0.1	7.3	2.7
Average sample excess returns	-23.5	-24.4	-29.7	-41.7	-54.0	-81.3	18.7	5.2	-0.1	7.3	2.6
p-value	(0.000)	(0.000)	(0.000)	(0.000)	(0.000)	(0.000)	(0.000)	(0.133)	(0.490)	(0.065)	(0.295)
DAX excess returns	-25.3	-26.2	-31.4	-43.4	-55.7	-82.9	17.1	3.6	-1.8	5.6	1.0
p-value	(0.000)	(0.000)	(0.000)	(0.000)	(0.000)	(0.000)	(0.000)	(0.230)	(0.357)	(0.122)	(0.422)
Panel B: Submitted orders											
High-low portfolio returns	-33.6	-36.4	-37.3	-47.4	-59.3	-32.4	15.6	7.4	6.4	5.0	1.7
Average sample excess returns	-33.3	-36.1	-37.0	-47.1	-59.0	-32.3	15.8	7.6	6.6	5.2	1.9
p-value	(0.000)	(0.000)	(0.000)	(0.000)	(0.000)	(0.000)	(0.000)	(0.044)	(0.072)	(0.126)	(0.340)
DAX excess returns	-35.1	-37.8	-38.7	-48.8	-60.7	-33.9	14.2	6.0	5.0	3.6	0.2
p-value	(0.000)	(0.000)	(0.000)	(0.000)	(0.000)	(0.000)	(0.001)	(0.097)	(0.139)	(0.217)	(0.478)

Momentum

Momentum is the empirically observed tendency for rising stock prices to rise further. Jegadeesh and Titman (1993) find that strategies which buy stocks that have performed well in the past and sell stocks that have performed poorly in the past generate significantly positive returns. These results have been well accepted in the finance literature, although the source of these "momentum profits" is still widely debated. It can be argued that momentum returns provide strong evidence of market inefficiency, but also that momentum returns are a compensation for additional risk factors.

Momentum in stock prices is controlled for by constructing momentum portfolios as follows: On the portfolio formation day (t=0), the decile of stocks with the highest returns forms the momentum portfolio and their equally-weighted return is then subtracted from the high-low sentiment portfolio excess returns.

Table 6.5 presents the high-low sentiment portfolio returns, the corresponding momentum returns, and the momentum excess returns, i.e. the sentiment returns minus the momentum returns.

Table 6.5: Controlling for Momentum

This table presents portfolio return statistics as a result of controlling for momentum returns. Statistics are restricted to sentiment based on leverage products. Panel A shows portfolio returns formed on the basis of executed market orders in leverage products. Panel B shows portfolio returns formed on the basis of submitted orders in leverage products. Momentum returns are the average returns of a momentum portfolio consisting of the sample stocks with the highest returns on the formation day. Momentum excess returns are calculated by subtracting the sample momentum returns from the high-low sentiment portfolio returns. p-values in brackets show the results of a t-test that tests whether excess returns are different from 0.

Leverage Products	Return Day										
	-5	-4	-3	-2	-1	0	1	2	3	4	5
Panel A: Executed market orders											
High-low portfolio returns	-23.5	-24.5	-29.7	-41.8	-54.1	-81.2	18.8	5.3	-0.1	7.3	2.7
Momentum returns	-3.3	-4.9	-6.5	-9.4	-4.0	384.7	3.4	-2.6	-4.1	-5.6	-0.5
	(0.244)	(0.175)	(0.106)	(0.028)	(0.228)	(0.000)	(0.233)	(0.294)	(0.183)	(0.103)	(0.458)
Momentum excess returns	-20.2	-19.6	-23.2	-32.3	-50.1	-465.9	15.4	7.9	4.0	13.0	3.2
	(0.000)	(0.000)	(0.000)	(0.000)	(0.000)	(0.000)	(0.002)	(0.069)	(0.209)	(0.004)	(0.266)
Panel B: Submitted orders											
High-low portfolio returns	-33.6	-36.4	-37.3	-47.4	-59.3	-32.4	15.6	7.4	6.4	5.0	1.7
Momentum returns	-3.3	-4.9	-6.5	-9.4	-4.0	384.7	3.4	-2.6	-4.1	-5.6	-0.5
	(0.244)	(0.175)	(0.106)	(0.028)	(0.228)	(0.000)	(0.233)	(0.294)	(0.183)	(0.103)	(0.458)
Momentum excess returns	-30.3	-32.0	-30.4	-37.7	-56.1	-417.7	12.8	10.5	10.6	11.1	3.0
	(0.000)	(0.000)	(0.000)	(0.000)	(0.000)	(0.000)	(0.005)	(0.021)	(0.016)	(0.010)	(0.271)

As expected, momentum returns on the day of portfolio formation are highly positive since only the stocks with the highest returns are selected. Following the momentum hypothesis, these stocks continue to perform well, at least on the following day (though not statistically significant). After that, the selected stocks perform poorly on average.

Subtracting the momentum portfolio returns from the high-low sentiment portfolio returns yields the momentum excess returns which are highly positive. On the first day after portfolio formation (t=1), momentum excess portfolio returns of 15.4 basis points (12.3 basis points) on the basis of executed market orders (submitted orders) in leverage products can be observed. This is statistically significant. It can be concluded that momentum is not a source of excess returns in the high-low sentiment portfolio.

Market Capitalization

The theory suggests that there are higher limits of arbitrage in small market capitalization stocks than in large capitalization stocks and that the share of retail investor trading is highest among smaller companies (see Chapter 2). If this is correct, differences in prediction quality of retail investor sentiment on portfolio returns are expected depending on market capitalization.

To investigate this issue, all 244 stocks are sorted into three market capitalization subgroups (small caps, medium caps, and large caps), and the portfolio construction methodology is applied for each of the three subgroups of stocks. In other words, all stocks within a market capitalization subgroup are ranked according to sentiment values, and the ten percent with the highest sentiment values are used to construct the high sentiment portfolio, and the ten percent with the lowest sentiment values are used to construct the low sentiment portfolio. The requirement for the minimum average number of orders per stock and trading day is set to 3 as before. Average low and high sentiment portfolio returns are calculated and the average high minus low sentiment portfolio returns for executed market and submitted orders in leverage products are presented in Table 6.6.

Table 6.6: Controlling for Market Capitalization

This table presents portfolio return statistics by market capitalization of the underlying stocks. Statistics are restricted to sentiment based on leverage products. Panel A presents statistics of high-low sentiment portfolios formed on the basis of executed market orders in leverage products. Panel B presents statistics of high-low excess portfolios formed on the basis of submitted orders in leverage products. p-values in brackets show the results of a t-test that tests whether high-low sentiment excess returns are different from zero.

Leverage Products	Return Day										
	-5	-4	-3	-2	-1	0	1	2	3	4	5
Panel A: Executed market orders											
Small Caps	-25.0	-27.2	-34.5	-51.0	-62.9	-69.5	41.8	16.3	5.8	3.4	4.6
	(0.000)	(0.000)	(0.000)	(0.000)	(0.000)	(0.000)	(0.000)	(0.005)	(0.171)	(0.281)	(0.217)
Medium Caps	-18.7	-25.2	-30.7	-40.2	-57.7	-90.6	13.0	3.7	0.6	2.7	5.5
	(0.000)	(0.000)	(0.000)	(0.000)	(0.000)	(0.000)	(0.005)	(0.202)	(0.450)	(0.279)	(0.131)
Large Caps	-19.9	-21.0	-23.2	-32.1	-47.6	-77.9	-0.9	0.2	-4.0	1.3	-3.5
	(0.000)	(0.000)	(0.000)	(0.000)	(0.000)	(0.000)	(0.418)	(0.479)	(0.152)	(0.371)	(0.209)
Panel B: Submitted orders											
Small Caps	-40.0	-41.6	-47.7	-55.8	-72.4	-40.9	39.6	19.4	16.1	2.1	6.6
	(0.000)	(0.000)	(0.000)	(0.000)	(0.000)	(0.000)	(0.000)	(0.000)	(0.001)	(0.339)	(0.108)
Medium Caps	-27.6	-35.4	-39.2	-51.8	-68.5	-36.1	8.8	2.5	1.6	4.0	-0.1
	(0.000)	(0.000)	(0.000)	(0.000)	(0.000)	(0.000)	(0.025)	(0.281)	(0.356)	(0.180)	(0.491)
Large Caps	-26.2	-23.3	-24.8	-33.8	-40.8	-28.4	6.5	5.8	0.7	8.2	-4.6
	(0.000)	(0.000)	(0.000)	(0.000)	(0.000)	(0.000)	(0.028)	(0.045)	(0.409)	(0.004)	(0.083)

The results in Table 6.6 confirm the theory for both executed market orders and submitted orders: High-low sentiment portfolio returns for small capitalization stocks are larger than those of medium and large capitalization stocks during the first days of trading after portfolio formation. For executed orders, excess returns are 41.8 basis points on the first trading day using small cap stocks, in contrast to 13.0 bp and -0.9 bp for medium and large cap stocks, respectively. Submitted orders show the same pattern: On the first trading day after portfolio formation, 39.6 basis points could be earned with the high-low sentiment portfolio for small cap stocks, whereas returns for medium and large cap stock portfolios are 8.8 bp and 6.5 bp, respectively.

The difference between executed market and submitted orders is very small: Statistical significance is higher for submitted orders than executed market orders on the second and third trading day meaning that sentiment measured at the time of order submission regardless of execution is a better predictor for subsequent stock returns than sentiment based on the execution of near-market orders.

6.3.3. Portfolio Holding Returns

Having established that there are significant excess returns for a portfolio strategy that buys high sentiment stocks and sells low sentiment stocks, this section's purpose is to analyze the portfolio holding returns of this strategy over a period of up to 25 trading days. The average cumulative returns of the high and the low sentiment portfolio as well as the resulting high-low sentiment portfolio are investigated in detail. Since the last section has shown that only sentiment based on leverage products has produced statistically significant results, this section focuses on sentiment based on leverage products only.

Table 6.7 reports portfolio holding return statistics for portfolios that are formed based on executed market orders (Panel A) as well as submitted orders (Panel B) over a period of up to 25 trading days.

The first lines of each Panel (all market caps) report average cumulative returns for the high-low sentiment portfolio. For executed market orders, the maximum return is reached on trading day 7 at 35.3 bp. For submitted orders, the maximum return is 44.7 bp on trading day 12. This difference suggests that the use of submitted orders might identify high potential stocks earlier than the use of executed market orders.

Figure 6.1 depicts the portfolio returns graphically. The high sentiment portfolio yields higher average returns than the low sentiment portfolio. The difference is the high-low sentiment portfolio with returns that are significantly different from zero. Table 6.7 provides p-values of the appropriate t-tests. Figure 6.1 also shows that the positive returns of the high-low sentiment portfolio are primarily caused by the negative returns of the low sentiment portfolio. Although the high sentiment portfolio yields significantly positive returns over the first five trading days, the cumulative returns become negative afterwards. The low sentiment portfolio, on the other hand, starts with negative returns and stays negative over the whole sample period of 25 trading days. Together, these two portfolios form the high-low sentiment portfolio and cause its returns to first increase and then revert to zero.

Figure 6.1 shows clearly that there is a pattern of reverting stock prices after initial periods of intense buying as predicted by theory and found by many empirical studies. However, a tendency of low-sentiment stock prices to revert cannot be found: Stock prices continue to decrease within the observation period of 25 trading days.

Table 6.7: Portfolio Holding Return Statistics

This table presents return statistics when portfolios are held over a period of up to 25 trading days. Statistics are presented for sentiment based on leverage orders only. Panel A presents return statistics for portfolios constructed using executed market orders in leverage products. Panel B presents statistics for portfolios constructed using submitted orders. Each row presents holding returns of a high-low sentiment portfolio formed in t=0. Return statistics are reported separately for all market caps, as well as broken into three size groups. p-values are reported in brackets. Bold numbers mark the maximum return for each row.

	Holding Day																								
	1	2	3	4	5	6	7	8	9	10	11	12	13	14	15	16	17	18	19	20	21	22	23	24	25
Panel A: Executed market orders																									
All market caps	18.8	24.1	24.0	31.4	34.0	30.5	**35.3**	33.4	28.7	28.7	25.8	25.5	20.2	17.1	12.9	7.7	5.1	6.2	4.6	6.6	5.2	0.5	-0.2	-2.6	-1.1
	(0.000)	(0.000)	(0.000)	(0.000)	(0.000)	(0.000)	(0.000)	(0.000)	(0.001)	(0.001)	(0.004)	(0.005)	(0.024)	(0.054)	(0.125)	(0.252)	(0.335)	(0.306)	(0.360)	(0.305)	(0.349)	(0.487)	(0.496)	(0.428)	(0.471)
Small caps	41.8	58.1	63.9	67.3	71.9	82.8	83.2	83.5	80.2	**87.4**	81.0	73.6	73.9	70.6	65.2	57.9	59.1	65.0	68.3	67.9	72.9	70.0	68.7	73.0	69.8
	(0.000)	(0.000)	(0.000)	(0.000)	(0.000)	(0.000)	(0.000)	(0.000)	(0.000)	(0.000)	(0.000)	(0.000)	(0.000)	(0.001)	(0.002)	(0.006)	(0.006)	(0.003)	(0.003)	(0.004)	(0.003)	(0.006)	(0.009)	(0.006)	(0.009)
Medium caps	13.0	16.7	17.3	20.0	**25.5**	21.6	17.9	11.5	4.9	2.8	2.1	0.7	-4.7	-5.0	-11.6	-16.8	-17.1	-14.5	-16.8	-18.9	-15.9	-20.7	-25.6	-31.4	-32.6
	(0.005)	(0.007)	(0.018)	(0.016)	(0.007)	(0.033)	(0.086)	(0.199)	(0.362)	(0.422)	(0.443)	(0.482)	(0.384)	(0.381)	(0.251)	(0.177)	(0.179)	(0.225)	(0.200)	(0.174)	(0.219)	(0.162)	(0.117)	(0.080)	(0.079)
Large caps	-0.9	-0.7	-4.8	-3.4	-7.0	-15.4	-17.0	-15.7	-17.0	-25.6	-31.0	-23.5	-28.0	-31.6	-31.7	-37.1	-45.2	-50.7	-55.8	-54.2	-61.0	-66.6	-68.9	-70.7	-66.6
	(0.418)	(0.453)	(0.257)	(0.337)	(0.222)	(0.056)	(0.051)	(0.076)	(0.070)	(0.017)	(0.009)	(0.044)	(0.026)	(0.018)	(0.018)	(0.008)	(0.002)	(0.001)	(0.001)	(0.001)	(0.000)	(0.000)	(0.000)	(0.000)	(0.000)
Panel B: Submitted orders																									
All market caps	15.6	23.1	29.5	34.5	36.1	36.3	35.8	37.0	37.3	41.8	43.2	**44.7**	40.9	37.7	35.2	33.4	32.4	29.7	30.0	27.9	24.2	20.6	18.3	13.9	9.[illegible]
	(0.000)	(0.000)	(0.000)	(0.000)	(0.000)	(0.000)	(0.000)	(0.000)	(0.000)	(0.000)	(0.000)	(0.000)	(0.000)	(0.000)	(0.000)	(0.000)	(0.001)	(0.002)	(0.002)	(0.005)	(0.015)	(0.036)	(0.057)	(0.121)	(0.227)
Small caps	39.6	59.0	75.1	77.2	83.8	96.1	101.0	106.4	113.9	120.4	117.5	125.4	123.5	122.5	122.5	127.9	127.0	132.2	**133.1**	131.2	121.9	120.7	114.4	112.3	112.5
	(0.000)	(0.000)	(0.000)	(0.000)	(0.000)	(0.000)	(0.000)	(0.000)	(0.000)	(0.000)	(0.000)	(0.000)	(0.000)	(0.000)	(0.000)	(0.000)	(0.000)	(0.000)	(0.000)	(0.000)	(0.000)	(0.000)	(0.000)	(0.000)	(0.000)
Medium caps	8.8	11.3	12.9	**16.9**	16.8	14.3	8.0	6.0	4.8	7.3	10.1	10.9	3.9	1.9	-1.5	-7.0	-6.2	-13.9	-18.0	-22.0	-24.0	-26.5	-31.0	-38.1	-46.1
	(0.025)	(0.028)	(0.047)	(0.029)	(0.042)	(0.079)	(0.220)	(0.292)	(0.339)	(0.275)	(0.213)	(0.203)	(0.389)	(0.448)	(0.458)	(0.321)	(0.346)	(0.194)	(0.137)	(0.099)	(0.085)	(0.068)	(0.043)	(0.019)	(0.007)
Large caps	6.5	12.3	13.1	**21.3**	16.7	10.4	8.4	10.9	12.0	9.0	8.9	3.7	-3.6	-7.4	-8.4	-10.9	-14.1	-14.6	-8.7	-8.9	-11.3	-17.7	-16.3	-18.4	-15.1
	(0.028)	(0.003)	(0.008)	(0.000)	(0.008)	(0.082)	(0.144)	(0.096)	(0.083)	(0.168)	(0.184)	(0.364)	(0.375)	(0.268)	(0.246)	(0.188)	(0.135)	(0.134)	(0.259)	(0.262)	(0.225)	(0.122)	(0.144)	(0.115)	(0.165)

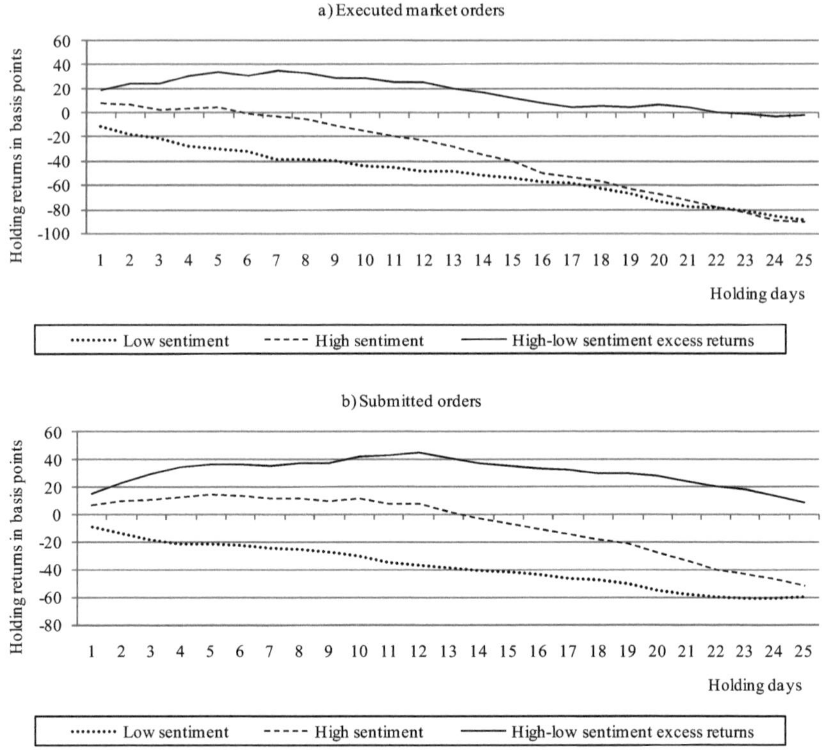

Figure 6.1: Portfolio Holding Returns

This figure presents average cumulative returns of portfolios that are held from the day of portfolio formation to up to 25 trading days. Returns of the low sentiment portfolio are represented by the dotted line, those of the high sentiment portfolio by the dashed line. The high-low sentiment portfolio excess returns are represented by the solid line. Graph a) shows the results for sentiment on executed market orders in leverage products; graph b) shows the results for sentiment on submitted orders in leverage products.

The previous section has also shown that controlling for market capitalization is essential because portfolio excess returns depend on firm size. Table 6.7 also presents portfolio return statistics separately for different firm size groups: small caps, medium caps, and large caps. Again, the maximum return is marked by a bold number.

The results reveal that the significantly positive returns of the high-low sentiment portfolio are primarily driven by small capitalization stocks: For executed market orders, small cap portfolio returns are 87.4 bp in the maximum, whereas mid caps only yield 25.5 bp. The large caps portfolio does not yield any positive returns for the high-low sentiment strategy. Figure 6.2 depicts portfolio holding returns by firm size graphically.

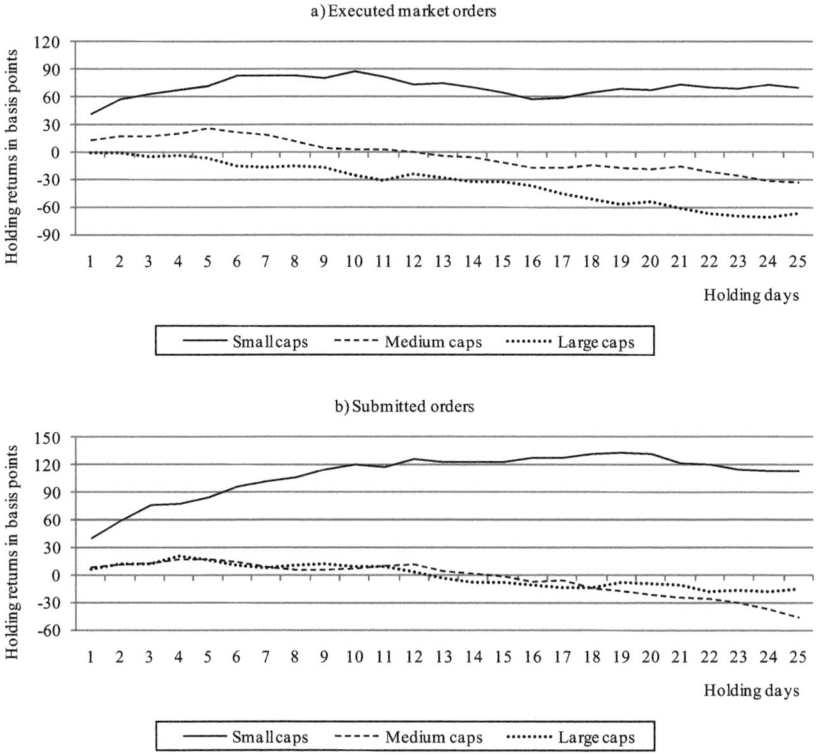

Figure 6.2: Portfolio Holding Returns by Market Capitalization

This figure presents average cumulative returns of high-low sentiment portfolios that are held from the day of portfolio formation to up to 25 trading days. The solid line shows results for the small cap portfolio, the dashed line for the medium cap portfolio, and the dotted line for the large cap portfolio. Graph a) shows the results for sentiment on executed market orders in leverage products; graph b) shows the results for sentiment on submitted orders in leverage products.

Figure 6.2 shows very convincingly that the strategy of buying high sentiment stocks and selling low sentiment stocks only works for small capitalization stocks. Returns for mid and large caps are very low or even negative. In addition, the maximum return point for this strategy on mid and large caps is reached within 4 or 5 trading days whereas the strategy for small caps reaches its maximum return on the 10th or 19th trading day (depending on the type of order used).

Figure 6.3 shows that – in comparison to the portfolios containing stocks of all sizes – the portfolios containing only high sentiment small firms show a longer tendency to yield significantly positive returns with a maximum on trading day 9, followed by decreasing holding returns before turning negative after trading day 21 (using sentiment based on submitted orders). Again, the negative sentiment portfolio does not seem to experience a reversion within the observation period of 25 trading days.

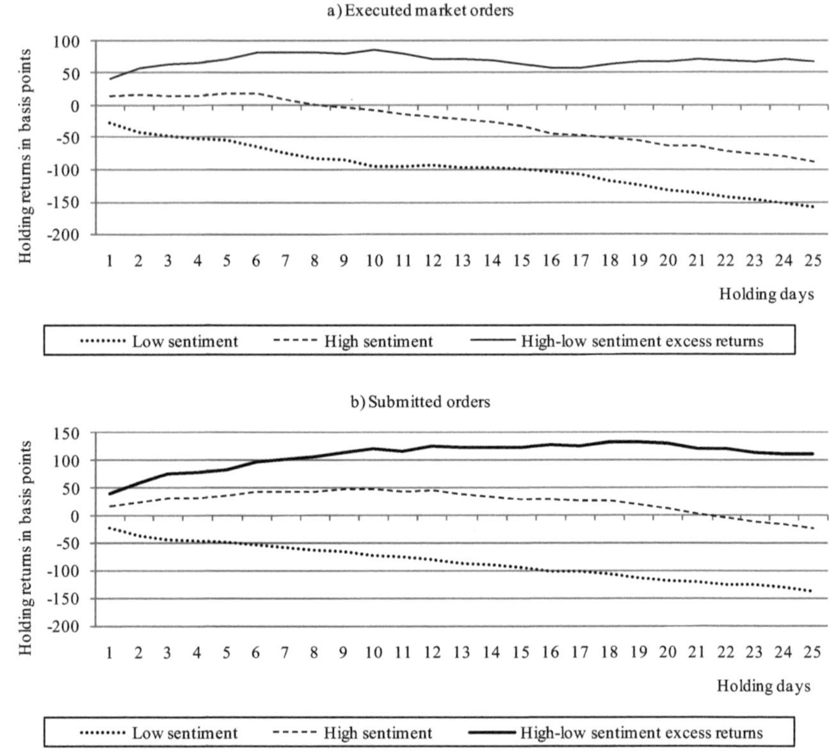

Figure 6.3: Portfolio Holding Returns for Small Caps

This figure presents average cumulative returns of portfolios consisting of small firms that are held from the day of portfolio formation to up to 25 trading days. Returns of the low sentiment portfolio are represented by the dotted line, those of the high sentiment portfolio by the dashed line. The high-low sentiment portfolio excess returns are represented by the solid line. Graph a) shows the results for sentiment on executed market orders in leverage products; graph b) shows the results for sentiment on submitted orders in leverage products.

To sum up, a trading strategy consisting of buying small high sentiment stocks and selling small low sentiment stocks, with the sentiment based on all submitted orders in leverage products, generate economically and statistically significant excess returns of up to 133 basis points for a 19-day period.

6.4. Robustness Checks

Several robustness checks are performed to assess the overall robustness of the results presented in the previous section.

Portfolio Formation

Whether deciles, quintiles, or terciles should be used when constructing the high and low sentiment portfolios, cannot be unambiguously answered. Dorn, Huberman, and Sengmueller (2008) use terciles, Kaniel, Saar, and Titman (2008) use both deciles and quintiles, Pan and Poteshman (2006) and Barber, Odean, and Zhu (2009a) form quintiles, and Hvidkjaer (2008) uses deciles. There is no guidance in the former literature that would prefer any alternative.

However, the idea behind the portfolio formation technique is that only extreme sentiment should be captured and that portfolio excess returns are higher the more extreme the sentiment expression. Therefore, all portfolio calculations are performed with deciles as well as quintiles. The intuitive hypothesis that excess returns are larger when using more extreme sentiment can be confirmed. For example, excess returns for a high-low sentiment portfolio strategy involving submitted orders on leverage products are 12.97 basis points for quintiles compared to 15.65 basis points for deciles.

We can conclude that the choice of the portfolio quantile influences the magnitude of the portfolio excess returns. In choosing it, however, the absolute number of stocks in one portfolio must be considered resulting in a meaningful portfolio size.

Volume- or Trade-Based Measure

Section 6.2.2 investigates the sentiment measure based on the number of executed orders instead of the volume based measure. As discussed in chapter 4, the number based sentiment and the volume based sentiment measures produce similar results with the difference that the former is robust to very large trades from a few individuals. After all, the number based measure is a better representation of the sentiment of retail investors as a whole.

A comparison of portfolio formation results using the volume based sentiment and the number based sentiment measure shows that the portfolio excess returns are not as large for the volume based measure as the excess returns for the number based measure, especially on the first day of the holding period. For example, instead of an excess return of 12.97 basis points (using quintiles of submitted orders on leverage products) for the number based measure, the value based measure yields an excess return of 10.85 basis points.

It can be shown that the volume based measure produces significantly positive excess returns but also that these excess returns are smaller in magnitude than the ones yielded when using the number based measure.

Minimum Number of Orders

The minimum number of orders restriction is crucial for meaningful sentiment values. Without it, extreme sentiment values could be constructed based on only one order resulting in a sentiment of plus one or minus one. As mentioned in section 6.2.2, additional tests using a minimum number of 5 or 10 orders per day and underlying show that the results are not changed significantly.

Portfolio Formation Period

Hvidkjaer (2008) uses portfolio formation periods of different lengths (from 1 to 24 months) and presents portfolio returns for different holding periods (from 1 to 36 months). Both Kaniel, Saar, and Titman (2008) and Barber, Odean, and Zhu (2009a) use a weekly formation period.

In the previous section, a portfolio formation period of one trading day is used in combination with portfolio holding periods of up to 30 trading days. In robustness checks, the formation period is increased to up to one week (5 trading days) to assess the influence on excess portfolio returns. These tests show that portfolio excess returns are highest when using a one-day portfolio formation period and are gradually lower when using a longer formation period of up to 5 trading days. For example, on the first trading day the excess returns of a strategy involving submitted orders on leverage products are 15.65 basis points using a formation period of one trading day, gradually declining to 11.66 basis points when using a formation period of five trading days.

In general, excess portfolio returns are highest when using the shortest formation period of one trading day. However, excess returns are still substantial and significant when using longer formation periods of up to five trading days.

Annual Results

Another robustness check involves testing whether the results of section 6.3.3 are constant over time. In order to investigate this issue, average portfolio returns for the five different years in the sample are calculated and presented in Table 6.8. Only returns for strategies involving executed market orders and submitted orders for leverage products on small capitalization stocks are considered.

Table 6.8: Annual Portfolio Holding Returns

This table presents portfolio holding returns for a high-low sentiment portfolio of small capitalization stocks using orders in leverage products for portfolio formation. Results are reported for each year of the sample period separately. Panel A shows results for executed market orders; Panel B shows results for submitted orders. p-values are reported in brackets.

	Holding day									
Year	1	2	3	4	5	6	7	8	9	10
Panel A: Executed market orders										
High-low sentiment portfolio returns										
2004	38.9	52.7	55.1	53.5	41.6	77.7	64.8	55.7	44.8	65.0
	(0.027)	(0.026)	(0.040)	(0.061)	(0.131)	(0.032)	(0.075)	(0.125)	(0.182)	(0.100)
2005	26.6	54.8	61.1	48.3	65.1	73.3	72.0	75.0	71.5	68.9
	(0.012)	(0.003)	(0.003)	(0.026)	(0.010)	(0.005)	(0.015)	(0.015)	(0.024)	(0.036)
2006	41.5	56.7	51.5	38.8	45.4	59.5	68.3	82.6	85.1	94.8
	(0.003)	(0.002)	(0.007)	(0.050)	(0.039)	(0.015)	(0.013)	(0.006)	(0.007)	(0.003)
2007	25.1	29.3	43.8	61.6	65.0	60.6	52.1	37.8	37.3	38.5
	(0.008)	(0.030)	(0.009)	(0.003)	(0.004)	(0.010)	(0.030)	(0.112)	(0.126)	(0.123)
2008	77.1	96.8	107.6	133.8	141.9	142.5	158.4	166.5	162.3	169.9
	(0.000)	(0.000)	(0.000)	(0.000)	(0.000)	(0.000)	(0.000)	(0.000)	(0.001)	(0.000)
Panel B: Submitted orders										
High-low sentiment portfolio returns										
2004	21.8	67.9	81.8	66.6	58.0	54.4	67.3	67.0	76.7	81.0
	(0.055)	(0.000)	(0.000)	(0.009)	(0.030)	(0.050)	(0.028)	(0.031)	(0.023)	(0.025)
2005	38.2	55.5	81.7	93.6	120.3	137.8	133.4	152.9	157.0	168.4
	(0.000)	(0.000)	(0.000)	(0.000)	(0.000)	(0.000)	(0.000)	(0.000)	(0.000)	(0.000)
2006	38.4	43.6	46.9	42.6	44.3	61.5	62.5	74.3	76.1	77.3
	(0.000)	(0.001)	(0.001)	(0.008)	(0.016)	(0.003)	(0.003)	(0.001)	(0.002)	(0.002)
2007	31.8	36.7	53.1	63.4	64.4	56.8	49.2	22.4	14.5	20.0
	(0.000)	(0.002)	(0.000)	(0.000)	(0.001)	(0.009)	(0.032)	(0.204)	(0.303)	(0.247)
2008	68.0	90.8	111.7	119.9	132.8	171.5	193.5	217.2	246.9	256.7
	(0.000)	(0.000)	(0.000)	(0.000)	(0.000)	(0.000)	(0.000)	(0.000)	(0.000)	(0.000)

The results indicate that in all five different annual periods excess returns are significantly positive, at least for the first days of the holding period. Of course there are differences in magnitude with the year 2008 being the period with the highest excess returns and the year 2007 the one with the lowest – considering the maximum returns are within the first 10 holding days.

Overall, these results confirm the robustness of the trading strategy involving the high minus low sentiment portfolio formation to the specific time period.

6.5. Conclusion

In this chapter, sentiment measures for different stocks are being developed based on Euwax Sentiment measures for single underlyings. It is shown that a trading strategy based on these sentiment measures is able to generate abnormal returns.

Related studies provide a mixed picture of whether retail sentiment data can be used to predict returns. In most cases, this is clearly a shortcoming of the data set used. Data sets usually differ in the following ways: origin of the data, exact identification of trade direction, exact identification of retail trades, country of origin, and short-sale restrictions. The unique data set used in this chapter tries to avoid known problems by including only retail investor orders from different brokerages, the explicit trade direction, and the possibility of expressing negative sentiment through put options. In addition, order types, product types, and market capitalization of the underlying firms are distinguished. Furthermore, the data set used in this work is the first data set using submitted orders to create order imbalance measures.

The methodology applied in this chapter is especially useful for detecting differences between extreme high sentiment and extreme low sentiment measurements. A high sentiment portfolio is constructed using stocks with extreme positive sentiment readings, and a low sentiment portfolio is constructed consisting of stocks with extreme negative sentiment readings. The returns of a long-short strategy involving buying the high sentiment portfolio and selling the low sentiment portfolio indicate that high sentiment stocks perform better than low sentiment stocks, and that the trading strategy yields abnormal returns.

Several filters are used on the data to assess the influence of distinguishing between product and order type as well as using submitted or executed orders. In general, sentiment based on market orders in leverage products has predictive power for the next trading days' returns whereas no such results can be found for sentiment based on limit orders and investment certificates. Furthermore, sentiment based on submitted orders shows the same predictive power, with even stronger returns on the first four trading days after portfolio formation.

Results remain statistically and economically significant even when controlling for market returns and momentum. However, controlling for market capitalization reveals that only small firm sentiment has significant predictive power whereas sentiment based on large firms does not produce significant results. This does not weaken the overall results. Calculating three separate portfolios for small, medium, and large firms rather controls for the SMB (small minus big) effect resulting in three high-low sentiment portfolios that are not influenced by this effect. Moreover, the results are in line with existing theory on noise trading and sentiment finding that small firm stocks are more likely to be influenced by retail investor trades.

7 Conclusion and Future Work

This chapter concludes this work. Section 7.1 reviews the research questions from Chapter 1 and briefly summarizes the answers provided in the various chapters of this work. Section 7.2 points out the key contributions, and section 7.3 completes this chapter with an overview of open questions and avenues of future research.

7.1. Conclusion

This section revisits the research questions as they are developed in the introduction of this work and briefly summarizes the answers given in the chapters following the introduction.

> *Research Question 1:*
>
> How can investor sentiment be measured and how are different sentiment indicators related?

Investor sentiment measures can be categorized according to the way they are created: Direct sentiment measures are surveys in which investors are asked directly about their attitude towards the economic situation or the stock market in particular. Indirect sentiment measures are usually created from financial variables and therefore measure sentiment only indirectly. Meta-measures are sentiment measures that are neither based on surveys nor pure financial data but involve meta-information about investor sentiment.

To investigate the differences between existing sentiment measures, two methodologies have been used: First, correlation of all sentiment indicators *within* a category as determined for the first part of the question is calculated to evaluate these against each other. In addition, correlation of all sentiment indicators *between* two categories is calculated to check whether they all rest on the same sources. Second, all sentiment indicators are compared to various contemporaneous market returns since sentiment measures and market returns should be correlated.

In general, most of the measures, regardless of whether they are indirect or direct, have a high pairwise correlation indicating that they indeed pick up the same sentiment signal. Furthermore, most of the sentiment indicators correlate well with market returns, with high-frequency indirect measures having the highest correlation and lower-frequency indirect measures a lower correlation with the market.

To conclude, there are many different measures of investor sentiment in research and practice but their evaluation remains difficult. A high correlation among each other and with market returns is a good indication that they react to the same underlying factor but does not serve as a necessary or sufficient condition. Future research is needed to identify this factor which will make it easier to construct new measures and evaluate existing ones.

Research Question 2:

Can an index be created from retail order flow data to describe investor sentiment?

This research question is being answered by developing a retail investor sentiment index as a proof-of-concept using data that has not been used before for that purpose. The Euwax Sentiment Index is based on executed retail investor orders in leverage products on the DAX and includes only market orders.

The unique data set from Boerse Stuttgart has several advantages over previously used data sets: First, it consists of retail investor orders only, i.e. there is no need for a trade classification by trade size as it has to be done for other data sets. Second, orders can be exactly classified as buy and sell orders without the need to infer the trade direction using signing algorithms such as the one by Lee and Ready (1991). Third, the data set allows for a more symmetric expression of retail sentiment since retail investors have the opportunity to invest in puts to express negative sentiment. Fourth, in addition to executed orders, the data set comprises submitted orders which provide further insights into the dynamic relationship between order submission and execution.

The results can be summarized as follows: First, sentiment extracted from orders in leverage products has a higher correlation with market returns than sentiment from orders in investment products. Second, market orders better represent sentiment because changes in sentiment are captured exactly when the order decision is made by the investor. In contrast, limit orders are executed without the necessity of a simultaneous order submission. Therefore, sentiment extracted from executed limit orders may include orders that have been submitted much earlier and do not represent actual sentiment. As an alternative to executed market orders, sentiment may also be extracted from submitted orders to circumvent the problem of delayed order execution.

However, the regression results reveal that sentiment is negatively correlated to market returns *regardless* of whether submitted orders, executed limit orders or executed market orders are used to generate the sentiment measure. The results confirm that retail investors act as contrarians, and that this is not just because their limit order trades lead us to believe it as suggested by Linnainmaa (2009).

The comparison with other existing sentiment measures shows that in the majority of cases there is a significant correlation between sentiment measures. However, the exact causality for this correlation cannot be determined. It is possible that different sentiment measures are driven by the same factors, but that these factors influence sentiment in different ways. For example, a large negative correlation between the Euwax Sentiment and the weekly German investor sentiment surveys can be documented. The negative correlation means that sentiment extracted from order flow data is contrary to that extracted from investor surveys. On the other hand, there are large positive correlations between Euwax Sentiment and other indirect measures of sentiment. It can be concluded that most of the sentiment measures are related but the unambiguous interpretation remains open and subject of future research.

Research Question 3:

Do retail investors herd?

The answer of this question needs an unambiguous definition of herding which does not exist in the literature. For the purpose of this study, the definition by Lakonishok, Shleifer, and Vishny (1992) is followed who define herding as "buying (selling) simultaneously the same stocks as others buy (sell)" but extend the definition to assets in general. Therefore, the order flow data from Boerse Stuttgart can be used to determine the level of herding for retail investors.

Herding as defined above has two dimensions: choice of time and choice of assets. The first dimension refers to retail investors (de-)investing in the market at the same time. This tendency is also called market-level herding. Market-level herding is analyzed by looking at aggregate retail investor order flow measures in securitized derivatives on the DAX. The second dimension of herding refers to retail investors choosing the same securities at the same time which is also called stock-level herding. Instead of the stocks themselves, securitized derivatives on those stocks are analyzed to detect stock-level herding.

On the market level, retail investors show a strong tendency of herding: More than 10% of all investors than expected by chance are on the same side of the market each day. This result holds across order types proving that this is not a result of automatic limit order execution. Furthermore, it is shown that optimistic herding, i.e. herding when most investors are optimistic about the market, is more prevalent in bear markets than in bull markets, and that pessimistic herding is more prevalent in bull than in bear markets. This finding supports the finding that retail investors act as contrarians. Moreover, herding is higher in bear markets than in bull markets, indicating that retail investors are collectively seeking investment opportunities in bear markets.

This finding is not a broker-specific phenomenon: The additional analysis shows that a substantial amount of herding is detected across all brokers and all types of brokers although there are differences between broker types: Analyzing the order flows of 22 different brokers in four distinct categories reveals that the level of herding is highest among public brokers with a rather conservative clientele and lowest among online brokers that neither give investment advice nor operate any branches.

On the stock level, the level of herding is similar to that found on the market level, and to those reported in other recent studies: Retail investors herd into and out of the same assets (underlying stocks) at the same time.

With respect to the theory, the empirical evidence supports the hypothesis that retail investors act in concert and that their trades are correlated. This is contrary to arguments made by efficient markets proponents who argue that trades by uninformed investors (noise traders) cancel each other out and therefore do not have the ability to influence asset prices. Therefore, the correlated behavior of retail investors in the stock market should be studied more closely. The development of a herding measure can be regarded as a first step towards this goal.

Research Question 4:

Does sentiment predict returns?

In recent years, several studies using some sort of order imbalance measures have tried to answer this question. However, the studies provide a mixed picture of whether retail sentiment data can be used to predict returns. In most cases, this is a shortcoming of the data set used. The data sets used by related work differ in many ways: There are differences concerning the source of the data, its frequency and period, regional focus, target group, and the construction of the imbalance measure.

In this work, a unique data set with executed and submitted retail investor orders on 244 underlying stocks is used to calculate sentiment measures for each stock. The relationship between sentiment measures and the corresponding returns is analyzed to evaluate whether sentiment positively predicts returns, i.e. high sentiment is followed by positive returns, and low sentiment is followed by negative returns.

This is done with a portfolio construction methodology: A high sentiment portfolio is constructed using stocks with extreme positive sentiment readings, and a low sentiment portfolio is constructed consisting of stocks with extreme negative sentiment readings. If high sentiment stocks perform better than low-sentiment stocks, a long-short trading strategy involving buying the high sentiment portfolio and selling the low sentiment portfolio should yield positive excess returns. This methodology is especially useful for detecting differences between extreme high sentiment and extreme low sentiment measurements. In addition, it provides a direct assessment of the economic significance, i.e. the absolute excess returns of the trading strategy.

The results reveal that sentiment – measured by retail investor market orders in leverage products – indeed positively predicts stock returns. Submitted orders in leverage products have the highest predictive power but only for small firms: The analysis of the five year historical data set shows that holding the long-short portfolio for 10 consecutive days yields 120 basis points excess returns.

Overall, the results show that the average retail investor order flow does not represent "dumb money" as suggested by market folklore – at least not for EUWAX investors. The results shows that retail investors have a rather good feeling for market timing as well as for picking stocks that do well in the short term.

7.2. Summary of Contributions

Reconciliation of Empirical Findings

The growing body of empirical research on order flow and prices demands a more detailed analysis and a critical comparison of the related findings. Recent research shows that findings concerning correlated trading and return predictability may be different and even contradictory. The literature currently does not present a reconciliation of all relevant studies[25]. Section 2.4 in Chapter 2 aims to close this gap and presents a structured overview of recent findings and offers explanations for any differences found.

Extensive Overview and Comparison of Investor Sentiment Measures

Many investor sentiment measures have been developed and are currently used in practice. There is a relatively large body of research covering single sentiment measures and especially their relation to returns and volatility. An overview of current sentiment measures and a correlation analysis, however, are missing[26]. Chapter 3 evaluates existing direct and indirect sentiment measures and presents correlation coefficients among them as well as correlation to contemporaneous market returns.

Construction of a New Sentiment Index

One of the main contributions of this work is the construction of a new sentiment index based on a unique data set using retail investor orders to the European Warrant Exchange in Chapter 4. Moreover, this work is among the first to use data on securitized derivatives[27]. These products are especially suited for the creation of a retail investor sentiment measure because retail investors have the possibility to express both positive and negative market sentiment with the purchase of a single product.

Investigation of Herding Behavior of Retail Investors

Chapter 5 focuses on the herding behavior of retail investors using the same data set on retail investor orders to EUWAX. There are not many studies about retail investor herding[28] as most of the related work is concerned with the herding of institutional investors. In addition,

[25] Barber, Hvidkjaer, Odean, and Zhu (2006) only present a reconciliation of their own work.
[26] Brown and Cliff (2004) present an overview of sentiment measures, but do not include important German survey measures.
[27] Schmitz, Glaser, and Weber (2007) use warrant data, a subset of the securitized derivatives data.
[28] Dorn, Huberman, and Sengmueller (2008) explicitly calculate an individual investor herding measure.

two types of herding are distinguished: market-level herding and stock-level herding whereas most other studies exclusively investigate stock-level herding while omitting the fact that investors may move into and out of the market at the same time.

Moreover, the herding analysis is broken down to a broker level and sheds light on the question whether customers of different brokerages also show a different herding behavior. The order flow data enriched with non-public broker IDs allows for a classification into four distinct broker types that is typical for the German brokerage landscape. There is currently no other research that investigates the retail investor herding behavior of different German brokers.

Analysis of Submitted Retail Investor Orders

Recent research[29] on order imbalance measures argues that the use of executed retail investor orders may lead to wrong conclusions with respect to the contrarian behavior of retail investors. This work alleviates these concerns by using submitted orders instead of executed Orders. This is the first study to use the order submission time for this purpose.

Development of a Trading Strategy

For evaluation purposes, a trading strategy is developed in Chapter 6 which consists of buying high sentiment stocks and selling low sentiment stocks resulting in a zero-cost portfolio that generates abnormal returns. While this methodology has also been used by other recent empirical studies[30], it provides several new aspects regarding the use of different order types, the exact classification of buy and sell orders, the influence of market capitalization, and the use of submitted instead of executed orders. No other related work addresses all of these aspects and provides such a high degree of detail in its analysis.

7.3. Future Work

While many issues have been addressed, there are still open questions which have arisen in the process of this work and which provide possible future research directions which are outlined briefly in this section.

Unified Investor Sentiment Theory

While this work focuses on the empirical investigation of retail investor sentiment, a unified theory of investor sentiment that brings together theory and empiricism is still missing. There have been some attempts to create a theory of investor sentiment but these do not explain all empirical findings.

[29] Linnainmaa (2009) argues that individual investors have been falsely classified as contrarian.

[30] Jackson (2003), Pan and Poteshman (2006), Kaniel, Saar, and Titman (2008), Dorn, Huberman, and Sengmueller (2008), and Barber, Odean, and Zhu (2009a) use similar portfolio construction methodologies.

In particular, a theory should incorporate short-term as well as long-term considerations since empirical research[31] indicates that short-term effects differ from long-term effects. These different patterns still have to be explained by market microstructure theory.

Individual Retail Investor Behavior

While this work focuses on the aggregate behavior of retail investors, a detailed investigation of individual investor behavior is needed to better understand the motivation of retail investors for trading. Although the data set used in this work presents valuable insights into retail investor behavior, its main drawback is the missing link to individual account data.

Future work on individual account data[32] – collected from large banks or brokers – which allows to track executed or submitted orders to individual accounts should focus on the motivation of retail investors to submit orders in particular stocks.

Moreover, individual account data offers the opportunity to investigate whether individual investors profit from trading by actually examining the exact holding period and account settlement data. In addition, individual retail investor account data allows for the identification of high-performance investors who continuously make profitable trading decisions and low-performance investors who usually make unprofitable decisions. If the distinction between high- and low-performance investors is persistent, then future research should be conducted to analyze the reason for this performance difference.

Experimental Evidence

One possibility to get more insights into the thinking and behavior of retail investors is to conduct field or laboratory experiments. These experiments should be targeted towards finding evidence about their individual motivation to trade assets and the timing of their trading decision.

Survey Evidence

Some of the open research questions mentioned above could be addressed by conducting surveys among retail investors. Surveys offer the possibility to directly ask investors about their motivation to trade and about possible information sources they have used to come to their concrete trading decision.

Explanation of Contrarian and Herding Behavior

The empirical evidence in this work shows that retail investors – at least EUWAX investors trading securitized derivatives – act as contrarians, i.e. they buy when the market declines and

[31] Barber, Hvidkjaer, Odean, and Zhu (2006) empirically show that the same analysis conducted on the same data sets for a monthly frequency and a weekly frequency is able to result in opposite patterns.

[32] Data sets including individual account data are used e.g. in Schmitz, Glaser, and Weber (2007), Dorn, Huberman, and Sengmueller (2008), and Barber, Odean, and Zhu (2009b).

sell when the market rises. However, the reason why retail investors show a contrarian behavior remains opaque. Further research is needed to figure out why investors think that they could earn abnormal returns by following a contrarian strategy, and whether they actually succeed by doing so.

Closely related to the contrarian behavior, the exact reasons for the herding behavior of retail investors remain to be subject of future research. While much has been done to explain the herding behavior of institutional investors theoretically, retail investors have not received such a great deal of attention. The question is whether they are following each others' trades (which is unlikely since their trades are generally not public) or whether they are following the same signals.

Moreover, if following the same signals lead retail investors to act as contrarians, then both research questions are closely related and must be considered together.

Appendix

A Appendix to Chapter 4

Table A.1: Summary Statistics on Executed Order Volume

This table reports summary statistics about the volume of executed orders by derivative product group (warrants, knock-outs, and investment certificates). Panel A groups the orders by option type and trade direction, Panel B by order type, and Panel C by underlying type. The percentages in brackets provide information about the relative use of the different order classes within each product group.

Panel A: Executed order volume (in million €) by option type

		Warrants		Knock-outs		Investment certificates		Total	
Call	Buy	15,900	(37.9%)	24,226	(35.6%)	50,494	(49.7%)	90,620	(42.8%)
	Sell	15,995	(38.1%)	25,417	(37.3%)	48,424	(47.6%)	89,836	(42.4%)
Put	Buy	5,017	(12.0%)	8,923	(13.1%)	1,325	(1.3%)	15,265	(7.2%)
	Sell	5,019	(12.0%)	9,487	(13.9%)	1,456	(1.4%)	15,962	(7.5%)
Total		41,931		68,053		101,699		211,683	

Panel B: Executed order volume (in million €) by order type

	Warrants		Knock-outs		Investment certificates		Total	
Market Orders	24,619	(58.7%)	42,758	(62.8%)	79,733	(78.4%)	147,110	(69.5%)
Limit Orders	14,989	(35.7%)	17,330	(25.5%)	19,696	(19.4%)	52,015	(24.6%)
Stop Orders	2,323	(5.5%)	7,965	(11.7%)	2,270	(2.2%)	12,558	(5.9%)
Total	41,931		68,053		101,699		211,683	

Panel C: Executed order volume (in million €) by underlying type

	Warrants		Knock-outs		Investment certificates		Total	
Stocks	20,407	(48.7%)	10,486	(15.4%)	41,111	(40.4%)	72,004	(34.0%)
Indices	17,152	(40.9%)	48,002	(70.5%)	52,629	(51.8%)	117,784	(55.6%)
Fixed Income	165	(0.4%)	758	(1.1%)	1,421	(1.4%)	2,344	(1.1%)
Currencies	2,138	(5.1%)	2,062	(3.0%)	106	(0.1%)	4,306	(2.0%)
Commodities	2,041	(4.9%)	2,062	(3.0%)	5,717	(5.6%)	9,820	(4.6%)
Other	28	(0.1%)	4,683	(6.9%)	714	(0.7%)	5,424	(2.6%)
Total	41,931		68,053		101,699		211,683	

Table A.2: Summary Statistics on Submitted Orders

This table reports summary statistics on the number of submitted orders by derivative product group (warrants, knock-outs, and investment certificates). Panel A groups the orders by option type and trade direction, Panel B by order type, and Panel C by underlying type. Panel D provides information about the execution status of submitted orders, i.e. whether they were filled or not. The percentages in brackets provide information about the relative use of the different order classes within each product group.

Panel A: Submitted orders by option type

		Warrants		Knock-outs		Investment certificates		Total	
Call	Buy	5,956,311	(41.2%)	4,841,590	(32.3%)	3,569,829	(50.0%)	14,367,730	(39.3%)
	Sell	4,881,688	(33.7%)	5,011,605	(33.5%)	3,408,494	(47.8%)	13,301,787	(36.4%)
Put	Buy	2,093,047	(14.5%)	2,481,306	(16.6%)	83,961	(1.2%)	4,658,314	(12.7%)
	Sell	1,538,033	(10.6%)	2,643,003	(17.6%)	72,617	(1.0%)	4,253,653	(11.6%)
Total		14,469,079		14,977,504		7,134,901		36,581,484	

Panel B: Submitted orders by order type

	Warrants		Knock-outs		Investment certificates		Total	
Market Orders	5,814,127	(40.2%)	6,610,997	(44.1%)	4,930,479	(69.1%)	17,355,603	(47.4%)
Limit Orders	7,802,032	(53.9%)	5,229,371	(34.9%)	1,811,306	(25.4%)	14,842,709	(40.6%)
Stop Orders	852,920	(5.9%)	3,137,136	(20.9%)	393,116	(5.5%)	4,383,172	(12.0%)
Total	14,469,079		14,977,504		7,134,901		36,581,484	

Panel C: Submitted orders by underlying type

	Warrants		Knock-outs		Investment certificates		Total	
Stocks	8,186,319	(56.6%)	3,228,694	(21.6%)	2,983,092	(41.8%)	14,398,105	(39.4%)
Indices	4,960,704	(34.3%)	8,813,129	(58.8%)	3,352,323	(47.0%)	17,126,156	(46.8%)
Fixed Income	76,339	(0.5%)	247,922	(1.7%)	97,658	(1.4%)	421,919	(1.2%)
Currencies	626,141	(4.3%)	696,693	(4.7%)	12,749	(0.2%)	1,335,583	(3.7%)
Commodities	611,709	(4.2%)	1,604,189	(10.7%)	618,449	(8.7%)	2,834,347	(7.7%)
Other	7,867	(0.1%)	386,877	(2.6%)	70,630	(1.0%)	465,374	(1.3%)
Total	14,469,079		14,977,504		7,134,901		36,581,484	

Panel D: Submitted orders by execution status

	Warrants		Knock-outs		Investment certificates		Total	
filled	8,177,580	(56.5%)	11,328,863	(75.6%)	5,985,030	(83.9%)	25,491,473	(69.7%)
not filled	6,291,499	(43.5%)	3,648,641	(24.4%)	1,149,871	(16.1%)	11,090,011	(30.3%)
Total	14,469,079		14,977,504		7,134,901		36,581,484	

Bibliography

Andrade, S., Chang, C., Seasholes, M. S. (2008): Trading imbalances, predictable reversals, and cross-stock price pressure. *Journal of Financial Economics*, 88(2), 406-423.

Antweiler, W., Frank, M. Z. (2004): Is All That Talk Just Noise? The Information Content of Internet Stock Message Boards. *The Journal of Finance,* 59(3), 1259-1294.

Baker, M., Stein, J.C. (2004): Market liquidity as a sentiment indicator. *Journal of Financial Markets,* 7(3), 271-299.

Baker, M., Wurgler, J. (2006): Investor Sentiment and the Cross-Section of Stock Returns. *The Journal of Finance*, 61(4), 1645-1680.

Baker, M., Wurgler, J. (2007): Investor Sentiment and the Stock Market. *The Journal of Economic Perspectives*, 21(2), 129-151.

Bandopadhyaya, A., Jones, A. L. (2006): Measuring Investor Sentiment in Equity Markets. *Journal of Asset Management*, 7(3), 208-215.

Bandopadhyaya, A., Jones, A. L. (2008): Measures Of Investor Sentiment: A Comparative Analysis Put-Call Ratio Vs. Volatility Index. *Journal of Business & Economics Research*, 6(8), 27-34.

Barber, B. M., Hvidkjaer, S., Odean, T., Zhu, N. (2006): A Comparison of the Results in Barber, Odean, and Zhu (2006) and Hvidkjaer (2006). *Working Paper*, University of California, Davis.

Barber, B. M., Lee, Y., Liu, Y., Odean, T. (2005): Do Day Traders Make Money? *Working Paper*, University of California, Davis.

Barber, B. M., Lee, Y., Liu, Y., Odean, T. (2009): Just How Much Do Individual Investors Lose by Trading? *Review of Financial Studies*, 22(2), 609-632.

Barber, B. M., Odean, T., Zhu, N. (2009a): Do Retail Trades Move Markets? *Review of Financial Studies*, 22(1), 151-186.

Barber, B. M., Odean, T., Zhu, N. (2009b): Systematic noise. *Journal of Financial Markets,* 12(4), 547-569.

Barberis, N., Shleifer, A., Vishny , R. (1998): A model of investor sentiment. *Journal of Financial Economics,* 49(3), 307-343.

Beaumont, R., van Daele, M., Frijns, B., Lehnert, T. (2005): On Individual and Institutional Noise Trading, W*orking Paper*, Maastricht University.

Berkman, H., Koch, P.D. (2008): Noise trading and the price formation process, *Journal of Empirical Finance*, 15(2), 232–250.

Black, F. (1986): Noise. *The Journal of Finance,* 41(3), 529-543.

Black, F., Scholes, M. (1973): The Pricing of Options and Corporate Liabilities, *Journal of Political Economy*, 81, 637–654.

Boehmer, E., Wu, J. (2008): Order Flow and Prices, *AFA 2007 Chicago Meetings Paper.*

Brown, G. W. (1999): Volatility, Sentiment, and Noise Traders. *Financial Analysts Journal*, 55(2), 82-90.

Brown, G. W., Cliff, M. T. (2004): Investor sentiment and the near-term stock market. *Journal of Empirical Finance*, 11(1), 1-27.

Brown, G. W., Cliff, M. T. (2005): Investor Sentiment and Asset Valuation. *Journal of Business*, 78(2), 405-440.

Burghardt, M. (2007): Investment Decisions and Behavior: Indicators for Investor Confidence. *Proceedings of the Conference on Group Decision and Negotiation* (Montreal, Canada) (Kersten, G. E.; Rios, J.; Chen, E., eds.).Volume I, 274–276.

Burghardt, M., Riordan, R. (2009): Know the Flow: Sentiment Extraction from Retail Order Flow Data. *Proceedings of the FinanceCom 2008*, Lecture Notes in Business Information Processing, 23 (D. Kundisch et al., ed.). Springer-Verlag. 31–46.

Campbell, J. Y., Kyle, A. S. (1993): Smart Money, Noise Trading and Stock Price Behaviour. *The Review of Economic Studies*, 60(1), 1-34.

Carhart, M. M. (1997): On Persistence in Mutual Fund Performance, *The Journal of Finance*, 52(1), 57-82.

Charoenrook, A. (2003): Does Sentiment Matter? *Working Paper*, Vanderbilt University.

Chordia, T., Roll, R., Subrahmanyam, A. (2002): Order imbalance, liquidity, and market returns. *Journal of Financial Economics*, 65(1), 111-130.

Chordia, T., Roll, R., Subrahmanyam, A. (2005): Evidence on the speed of convergence to market efficiency, *Journal of Financial Economics*, 76(2), 271-292.

Chordia, T., Subrahmanyam, A. (2004): Order imbalance and individual stock returns: Theory and evidence. *Journal of Financial Economics*, 72(3), 485–518.

Ciccone, S. (2003): Does Analyst Optimism About Future Earnings Distort Stock Prices? *The Journal of Behavioral Finance,* 4(2), 59-64.

Clarke, R. G., Statman, M. (1998): Bullish or Bearish? *Financial Analysts Journal*, 54(3), 63-72.

Coval, J. D., Hirshleifer, D. A., Shumway, T. (2005): Can Individual Investors Beat the Market? *HBS Finance Working Paper No. 04-025*, Harvard Business School.

Daniel, K., Hirshleifer, D., Subrahmanyam, A. (1998): Investor Psychology and Security Market Under- and Overreaction. *The Journal of Finance*, 53(6), 1839-1885.

Das, S. R., Chen, M. Y. (2007): Yahoo! for Amazon: Sentiment Extraction from Small Talk on the Web, *Management Science*, 53(9), 1375-1388.

Das, S., Martínez-Jerez, A., Tufano, P. (2005): eInformation: A Clinical Study of Investor Discussion and Sentiment. *Financial Management*, 34(3), 103-137.

De Bondt, W. F. M. (1998): A portrait of the individual investor. *European Economic Review,* 42(3-5), 831-844.

De Bondt, W. F. M., Thaler, R. (1985): Does the Stock Market Overreact? *The Journal of Finance*, 40(3), 793-805.

De Long, J. B., Shleifer, A., Summers, L., Waldmann, R. (1990): Noise Trader Risk in Financial Markets. *Journal of Political Economy,* 98(4), 703-738.

Dorn, D., Huberman, G. (2005): Talk and Action: What Individual Investors Say and What They Do. *Review of Finance*, 9(4), 437-481.

Dorn, D., Huberman, G., Sengmueller, P. (2008): Correlated Trading and Returns. *The Journal of Finance*, 63(2), 885-920.

Edwards, W. (1968): Conservatism in human information processing. In B. Kleinmuntz (Ed.), Formal representation of human judgment. Wiley, New York.

Fabozzi, F. J., Francis, J. C. (1977): Stability Tests for Alphas and Betas over Bull and Bear Market Conditions. *The Journal of Finance*, 32(4), 1093-99.

Fama, E. F. (1965): The Behavior of Stock-Market Prices, *The Journal of Business*, 38(1), 34-105.

Fama, E. F. (1970): Efficient Capital Markets: A Review of Theory and Empirical Work. *The Journal of Finance*, 25(2), 383-417.

Fama, E. F. (1998): Market efficiency, long-term returns, and behavioral finance. *Journal of Financial Economics*, 49, 283-306.

Fama, E.F., Fisher, L., Jensen, M.C., Roll, R. (1969): The Adjustment of Stock Prices to New Information, *International Economic Review*, 10(1), 1 -21.

Fama, E.F., French, K. (1992): The cross-section of expected stock returns. *The Journal of Finance*, 47(2), 427-465.

Fama, E.F., French, K. (1993): Common risk factors in the returns on bonds and stocks. *Journal of Financial Economics*, 33(1), 3-56.

Fisher, K. L., Statman, M. (2000): Investor Sentiment and Stock Returns. *Financial Analysts Journal*, 56(2), 16-23.

Fisher, K. L., Statman, M. (2003): Consumer Confidence and Stock Returns. *The Journal of Portfolio Management*, 30(1), 115-127.

Frazzini, A., Lamont, O. A. (2008): Dumb Money: Mutual fund flows and the cross-section of stock returns. *Journal of Financial Economics*, 88(2), 299-322.

Friedman, M. (1953): The case for flexible exchange rates. *Essays in Positive Economics*. Chicago: University of Chicago Press.

Griffin, J. M., Harris, J. H., Topaloglu, S. (2003): The Dynamics of Institutional and Individual Trading. *The Journal of Finance*, 58(6), 2285-2320.

Grinblatt, M., Titman, S., Wermers, R. (1995): Momentum Investment Strategies, Portfolio Performance, and Herding – A Study of Mutual Fund Behavior. *The American Economic Review*, 85(5), 1088-1105.

Grossman, S. J., Stiglitz, J. E. (1980): On the Impossibility of Informationally Efficient Markets. *The American Economic Review*, 70(3), 393-408.

Groves, R. M. (1989): Survey Errors and Survey Costs. Wiley, New York.

Han, B. (2008): Investor Sentiment and Option Prices. *Review of Financial Studies,* 21(1), 387-414.

Honcoop, D., Lehnert, T. (2007): Can Sentiment be predicted to have Cross-Sectional Effects? *Working Paper*, Maastricht University.

Hong, H., Stein, J. C. (1999): A Unified Theory of Underreaction, Momentum Trading, and Overreaction in Asset Markets. *The Journal of Finance*, 54(6), 2143-2184.

Hull, J. C. (2006): Options, futures, and other derivatives. 6th edition. Prentice Hall, Upper Saddle River, New Jersey.

Hvidkjaer, S. (2008): Small Trades and the Cross-Section of Stock Returns. *Review of Financial Studies*, 21(3), 1123-1151.

Jackson, A. (2003): The Aggregate Behaviour of Individual Investors. *Working paper*, London Business School.

Jayaraman, N., Frye, M. B., Sabherwal, S. (2001): Informed Trading around Merger Announcements: An Empirical Test Using Transaction Volume and Open Interest in Options Market. *The Financial Review*, 36, 45–74.

Jegadeesh, N, Titman, S. (1993): Profitability of Momentum Strategies: An Evaluation of Alternative Explanations. *The Journal of Finance*, 56(2), 699-720.

Kahneman, D., Tversky, A. (1979): Prospect Theory: An Analysis of Decision under Risk. *Econometrica*, 47(2), 263-291.

Kaniel, R., Saar, G., Titman, S. (2008): Individual Investor Trading and Stock Returns. *The Journal of Finance*, 63(1), 273-310.

Kraus, A., Stoll, H. R. (1972): Parallel Trading by Institutional Investors. *The Journal of Financial and Quantitative Analysis*, 7(5), 2107-2138.

Kumar, A., Lee, C. M. C. (2006): Retail Investor Sentiment and Return Comovements. *The Journal of Finance,* 61(5), 2451–2486.

Kurov, A. (2008): Investor Sentiment, Trading Behavior and Informational Efficiency in Index Futures Markets. *The Financial Review*, 43, 107-127.

Kyle, A. S. (1985): Continuous Auctions and Insider Trading. *Econometrica,* 53(6), 1315-1336.

Lakonishok, J., Shleifer, A., Vishny, R. W. (1992): The impact of institutional trading on stock prices. *Journal of Financial Economics*, 32(1), 23-43.

Lee, C. M. C., Radhakrishna, B. (2000): Inferring Investor Behavior: Evidence from TORQ, *Journal of Financial Markets*, 3(2), 83-111.

Lee, C. M. C., Ready, M. J. (1991): Inferring Trade Direction from Intraday Data. *The Journal of Finance*, 46(2), 733-46.

Lee, C. M. C., Shleifer, A., Thaler, R. H. (1991): Investor Sentiment and the Closed-End Fund Puzzle. *The Journal of Finance*, 46(1), 75-109.

Lee, W. Y., Jiang, C. X., Indro, D. C. (2002): Stock market volatility, excess returns, and the role of investor sentiment. *Journal of Banking & Finance*, 26, 2277-2299.

Lee, Y., Liu, Y., Roll, R., Subrahmanyam, A. (2004): Order Imbalances and Market Efficiency: Evidence from the Taiwan Stock Exchange. *The Journal of Financial and Quantitative Analysis*, 39(2), 327-341.

Lemmon, M., Portniaguina, E. (2006): Consumer Confidence and Asset Prices: Some Empirical Evidence. *Review of Financial Studies*, 19(4), 1499-1529.

Linnainmaa, J. (2009): Do Limit Orders Alter Inferences about Investor Performance and Behavior? *The Journal of Finance, forthcoming.*

Lo, A. W., ed. (1997): Market Efficiency: Stock Market Behaviour in Theory and Practice. Volumes I and II. Cheltenham, UK: Edward Elgar Publishing Company.

Martikainen, T., Puttonen, V. (1996): Call-put signal predict Finnish stock returns. *Applied Economics Letters,* 3(10), 645–648.

McHattie, A. (2002): Covered Warrants – New opportunities in an exciting new market. Harriman House Publishers, Petersfield, Great Britain.

Milgrom, P., Stokey, N. (1982): Information, Trade and Common Knowledge. *Journal of Economic Theory,* 26(1), 17-27.

Odean, T. (1998): Are Investors Reluctant to Realize Their Losses? *The Journal of Finance,* 53(5), 1775-1798.

Odean, T. (1999): Do Investors Trade Too Much? *The American Economic Review,* 89(5), 1279-1298.

Oehler, A. (1998): Do mutual funds specializing in German stocks herd? *Finanzmarkt und Portfolio Management,* 12(4), 452-465.

Otoo, M. W. (1999): Consumer Sentiment and the Stock Market. *FEDS Working Paper* No. 99-60.

Pan, J., Poteshman, A. M. (2006): The Information in Option Volume for Future Stock Prices. *Review of Financial Studies,* 19(3), 871-908.

Qiu, L. X., Welch, I. (2006): Investor Sentiment Measures. *Working Paper*, Brown University.

Ross, S. A. (2002): Neoclassical Finance, Alternative Finance and the Closed End Fund Puzzle. *European Financial Management,* 8(2), 129-137.

Ross, S. A., Westerfield, R. W., Jaffe, J. (2001): Corporate Finance. 6th Edition, McGraw-Hill.

Rozeff, M. S., Kinney, W. R. (1967): Capital market seasonality: The case of stock returns. *Journal of Financial Economics*, 3(4), 379-402.

Schmeling, M. (2007): Institutional and individual sentiment: Smart money and noise trader risk? *International Journal of Forecasting*, 23(1), 127-145.

Schmitz, P., Glaser, M., Weber, M. (2007): Individual Investor Sentiment and Stock Returns - What Do We Learn from Warrant Traders? *Working Paper*, Universität Mannheim.

Sharpe, W. F., Alexander, G. J. (1990): Investments. Prentice Hall, Englewood Cliffs, NJ.

Shefrin, H., Statman, M. (1985): The Disposition to Sell Winners Too Early and Ride Losers Too Long: Theory and Evidence. *The Journal of Finance,* 40(3), 777-790.

Shiller, R. J. (1984): Stock Prices and Social Dynamics. *Brookings Papers on Economic Activity*, 457-98.

Shiller, R. J. (2000): Measuring Bubble Expectations and Investor Confidence. *The Journal of Psychology and Financial Markets,* 1(1), 49-60.

Shleifer, A. (2000): Inefficient Markets – An Introduction to Behavioral Finance. Clarendon Lectures in Economics. Oxford University Press. Oxford.

Shleifer, A., Summers, L. H. (1990): The Noise Trader Approach to Finance. *The Journal of Economic Perspectives*, 4(2), 19-33.

Shleifer, A., Vishny, R. W. (1997): The Limits of Arbitrage. *The Journal of Finance*, 52(1), 35-55.

Sias, R.W. (2004): Institutional Herding. *Review of Financial Studies*, 17(1), 165-206.

Simon, D. P., Wiggins, R. A. (2001): S&P Futures Returns and Contrary Sentiment Indicators. *The Journal of Future Markets*, 21(5), 447-462.

Solt, M. E., Statman, M. (1988): How Useful Is the Sentiment Index? *Financial Analysts Journal*, 44(5), 45-55.

Subrahmanyam, A. (2005): Distinguishing Between Rationales for Short-Horizon Predictability of Stock Returns. *The Financial Review*, 40, 11-35.

Subrahmanyam, A. (2007): Behavioural Finance: A Review and Synthesis. *European Financial Management*, 14(1), 12-29.

Subrahmanyam, A. (2008): Lagged order flows and returns: A longer-term perspective. *The Quarterly Review of Economics and Finance*, 48, 623-640.

Tetlock, P. C. (2007): Giving Content to Investor Sentiment: The Role of Media in the Stock Market. *The Journal of Finance*, 62(3), 1139-1168.

Tversky, A. and Kahneman, D. (1974): Judgment under Uncertainty: Heuristics and Biases. *Science,* 185(4157), 1124-1131.

Wang, Y., Keswani, A. Taylor, S. J. (2006): The relationships between sentiment, returns and volatility. *International Journal of Forecasting*, 22(1), 109-123.

Whaley, R. E. (2000): The investor fear gauge. *Journal of Portfolio Management*, 26(3), 1-6.

Zwergel, B., Klein, C. (2006): On the Predictive Power of Sentiment - Why Institutional Investors are Worth Their Pay. *Working Paper,* Universität Augsburg.

MIX
Papier aus verantwortungsvollen Quellen
Paper from responsible sources
FSC® C105338

FSC
www.fsc.org

If you have any concerns about our products,
you can contact us on
ProductSafety@springernature.com

In case Publisher is established outside the EU,
the EU authorized representative is:
Springer Nature Customer Service Center GmbH
Europaplatz 3, 69115 Heidelberg, Germany

Printed by Libri Plureos GmbH
in Hamburg, Germany

SpringerBriefs in Philosophy

SpringerBriefs present concise summaries of cutting-edge research and practical applications across a wide spectrum of fields. Featuring compact volumes of 50 to 125 pages, the series covers a range of content from professional to academic. Typical topics might include:

- A timely report of state-of-the art analytical techniques
- A bridge between new research results, as published in journal articles, and a contextual literature review
- A snapshot of a hot or emerging topic
- An in-depth case study or clinical example
- A presentation of core concepts that students must understand in order to make independent contributions

SpringerBriefs in Philosophy cover a broad range of philosophical fields including: Philosophy of Science, Logic, Non-Western Thinking, and Western Philosophy. We also consider biographies, full or partial, of key thinkers and pioneers.

SpringerBriefs are characterized by fast, global electronic dissemination, standard publishing contracts, standardized manuscript preparation and formatting guidelines, and expedited production schedules. Both solicited and unsolicited manuscripts are considered for publication in the SpringerBriefs in Philosophy series. Potential authors are warmly invited to complete and submit the Briefs Author Proposal form. All projects will be submitted to editorial review by external advisors.

SpringerBriefs are characterized by expedited production schedules with the aim for publication 8 to 12 weeks after acceptance and fast, global electronic dissemination through our online platform SpringerLink. The standard concise author contracts guarantee that

- an individual ISBN is assigned to each manuscript
- each manuscript is copyrighted in the name of the author
- the author retains the right to post the pre-publication version on his/her website or that of his/her institution.

Xabier E. Barandiaran · Arantza Etxeberria
Editors

Outonomy: Fleshing out the Concept of Autonomy Beyond the Individual

Springer

Editors
Xabier E. Barandiaran
IAS Research Group for Life, Mind
and Society, Department of Philosophy
University of the Basque Country
San Sebastian, Spain

Arantza Etxeberria
IAS Research Group for Life, Mind
and Society, Department of Philosophy
University of the Basque Country
San Sebastian, Spain

ISSN 2211-4548 ISSN 2211-4556 (electronic)
SpringerBriefs in Philosophy
ISBN 978-3-032-05500-2 ISBN 978-3-032-05501-9 (eBook)
https://doi.org/10.1007/978-3-032-05501-9

This Springer imprint is published by the registered company Springer Nature Switzerland AG
The registered company address is: Gewerbestrasse 11, 6330 Cham, Switzerland

Preface

This book brings together a rich and multifaceted exploration of autonomy in interactions, exploring its dimensions within philosophy of biology and origins of life, philosophy of mind and enactivism, philosophy of medicine, technology, and politics. The chapters span theoretical foundations, the emergence and dynamics of life, the embodied self, and the sociotechnical and ecological dimensions of autonomous systems. Through this structure, the book provides a coherent yet diverse perspective on the new concept of *outonomy*, one aiming to expand new insights and critical engagements across disciplines about how autonomy is also related to the environment and to others.

We are especially grateful to the contributing authors, who were actively involved at every stage of the project. In addition to writing their chapters, they served as reviewers for each other's work, ensuring a robust and constructive peer review process. Their careful feedback and intellectual generosity greatly enhanced the coherence and quality of this volume.

We also benefited from the input of several external reviewers, whose independent evaluations provided valuable perspectives and helped sharpen the contributions further. We warmly thank the following external reviewers: JuanBa Bengoetxea, Alejandro Fabregas-Tejeda, Laura Nuño de la Rosa, Miguel Segundo-Ortin, Laura Mójica, Antonio Casado da Rocha, Mirko Prokop, and Ion Arrieta.

This book is the result of sustained collaboration within an ongoing research network, and we would like to express our deep appreciation to the projects and initiatives that supported it. In particular, we are grateful to the Principal Investigators who have guided and nurtured this work over the years. We especially thank Leonardo Bich for his insights and commitment to the project that made this publication possible.

The resulting collection reflects not only the maturity of current discussions around autonomy and related concepts, but also the openness of this research community to novel approaches and applications. We hope this volume will serve as a valuable resource for scholars across disciplines, and that it will stimulate further inquiry and debate in the years to come.

San Sebastian, Spain

Xabier E. Barandiaran
Arantza Etxeberria

Acknowledgements

This book started developing as a result of research project Outonomy, PID2019-104576GB-I00 funded by MCIU/AEI/10.13039/501100011033 and continued under project Outagencies, PID2023-147251NB-I00 funded by MCIU/AEI/10.13039/501100011033 and FEDER/UE. Funding for the OA publication of this book was provided by the *IAS-Research group on Life, Mind and Society* funding IT1668-22 from Basque Government.

Contents

Contributors

Xabier E. Barandiaran IAS Research Centre for Life, Mind and Society, Department of Philosophy, University of the Basque Country (UPV/EHU), Donostia—San Sebastián, Spain

William Bechtel Department of Philosophy, University of California, La Jolla, CA, USA

Leonardo Bich IAS-Research Centre for Life, Mind and Society, Department of Philosophy, University of the Basque Country (UPV/EHU), Leioa, Spain

Violeta Cabello Basque Centre for Climate Change, Bilbao, Spain

Antonio Calleja-López Open University of Catalonia (UOC), Barcelona, Spain

David Cortés-García IAS Research Centre for Life, Mind and Society, Department of Philosophy, University of the Basque Country (UPV/EHU), Donostia-San Sebastián, Spain

Arantza Etxeberria IAS Research Centre for Life, Mind and Society, Department of Philosophy, University of the Basque Country, EHU, Donostia/San Sebastián, Spain

Enara García Department of Psychology, University of Southern Denmark, Odense, Denmark

Michelle L. Maiese Emmanuel College, Boston, MA, USA

María Mancilla Stockholm Resilience Centre, University of Stockholm, Stockholm, Sweden

Alejandra Martínez-Quintero IAS Research Centre for Life, Mind and Society, Department of Philosophy, University of the Basque Country (UPV/EHU), Bilbao, Spain

Laura Menatti IHPST, Institut d'Histoire et de Philosophie des Sciences et des Techniques, Université Paris 1 Panthéon-Sorbonne & CNRS, Paris, France

Alejandro Merlo IAS-Research Center for Life, Mind, and Society, Department of Philosophy, University of the Basque Country (UPV/EHU), Donostia-San Sebastián, Spain

Alberto Monterde-Fuertes IAS-Research Centre for Life, Mind and Society, Department of Philosophy, University of the Basque Country (UPV/EHU), Donostia-San Sebastián, Spain

Alvaro Moreno Donostia International Physics Center (DIPC), Donostia-San Sebastian, Spain

Ainhoa Rodríguez Muguruza IAS Research Centre for Life, Mind and Society, Department of Philosophy, University of the Basque Country (UPV/EHU), Bilbao, Spain

Marta Pérez-Verdugo IAS Research Centre for Life, Mind and Society, Department of Philosophy, University of the Basque Country (UPV/EHU), Donostia—San Sebastián, Spain

Kepa Ruiz-Mirazo IAS-Research Centre for Life, Mind and Society, Department of Philosophy, University of the Basque Country (UPV/EHU), Donostia-San Sebastián, Spain;
Biofisika Institute (CSIC, UPV/EHU), Leioa, Spain

Ben Shirt-Ediss Donostia International Physics Center (DIPC), Donostia-San Sebastian, Spain

Jesús M. Siqueiros Instituto de Investigaciones en Matemáticas Aplicadas y en Sistemas, UAEY-IIMAS, UNAM, Mexico City, México

Jon Umerez IAS Research Centre for Life, Mind and Society, Department of Philosophy, University of the Basque Country (UPV/EHU), Donostia-San Sebastián, Spain

Mikel Urdangarin Department of Philosophy, University of the Basque Country (UPV/EHU), Donostia-San Sebastián, Spain

Louis Virenque Institut d'Histoire Et de Philosophie Des Sciences Et Des Techniques (IHPST), Panthéon-Sorbonne, CNRS, Université Paris, Paris, France

Part I
Theoretical Insights

Chapter 1
Outonomy, the Very Idea

Xabier E. Barandiaran and Arantza Etxeberria

Abstract The concept of autonomy, as the capacity of a system to govern itself according to its own normativity, is central to modernity. Its theoretical significance spans across various scientific and philosophical fields. Traditionally, however, autonomy has been conceived as arising within the boundaries attributed to the individual in an abstract, internalist and self-sufficient manner. During the last decades, this conception has been challenged at different scales and requires a revision that crosses the boundaries of the individual and takes into account the material embeddedness, open interactivity, and deep interdependency of natural and social phenomena. We propose that autonomous systems are better understood as emerging-from and depending-on different scales of interactivity, collectivity, extensionality, environmentality, and through the lenses of integrativity and sustainability. This updated approach we call *Outonomy*.

Keywords Autonomy · Outonomy · Individuality · Interaction · Integration · Sustainability · Collectivity · Environmentality

1.1 The Concept of Autonomy in the Philosophy of Life, Mind, and Society

The concept of autonomy (*autos* = self, *nomos* = norm) originated in classical Greece and was reborn in modernity, coming to occupy a central place in the conceptual foundations of our societies, human self-understanding, and our comprehension of the living. This notion, often conceptualized as self-determination, refers to the capacity of systems to operate according to their own normativity, in a manner that

X. E. Barandiaran (✉) · A. Etxeberria
Department of Philosophy, IAS-Research Centre for Life, Mind, and Society, University of the Basque Country (UPV/EHU), Donostia-San Sebastián, Spain
e-mail: xabier.barandiaran@ehu.eus

A. Etxeberria
e-mail: arantza.etxeberria@ehu.eus

X. E. Barandiaran and A. Etxeberria (eds.), *Outonomy*,
SpringerBriefs in Philosophy, https://doi.org/10.1007/978-3-032-05501-9_1

is not reducible-to nor specified-by its environment or constituent components in isolation. Although it has multiple interpretations across philosophical and scientific disciplines, it has traditionally been associated with the rational, self-sufficient individual, emphasising self-governance and independence in Modern thought.

Nowadays, the concept of autonomy is fundamental to account for the defining character of the living (Moreno and Mossio 2015), its origins (Lauber et al. 2021; Shirt-Ediss et al. 2017), and how organisms maintain themselves as cohesive units through change (Bechtel 2007; Ruiz-Mirazo and Moreno 2012), development (Nuño de la Rosa 2010; Bich and Skillings 2024), and evolution (Cortés-García and Etxeberria Agiriano 2023; Walsh 2015). It also acts as a conceptual anchor for the notions of *function* (Christensen and Bickhard 2002; Mossio et al. 2009), *teleology* (Mossio and Bich 2017) and *agency* (Barandiaran et al. 2009) within biological and cognitive sciences, as well as *normativity* with respect to concepts of health and disease (Etxeberria 2016; García and Barandiaran 2025). In *metaphysics* autonomy is key to categorize actions in contrast to mere events (Buss 2014), to naturalize free-will (Newsome 2009; Walter 2001), or to characterize emergence and downward causation in metabolic and neurobehavioural domains (Ruiz-Mirazo and Moreno 1998; Thompson and Varela 2001).

Following the Kantian legacy in *ethics*, autonomy is an analytical and regulative concept strongly associated with the values of freedom (Mele 1995) and responsibility (MacKenzie and Stoljar 2000). In social and *political theory,* autonomy addresses the notion of political subject (Hardt and Negri 2005), the identity of different social systems (Luhmann and Knodt 1996), the collective dimension of emancipation (Zibechi 2007), or the creative and democratic power of the social (Castoriadis 1991; Escobar 2018).

These myriad approaches rarely share the exact same concept of autonomy. But two points are worth making. First, there is a continuous circulation of sources of inspiration, conceptual pollination, and methodological exchanges among all these fields: from biological autonomy to political autonomy (Castoriadis and Varela 1995; Luhmann and Knodt 1996), from biological to cognitive autonomy (Di Paolo et al. 2017), from cognitive to moral autonomy (Korsgaard 2009), from ecological to technological autonomy (Escobar 2018). Second, albeit at varying degrees, and not without conflict, many contemporary approaches continue to gravitate around a robust cluster of properties inherited from modernity: the self-sufficient, internalist, and abstract nature of the individual of which autonomy is predicated (Metzinger 2015; Pinker 2021). This conception of the individual is in crisis, and the concept(s) of autonomy that cut across these disciplines and scales need to address it.

1.2 Contemporary Challenges to Autonomy

Recent advances in the biological and social sciences have raised some fundamental challenges to the concepts of individuality and identity, particularly through the increasing acknowledgement of the interconnectedness and mutual dependence of natural and social phenomena. As a result, the boundaries of the system become blurry, porous and difficult to identify; pressing the need for a deeper understanding of the biological and social complexity underlying the interactive, relational dimension of autonomy.

The discovery of complex biological associations (symbionts, holobionts, colonies) compels us to reconsider the notion of organism and of individuality (Gilbert et al. 2012, p. 201; Haraway 2016). In cognitive science, the rise of dynamicist, embodied and anti-representationalist approaches (Chemero 2009), along with the expansion of computationalism to include body and environment (Clark and Chalmers 1998) have reshaped the bounds of the cognitive subject, spreading them to living (Lyon et al. 2021) and non-living entities (Hayles 2017).

In the moral dimension, feminist philosophers have rejected (Code 1987), or called for a revision (MacKenzie and Stoljar 2000) of, the individualistic and internalist character of modernity's conception of (masculine) autonomy. They argue that autonomy is "constituted, in large part, by the external, social relations people find themselves in" (Oshana 1998, p. 81), rather than being intrinsic to the rationally self-sufficient individual (Urdangarin and Umerez 2026, this volume). The category of identity in social sciences has also been questioned (Brubaker and Cooper 2000). Similarly, identifying genuine forms of collective autonomous agency remains difficult (Carter et al. 2018), which undermines its application to social ensembles.

Alongside the relative dissolution of the subject,[1] the role of natural and artificial scaffolding in the viability, development, and evolution of autonomous systems has gained recognition (Caporael et al. 2013). The environment is no longer seen as passive but as a complex, dynamic milieu that relationally sustains autonomy (Etxeberria 2026, this volume). Beyond epistemic challenges, contemporary sociotechnical environments jeopardize human and living autonomy. Threats to democratic self-governance and collective agency (Steinhoff 2021; Zuboff 2019) posed by the rising domination of technology and capital which have grown beyond human control (Winner 1978), epitomized by so-called Artificial Intelligence. Similarly, Stengers' "intrusion of Gaia" (2017) highlights how anthropogenic perturbations of the Earth System destabilize the material conditions necessary for the autonomous continuity and reproduction of human societies (Lenton et al. 2020).

* * *

It might be tempting to put into question the very concept of autonomy altogether. But next to these obstacles, we also find new opportunities, theoretical trends and pressing societal and philosophical challenges calling for an updated version of this notion. On the one hand, understanding life, mind, and society beyond the limitations

[1] See, for example, the post-structuralist critique of the subject in the works of Foucault and Derrida, feminist approaches in Butler and Fraser, the moral philosophy of Korsgaard and MacIntyre, biocognitive theories in Canguilhem and Damasio, phenomenological perspectives in Merleau-Ponty and followers, and posthumanist thought in Braidotti. These thinkers collectively challenge traditional notions of the autonomous subject by emphasizing relational, social, and embodied dimensions of agency.

of molecular, genetic, neural, computational or economic reductionism is crucial, especially as personal, collective, and social-ecological challenges demand respect for autonomy in an increasingly hostile context. At the same time, new capacities for addressing those challenges are emerging through the growing availability of digital data, advances in simulation and modelling techniques, and a philosophical shift toward processual, relational, and materialist understandings of life and cognition. Those help transcend traditional dichotomies and develop conceptual resources to support new accounts of autonomy.

In fact, a family of theoretical approaches is well suited to meet the demands of these challenges and opportunities: organicist (Etxeberria and Umerez 2006; Nicholson and Gawne 2015), organizational (Bich 2024; Moreno and Mossio 2015), and enactive (Barandiaran 2017; Stewart et al. 2010; Varela et al. 1991) theories have advanced non-reductive biological, cognitive and social sciences. They share a common tradition in theoretical biology and the naturalizing project it affords. Autonomy is here developed in terms of emergent self-organization, operational closure between interdependent and mutually enabling processes, and the capacity of living systems to regulate themselves both internally and through their environments.

This understanding is linked to the Aristotelian roots of organicism, Spinoza's concept of *conatus*, and Kant's understanding of organisms as self-organized, which underlies German idealism and *Naturphilosophie*. It continued later in a scientific context, as seen in the work of Claude Bernard, Walter B. Cannon, and Kurt Goldstein. Cybernetics and Systems theory paved the way to reintroduce the concepts of *autopoiesis* and autonomy in bio-cognitive sciences (Varela 1979) and their artificial spinoffs: A Life and AI (Boden 1996). From a thermodynamic perspective, Kauffman (2000) characterised autonomy as closure sustaining *work-constraint cycles*. Margulis' symbiogenesis came to fill an important gap within this tradition: that autonomy can be compatible with collaborative relationships and interdependent ontologies. This latter framework is close to what we refer to here as *outonomy*. Aiming to move beyond purely idealized, rationalist views of autonomy, scientific approaches have consistently sought to naturalize the concept by explaining autonomous organization in biological terms—despite Kant's well-known skepticism (Weber and Varela 2002). Together, organismic, organizational, and enactive approaches contribute to a unified vision of autonomy as a dynamic, relational process that is context-dependent and continuously shaped by interactions with the environment. This emerging vision holds promise for advancing also in social, technological and ecological domains.

1.3 Outonomy and Its Properties

Departing from the legacy of modern individualistic views of autonomy, we introduce and elaborate an renewed approach by the term *Outonomy*, after the language game of "out", to break the self-referential appeal of the "autos" (self). In this book, we present outonomy as a further elaboration of the organismic, organizational and enactive conceptions of autonomy in life, mind, and society. This framework highlights six key properties. Four of them involve expanding beyond individual boundaries towards the environment in the enabling and constitution of autonomy.

1. ***Interactivity****: Autonomy results, not only from internal processes, but also from interactions with the environment and other organisms.* The interactions across membrane, skin, skull, or border that differentiate the individual from its environment are not just resource consumption but active forms of constitution (Etxeberria et al. 2021). Breathing and touching are not simply means to extract oxygen and information from the environment to be internally deployed to produce the individual just by itself, but forms of interaction through which the autonomy of the individual is constituted. Moreover, complex sensorimotor systems also emerge as autonomous processes themselves, further enabling an open interactive dimension extending beyond the individual into the world (Di Paolo et al. 2017; see also Virenque 2026, this volume). Even typically internalist notions, like pain or menstrual health, are ultimately open to social and environmental interactions (see Martínez-Quintero and Rodriguez-Muguruza 2025; Monterde Fuertes 2026, this volume). Autonomy, in this sense, includes specific qualitative forms of interaction. We shall elaborate them next.
2. ***Collectivity****: All forms of autonomy are doubly enabled and restricted by interactions with other agents, forming various assemblages, and opening-up to higher-level autonomous organizations.* From the very origins of life (see Ruiz-Mirazo et al. 2026 this volume) the individual's autonomy is interwoven with that of others. This relational character is particularly evident in inter-organismal reproductive processes (Cortés-García 2026, this volume; Etxeberria et al. 2023), as well as for conceiving the moral and political autonomy of the subject as relational and interdependent (see Urdangarin and Umerez 2026 this volume).
3. ***Extensionality****: Autonomy often (if not always) extends beyond the individual into sedimented structures that are the result of recurrent interactions and those of other autonomous systems.* Technologies and institutions are the most familiar forms of extensionality in humans, but many, if not all, forms of life extend their autonomous processes into their environments. From biofilms in bacteria, to stigmergic structures in insect colonies, or nests in birds, autonomous systems build their environments, organizing the inorganic to extend their autonomy beyond themselves. In some cases, these extensions are so wide and complex, that their increasing autonomy or automaticity hinders that of its creators (see Calleja-López et al. 2026, this volume). In all cases such extensions define relations of co-dependence that produce normative conflicts that challenge the autonomy of the individual in various ways, from oppression (Maiese 2026, this volume) to mental health (García 2026, this volume).
4. ***Environmentality***: *Every autonomous system depends on a larger environment that in turn actively sustains its activities, assemblages and extensions, and which, to a large extent, is constructed by those or other interdependent autonomous systems.* The scale of environmentality situates autonomy within its ecological context, emphasizing the interdependence between agents and their ecosystems.

The environment here is not a passive backdrop but an active and long-term participant in the dynamics of autonomy. As an emergent property of social-ecological systems, autonomy challenges anthropocentric models of governance and advocates for more integrated approaches that account for the interconnectedness of life systems (Cabello et al. 2026, this volume).

The other two properties affect the way of conceiving the self (*autos)* and the normative (*nomos*) aspects of autonomy, across the previous four scales of interaction beyond the individual.

5. ***Integration***: *Autonomy manifests through the (degree of) integration of processes that participate in individuation.* The type and degree of this integration serve as good criteria for determining the self or identity of an autonomous system, especially within the messy, fine-grained world of real process interactions. From the outonomy perspective, integration refers to how heterogeneous, interdependent subsystems or components constitute cohesive systems. It involves coordinating the regulation and control of component behaviours such that they contribute to the system´s maintenance (Bich and Bechtel 2026, this volume). It rests to be explored how autonomy could be conceived as a gradual achievement, with integration being a criterion for determining the self or identity of the autonomous system, potentially complementing (or substituting) the concept of closure (whether of constraints, operations, organization, information or otherwise).
6. ***Sustainability***: *The normative matrix that characterizes autonomous systems incorporates the care for the sustainability of what is beyond the individual.* Care is understood as the activity that sustains bodies, communities, and environments through a web of life-supporting practices (Puig de la Bellacasa 2017). Autonomy is here reframed to incorporate the inherent precariousness of systems at relational scales that not only support but also demand and implicate individuals and collectivities across multiple levels. This vulnerability takes diverse forms, as considered throughout this volume, ranging from the prebiotic, cellular and organismal scales to human, social and techno-ecological domains.

Acknowledgements XEB and AE acknowledge IAS-Research group funding IT1668-22 from Basque Government, grants PID2019-104576GB-I00 for project Outonomy and PID2023-147251NB-I00 for Outagencies funded by MCIU/AEI/10.13039/501100011033 and FEDER/UE.

References

Barandiaran XE (2017) Autonomy and enactivism: towards a theory of sensorimotor autonomous agency. Topoi 36(3):409–430. https://doi.org/10.1007/s11245-016-9365-4

Barandiaran XE, Di Paolo E, Rohde M (2009) Defining agency: individuality, normativity, asymmetry, and spatio-temporality in action. Adapt Behav 17(5):367–386. https://doi.org/10.1177/1059712309343819

Bechtel W (2007) Biological mechanisms: organized to maintain autonomy. In: Boogerd FC, Bruggeman FJ, Hofmeyr J-HS, Westerhoff HV (eds) Systems biology: philosophical foundations. Elsevier, pp 269–302

Bich L (2024) Biological organization (1st ed.). Cambridge University Press. https://doi.org/10.1017/9781009393959

Bich L, Bechtel W (2026) Autonomy and heterarchy: organizing control in biological organisms. In Barandiaran XE, Etxeberria A (eds), Outonomy: fleshing out the concept of autonomy beyond the individual. Springer

Bich L, Skillings D (2024) There are no intermediate stages: an organizational view on development. In: Mossio M (ed) Organization in biology, pp 241–262. Springer International Publishing. https://doi.org/10.1007/978-3-031-38968-9_11

Boden MA (1996) The philosophy of artificial life. Oxford University Press

Brubaker R, Cooper F (2000) Beyond "identity." Theory Soc 29(1):1–47. https://doi.org/10.1023/A:1007068714468

Buss S (2014) Personal autonomy. In: Zalta EN (ed) The Stanford encyclopedia of philosophy (Winter 2014). http://plato.stanford.edu/archives/win2014/entries/personal-autonomy/

Cabello V, Merlo A, Mancilla M, Siqueiros J, Barandiaran XE (2026) Autonomy and its limits in social-ecological systems. In Barandiaran XE, Etxeberria A (eds) Outonomy: fleshing out the concept of autonomy beyond the individual, Springer (p. in press)

Calleja-López A, Pérez-Verdugo M, Barandiaran XE (2026) Autonomy and technology: from instrumentalism to technocomplexity. In Barandiaran XE, Etxeberria A (eds) Outonomy: fleshing out autonomy beyond the individual, Springer (p. In press)

Caporael LR, Griesemer JR, Wimsatt WC (2013) Developing scaffolds in evolution, culture, and cognition. MIT Press Ltd

Carter JA, Clark A, Kallestrup J, Pritchard D (eds) (2018) Extended epistemology, 1st edn. Oxford University Press

Castoriadis C (1991) Philosophy, politics, autonomy (trans: Curtis DA). Oxford University Press, Oxford. http://autonomousuniversity.org/sites/default/files/Castoriadis_Power-Politics-Autonomy.pdf

Castoriadis C, Varela FJ (1995) Entretien Cornelius Castoriadis—Francisco Varela. D, 59–82

Chemero A (2009) Radical embodied cognitive science. The MIT Press

Christensen WD, Bickhard MH (2002) The process dynamics of normative function. Monist 85(1):3–29

Clark A, Chalmers D (1998) The extended mind. Analysis 58(1):7

Code L (1987) Second persons. Can J Philos Suppl 13:357–382. https://doi.org/10.1080/00455091.1987.10715942

Cortés-García D (2026) Biological outonomy and reproduction. In: Barandiaran XE, Etxeberria A (eds), Outonomy: fleshing out the concept of autonomy beyond the individual. Springer

Cortés-García D, Etxeberria Agiriano A (2023) Ontologies in evolutionary biology: the role of the organism in the two syntheses. In: Viejo JM, Sanjuán M (eds), Life and mind: new directions in the philosophy of biology and cognitive sciences, pp 185–205. Springer International Publishing. https://doi.org/10.1007/978-3-031-30304-3_9

Di Paolo EA, Buhrmann T, Barandiaran XE (2017) Sensorimotor life: an enactive proposal. Oxford University Press. https://doi.org/10.1093/acprof:oso/9780198786849.001.0001

Escobar A (2018) Designs for the pluriverse: radical interdependence, autonomy, and the making of worlds. Duke University Press

Etxeberria A (2016) Biological organization and pathology: three views on the normativity of medicine. In: Giroux E (ed) Naturalism in the philosophy of health: issues and implications, Springer International Publishing, pp 121–142. https://doi.org/10.1007/978-3-319-29091-1_8

Etxeberria A (2026) Environment(s), autonomy and (a)symmetries. In: Barandiaran XE, Etxeberria A (eds) Outonomy: fleshing out the concept of autonomy beyond the individual. Springer

Etxeberria A, Cortés García D, Torres Aldave M (2023) Organisms, life relations, and evolution: inter-dependencies after Kropotkin's mutual aid. ArtefaCToS. Revista de Estudios Sobre La Ciencia y La Tecnología 12(1):79–204. https://doi.org/10.14201/art2023121179204
Etxeberria A, Damiano L, Ruiz-Mirazo K (2021) Editorial: 'Inter-identities' in life, mind, and society. Front Psychol 12. https://doi.org/10.3389/fpsyg.2021.704772
Etxeberria A, Umerez J (2006) Organismo y organización en la biología teórica: ¿Vuelta al organicismo? Ludus vitalis: revista de filosofía de las ciencias de la vida = journal of philosophy of life sciences = revue de philosophie des sciences de la vie 14(26):3–38
García E (2025) Process and relational ontology in enactive psychiatry. In: Barandiaran XE, Etxeberria A (eds) Outonomy: fleshing out the concept of autonomy beyond the individual. Springer
García E, Barandiaran XE (2026) Varieties of normativity and mental health: an enactive approach. Synthese 205(2):1–29. https://doi.org/10.1007/s11229-024-04854-y
Gilbert SF, Sapp J, Tauber AI (2012) A symbiotic view of life: we have never been individuals. Q Rev Biol 87(4):325–341. https://doi.org/10.1086/668166
Haraway DJ (2016) Staying with the trouble. Duke University Press
Hardt M, Negri A (2005) Multitude: war and democracy in the age of empire. Penguin
Hayles NK (2017) Unthought: the power of the cognitive nonconscious. University of Chicago Press. https://doi.org/10.7208/chicago/9780226447919.001.0001
Kauffman SA (2000) Investigations. Oxford University Press
Korsgaard CM (2009) Self-constitution: agency, identity, and integrity. Oxford University Press
Lauber N, Flamm C, Ruiz-Mirazo K (2021) "Minimal metabolism": a key concept to investigate the origins and nature of biological systems. BioEssays News Rev Mol Cell Dev Biol 43(10):e2100103. https://doi.org/10.1002/bies.202100103
Lenton TM, Dutreuil S, Latour B (2020) Life on earth is hard to spot. Anthrop Rev 7(3):248–272. https://doi.org/10.1177/2053019620918939
Luhmann N, Knodt EM (1996) Social systems (trans: Baecker JB Jr D, 1st edn). Stanford University Press
Lyon P, Keijzer F, Arendt D, Levin M (2021) Reframing cognition: getting down to biological basics. Philos Trans Royal Soc B Biol Sci 376(1820):20190750. https://doi.org/10.1098/rstb.2019.0750
MacKenzie C, Stoljar N (eds) (2000) Relational autonomy: feminist perspectives on autonomy, agency, and the social self. Oxford University Press
Maiese M (2026) Mindshaping and adaptive preferences. In: Barandiaran XE, Etxeberria A (eds) Outonomy: fleshing out the concept of autonomy beyond the individual, Springer (p. in press)
Martínez-Quintero A, Rodriguez-Muguruza A (2025) Autonomy and alienation in menstrual health. In: Barandiaran XE, Etxeberria A (eds) Outonomy: fleshing out the concept of autonomy beyond the individual. Springer
Mele AR (1995) Autonomous agents: from self-control to autonomy. Oxford University Press. http://gen.lib.rus.ec/book/index.php?md5=af29b834ad96c44388b21df15684313c
Metzinger T (2015) M-Autonomy. J Conscious Stud 22(11–12):270–302
Monterde Fuertes A (2026) Pain beyond nociception: a biological autonomy perspective. In Barandiaran XE, Etxeberria A (eds) Outonomy: fleshing out the concept of autonomy beyond the individual. Springer
Moreno A, Mossio M (2015) Biological autonomy: a philosophical and theoretical enquiry. Springer
Mossio M, Bich L (2017) What makes biological organisation teleological? Synthese 194(4):1089–1114. https://doi.org/10.1007/s11229-014-0594-z
Mossio M, Saborido C, Moreno A (2009) An organizational account of biological functions. Br J Philos Sci 60(4):813–841. https://doi.org/10.1093/bjps/axp036
Newsome W (2009) Human freedom and "emergence." In Murphy N, Ellis GFR, O'Connor T (eds) Downward causation and the neurobiology of free will (1st edn). Springer, pp 52–62

Nicholson DJ, Gawne R (2015) Neither logical empiricism nor vitalism, but organicism: what the philosophy of biology was. Hist Philos Life Sci 37(4):345–381. https://doi.org/10.1007/s40656-015-0085-7

Nuño de la Rosa L (2010) Becoming organisms: the organisation of development and the development of organisation. Hist Philos Life Sci 32(2–3):289–315

Oshana MAL (1998) Personal autonomy and society. J Soc Philos 29(1):81–102. https://doi.org/10.1111/j.1467-9833.1998.tb00098.x

Pinker S (2021) Rationality: what it is, why it seems scarce, why it matters. Viking

Puig de la Bellacasa M (2017) Matters of care: speculative ethics in more than human worlds (3rd edn). University of Minnesota Press

Ruiz-Mirazo K, Moreno A (1998) Autonomy and emergence: how systems become agents through the generation of functional constraints. Acta Polytech Scand Ma91:273–282

Ruiz-Mirazo K, Moreno A (2012) Autonomy in evolution: from minimal to complex life. Synthese 185(1):21–52. https://doi.org/10.1007/s11229-011-9874-z

Ruiz-Mirazo K, Moreno Á, Shirt-Ediss B (2026) Outonomy at the origins of life. In Barandiaran XE, Etxeberria A (eds) Outonomy: fleshing out the concept of autonomy beyond the individual. Springer

Shirt-Ediss B, Murillo-Sánchez S, Ruiz-Mirazo K (2017) Framing major prebiotic transitions as stages of protocell development: three challenges for origins-of-life research. Beilstein J Org Chem 13(1):1388–1395. https://doi.org/10.3762/bjoc.13.135

Steinhoff J (2021) Automation and autonomy: labour, capital and machines in the artificial intelligence industry. Springer International Publishing. https://doi.org/10.1007/978-3-030-71689-9

Stengers I (2017) Autonomy and the intrusion of Gaia. South Atlantic Q 116(2):381–400. https://doi.org/10.1215/00382876-3829467

Stewart JR, Gapenne O, Di Paolo EA (eds) (2010) Enaction: toward a new paradigm for cognitive science. MIT Press

Thompson E, Varela FJ (2001) Radical embodiment: neural dynamics and consciousness. Trends Cogn Sci 5(10):418–425. https://doi.org/10.1016/S1364-6613(00)01750-2

Urdangarin M, Umerez J (2026) Rethinking the autonomy of subjects-in-common. In: Barandiaran XE, Etxeberria A (eds) Outonomy: fleshing out the concept of autonomy beyond the individual. Springer

Varela FJ (1979) Principles of biological autonomy. North Holland http://openlibrary.org/b/OL4416494M/Principles_of_biological_autonomy

Varela FJ, Thompson E, Rosch E (1991) The embodied mind: cognitive science and human experience. MIT Press

Virenque L (2026) Enactivism and intrinsic purposiveness. In: Barandiaran XE, Etxeberria A (eds) Outonomy: fleshing out the concept of autonomy beyond the individual. Springer

Walsh DM (2015) Organisms, agency, and evolution (1st edn). Cambridge University Press. https://doi.org/10.1017/CBO9781316402719

Walter H (2001) Neurophilosophy of free will: from libertarian illusions to a concept of natural autonomy (trans: Klohr C). A Bradford Book

Weber A, Varela FJ (2002) Life after Kant: natural purposes and the autopoietic foundations of biological individuality. Phenomenol Cogn Sci 1(2):97–125

Winner L (1978) Autonomous technology: technics-out-of-control as a theme in political thought. MIT Press

Zibechi R (2007) Autonomías y emancipaciones. América Latina en movimiento. Fondo Editorial de la Facultad de Ciencias Sociales, Unidad de Post Grado, UNMSM

Zuboff S (2019) Surveillance capitalism and the challenge of collective action. New Labor Forum 28(1):10–29. https://doi.org/10.1177/1095796018819461

Chapter 2
Intrinsic Purposiveness and Autonomy in Interaction

Louis Virenque

Abstract Autonomy Theory characterizes agency as a subset of functions of an autonomous entity that controls the interactions of the living being with its environment so as to maintain its organization, considered as its intrinsic purpose. Yet, this understanding of agency faces a major philosophical and theoretical problem: there seems to be many purposive interactive behaviors that do not directly contribute to survival, or even run contrary to it, such as playing or smoking a cigarette. The challenge, therefore, is to elucidate these more complex interactive capacities within the framework of the Autonomy Theory. In this chapter, I explore three key hypotheses to address this challenge: first, the idea that such behaviors might respond to underlying biological "needs"; second, the idea that, as emphasized by the enactivist perspective, these behaviors are embedded in a sensorimotor level of organization; and third the idea that these behaviors relate to a social level of closure.

Keywords Autonomy · Intrinsic purposiveness · Agency · Self-determination

2.1 Introduction

In recent years, several scholars have contributed to reviving the concept of *autonomy*, initially introduced by Francisco Varela (1979) to describe the distinctive organization of living systems (Barandiaran and Moreno 2008; Moreno and Etxeberria 2005; Ruiz-Mirazo and Moreno 2004). Autonomy means "self-law" and designates, when applied to the Life Sciences, the particular capability of living systems to self-determine, by realizing a network of reciprocal productive relations among their constituents (the so-called *autopoiesis*). Some proponents of Autonomy Theory (hereafter AT) have refined the original concept by emphasizing that autonomy encapsulates three fundamental concepts, which are: organizational *closure* of constraints,

L. Virenque (✉)
Institut d'Histoire Et de Philosophie Des Sciences Et Des Techniques (IHPST), Panthéon-Sorbonne, CNRS, Université Paris, Paris, France
e-mail: Louis.Virenque@etu.univ-paris1.fr

X. E. Barandiaran and A. Etxeberria (eds.), *Outonomy*,
SpringerBriefs in Philosophy, https://doi.org/10.1007/978-3-032-05501-9_2

agency, and *regulation* (see Moreno and Mossio 2015, for a synthesis). In this framework, on which I rely here, a living autonomous system is a self-sustaining network of constraints that controls the thermodynamic flow and, thereby, determines by itself its metabolic organization.[1] Philosophically, living autonomous systems can be said to realize intrinsic purposiveness, insofar as the effects of their activity contribute to determining and maintaining their own conditions of existence (Mossio and Bich 2017).

As we shall see, however, this conception of autonomy and purposiveness leads to a dilemma: either any behavior which is deemed purposive can be shown to contribute to self-determination (and then be functional); or non-functional behaviors (e.g., playing or smoking) should not be considered purposive (which would be strongly counter-intuitive). This philosophical dilemma highlights a theoretical problem for AT, when it comes to account for a whole range of behaviors, which do not appear to contribute to the autonomy of the living system.

2.2 Non-Functional Behaviors or Fulfillment of Needs?

A living organism is a dissipative system. While maintaining this constant flow, the system retains its own individuality. A cell, for example, conserves its identity through operations such as the sodium–potassium pump, which actively transports sodium ions out and potassium ions into its membrane, maintaining electrochemical gradients. Despite the perpetual turnover of ions and other components, the cell maintains its identity by performing work (Kauffman 2000). The concept of "*closure of constraints*" captures this idea of self-individuation through self-determination.

A constraint is an entity that channels or limits the activity of other entities, such as the chemical bond for atoms, an inclined plane for a ball, the skeleton for an organism, etc. A closure of constraints characterizes the relationship of mutual determination of a network of constraints, each channeling physico-chemical processes to perform a functional work (see Montévil and Mossio 2015 for a detailed discussion). Some advocates of AT claim that closure of constraints achieves intrinsic normativity and purposiveness. Indeed, the effects of the activities of constraints achieve one overarching goal: the determination of the system's conditions of existence, that are set (at least in part) by the system itself (Barandiaran and Moreno 2008; Mossio and Bich 2017). This causal regime (i.e., intrinsically purposive organization) also provides a natural basis for functional explanations. In fact, in AT, each constraint performs a specific function insofar as it both depends on and enables the activity of other constraints (Mossio et al. 2009; Moreno and Mossio 2015). However, as we shall see, this theoretical framework can face challenges, particularly in relation to agency.

[1] By 'metabolic organization' I mean the set of functions that maintains an agent as a biological individual far from thermodynamic equilibrium.

According to one version of AT that I follow here,[2] agency is defined in its *minimal* meaning as a subset of interactive functions, i.e. constraints that are functionally exerted on the system's environment. In fact, two nested kinds of functions are part of the closure: constitutive and interactive ones. While the effects of the former take place inside the closure, the effects of the latter operate outside the whole system, on its environment. As a subset of interactive functions (or interactive constraints), agency must be directed toward the self-determination of the system (Moreno and Mossio 2015). For example, behaviors like sneezing or coughing are constitutive but not interactive (agential) functions because, although they modify the environment, these modifications do not promote the continued existence of the system (Arnellos and Moreno 2015).

In contrast, the flagellar rotations of a bacterium that propels itself toward a sugar gradient (chemotaxis) modify the relation of the whole system with its environment. This shift in the interaction with the environment is functional since it contributes to the determination of the system's existence (Moreno 2018). Moreover, bacterial chemotaxis, as any realization of agency in living beings, is a case of *adaptive*[3] behavior. The bacterium is an adaptive agent because it not only performs actions but also adapts such actions to new environmental conditions, i.e., by *regulating* its own flagellar movement while approaching a nutrient source. This is why, in AT, adaptive agency entails *regulation.*

According to AT, regulation consists in the modulation of the system's functions (or organization) by a dedicated subsystem (constituted by a set of second-order functions) in response to environmental disturbances (see Barandiaran and Moreno 2008; Bich et al. 2015; Bich and Moreno 2016). The regulatory activity of second-order functions applies both to the constitutive functions of metabolism and to its interactive functions. Thus, for example, lac operon and chemotaxis are two types of regulation, one acting within the system, the other on its boundaries (see Barandiaran 2008; Bich et al. 2015). According to AT, all organisms are adaptive agents in that they continuously adapt to their environment. If they are adapting, it means that they must have some kind of meaningful relation with what they are adapting to. Consequently, for AT, all adaptive agents "make sense" of their environment in order to survive (Weber and Varela 2001).

The challenge for this conception of agency emerges when one attempts to account for behaviors that do not seem *prima facie* oriented toward metabolic organization but are commonly (and intuitively) deemed to be purposive and therefore agential—such as playing, exploring, smoking or even committing suicide. Now, if one understands intrinsic purposiveness in AT's terms, then a philosophical and theoretical dilemma emerges: either any purposive behavior can be shown to be functional according to AT's definition, or one must conclude that non-functional behaviors

[2] I rely here on Moreno and Mossio (2015), which distinguishes minimal agency from adaptive agency. For partly different but largely converging definitions of agency within AT, see Barandiaran and Moreno (2008) and Barandiaran et al. (2009).

[3] I rely here on Di Paolo (2005)´s work on adaptivity, characterized as the monitoring and regulation of the tendencies of the system with respect to its boundaries of viability (I thank a reviewer for this compact formulation).

should not be considered purposive. Either way, it's a difficult position to argue for. Behind the philosophical issue lies a theoretical problem: regardless of the term employed, how could AT account for non-(obviously) functional behaviors such as smoking or playing, which are important aspects of an organism's interactions with its environment?

The first possible answer to this dilemma requires taking a step back. Indeed, the dilemma presupposes that behaviors such as playing or smoking are non-functional for the individual that produces them. However, it is possible that our understanding is incomplete, insofar as these behaviors might be fulfilling underlying *needs* of the organism and, therefore, be functional. For example, smoking might fulfil some physiological needs by reducing anxiety and enhancing the feeling of concentration, and therefore perform a function, at least at a relatively short time scale and at limited doses. Similarly, in ethology, playing is not defined as being *fully* functional, that is, as contributing to the immediate survival of the system (Burghardt 2005, p. 71). Therefore, one might consider that playing satisfies a comparable need (e.g., releasing energy or having fun), whose fulfillment also contributes to the metabolic organization. Committing suicide is obviously a more complex challenge, as it does not contribute neither to the short-term nor long-term determination. Yet, let us conjecture that even suicide might possibly respond to a certain biological need (e.g., one might feel a 'metabolic need' to eliminate despair, torment, etc.).

Reconceptualizing apparent non-functional behaviors as behaviors fulfilling individual needs, while providing an original answer to the dilemma, would inevitably face several open questions. What kind of objects are 'needs' in AT? What is their relationship to the system's organization if they can, in some cases, threaten or even undermine it? Relatedly, how exactly would the fulfilment of needs be interpreted as a function? Given that AT currently lacks a workable concept of 'need', I will explore in the next section alternative answers, which presuppose that the behaviors in question are *non*-functional with regards to the metabolic organization that produces them.

2.3 Sensorimotor Relations?

In 2017, enactivist theorists Di Paolo, Buhrmann, and Barandiaran (DPBB hereafter) introduced the notion of sensorimotor closure as enabling new relationships between the organism and its environment (Di Paolo et al. 2017). Their approach offers a potential way for AT to address the above dilemma. For DPBB, those behaviors, which are more complex than those related to the system's metabolic organization, pertain to a "sensorimotor organization" grounded in the concept of *habit* (Barandiaran and Di Paolo 2014).

For DPBB, habits are primarily "self-sustaining precarious sensorimotor schemes," (Di Paolo et al. 2017, p. 144), i.e., behaviors that require repetition to be maintained. However, habits are never "enacted" alone, but always as part of a larger whole that the authors call "activities," which are "bundles of habits" (p. 147). For

DPBB, this interconnectivity between sensorimotor patterns (i.e., between habits) achieves a distinct "layer" of closure, i.e., of self-individuation.

In fact, in a sensorimotor closure, each sensorimotor scheme depends on at least one support structure within the network (p. 151). A support structure is a set of variables that are necessarily associated with an event. For instance, as I understand it, in a sensorimotor scheme such as "bottle feeding," suckling, swallowing and breathing are processes that need a support structure in the body (e.g., swallow support, suckle support, breathe support) and in the environment (e.g., milk, bottle, air). Air, milk, swallowing, and sucking are all necessary variables in the bottle-feeding habit. However, this is a single sensorimotor scheme (or habit). When realizing a sensorimotor closure, several schemes and support structures are interdependent (p. 151). For example, the "running" scheme depends on at least one support structure that also supports "bottle-feeding" (e.g., breathing support), just as "bottle-feeding" also depends on at least one support structure of another scheme, such as eating (i.e., swallowing support). Sensorimotor schemes thus depend on each other in their realization (e.g., in the order of an action), and on the support structures that sustain them within a network that is neither in the environment nor in the agent (pp. 151 and 157). Thus, for DPBB sensorimotor closure has no physical boundary (p. 152). The network of sensorimotor schemes then achieves an asymmetrical coupling with the environment understood as everything that influences the enabling relationship between habits; (p. 153). According to the authors, the network is even adaptive, i.e., it can modulate its relationship with its environment to ensure the viability of a scheme or a succession of schemes (e.g., in the succession of schemas for lighting a cigarette, protect the flame from the wind with your hand (pp. 156–157). Finally, sensorimotor schemes are underdetermined by metabolic normativity. They can respond to it and contribute to it, but also have their own norms of viability. The success or failure of a pattern affects the entire network, including the supporting structures that sustain it, by enabling (or disabling) the continuation of an activity (pp. 157–156).

In brief, according to DPBB, just as metabolic/physiological closure achieves agency through self-individuation, asymmetric coupling, and normativity, sensorimotor closure exhibits *sensorimotor agency*, which may help resolve the dilemma regarding explanations for seemingly non-functional behaviors. In fact, it could be argued that behaviors such as playing or smoking are related to the intrinsic purposiveness and normativity *of the sensorimotor organization*, and not to the metabolic organization. Accordingly, playing or smoking would be functions of the sensorimotor closure.

This hypothesis implies at least one intriguing consequence. As DPBB suggests (p. 147), a habit within sensorimotor closure is analogous to an autocatalytic reaction within metabolic closure: just as the latter sustains the metabolic organization, the former appears to uphold sensorimotor closure. If this is the case, then it follows that the function of the smoking scheme (beyond any extrinsic purpose it may have) consists in maintaining the sensorimotor closure to which it is subject. In turn, this means that the fundamental purpose of performing habits is… the preservation of the very network of habits. Habits then appear not only as underdetermined, but (and crucially) as functionally separated from (although dynamically coupled to) metabolic closure. The theoretical move that consists in distinguishing these two closures, each with its own intrinsic purposiveness, may be open to criticism, precisely because it leads to the conclusion that a habit situated in a sensorimotor network would aim at its own maintenance, or the maintenance of habits situated in the same network (e.g., running aimed at running or maintaining other linked schemes such as squatting or jumping). However, it may be argued that this is too restrictive, as behaviors generally seem to be directed towards something extrinsic to themselves: I run to get away from someone, to have fun, to train for a race, etc..... If so, habits should be understood as contributing to another purpose (and then be subject to another closure), be it metabolic, social or of a different kind.[4] In any event, this hypothesis does indicate a way to address the dilemma by positing the existence of different levels of closure. As a matter of fact, such a strategy can be further expanded to consider broader levels of autonomy, beyond sensorimotor closure.

2.4 Social Relations?

The hypothesis that autonomy can emerge at levels beyond the metabolic one exists since the foundational work of Maturana and Varela, who already postulated forms of autonomy at the immune, nervous, and even social level (Maturana and Varela 1980). The challenge, however, consists of specifying the conditions at which the central tenets of AT can be legitimately applied to different levels of description.

Consider again the example of smoking. As Jarvis (2004) or Nichter et al. (2007) suggest, various aspects of addiction, such as its social dimensions, help explain why people smoke. From this perspective, an alternative way to address the intrinsic purposiveness's dilemma is to propose that behaviors like playing or smoking are indeed purposive, because they perform a function within a higher, collective organization, distinct from their own metabolic and sensorimotor closures.

In *Linguistic Bodies* (2018), Di Paolo, Cuffari, and De Jaegher advance a theory of social interactions that can account for norms extending beyond those imposed by the metabolic (and sensorimotor) organization. According to the authors, bodies are not isolated or static entities, but are rather dynamic processes that interact with both their environment and each other (p. 7). These relationships may, on occasion, give rise to social interactions. Such *social interactions* can result in the formation of a new dynamic organization that possesses its own autonomy without threatening the autonomy of the individuals involved. A *social interaction* is defined as the "regulated coupling between at least two autonomous agents where the regulation is aimed at aspects of the coupling itself" (De Jaegher and Di Paolo 2007, p. 493). The encounter of two agents, as sense-makers, modifies their respective sense-making processes and generates an autonomous relational domain that has its own norms, different from

[4] Mojica (2021) raises a similar issue and offers a solution by developing an account of 'external normativity' emerging from the interaction of individuals.

individuals' ones. The modification of the social domain by the interacting agents gives rise to *social agency*. An illustrative example of social agency is a conversation. In a conversation both regulate their respective relations to the autonomous domain of the interaction in order to maintain the conversation. To illustrate this further, if I wish to continue a conversation, at a social gathering, with someone who smokes, the social interaction with that person may prompt me to accompany them outside for a cigarette, which would explain my behavior—which is detrimental to my health.

The hypothesis that the interaction between two individuals realizes a distinct autonomous domain viz. a different level of normativity (see for instance Mojica 2021) is debatable, especially if one considers, as I do, that this requires showing that such interaction realizes a distinct level of constraints closure. In their analysis, however, Di Paolo et al. (2018) do not limit themselves to social interactions between a few individuals. While these individuals may engage in specific interactions, they can also be embedded in larger social systems that influence them to reproduce certain behaviors (Di Paolo et al. 2018, p. 84, see also Maiese 2025, this issue). Accordingly, smoking might, in fact, be functional for the agent embedded in this larger social system, insofar as such behavior could confer benefits, such as the fact of belonging to a specific social group, facilitating encounters, making friends, etc.

From this perspective, complex behaviors of this kind would occur in relation to a higher-level closure, within which they would serve a "social function" and would be only indirectly related to the survival of the individual agent (as a part of the larger system). The closure of this broader social organization could even possibly generate new "needs" for individual agents (e.g., the "need" to feel different, rebellious, mysterious, and so on) and provide a more sophisticated explanation for the act of smoking. Although there exists a literature on the organization of social systems that converge with AT (see for instance Luhmann 1995) it remains conjectural whether social organizations can adequately be understood in terms of closure of constraints and, if so, whether this concept of closure would need to be adapted when applied to such an object.

The idea of *outonomy* explored in this book (see Barandiaran and Etxeberria 2026, this volume) might be specifically interpreted as referring to this particular mode of agency, by which an individual autonomous agent performs functional behaviors that contribute to the self-determination (and therefore to the intrinsic purposiveness) of an encompassing social organization to which it belongs. In other words, outonomy would refer to the *interplay* between different levels of autonomy, such that individual agents contribute to an encompassing autonomous system which is, in a sense, external to them, "out there".

2.5 Conclusion

In this brief discussion, my goal was to explore how the concept of agency elaborated by AT could account for more complex interactions between living beings and their environment. As mentioned, such behaviors raise a problem insofar as, while being commonly (and intuitively) understood as instances of purposive agency, they do not seem to fulfil AT's requirements. I have outlined the several ways in which AT can solve the dilemma:

- Firstly, through a reinterpretation of seemingly non-functional behaviors as responding to a "need" of an organism;
- Secondly, through DPBB's hypothesis of sensorimotor closure, which involves a distinct individual dimension of purposiveness and therefore of functionality;
- Finally, through the DPCDJ's hypothesis of a social level of organizational closure, which would ground distinct social "needs" and functions.

Each of these hypotheses is as intriguing as it is ambitious. In fact, each of them addresses at least one fundamental aspect of AT, either by reexamining the notion of organizational function or by reassessing the limits of organizational closure. Consequently, behaviors that do not appear to be directly linked to the self-determination of an individual autonomous biological agent are open to different explanations consistent with AT or, more likely, to a combination of them.

Acknowledgements Thanks to Matteo Mossio, Xabier Barandiaran, Arantza Etxeberria, Laura Mojica, and Miguel Segundo Ortin, for insightful comments and criticisms on earlier versions.

References

Arnellos A, Moreno A (2015) Multicellular agency: an organizational view. Biol Philos 30(3):333–357. https://doi.org/10.1007/s10539-015-9484-0

Barandiaran X (2008) Mental Life. A naturalized approach to the autonomy of cognitive agents. PhD Thesis at the University of the Basque Country, Spain. http://barandiaran.net/phdthesis/

Barandiaran XE, Etxeberria A (2026) Outonomy, the very idea. In: Barandiaran XE, Etxeberria A (eds) Outonomy: fleshing out the concept of autonomy beyond the individual, Springer (in press)

Barandiaran X, Moreno A (2008) Adaptivity: from metabolism to behavior. Adapt Behav 16(5):325–344. https://doi.org/10.1177/1059712308093868

Barandiaran XE, Di Paolo E, Rohde M (2009) Defining agency: individuality, normativity, asymmetry, and spatio-temporality in action. Adapt Behav 17(5):367–386. https://doi.org/10.1177/1059712309343819

Barandiaran XE, Di Paolo EA (2014) A genealogical map of the concept of habit. Front Hum Neurosci 8:522

Bich L, Moreno A, (2016) The role of regulation in the origin and synthetic modelling of minimal cognition. BioSystems 148: 12–21. https://doi.org/10.1016/j.biosystems.2015.08.002

Bich L, Mossio M, Ruiz-Mirazo K, Moreno A (2015) Biological regulation: controlling the system from within. Biol Philos 31(2):237–265. https://doi.org/10.1007/s10539-015-9497-8

Burghardt GM (2005) Creativity, play and the pace of evolution. In: Kaufman AB, Kaufman JC (eds) Animal creativity and innovation. Elsevier

De Jaegher H, Di Paolo EA (2007) Participatory sense-making: an enactive approach to social cognition. Phenomenol Cogn Sci 6:485–507. https://doi.org/10.1007/s11097-007-9076-9

Di Paolo EA (2005) Autopoiesis, adaptivity, teleology, agency. Phenomenol Cogn Sci 4(4):429–452. https://doi.org/10.1007/s11097-005-9002-y

Di Paolo E, Buhrmann T, Barandiaran X (2017) Sensorimotor life: an enactive proposal (1st edn). Oxford University Press
Di Paolo EA, Cuffari EC, De Jaegher H (2018) Linguistic bodies: the continuity between life and language. MIT Press
Jarvis MJ (2004) Why people smoke. BMJ (Clinical Research Ed.) 328(7434):277–279. https://doi.org/10.1136/bmj.328.7434.277
Kauffman S (2000) Investigations. Oxford University Press, Oxford
Luhmann N (1995) Social systems. Stanford University Press
Maiese M (2025) Mindshaping and adaptive preferences. In: Barandiaran, XE, Etxeberria, A. (eds), Outonomy: fleshing out the concept of autonomy beyond the individual, Springer (p. in press)
Maturana H, Varela FJ (1980). Autopoiesis and cognition: the realization of the living. Dordrecht, The Netherlands, D. Reidel
Mojica L (2021) The enactive naturalization of normativity: from self-maintenance to situated interactions. Hist Philos Life Sci 43(4):127. https://doi.org/10.1007/s40656-021-00479-3
Montévil M, Mossio M (2015) Biological organisation as closure of constraints. J Theor Biol 372:179–191. https://doi.org/10.1016/j.jtbi.2015.02.029
Moreno A (2018) On minimal autonomous agency: natural and artificial. Complex Syst 27(3):289–313. https://doi.org/10.25088/ComplexSystems.27.3.289
Moreno A, Etxeberria A (2005) Agency in natural and artificial systems. Artif Life 11(1–2):161–176. https://doi.org/10.1162/1064546053278919
Moreno A, Mossio M (2015). Biological autonomy: a philosophical and theoretical enquiry (Vol. 12). Springer Netherlands. https://doi.org/10.1007/978-94-017-9837-2
Mossio M, Bich L (2017) What makes biological organisation teleological? Synthese 194(4):1089–1114. https://doi.org/10.1007/s11229-014-0594-z
Mossio M, Saborido C, Moreno A (2009) An organizational account of biological functions. Br J Philos Sci 60(4):813–841. https://doi.org/10.1093/bjps/axp036
Nichter M, Nichter M, Carkoglu A, Tobacco Etiology Research Network (2007) Reconsidering stress and smoking: a qualitative study among college students. Tobacco Control 16(3):211–214. https://doi.org/10.1136/tc.2007.019869
Ruiz-Mirazo K, Moreno A (2004) Basic autonomy as a fundamental step in the synthesis of life. Artificial Life 10:235–259. https://doi.org/10.1162/1064546041255584
Varela FJ (1979) Principles of biological autonomy. North Holland, New York
Weber A, Varela FJ (2001) Life after Kant: Natural purposes and the autopoietic foundations of biological individuality. Phenomenol Cogn Sci 1:97–125. https://doi.org/10.1023/a:1020368120174

Chapter 3
Autonomy and Heterarchy: Organizing Control in Biological Organisms

Leonardo Bich and William Bechtel

Abstract In order to maintain themselves as systems far from equilibrium with their environment, organisms must control the operation of numerous production mechanisms. Control involves mechanisms that make or are responsive to measurements of conditions within or in the environment of the organism and that operate on flexible constraints in other mechanisms to adjust their operation. A frequent assumption of humans is that control mechanisms are organized in a hierarchical pyramid. However, control in biological organisms commonly deviates from several principles of hierarchical organization and is better characterized as organized heterarchically. To provide a positive understanding of autonomy, this paper advances several features of its heterarchical organization and illustrates them using control of glucose regulation in mammals as an exemplar.

Keywords Autonomy · Control · Organization · Hierarchy · Heterarchy

3.1 Introduction

Organisms consist of components that tend to degrade, yet they maintain themselves far from equilibrium with their environment through a host of mutually dependent activities. These activities include procuring and taking in resources (matter and energy), processing them, and using them to select and run their internal processes in ways that are appropriate to circumstances, to build and repair themselves, and to generate, modulate and sustain behaviors that allow them to move in and interact with their environment. They do not operate under a fixed set of conditions but exhibit diverse activities so as to cope with continuously changing conditions not only in their environment but also within themselves.

L. Bich (✉)
IAS-Research, Department of Philosophy, University of the Basque Country (UPV/EHU), Leioa, Spain
e-mail: leonardo.bich@ehu.eus

W. Bechtel
Department of Philosophy, University of California, La Jolla, CA, USA

X. E. Barandiaran and A. Etxeberria (eds.), *Outonomy*,
SpringerBriefs in Philosophy, https://doi.org/10.1007/978-3-032-05501-9_3

Since organisms do these things for themselves, they are properly characterized as autonomous (Moreno and Mossio 2015). As we develop in the next section, biological autonomy involves not just organisms producing themselves but controlling themselves: they must determine when and how to carry out the various activities that enable them to maintain themselves. Our concern, to which we turn in sect. 3, is how control processes are organized. Although humans have tended to think in terms of hierarchical pyramids or centralized systems, we argue that biological organisms violate several of the characteristic features of such pyramids and instead are organized heterarchically. *Heterarchy* is often characterized as involving deviation from hierarchy, but in sect. 4 we offer some positive characteristics of heterarchy and discuss how biological organisms have come to be organized in heterarchical ways that are adequate to maintaining themselves.

3.2 Biological Autonomy: Self-Production and Self-Control

In their pioneering contributions to understanding biological organisms as autonomous, Varela et al. (1974) emphasized that organisms are autopoietic—they make all of their own components. To do this, they deploy a host of production mechanisms that enable them to transform materials that they take into themselves and to act in the environment around them, both moving themselves and moving (or otherwise changing) other entities in their environment (see also Ruiz-Mirazo et al. and Virenque, this volume). These are crucial to the ability of organisms to maintain themselves. But these mechanisms also need to be controlled if they are to operate when and in the manner needed to maintain the organism (Bich et al. 2016). Production mechanisms do not operate whenever their substrates and energy are available. Organisms *control* (activate, inhibit, modulate) their production mechanisms and more generally modify themselves and what they (and their parts) do based on their internal physiological state and environmental conditions. For example, consider the activity of metabolizing glucose to pyruvic acid (or alcohol), a process known as glycolysis. It generates ATP, which provides energy for most biological activities. If glycolysis occurred whenever glucose was available and continued until all glucose was consumed, it would waste free energy when it is not needed and deprive the organism of it when it is needed. Accordingly, glycolysis is controlled so as to occur when it is needed.

As we understand control, it involves control mechanisms operating on production mechanisms (or other control mechanisms), changing how they operate. Both production and control mechanisms produce activities by constraining flows of free energy (Winning and Bechtel 2018). Some of the constraints that enable them to perform their activities are (relatively) fixed during the operation of the mechanism, but others are flexible. It is by acting on flexible constraints that control mechanisms can change how other mechanisms operate. In the case of glycolysis, the conformation of enzymes is subject to modification so as either to allow glycolysis to proceed or to divert glucose to another reaction that transforms it into a storage molecule, glycogen, from which it can again be generated when it is needed.

Control involves not just acting on another mechanism, but doing so in response to information about circumstances relevant to whether the activity of the mechanism is required. As discussed by Pattee (1971), such information is acquired by making measurements. This results in changing constraints within the control mechanism, as illustrated by a mechanical thermostat—when ambient temperature changes, constraints are changed (e.g., bimetallic strips straighten or bend) so as to complete (or break) an electric circuit, turning a furnace on (or off). Measurement processes can often be complex and carried out at a distance from the controlled mechanism. When the site of measurement is distant from the mechanism being controlled, a signal must be transmitted between them. Biology is replete with measurement and signalling devices. In the case of glycolysis, the enzyme that initiates the catabolism of glucose can also bind the energy transfer molecule, ATP, when it is plentiful, changing its conformation so that it no longer catabolizes glucose.

Both production and control mechanisms typically contain multiple constraints that together determine their activities. Accordingly, they can be acted on by multiple other control mechanisms or make multiple measurements. As a result, they can procure information about different conditions internal to the organism or in the world external to it, which they then integrate in producing their activity. How they integrate information and what action they perform is determined by how the mechanism itself is organized and how it interacts with other mechanisms in the organism (see Monterde, this volume, for an example). These are not mysterious processes. They are processes performed by a mechanism produced by the organism in the same way it produces other mechanisms—by taking materials, transforming them, and organizing the products in a particular way so that energy is directed through them. Control mechanisms just operate differently by modifying constraints in other mechanisms rather than making products or generating movement.

Control is performed by mechanisms that, together with production mechanisms, constitute the organism. Thus, when control is exercised, it is being exercised by and for the organism. Autonomous organisms (and any other autonomous systems) not only build themselves but control their own operation.

3.3 Organizing Control in Biological Organisms: Heterarchy Vs. Hierarchy

As we just noted, an organism consists of multiple production and control mechanisms. However, it is not just a collection of them, but an organized system. How the component mechanisms are organized is critical —the same components differently organized can generate different behaviors. Since we also noted that control mechanisms can operate on other control mechanisms, a critical challenge in understanding autonomous systems is to understand how control mechanisms are themselves organized (Bich and Bechtel 2022b).

When humans establish social systems—companies, universities, militaries, etc.—they tend to initially organize them hierarchically, generating a pyramid in which groups of workers at the bottom report to one supervisor, several supervisors report to a common higher-level supervisor, and ultimately everyone reports to one chief executive. The assumption is that such a hierarchy is most likely to ensure that all those in the organization are working to promote the whole institution. Central to such organization is a clear ordering of levels from bottom to top. In a variety of contexts such structuring of levels is violated. One such context is with nontransitive preferences in which A is preferred to B, B to C, but C to A. Such preferences clearly violate the hierarchy of levels. McCulloch (1945) introduced the term *heterarchy* for such nontransitive preferences. Heterarchy can be extended to modes of organization that deviate from different features of the pyramid organization. One individual may be subordinate to multiple supervisors. There may be no one agent in charge. There could even be more supervisors than individuals supervised. Crumley (2015) characterizes heterarchies as tangled networks in which elements potentially can be ranked in a number of different ways (see also Pattee 1991). On this view, supervisors and supervised individuals are not defined univocally as belonging to well-delineated levels, but only in regard to a specific activity or relationship. Any supervisor can be in turn supervised by one or more of the individuals she supervises, even skipping intermediate levels. The idea of heterarchy stresses the importance of considering not just top-down but also bottom-up and lateral processes. It identifies a mixed type of organization of control that employs and combines features of both hierarchies (vertical relationship) and networks (horizontal relationship) (Cumming 2016).

3.4 Some Principles of Heterarchy

Heterarchy is usually defined negatively as non-hierarchical. That is both extremely expansive, as it includes every form of organization that is not hierarchical, and non-informative. The challenge is to provide a more positive characterization of the features to be associated with heterarchy so as to be in a position to understand the implications of such features in enabling autonomy.

Considering the space of possible modes of organization, at the opposite extreme from hierarchy are flat networks as studied in graph theory. A graph consists of nodes and edges connecting the nodes. Graph theorists can explain some behavior of systems corresponding to a particular graph in terms of basic metrics such as the mean shortest path between nodes and the average number of connections a node has to its neighbors. Watts and Strogratz (1998) showed that many real-world networks exhibit relatively short mean shortest pathlength and high clustering. Such *small world* networks enable rapid communication across the whole network. Barabási and Albert (1999) explored another metric of network design—the number of other nodes to which a node is connected. In many real-world networks, that is distributed according to a power-law so that many nodes have very few connections, but a few (referred to as *hubs*) have a great many. Such *scale-free* networks are robust against perturbations to nodes or edges.

As useful as such graph-theoretic analyses are in explaining features of real-world systems, they do not distinguish control relations from other interactions between entities. We will develop an account of several features of heterarchical organization according to which it occupies the space between hierarchical pyramids and flat networks and is equipped to explain how control in autonomous systems enables them to sustain themselves.

A first feature of heterarchy that clearly positions it between hierarchy and flat networks is that it maintains a notion of levels, but only defined locally. As we characterized them, control mechanisms operate on the flexible constraints in controlled mechanisms. This allows us to say that a control mechanism is at a higher-level than that which it controls. Sometimes this can be extended to multiple levels—the control mechanism operating on a control mechanism is at a still higher level. In the case of glucose regulation in mammals: glucagon and insulin, released by α- and β-pancreatic cells respectively, control production mechanisms in the liver (also in muscle and adipose tissue) that transform glucose into glycogen for storage. The secretive activities of pancreatic cells are controlled in turn by further higher-order control constraints in the system. These include neurons in the brainstem that stimulate the release of insulin when they receive signals from the gut that food has entered the digestive system or from the eyes when food is visible. On this scheme, the brainstem neurons are at a higher level than β-pancreatic cells which are, in turn, at a higher level than liver cells. But this hierarchical relationship can break down at any point, as with McCulloch's example of non-transitive preferences. For example, it breaks when insulin from β-pancreatic cells modulates the release of neuropeptides. A negative feedback system illustrates this—constraints in the control mechanism operating on a production mechanism are themselves acted on by the product of the production mechanism. Or when two entities both control a production mechanism, one of them may also act on soft constraints in the other, controlling it. The two controllers may be at the same level with respect to the production mechanism that is controlled, but at different levels vis a vis each other. Globally, levels are not well defined in heterarchical systems.

A second feature of heterarchy is that multiple controllers can act independently on one lower-level production mechanism or controller. They may act either on the same constraint in the controlled mechanism, or on different constraints. In either case, conflict can result, with two controllers acting in opposing ways on the same production mechanism. This is comparable to an employee having multiple independent bosses who demand that a given action be performed differently or that each demands an action that is incompatible with performing what the other demands. Sometimes the conflict can be resolved by another locally higher-level controller regulating the controllers making conflicting demands. But often, in both business and biology, that is not the case. The resolution typically rests with the controlled employee or mechanism determining which, if either, of the directives to follow. To continue the above example, circadian regulation and brainstem regulation of the liver can conflict, as when eating occurs at an unexpected time; in such circumstances it is the liver that determines how glucose will be processed.

From the hierarchical perspective, the higher-level controller is in charge—it makes the decision about what those beneath it ought to do. To do so, it brings together information from a variety of sources, often including the entities it regulates, evaluates them according to its own principles (realized as constraints operating within it), and delivers commands. The case of conflicting controllers reveals that in fact the final decision rests with the lower-level controller, or even the production mechanism, the liver in our example. In many cases, a control mechanism integrates inputs both from below and from above in deciding what to do. For example, the brainstem neurons that act on the liver receive inputs not only from the digestive tract but from nuclei in the hypothalamus (to which they also supply information). When multiple lower-level entities provide input to one higher-level entity, and one lower-level entity receives input from several higher-level entities, all act to integrate information and respond to it.

A third feature of heterarchies is that local control hierarchies can be reversed, with mechanisms that are controlled with respect to a given source of information in turn controlling their control mechanisms with respect to another source. Within the local control-hierarchy perspective, lower-level entities act on higher-level controllers by providing information—the measurements they make are communicated by signals that end up altering the constraints in the controller. But they can also act on the controller (or even on a controller acting on the controller)—that is, their output, determined by constraints within them, operates to change constraints in the controller (or, again, in a controller operating on it). In this respect, it is at a higher level than the controller that operates on it. This undermines the prospect of identifying levels globally. For example, insulin released in response to a meal stimulates, among others, pro-opiomelanocortin neurons in the hypothalamus, thus triggering signaling pathways that decrease food intake (Röder, et al. 2016).

A fourth feature of heterarchies is crosstalk. A feature of hierarchical control schemes that we haven't addressed so far is that control at lower levels is segregated—different control streams are independent of each other until they are integrated at a higher level, with some streams only being integrated at the very highest level. This feature is violated if there is crosstalk between the streams. Crosstalk often results when the same components are involved in different control mechanisms, enabling the information procured in regulating one production mechanism to also contribute to the regulation of other production mechanisms. That often happens in regulatory signalling pathways (Bich and Bechtel 2022a). One advantage of crosstalk is that it enhances the likelihood that the activity of one controller will be consistent with that of others, leading to coherent actions. But failure of segregation of different lines of control may also lead to lack of specificity, with controllers failing to respond to local information to which they would otherwise respond. It also makes it much harder to identify the control elements that are responsible for failures so as to address them. The nuclei of the hypothalamus illustrate crosstalk. For many nuclei it is possible to assign one or more physiological or behavioral activity they regulate—the arcuate nucleus regulates eating, the lateral hypothalamus regulates wakefulness, the posterior hypothalamus regulates body temperature, and the suprachiastmatic nucleus maintains circadian time. But the various nuclei project to each other so that, as each regulates one activity, it is modulated by other nuclei regulating other activities.

3.5 Conclusions

We have identified some of the features of heterarchical organizations, features that may provide useful resources to organisms as they organize and integrate their activities. We focused on physiological examples, but these heterarchical control relations can be also instantiated when control relationships are extended in the environment involving two or more autonomous systems, such as in biofilms, multicellular organisms, and symbiotic associations.

A major challenge remains—explaining how a heterarchically organized system can act in ways that enable it to maintain itself as an autonomous system. Those designing machinery to operate in a given environment typically impose a hierarchical design. In such a design, they can anticipate how the system will respond to each perturbation, processing information and generating responses. One problem with this type of organization is that controllers higher in the hierarchy need to be increasingly complex and able to manage more and more information. Another problem is that a failure in one control mechanism high in the hierarchy can have cascading effects on the operation of all the lower-level mechanisms whose behavior depends on it. Heterarchical organizations instead are much more flexible. Distribution of control and the fact that final decisions often rest with the lower-level mechanisms does not require centralization of information processing and so makes systems less subject to cascading failures. Heterarchical systems, however, are much more difficult to understand as information flows in diverse ways through the system, and individual control components often alter the operation of multiple production mechanisms. This presents challenges to someone trying to modify or repair such a system—a given change in the system can have multiple effects beyond those anticipated. It also presents challenges to understanding how a heterarchical organization could enable organisms to maintain themselves as autonomous systems. A randomly assembled system would be unlikely to maintain itself. Among the possible ways of organizing the same components, probably very few would actually suffice to keep the organism going.

If a system is being designed by rational agents, it may indeed be difficult for them to arrive at a successful heterarchical design. But biological systems are not designed. They have evolved over an extremely long period of time in which variations are successively introduced and those variants that succeed in maintaining organisms sufficiently long to leave offspring are maintained. Although approaching the organization of organisms as an engineering problem is problematic, some insight can be acquired by considering a scenario in which you are charged with improving the performance of a system (e.g., a computer program or a company) that is operating moderately well. Unlike biological systems, let's further assume that the system assigned to you was initially organized in a hierarchical pyramid. You identify a particular context in which performance might be improved and hypothesize that it would be improved if a new control relation was added that violated the pyramidal organization—e.g., you allowed a second controller to act on the same controlled component. You make many additional changes in the same way: if, in the context in which the system is supposed to operate, overall performance improves, or at least doesn't deteriorate too much, the modifications will be incorporated into the system. When your successor takes over, she proceeds in the same way. Along the way the control exercised by the top-level controller is diminished as you add additional lower-level controllers, or connections between them, that improve performance. Before long, any semblance of the hierarchical pyramid will be lost. The explanation for how such a heterarchical organization could become instantiated is that it developed over time, with each addition being added when it maintained or improved performance.

This thought experiment offers a small example of the processes by which organisms acquire organization through evolution (except that they almost certainly did not start out with a hierarchical pyramid). As Partridge (1982) argues, evolution is not engineering, and the organization that results may not be one that is readily understood by us. The relevant consideration is whether it enables the organism to maintain itself as an autonomous system. To better approximate biological evolution, we need to take into account the fact that the environment in which organization is evaluated does not stay fixed but is constantly modified, both as the physical environment changes and as other organisms change. In the changed environment, what matters is that the modification enabled the organism to continue to maintain itself and reproduce (see also Menatti, this volume). But when we consider changing environments, we can identify a further virtue of the heterarchical organization. In a strict hierarchy, the loss of a component is likely to have a distinct effect (typically negative) on performance. But as a component is subject to multiple controllers, and these control relations become more entangled, there are more pathways by which it may get the information needed to perform. It is not dependent on a single supervisor doing its job (or doing it well). As a result, heterarchical control schemes that have developed through iterated modifications as in evolution are likely to be more robust. Accordingly, they advance autonomy.

3.6 Funding

LB acknowledges funding from IAS-Research group funding IT1668–22 (Basque Government); grants PID2019-104576GB-I00 "Outonomy" and PID2023-147251NB-I00 "Outagencies", funded by MCIU/AEI/10.13039/501100011033 and FEDER/UE.

References

Barabási AL, Albert R (1999) Emergence of scaling in random networks. Science 286:509–512

Bich L, Bechtel W (2022a) Control mechanisms: explaining the integration and versatility of biological organisms. Adapt Behav 30(5):389–407. https://doi.org/10.1177/10597123221074429

Bich L, Bechtel W (2022b) Organization needs organization: understanding integrated control in living organisms. Stud Hist Phil Sci 93:96–106. https://doi.org/10.1016/j.shpsa.2022.03.005

Bich L, Mossio M, Ruiz-Mirazo K, Moreno A (2016) Biological regulation: controlling the system from within. Biol Philos 31(2):237–265. https://doi.org/10.1007/s10539-015-9497-8

Crumley CL (2015) Heterarchy. In: Scott RA (ed) Emerging trends in the social and behavioral sciences. Wiley, pp 1–14

Cumming GS (2016) Heterarchies: reconciling networks and hierarchies. Trends Ecol Evol 31(8):622–632. https://doi.org/10.1016/j.tree.2016.04.009

McCulloch WS (1945) A heterarchy of values determined by the topology of nervous nets. Bull Math Biophys 7(2):89–93. https://doi.org/10.1007/BF02478457

Menatti L (2025) Salutogenesis, adaptivity and the continuum of health. In: Barandiaran X, Etxeberria A (eds) Outonomy: fleshing out autonomy beyond the individual. Springer

Monterde-Fuertes A (2025) Pain beyond nociception: a biological autonomy perspective. In: Barandiaran X, Etxeberria A (eds) Outonomy: fleshing out autonomy beyond the individual. Springer

Moreno A, Mossio M (2015) Biological autonomy: a philosophical and theoretical inquiry. Springer, Dordrecht

Partridge LD (1982) The good enough calculi of evolving control systems: evolution is not engineering. Am J Phys Regul Integr Comp Phys 242(3):R173–R177. https://doi.org/10.1152/ajpregu.1982.242.3.R173

Pattee HH (1971) Physical theories of biological co-ordination. Q Rev Biophys 4(2):255–276

Pattee HH (1991) Measurement-control heterarchical networks in living systems. Int J Gen Syst 18(3):213–221

Röder PV, Wu B, Liu Y, Han W (2016) Pancreatic regulation of glucose homeostasis. Exp. Mol. Med. 48:e219. https://doi.org/10.1038/emm.2016.6

Ruiz-Mirazo K, Moreno A, Shirt-Ediss B (2025) Outonomy at the origins of life. In: Barandiaran X, Etxeberria A (eds) Outonomy: fleshing out autonomy beyond the individual. Springer

Varela FJ, Maturana HR, Uribe R (1974) Autopoiesis: the organization of living systems, its characterization and a model. Biosystems 5:187–196

Virenque L (2025) Intrinsic purposiveness and autonomy in interaction. In: Barandiaran X, Etxeberria A (eds) Outonomy: fleshing out autonomy beyond the individual. Springer

Watts D, Strogratz S (1998) Collective dynamics of small worlds. Nature 393:440–442

Winning J, Bechtel W (2018) Rethinking causality in neural mechanisms: constraints and control. Mind Mach 28(2):287–310. https://doi.org/10.1007/s11023-018-9458-5

Part II
The Fabric of Life

Chapter 4
Environment(s), Autonomy and (A)Symmetries

Arantza Etxeberria

Abstract This chapter examines conceptualizations of the environment in biology and addresses the different organism/environment asymmetries appearing in autonomy views and evolutionary theories. It argues for recognizing the environment not merely as an external background, but also as co-constitutive and relational, insofar as life is shaped by epigenetic, exposomic, and interorganismal dynamics. Two perspectives emerge, environments as surroundings and as entanglements, both required for developing an "outonomy" framework that expands biological autonomy theory to include environmental agency and interdependence.

Keywords Epigenetics · Exposome · Milieu · Plasticity · Relationality · Holobiosis

> *"The notion of milieu is becoming a universal and obligatory mode of apprehending the experience and existence of living beings; [...]it is now being constituted as a category of contemporary thought [...] philosophy must take the initiative in synoptically investigating the meaning and value of this concept."* (Canguilhem 2008, 98)

4.1 Introduction

The environment is an elusive concept, highly polysemous, deeply entangled with history, and difficult to define precisely in science and medicine. Yet, in recent years, it has emerged as a philosophical subject in its own right, demanding attention beyond its conventional role of being merely the background to living beings. This shift signals a growing recognition of the environment's complex multifaceted philosophical significance across disciplines, particularly in biology, medicine, and environmental philosophy. Conceptually, it is riddled with tensions: whether the environment

A. Etxeberria (✉)
IAS Research Centre for Life, Mind and Society, Department of Philosophy, University of the Basque Country, EHU, Donostia/San Sebastián, Spain
e-mail: arantza.etxeberria@ehu.eus

X. E. Barandiaran and A. Etxeberria (eds.), *Outonomy*,
SpringerBriefs in Philosophy, https://doi.org/10.1007/978-3-032-05501-9_4

is a passive stage or an active force, an external domain or an internal one, and whether it is defined by intrinsic properties or by relations. These questions could reshape our understanding of the environment and prompt a reconsideration of its role in shaping life itself.

This chapter outlines the role of the environment in biological thought, contrasting its significance in organizational and evolutionary theories within biology. It provides an overview of key narratives about the concept of the environment in science and philosophy, explores organism-environment systems, and the symmetries and asymmetries shaping their mutual influences. The analysis suggests that accounts of autonomous systems require expanding to embrace relational dimensions, with the recognition of the environment as an active participant being central to conceiving autonomy as *outonomy*.

4.2 What Is/Are (the) Environment(s)?

Several distinct narratives of the environment can be identified in current science and philosophy, each serving a different purpose. One of them, articulated by Georges Canguilhem in *The Living and its Milieu* (Canguilhem 2008), examines the environment as a counterpart to the organism. Canguilhem traces the history of the milieu within the organism-environment pair, arguing that organisms are internally regulated systems that, as wholes, maintain relations with their milieu similar to the interactions among the parts that constitute the system itself, engaging in mutual influence rather than a simple cause-and-effect (Etxeberria 2020). The concept of milieu, originating in Newtonian mechanics as a fluid medium (ether) that mediated between bodies and transmitted causal action, later appeared in biology with Lamarck's "milieux" and Darwin's "conditions of existence." Although Darwin didn't use "environment" in *On the Origin of Species*, Herbert Spencer popularized the term in the late nineteenth century (Pearce 2010). At this point, "environment" emerged as a singular, abstract concept, meaning the external correlate of the organism, itself an abstract concept. The concept evolved further, with Bernard introducing the "internal milieu" for physiological regulation, Comte unifying physical surroundings and influential circumstances, von Humboldt conceptualizing a global environment, and von Uexküll defining "Umwelt" as each species' enacted sphere of significance. For further elaborations, see Pearce (2010), Casetta (2025), and Fábregas-Tejeda (2025).

A second line of thought addresses our understanding of environmental phenomena in relation to planetary life in fields like *Earth Systems Science* (Warde et al. 2018). This perspective presents *the environment* as a singular, global concept emerging post-World War II, highlighting its status as both a scientific and social construct, particularly in its modern, global dimension. Unlike "nature", which is often associated with intrinsic properties, "environment" is frequently understood as relational, constituted by interdependencies among systems.

A third perspective regards environments as inherently plural, reflecting diverse cultural understandings, roles (such as resource, habitat, threat, or partner), and approaches ranging from indigenous knowledge to modern science. This plurality suggests that environmental thinking resists reduction to a single framework, instead drawing its richness from multiple interpretations: as physical space, relational network, cultural construct, and field of action (Benson 2020).

The essay will primarily focus on how the environment is conceptualized in relation to organisms in biology and medicine, while also returning at the end to how expansions of biological views influence the other two main understandings of the concept.

4.3 Organism/Environment Asymmetries

The organism/environment system was conceptualized through opposed asymmetries in autonomous systems accounts and evolutionary theories.

4.3.1 The Internalist Asymmetry of the Autonomy Perspective

The autonomy theory of the organism can be traced across a historical critique of various deterministic accounts of life and living systems, ranging from mechanistic conceptions of organisms as machines, to notions of the *milieu* as a deterministic force, to evolutionary externalist accounts emphasizing the role of selection as a form of design.

The development of biological autonomy theory traces a rich intellectual lineage, starting from Kant's idea of self-organized beings. Key further contributors include Claude Bernard's work on internal stability and Walter Cannon's concept of homeostasis (Bernard 1974; Cannon 1929). These notions laid the groundwork for understanding biological self-regulation, which proved highly influential for cybernetics. This framework was further developed by second-order cybernetics theorists, particularly Maturana and Varela's theory of autopoiesis, while Stuart Kauffman contributed about how internal constraints generate biological autonomy against entropic tendencies. This theoretical progression led to the organizational approach, including the one developed by the San Sebastian group, which emphasizes how living systems maintain themselves through complex self-regulatory processes that generate their own constraints and enable their continued existence (Moreno et al. 2008; Moreno and Mossio 2015).

This tradition of biological autonomy has frequently relegated the environment to a secondary role, either as a mere facilitator of autonomous processes or as a source of disturbances to be resisted. Various philosophical perspectives, such as Spinoza's idea that passive affections are harmful, have contributed to this negative view of environmental influences, and Bernard's notion of the constancy of the *milieu intérieur* as a condition for a free and independent life was especially influential (Bernard 1974). More recently, this view states that a "broad agential autonomy implies that the organization of the system causes the processes exerted on the environment, whereas those of the environment towards the system are monitored according to internally defined needs" (Moreno et al. 2008, 312).

All this reveals an asymmetry in how organisms and environments are understood: organisms are seen as active agents, whereas the environment is reduced to a passive enabling background. This bias may stem from individualistic ideals, but the idea of autonomy as freedom from the environment requires reevaluation. As relational phenomena organisms are not fully independent, they are inherently open to environmental influences, constantly sensing and responding to change. This dimension is required for their goal-directed and purposeful existence.

4.3.2 The Externalist Asymmetry of Evolutionary Theory

In evolutionary thinking, the organism-environment relationship was framed through adaptation to selective pressures, favoring a functionalist view of organisms. While the earlier Kantian Cuvier saw functions as internally articulated, Darwin viewed traits as evolutionary solutions to environmental demands. With the "hardening" of the Modern Synthesis (Gould 1983), genes became the primary units of adaptation, reinforcing an externalist *asymmetry* where environmental pressures shape genes, but organisms do not act on the environment (Cortés-García and Etxeberria Agiriano 2023).

Philosophers of evolutionary biology have examined the role of the environment. Robert Brandon (1990) identifies three types: the external environment (all factors outside the organism), the ecological environment (those within a specific area), and the selective environment (factors affecting reproductive success). However, this framework focuses on shared environments influencing populations, not the dynamic, reciprocal relationships between organisms and environments. As Walsh (2022) notes, the shared environment is a theoretical abstraction that overlooks the occurring complex, multifaceted interactions organisms actually engage in (see also Fábregas-Tejeda 2025). Organisms actively shape their environments and developmental trajectories, as critics of adaptationism contend. Thus, organism-centered approaches to evolution challenge classical externalism recognizing that organisms actively influence, rather than passively adapt to fixed conditions (Levins and Lewontin 1985; Baedke et al. 2021). They emphasize the constructive capacities and internal organization of organisms (Walsh 2015; Alberch 1989; Etxeberria and Nuño de la Rosa 2021), while recognizing the active causal role of environmental factors. Some views of niche construction admit that the environmental influences can be either to change the environment or to change the organisms themnselves. Some perspectives within Niche Construction Theory hold that constructing a niche may entail both environmental changes and organismal modifications that reshape how they experience it (Chiu 2019). These perspectives soften the Modern Synthesis's externalist asymmetry and align closely with autonomy theory and enactivism.

4.4 Towards Organism/Environment Symmetries

The preceding discussion outlined how both autonomy theory and evolutionary biology often uphold asymmetries: the former minimizes the environment's role, while the latter treats organisms as passive responders. These views are increasingly contested by approaches that emphasize dynamic, reciprocal organism-environment relations. This section examines how epigenetics and exposomics reconceive the environment as an active, co-constitutive element in biological individuation.

4.4.1 Epigenetics

Epigenetics offers a key framework for understanding how the environment co-constitutes living systems, showing how social interactions and contingent relationships can influence gene expression without altering DNA. Neural epigenetics, for instance, links social experiences to molecular changes like DNA methylation, integrating environmental inputs into an organism's biological constitution (Nicoglou and Merlin 2017).

Conrad H. Waddington's early work conceived epigenetics broadly, taking into account the entire developmental process and its underlying causal basis. In contrast, contemporary molecular epigenetics focuses on specific pathways, such as chromatin modifications, maternal imprinting, and small RNAs, through which environmental factors affect gene regulation without altering the DNA sequence. Thus the environment's active role in gene regulation and biological development is highlighted, moving beyond the notion of a passive background for genetic programs (though see Loison 2022 for distinctions between them).

Epigenetics thus shifts our understanding of biological complexity from hierarchical control to interdependent organizations of connected elements, emphasizing notions of *connectivity*, *crosstalk*, and *exchange* among elements (Buklijas 2018), and calling for an analysis of heterarchies (Bich and Bechtel 2025, this volume). These insights suggest the need to revise autonomy theories to emphasize relational co-constitution. One way forward is to reconsider the distinction between constitutive and interactive autonomy proposed in the organizational framework (originally outlined in Moreno et al. 2008), particularly the assumption that organisms are constituted prior to their interactions. Barad's agential realism offers an alternative framework for this relational constitution (Barad 2007). In this light, processes such as learning, metabolic plasticity, and other adaptive changes can be seen as co-constitutive.

4.4.2 Exposures to Environmental Influences

The study of environmental exposures reveals the permeable nature of living bodies, constantly influenced and traversed by their environments, entangled with them rather than merely surrounded by external conditions. This challenges the conventional view of autonomy as self-production. Hannah Landecker (2017) critiques the metabolic conception of autonomy rooted in Claude Bernard's idea of digestion, where consumed material becomes "inert raw material" and fully assimilated into the eater. She argues instead that ingested genetic material can persist and function in the host, forming symbiotic or commensal relationships rather than being entirely broken down.

This biological porosity, documented in epidemiology and the emerging field of *exposomics*, contests the idea of strict boundaries between organisms and environments. Exposomics, developed in the post-genomic era, examines the full range of environmental exposures (i.e., the *exposome*) and their health effects by analyzing thousands of factors at once (Wild 2012). It redefines the concept of environment to include both external factors and the body's internal chemical landscape, encompassing both exogenous compounds and endogenous molecules alike (Rappaport and Smith 2010). Exposures thus refer not only to substances entering the body but also those produced within it, offering a notion of the exposome as everything in the body that is not genetic (Wild 2012; Canali and Leonelli 2022; Pontarotti and Merlin 2023).

Epidemiology offers two main perspectives on the environment (Shostak 2013) with a molecular approach, exemplified by exposomics and social epidemiology, which focuses on social variables such as "neighborhood effects", suggesting that where one lives (postal code) may be as biologically significant as one's genetic code. Nancy Krieger argues that it is bodies, not genes, that narrate stories of existence through exposure, susceptibility, and resistance, showing how social inequalities become biologically embodied, for example in the form disease (Krieger 2005).

The concepts of *exposed science* (Shostak 2013) and *permeable corporeality* (Begueria and Zafra 2019) stress that bodies are relational and dynamic, actively engaging with their surroundings. This permeability reflects a balance between receptivity and agency, where bodies both shape and are shaped by their environments (Menatti 2025, this volume). The notion of exposure shows how environments permeate organisms, and this reinforces a view of autonomy grounded not in isolation, but in ongoing relations.

4.5 Interorganismal Interdependences and Holobiosis

Previous sections examine how the environment is viewed as having a direct causal impact on organisms, rather than being a passive backdrop. However, this causal influence is typically understood in physical or chemical terms, such as temperature, light, or nutrient availability, rather than an influence exerted by other organisms. However, as Canguilhem observed, Darwin's approach differs in that it prioritizes inter-organismal relationships over the consideration of the milieu as merely physical surroundings (Etxeberria 2020, 2023): *"The fundamental biological relation, in Darwin's eyes, is the relation of one living being to others; it prevails over the relation between the living and the milieu conceived as an ensemble of physical forces. The first milieu an organism lives in is an entourage of living beings, which are for it enemies or allies, prey or predators"* (Canguilhem 2008, 105). Canguilhem rightly notes that Darwinian biology emphasizes inter-organismal relations, but these are largely framed as competitive interactions that impact individual fitness. This perspective is now changing as emerging views frame evolution as involving genuine organismal entanglements, challenging individualist paradigms. By treating organisms and their environments, including other organisms, as mutually constitutive, this shift redirects focus from discrete entities to processes of exchange and connectivity, demanding new ontological frameworks.

In this sense, Lynn Margulis's concept of the holobiont redefines our understanding of organisms, viewing them as assemblages or consortia of entities in symbiotic relationships (Margulis 1991; Baedke et al. 2021). Rooted in her theory of symbiogenesis, this framework explains how new kinds of living entities emerge through long-term collaborations, where relations become so integrated within new unified systems.

Such interconnectedness is further exemplified through biological and social relationships. Eutherian pregnancy, for instance, involves physiological and immunological interplay between gestator and embryo (Etxeberria and Nuño de la Rosa 2021, Etxeberria and Cortés-García 2024).

Early caregiving similarly influences development, through behavioral bonds which are the basis for "social markers", or measurable indicators of relationships that affect biological processes. These cases challenge the notion of organismal independence, showing that identity is co-constituted through lasting relationships with others. The perspective of holobiosis captures aspects of a broader shift in biology, according to which organisms are now increasingly understood as part of dense webs of interdependencies. The environment is now an active, dynamic network of relations that shape and are shaped by living systems (Barker et al. 2014).

This view becomes especially urgent in light of the growing interplay between natural and artificial environments—highlighted by the fact that anthropogenic mass now exceeds Earth's biomass (Elhacham et al. 2020). Within this context, decomposition is as fundamental to life as composition itself; the breaking down of materials is equally important as their assembly. Decomposition, decay, and death are not opposite to life, but essential processes that sustain its cycles and balance. From this entangled perspective, the environment is neither wholly external nor internal to organisms, who maintain identities linked to their environments, actively engaging in mutual influence.

4.6 Two Environments: Surroundings and Entanglements

This essay has examined two expanded concepts of the environment. The first understands environments as external surroundings, considering their influence on life and health. As *surroundings*, environments are the physical, chemical, and biological contexts that influence individuals and sustain communities, then including shared environments (Fábregas-Tejeda 2025). Thus although "the environment" appears as a global entity, environments as surroundings can also be multiple, partial, and specific to particular locations. In biology, it aligns with views of organisms as plastic and ecologically embedded, such as the holobiont concept. In medicine, it relates to research on exposures, microbial communities, and cultural practices.

As *entanglements*, the second perspective favors understanding environments as networks of entangled relations, thus primarily constituted by other organisms. Here, the environment is not an external force but a co-constitutive agent, changing how we understand ecological and relational networks. Biology increasingly adopts this view, seeing environments as dynamic systems of interdependence, beyond mere surroundings.

The two concepts of environment have different implications for how we understand life and ecological relationships science, philosophy, and environmental thought. The view of a global understanding of the environment as a matter of ethical and political concerns remains linked to a view of environment as surroundings which remains largely asymmetrical and is pictured as an independent entity which needs to be cared after. In contrast, the entanglement model aligns with biodiversity concerns and feminist and relational ontologies, which emphasize fluid boundaries and mutual constitution (Haraway 2016; Barad 2007; Cabello et al. 2025, this volume).

The symmetry perspective sees environments as agential, living or produced by living beings. Though unconventional, it reflects the reality that most environments are composed or constructed by other living forms. The internalist asymmetry is required to better examine the organization of living systems, which may include the generation of system boundaries, while the notion of 'outonomy' signals a shift toward recognizing their porous nature as co-produced, interconnected systems. Hence, both conceptions of the environment remain essential to contemporary scientific inquiry.

4.7 Acknowledgements

I thank the reviewers for their valuable comments. This research was supported by the Basque Government [IT1668–22], grants PID2019-104576GB-I00 for project Outonomy and PID2023-147251NB-I00 for Outagencies funded by MCIU/AEI/10.13039/501100011033 and FEDER/UE, and the 'Metaphysics of Biology' project [PID2021-127184NB-I00].

References

Alberch P (1989) The logic of monsters: evidence for internal constraint in development and evolution. Geobios 22:21–57

Baedke J, Fábregas-Tejeda A, Prieto GI (2021) Unknotting reciprocal causation between organism and environment. Biol Philos 36:48

Baedke J, Fábregas-Tejeda A, Nieves Delgado A (2020) The holobiont concept before Margulis. J Exp Zool B Mol Dev Evol 334(3):149–155

Barad K (2007) Meeting the universe halfway: quantum physics and the entanglement of matter and meaning. Duke University Press, Durham, NC

Barker, G., Desjardins, E. and Pearce, T., T. Eds. (2014). *Entangled life.* Springer

Begueria A, Zafra E (2019) Permeable corporalities: intersections between the environment and health. Rev. Antropol. Iberoam.Na 14(1):11–27

Benson ES (2020) Surroundings: a history of environments and environmentalisms. University of Chicago Press

Bernard, C. (1974). *Lectures on the phenomena common to animals and plants* (H. E. Hoff, R. Guillemin, & L. Guillemin, trans.). Charles C. Thomas. (Original work published 1878)

Bich, L & Bechtel, W. (2025) Autonomy and Heterarchy: organizing control in biological organisms. In X. E. Barandiaran & A. Etxeberria (Eds.), Outonomy: fleshing out autonomy beyond the individual (p. in press). Springer

Brandon RN (1990) *Adaptation and environment.* Princeton University Press

Buklijas T (2018) Histories and meanings of epigenetics. In: Meloni M, Cromby J, Fitzgerald D, Lloyd S (eds) *The Palgrave handbook of biology and society.* Palgrave Macmillan, pp 167–187

Cabello V, Merlo A, Mancilla M, Siqueiros J, Barandiaran X (2025) Autonomy and its limits in social-ecological systems. In: Barandiaran XE, Etxeberria A (eds) Outonomy: fleshing out autonomy beyond the individual (p. in press). Springer

Canali S, Leonelli S (2022) Reframing the environment in data-intensive health sciences. Stud Hist Phil Sci 93:203–214

Canguilhem, G. (2008). The living and its milieu. In *Knowledge of life* (S. Geroulanos & T. Meyers, Trans., pp. 98–120). Fordham University Press. (Original work published 1965).

Cannon W (1929) Organization for physiological homeostasis. Physiol Rev 9(3):399–431

Casetta E (2025) *Philosophy of the environment.* Routledge, Forthcoming

Chiu, L. (2019). Decoupling, commingling, and the evolutionary significance of experiential niche construction. In T. Uller & K. Laland Eds. *Evolutionary causation: biological and philosophical reflections,* pags. 299-322

Cortés-García, D., Etxeberria Agiriano, A. (2023). Ontologies in evolutionary biology: the role of the organism in the two syntheses. In: Viejo, J.M., Sanjuán, M. (eds) *Life and mind. Interdisciplinary evolution research,* vol 8. Springer, Cham. doi:https://doi.org/10.1007/978-3-031-30304-3_9

Elhacham E, Ben-Uri L, Grozovski J, Bar-On YM, Milo R (2020) Global human-made mass exceeds all living biomass. Nature 588(7838):442–444

Etxeberria A (2020) Regulation, milieu, and norms: Georges Canguilhem's individual organisms as relations. In: Méthot PO (ed) *Vital norms. Canguilhem's the Normal and the pathological in the twenty-first century* (pp. 291–328). Hermann Ed

Etxeberria A, Nuño de la Rosa L (2021) Pere Alberch (1954–1998). In: L N d l R, Müller G (eds). Evolutionary Developmental Biology: A Reference Guide, Springer, pp 339–353

Etxeberria A., Cortés-García D (2024). El embarazo en filosofía de la biología: un enfoque organísmico relacional. Ludus Vitalis, 30(1):1–22

Fábregas-Tejeda A (2025) *The organism-environment pairing: a historical and philosophical re-appraisal.* MIT Press, Forthcoming

Gould SJ (1983) The hardening of the modern synthesis. In: Grene M (ed) *Dimensions of Darwinism: themes and counterthemes in twentieth-century evolutionary theory.* Cambridge University Press, Cambridge, pp 71–93

Haraway DJ (2016). Staying with the trouble: Making kin in the Chthulucene. Durham, NC: Duke University Press
Krieger N (2005) Embodiment: a conceptual glossary for epidemiology. J Epidemiol Community Health 59(5):350–355
Landecker H (2017) Metabolism, autonomy, and individuality. In: Lidgard S, Nyhart L (eds) *Biological individuality: integrating scientific, philosophical, and historical perspectives*. University of Chicago Press, pp 225–248
Levins R, Lewontin RC (1985) *The dialectical biologist*. Harvard University Press, Cambridge
Loison L (2022) The environment: an ambiguous concept in Waddington's biology. Stud Hist Phil Sci 91:181–190
Menatti L (2025) Salutogenesis, adaptivity and the continuum of health: a perspective from biological autonomy. This volume
Margulis L (1991). Symbiogenesis and symbioticism. In L. Margulis & R. Fester (Eds.), Symbiosis as a source of evolutionary innovation: Speciation and morphogenesis (pp. 1–14). Cambridge, MA: MIT Press
Moreno A, Etxeberria A, Umerez J (2008) The autonomy of biological individuals and artificial models. Biosystems 91(2):309–319
Moreno A, Mossio M (2015) Biological autonomy. A philosophical and theoretical enquiry, Springer
Nicoglou A, Merlin F (2017) Epigenetics: a way to bridge the gap between biological fields. Stud Hist Philos Sci Part C: Stud Hist Philos Biol Biomed Sci 66:73–82
Pearce T (2010) From 'circumstances' to 'environment': Herbert Spencer and the origins of the idea of organism-environment interaction. Stud Hist Phil Biol Biomed Sci 41(3):241–252
Pontarotti G, Merlin F (2023) From Exposome to pathogenic niche. Looking for an operational account of the environment in health studies. In: Giroux É, Merlin F, Fayet Y (eds) *Integrative approaches in environmental health and Exposome research*. Palgrave Macmillan, Cham. https://doi.org/10.1007/978-3-031-28432-8_7
Rappaport SM, Smith MT (2010) Environment and disease risks. Science 330(6003):460–461. https://doi.org/10.1126/science.1192603
Shostak S (2013) *Exposed science*. University of California Press
Walsh D (2015) *Organisms, agency, and evolution*. Cambridge University Press
Walsh D (2022) Environment as abstraction *Biological theory* 17(1):68–79
Warde P, Robin L, Sorlin S (2018) *The environment: a history of the idea*. Johns Hopkins University Press
Wild CP (2012) The exposome: from concept to utility. Int J Epidemiol 41(1):24–32

Chapter 5
Outonomy at the Origins of Life

Kepa Ruiz-Mirazo, Alvaro Moreno, and Ben Shirt-Ediss

Abstract The first living beings, prokaryotes, were endowed with an extremely complex and dynamic individual organization: a compartmentalized metabolism in which diverse molecular components and transformation processes got functionally coupled, including a selectively permeable membrane, a set of energy currencies and a translation apparatus built upon a common genetic code. Each microorganism neatly distinguishes itself from the surrounding medium and is capable of generating and modulating its own rules of behaviour (i.e., it acts on its own behalf) so it can be interpreted as *autonomous* in a fundamental biological sense. However, the autonomy theoretical framework only covers part of the explanation for the striking complexity observed in minimal lifeforms. In fact, all known living cells depend on other cells for their sustenance, so they engage in diverse ecological relationships without which their survival would not be feasible. Furthermore, all living cells have arisen from pre-existing cells, through reproduction, within a long-term, open-ended evolutionary process. As we will argue below, the constitution of any biological domain requires a strong –though deeply asymmetric– causal interweaving between individual (*metabolic-physiological*) and collective (*ecological* and *evolutionary*) dynamics, covering different spatial and temporal scales that unfold in the course of abiogenesis.

Keywords Origins of life · Prebiotic *systems* evolution · Ecopoiesis · Biological autonomy · Agency · Dynamic decoupling

---

K. Ruiz-Mirazo (✉)
IAS-Research Centre for Life, Mind and Society, Department of Philosophy, University of the Basque Country (UPV/EHU), Donostia-San Sebastián, Spain
e-mail: kepa.ruiz-mirazo@ehu.eus

Biofisika Institute (CSIC, UPV/EHU), Leioa, Spain

A. Moreno · B. Shirt-Ediss
Donostia International Physics Center (DIPC), Donostia-San Sebastian, Spain

X. E. Barandiaran and A. Etxeberria (eds.), *Outonomy*,
SpringerBriefs in Philosophy, https://doi.org/10.1007/978-3-032-05501-9_5

5.1 Introduction: The 'Protocell Scenario' and a Few Preliminary Implications

The last universal common ancestor of all life on Earth (LUCA) was a population of prokaryotes. Although the specific properties, diet, local habitat or degree of phenotypic heterogeneity of those systems may still be controversial, few scientists doubt that they constituted a large group of unicellular organisms performing 'genetically-instructed' (i.e., ribosome-/code-mediated) metabolism (Moody et al. 2024). Before the appearance of that fundamental microbial threshold, we don't really know what happened. The absence of natural, physical–chemical systems of intermediate complexity could be due to life's voracity or to the fact that terrestrial conditions have changed so dramatically over the years that they no longer allow for the emergence of alternative lifeforms. However, this state of affairs is truly intriguing, because the compositional, organizational and behavioural complexity of individual microorganisms is many orders of magnitude higher than any other non-biological system we find in nature.

The huge 'complexity gap' between extant living vs. non-living systems[1] holds a profound message for us to unravel, and far-reaching implications that we just barely grasp. One has to do with the source of biological causality, a rather difficult, slippery topic. Current understanding of non-equilibrium physics and chemistry has moved beyond the classical Newtonian view of matter as passive and inert: we now consider that self-organizing forces/principles play fundamental roles in nature (Nicolis and Prigogine 1977), including biological phenomena at different levels (Saha and Galic 2018). Hence the trend to incorporate such intrinsic dynamics in our explanations about primordial biogenesis, as well (Nogal et al. 2023).

Yet, in addition to self-organization and self-assembly processes, probably combined in non-trivial ways (Showalter and Epstein 2015; Chen et al. 2022), a material system with biological potential entails the interplay of several, self-induced, control mechanisms at once. On these lines, we have claimed over the years (Ruiz-Mirazo and Moreno 2004; Lauber et al. 2021) that proto-biological organization requires the production and functional integration of molecular constraints of various kinds (i.e., *kinetic*, *spatial* and *energetic* controls) to actively maintain itself in non-equilibrium conditions and achieve what we coined 'basic autonomy', in an attempt to complement other, more abstract, classical proposals (Varela 1979; Ganti 1987; Rosen 1991; Kauffman 2000).

Incipient physical–chemical self-constraining/self-maintaining systems would thus develop into minimal metabolisms (Lauber et al. 2021) through coupling with organic compartments in aqueous, heterogeneous media. This hypothesis is supported by extensive experimental evidence on the prebiotic plausibility of the

[1] 'Infra-biological' entities, like viruses or other types of –molecularly very sophisticated– parasitic systems, which function thanks to the metabolic activity and machinery of prokaryotes, do not dwell in that intermediate region between physics/chemistry and biology: they definitely belong to the biological domain and play important roles within it, even if they are not living beings themselves (Moreira and Lopez-García 2009).

molecular building blocks and elementary reaction networks involved (Nogal et al. 2023) and has also been explored and tested through various computational models (Ruiz-Mirazo and Mavelli 2008; Piedrafita et al. 2017). In more general philosophical terms, conceiving protocells as primary autonomous systems has helped to elaborate a non-reductionist *organizational* account of biological functions (Mossio et al. 2009), or even to ground teleological explanations (Mossio and Bich 2017), starting from very early prebiotic stages. The self-determination dynamics of these minimal metabolic systems would inaugurate a novel and recursively cyclic causal regime (Moreno and Mossio 2015) upon which all subsequent living beings would build.

If we accept 'basic autonomy' as a key transition for the onset of life, a first 'internal/external' causal asymmetry slides into our prebiotic explanations, given the increasingly complex and distinct molecular transformations occurring within the compartment, as compared to its surrounding milieu. Furthermore, as non-equilibrium open systems, metabolizing protocells must continuously capture and release matter-energy to implement and maintain their identity, including their physical interface with the external world, which necessarily involves an *active* tuning of their local boundary conditions. In other words, self-constructing protocells cannot help being *agents* from the beginning, even if this should be taken in a minimalist, crudely foundational sense (Barandiaran et al. 2009). Thus, our approach puts a lot of emphasis on the individual system, the protocell, as the main axis of prebiotic activity, reinforcing the 'in–out' asymmetry not only in compositional but also in processual and behavioural terms. Protocells would constitute, in this way, the main loci and channel for biologically relevant processes to come forward, which can be spelled out as endogenous metabolic activity and outward action.

Accordingly, although we will defend that protocellular systems –if they are to turn cellular, fully biological– must establish additional collective and trans-generational causal relationships, it is important to highlight that these larger-scale spatial and temporal interactions *spring from* and *sediment in* their individual organization. In other words, under the theoretical framework we propose for primordial biogenesis, individual protocells remain both the source and sink of all the novel causal powers that unfold during the transition, even if those come thanks to their belonging to a *population* of interacting and reproducing autonomous entities. In such a scene, as described in the next two sections, collective action essentially takes shape in a twofold manner: ecological and evolutionary.

Many issues of interest can be discussed within this rich prebiotic arena (Ruiz-Mirazo et al. 2020), but our focus here will be on how some populations of protocells may come up with molecular mechanisms through which processes that expand beyond the individual sphere somehow feed back into it, making later protocells increasingly complex and adaptive. We shall argue that the appearance of 'hereditary templates' (oligomers whose characteristic linear sequences can be replicated through base-pairing and then transmitted via reproduction), as expected, must play a critical role in this regard, together with 'higher-order controls' (regulatory molecular constraints), because they enable the simultaneous increase of both protocell complexity and robustness, under highly variable environmental conditions. Therefore, by the time the origins-of-life process is completed, those protocells that manage to combine *regulatory* and *hereditary* mechanisms in such a way as to distil the learnings of all that prebiotic collective effort, across a huge number of subsequent generations, will no longer be protocells: they will already constitute living cells in their own right.

5.2 Matter and Energy Cycles Beyond the Individual: Ecological Networks and Collective Action as a Fundamental Requirement for Abiogenesis

Before we address the crucial impact that the development of reliable heredity and regulation had on protocell organization, functional/agent behaviour and proliferation, it is important to highlight that protocellular individuals never stood alone. Even at the first stages of abiogenesis, when protocells formed spontaneously and underwent diverse physical–chemical transformations (mostly due to exogenous forces), they were part of highly heterogeneous populations (similar to vesicle suspensions that one can prepare in vitro). The simpler the protocells, the simpler the features that reflect that heterogeneity: e.g., global size, shape, molecular composition, membrane permeability/fluidity, etc. (Piedrafita et al. 2017). In any case, the current picture of the process of origins consists in a progressive transition from primordial ('messy') instances of chemical/protocell heterogeneity (Szostak 2011) towards more and more sophisticated versions of it, eventually akin to those we observe in extant cell populations.

In this scenario, where molecular diversity is the rule rather than the exception, one can easily imagine different chemistries arising independently, in a variety of compartments, and then combining through protocell fusion events (Carrara et al. 2012), or coupling indirectly by means of a smaller pool of intermediate compounds that are cycled through the local environment (waste products, nutrients, etc.—depending on the type of protocell/proto-metabolism under consideration). As division events become more frequent and reliable, fostered by endogenous chemistries, protocell proliferation rates shall accordingly increase, and the material and/or energy resources required by these non-equilibrium systems will become a strong limiting factor. At that point, competition forces may appear and lead to the "survival of the fittest", inducing more homogeneity in the population (like autocatalysis could also do, at a more basic molecular level). However, nature is intrinsically stochastic, providing many sources for chemical and system variability. In addition, experimental and theoretical models of bacterial ecology have demonstrated that "cross-feeding" or "mutual sustenance" among cell species is not only possible but may well be the norm (Posfai et al. 2017; Pacheco et al. 2019).

In this way the origins of syntrophic relationships and "ecopoiesis" (Guerrero 1998) can be envisioned in a prebiotic scenario, since the first self-(re-)producing protocells would face not only scarcity of some essential nutrients but also the potential contamination of their local environments due to the accumulation of waste/

leakage products. Under such conditions, spontaneous metabolic shifts to adapt to the new circumstances should be naturally expected: namely, protocells benefiting from new feeding opportunities and collectively engaging with others in matter and energy exchanges that expand and, at the same time, interlock the endogenous chemical transformations that take place within each of them.

From this perspective, the development of agent capacities (i.e., diverse protocell-protocell interaction mechanisms) by the members of the population is pivotal: both for each individual to respond to external challenges and endure over time and for their collective maintenance, as a whole—which in turn contributes to more efficient versions of the metabolism performed by single protocells. Therefore, a reciprocal but asymmetric reinforcement occurs between two parallel dimensions of the phenomenon: (i) the metabolic dynamics carried out by protocells, thanks to the cyclic and highly integrated organization of their internal components; and (ii) the ecological relationships that involve global resource allocation/distribution (cross-feeding, etc.). This type of bolstering connection, which will re-materialize later, at different stages of evolution (see, e.g.: [Etxeberria 2025; Cabello et al. 2025, this issue]) is reciprocal because one dimension cannot exist without the other (there is no physiology without ecology, and vice-versa), but asymmetric in the sense that individual protocells remain the principal source of activity, the main "performers" or "transformers" of causal power and action. Thus, we speak about protocell *organization*, whereas (relatively less integrated or looser) ecological interconnections are regarded as *networks*.

5.3 Climbing the Ladder of Complexity Towards Biological Autonomy: 'Dynamic Decoupling' Mechanisms as the Key Towards Open-Ended Evolution

Even if some self-producing protocells could establish proto-ecological networks and become sufficiently robust to sustain themselves and proliferate on the planet, the long-term maintenance of the living phenomenon (across geological time scales) is still quite remarkable. And more so if one realizes that any material system, especially under precarious, non-equilibrium conditions, inherently tends to decay, accumulate defects, etc. How did nature overcome these difficulties, bringing about an incredibly wide range of efficient and adaptive metabolisms, colonizing the whole surface of the Earth and remaining there until the present day?

Answering this question brings us down to the problem of how a complex system may achieve its own *reproduction*. Biological organization is ensured and thrives, in practice, via growth and division of individual living beings, establishing a historical causal entailment through which they perpetuate. One could even say that the hard-core problem of the origins of life is achieving reliable reproduction of complex, self-producing, autonomous systems. But this challenge is huge because efficient and adaptive metabolisms require an increasingly complex organization, which involves very heavy material/energetic demands: in particular, reliable reproduction needs specific molecular recording mechanisms, arranged within a given system architecture, so that the intermediate levels of complexity generated on the way don't get degraded and lost. Almost a century ago, von Neumann had the deep insight that there is a threshold of complexity below which any "universal constructor" would decay and above which it would be able to maintain itself, via self-reproduction, and start a process of open-ended evolution (McMullin 2000; Ruiz-Mirazo et al. 2008). The formidable quest of natural physical systems that may eventually turn biological is, indeed, reaching the von Neumann threshold/architecture without disintegrating on the way.

Protocell reproduction plays a critical role here because it leads to *lineages*, which transform into actual *families* (groups of closely similar individuals, related via common ancestry) within the overall population. This adds a completely new historical dimension to the emerging phenomenon. The more reliably reproduction is accomplished, the deeper the protocell lineage, and the bigger the weight of the corresponding family, in the population, over time. New protocells, in this way, become the result of the self-making of previous protocells, transcending their individual sphere through consecutive growth and reproduction cycles (Ruiz-Mirazo et al. 2020). All of this, of course, has a significant impact on the overall population dynamics, including the potential to extend the influence of a change/innovation far beyond the spatial and temporal coordinates of the individual organization where it first occurs—by virtue of the role it plays in a later coming, similar individual.

Thus, protocell populations evolve across prebiotic times, comprising a high number of trans-generational trajectories that contingently intermingle, combining different factors (physiological, ecological, reproductive…) under global matter/energy limitations, which impose further restrictions and tension on the interactions. Natural selection and other evolutionary forces operating on the population shape the progressive, historical outcome of this multi-scale, collective process. The evolutionary process itself is transformed, thereby, as new individuals, with novel features, take over the population. In brief, prebiotic evolution transforming into proper *biological* evolution. For all of this to happen, the key lies in the development of molecular mechanisms that contribute to solve, at once, two hard –apparently unrelated– problems: (i) improving the robustness and adaptivity of the individual protocells and (ii) registering and transmitting, via efficient reproduction, their level of complexity (including potentially beneficial variations) to their offspring, in a way that allows subsequent protocells in the lineage to retain that complexity and avoid decay.

The solution to this double problem is particularly challenging because those molecular mechanisms must be embedded –and have direct effects– in the recursively cyclic and functionally integrated (metabolic) organization of each protocell, while making lineages more reliable and profound in a linear, historical sense. The first steps towards the end of this tunnel were surely taken when protocells started synthesizing molecular templates (e.g., RNA oligonucleotides) with capacity *both* for replication (sequence conservation) *and* for the specification of new (more elaborate and accurate) constraints on their individual metabolism: in other words, material 'records' that could not only be faithfully *transmitted* to other individuals in the population, but also physiologically *interpreted* by each of them (Pattee 1969).

Nevertheless, together with this incipient 'self-recording/self-interpreting infrastructure', the production of second-order control mechanisms was also crucial. The reason is that any complex dynamic organization, articulated through the synthesis and functional integration of its component parts (like the metabolizing protocells described above), needs to explore a wide range of states/behaviours, as it faces multiple variations of both internal and external conditions. Being precarious (non-equilibrium) systems, effective navigation of those large phenotypic spaces requires dedicated meta-control mechanisms so individuals can respond quickly and adequately to a given challenge, finding the specific stationary state –or behavioural strategy– that solves the problem, which ultimately requires the modification of primary controls on metabolism. But that's precisely what biological regulation involves (Bich et al. 2016): endogenously produced material controls operating on other controls in such a way that global system robustness and adaptivity are enhanced.

Although the primordial, natural origin of regulatory mechanisms is still an open question, in our view it is deeply connected to prebiotic evolutionary dynamics and, more precisely, to the capacity that some protocells developed to "learn" from the experience (i.e., from the "trials and errors") of previous and contemporary individuals in the population—outcompeting members of their own or other families, sharing and collaborating with some others, etc. (Ruiz-Mirazo and Moreno 2024; Shirt-Ediss et al. 2024). Thus, regulation might have appeared, for the first time, when protocells started implementing reversible metabolic shifts to face nutritional challenges (e.g., similar to the 'Lac-operon mechanism' in extant bacteria); or in the context of their response to viroid infections, leading to early versions of microbial immunity (e.g., something like the CRISPR-Cas defence system); or directly operating changes in external conditions (e.g., by means of selective secretion, or controlled change of spatial position) which become functional, feeding back into the protocell individual and enhancing its "adaptive agency" (Di Paolo 2005).

What is important to realise is that all these mechanisms serving as 'material memory' of the dynamics of a population, across generations –be them hereditary or regulatory– must operate "off-line" with regard to the internal functioning and external behaviour of individual systems: in other words, they are *dynamically decoupled* from the basic metabolic workings of the organism, even if they remain *hierarchically coupled* to them (Pattee 1969; Ruiz-Mirazo and Moreno 2024), contributing to the whole system robustness, plasticity and adaptive capacities. Such is the trick that nature invented to generate, maintain and potentially increase the complexity of the biological world: produce individuals with a highly sophisticated organization of controls, operating at different rates, which represent a much longer, historical and inherently collective process.

5.4 Conclusion

The estimated time window for primordial biogenesis to be completed was of the order of hundreds of million years. This incomprehensible figure makes perfect sense, because the process surely involved an enormous amount of protocell reproduction cycles and subsequent generations of similar systems in constant interaction and transformation. As a result, there must have been a strong and very long sorting/turnover among protocell families, or lineages, in their struggle for the material and energetic resources available on the surface of the primitive Earth. Furthermore, the limited nature of these resources surely made ecological and other types of competitive/cooperative relationships necessary, from early stages, for the long-term sustenance of the emergent phenomenon, taken as a whole.

Therefore, it is highly compelling to conceive the three main dimensions of life –physiology, ecology and evolution– unfolding together, though asymmetrically, during its actual origins. At the end of that process, the living phenomenon, realised in/by individual autonomous agents (prokaryotic cells—the major causal drivers of most biological processes), transcends any of those particular individuals, extending far beyond their spatial boundaries and lifetimes. In other words, becoming a living organism, right from the beginning, from the dawn of life, requires the collective effort of many previous (proto-)organisms, with which it shares a common historical path.

Acknowledgements Authors were supported by IAS-Research Group Grant IT1668-22 from the Basque Government, grants PID2019-104576GB-I00 and PID2023-147251NB-I00, funded by MCIU/AEI/https://doi.org/10.13039/501100011033 and FEDER/UE (for projects 'Outonomy' and 'Outagencies', respectively) and the John Templeton Foundation (JTF, Science of Purpose -- Grant No. 62220). This contribution improved thanks to helpful critical comments from two reviewers (Alejandro Merlo & Leonardo Bich) and the editors of the compilation (Arantza Etxeberria & Xabier Barandiaran).

References

Barandiaran XE, Di Paolo E, Rohde M (2009) Defining agency: individuality, normativity, asymmetry, and spatio-temporality in action. Adapt Behav 17(5):367–386. https://doi.org/10.1177/1059712309343819

Bich L, Mossio M, Ruiz-Mirazo K, Moreno A (2016) Biological regulation: controlling the system from within. Biol Philos 31(2):237–265. https://doi.org/10.1007/s10539-015-9497-8

Carrara P, Stano P, Luisi PL (2012) Giant vesicles "Colonies": A model for primitive cell communities. Chem Bio Chem 13(10):1497–1502. https://doi.org/10.1002/cbic.201200133

Cabello V et al (2025) Autonomy and its limits in social-ecological systems. In: Barandiaran XE, Etxeberria A (eds) Outonomy: fleshing out autonomy beyond the individual. Springer.

Chen X-M et al (2022) Light-activated photodeformable supramolecular dissipative self-assemblies. Nat Commun 13(1):3216

Di Paolo EA (2005) Autopoiesis, adaptivity, teleology, agency. Phenomenol Cogn Sci 4(4):429–452. https://doi.org/10.1007/s11097-005-9002-y

Etxeberria A (2025) Environment(s), autonomy and (a)symmetries. In: Barandiaran XE, Etxeberria A (eds) Outonomy: fleshing out autonomy beyond the individual. Springer.

Ganti T (1987) The principle of life. OMIKK, Budapest.

Guerrero R (1998) Crucial crises in biology: life in the deep biosphere. Int Microbiol 1:285–294

Kauffman SA (2000) Investigations. Oxford University Press

Lauber N, Flamm, C, Ruiz-Mirazo, K (2021) "Minimal metabolism": a key concept to investigate the origins and nature of biological systems. BioEssays 43(10). https://doi.org/10.1002/bies.202100103

McMullin B (2000) John von Neumann and the evolutionary growth of complexity: looking backward looking forward. Artif Life 6(4):347–361. https://doi.org/10.1162/106454600300103674

Moody ERR et al (2024) The nature of the last universal common ancestor and its impact on the early Earth system. Nat Ecol Evol 8:1654–1666. https://doi.org/10.1038/s41559-024-02461-1

Moreira D, López-García P (2009) Ten reasons to exclude viruses from the tree of life. Nat Rev Microbiol 7(4):306–311. https://doi.org/10.1038/nrmicro2108

Moreno A, Mossio M (2015) Biological autonomy: a philosophical and theoretical enquiry. Springer, Netherlands

Mossio M, Bich L (2017) What makes biological organisation teleological? Synthese 194(4):1089–1114. https://doi.org/10.1007/s11229-014-0594-z

Mossio M, Saborido C, Moreno A (2009) An organizational account of biological functions. Br J Philos Sci 60(4):813–841. https://doi.org/10.1093/bjps/axp036

Nicolis G, Prigogine I (1977) Self-organization in nonequilibrium systems: from dissipative structures to order through fluctuations. Wiley.

Nogal N et al (2023) The protometabolic nature of prebiotic chemistry. Chem Soc Rev 52(21):7359–7388. https://doi.org/10.1039/D3CS00594A

Pacheco AR, Moel M, Segrè D (2019) Costless metabolic secretions as drivers of interspecies interactions in microbial ecosystems. Nat Commun 10(1):103. https://doi.org/10.1038/s41467-018-07946-9

Pattee HH (1969) How does a molecule become a message? Developmental Biology Supplement 3:1–16

Piedrafita G et al (2017) Permeability-driven selection in a semi-empirical protocell model: the roots of prebiotic systems evolution. Sci Rep 7(1):3141. https://doi.org/10.1038/s41598-017-02799-6

Posfai A, Taillefumier T, Wingreen NS (2017) Metabolic trade-offs promote diversity in a model ecosystem. Phys Rev Lett 118(2):028103. https://doi.org/10.1103/PhysRevLett.118.028103

Rosen R (1991) Life itself: a comprehensive inquiry into the nature, origin, and fabrication of life. Columbia University Press

Ruiz-Mirazo K, Mavelli F (2008) On the way towards 'basic autonomous agents': Stochastic simulations of minimal lipid–peptide cells. Biosystems 91(2):374–387. https://doi.org/10.1016/j.biosystems.2007.05.013

Ruiz-Mirazo K, Moreno A (2004) Basic autonomy as a fundamental step in the synthesis of life. Artif Life 10(3):235–259. https://doi.org/10.1162/1064546041255584

Ruiz-Mirazo K, Moreno, A (2024) On the evolutionary development of biological organization from complex prebiotic chemistry. In: Mossio M (ed) Organisation in Biology, pp 187–218. https://doi.org/10.1007/978-3-031-38968-9_9

Ruiz-Mirazo K, Shirt-Ediss B, Escribano-Cabeza M, Moreno A (2020) The construction of biological 'inter-identity' as the outcome of a complex process of protocell development in prebiotic evolution. Front Physiol 11. https://doi.org/10.3389/fphys.2020.00530

Ruiz-Mirazo K, Umerez J, Moreno A (2008) Enabling conditions for 'open-ended evolution.' Biol Philos 23(1):67–85. https://doi.org/10.1007/s10539-007-9076-8

Saha T, Galic M (2018) Self-organization across scales: from molecules to organisms. Philosophical Transactions of the Royal Society B: Biological Sciences 373(1747):20170113. https://doi.org/10.1098/rstb.2017.0113

Shirt-Ediss et al (2024) Modelling the prebiotic origins of regulation & agency in evolving protocell ecologies. *BioRxiv* Preprint. https://www.biorxiv.org/content/10.1101/2024.11.20.624505v1

Showalter K, Epstein IR (2015) From chemical systems to systems chemistry. Chaos 25:097613. https://doi.org/10.1063/1.4918601

Szostak JW (2011) An optimal degree of physical and chemical heterogeneity for the origin of life? Philosophical Transactions of the Royal Society B: Biological Sciences 366(1580):2894–2901. https://doi.org/10.1098/rstb.2011.0140

Varela FJ (1979) Principles of biological autonomy. Elsevier North Holland.

Chapter 6
Biological Autonomy and Reproduction

David Cortés-García

Abstract This chapter encompasses a discussion about the understanding of reproduction in the theory of autonomy, emphasizing the need to expand traditional theories of autonomous self-reproduction to account for interorganismal and ecological interactions. Drawing from recent contributions in the philosophy of biology, the chapter examines some of the limitations of self-reproduction as an endogenous process derived from self-production, highlighting cases such as sexual reproduction or symbiotic dependencies that illustrate the relational and interactive nature of reproduction. I then argue for an extended framework that integrates relational dependencies and distributed organizational processes.

Keywords Biological Autonomy · Interdependence · Symbiosis · Relationality · Self-Reproduction · Self-Maintenance · Material overlap

6.1 Introduction

Biological autonomy is a central concept in understanding living systems, which captures their capacity to self-maintain and regulate their own functioning. However, our growing knowledge on the interconnectedness and mutual dependencies of the living is calling for a rethinking of the concept of biological autonomy. The limitations of traditional formulations of autonomy have been highlighted, emphasizing that autonomy must account for interactive aspects beyond internally regulated self-organization (Aguilera and Di Paolo 2019; Moreno et al. 2008). In particular, this chapter explores how reproductive processes, far from being merely internal functions or outputs, often depend on dynamic interactions with other organisms, developmental scaffolds, and environmental cues. These observations challenge the prevailing ideal of autonomous self-reproduction and invite a reconceptualization

---

D. Cortés-García (✉)
IAS Research Centre for Life, Mind and Society, Department of Philosophy, University of the Basque Country (UPV/EHU), Donostia-San Sebastián, Spain
e-mail: david.cortes@ehu.eus

X. E. Barandiaran and A. Etxeberria (eds.), *Outonomy*,
SpringerBriefs in Philosophy, https://doi.org/10.1007/978-3-032-05501-9_6

of reproduction within the organizational theories as a structurally dependent and ecologically embedded phenomenon (Etxeberria 2026, this volume).

Organizational theories of biological autonomy have traditionally subordinated reproduction to metabolic self-maintenance. However, several recent contributions have sought to incorporate reproductive functions into this framework. These include analyses of functional integration (Mossio et al. 2009; Saborido et al. 2011), organizational extended inheritance (Pontarotti 2015), intergenerational continuity (DiFrisco and Mossio 2020), reproductive individuality (Nuño de la Rosa et al. 2021), reproductive continuity (Etxeberria 2023), mutual dependencies (Etxeberria et al. 2023), reproductive agency (Nuño de la Rosa 2023) and reproductive traits (Cortés-García et al. 2024). These contributions have significantly advanced the discussion on how to integrate reproduction into organizational theories of biological autonomy. The perspective developed in this chapter is intended as a further contribution in this direction, by emphasizing the ecological and relational dimensions of reproductive processes, and exploring how these dimensions invite a reconceptualization of reproduction beyond the classical model of autonomous self-reproduction. By emphasizing the diversity of reproductive processes and their dependence on interactions within and across organisms, I argue that reproduction is not simply a capacity of autonomous individuals but a process that frequently exceeds and redefines the boundaries of individuality.

6.2 Autonomous Self-Reproduction

In the theory of autonomy, reproduction is understood as a second-order process, derived from the self-produced organization of the autonomous system. Within this framework, organization holds ontological primacy and is conceptualized as the determining factor of what constitutes a living being. Consequently, other processes such as reproduction or evolution are theorized as secondary, or second-order, processes, derived from autonomous self-organization. As Humberto Maturana and Francisco Varela explicitly state, "[reproduction] requires a unit that reproduces itself; this is why reproduction is an operation subsequent to the establishment of the unit and cannot enter as a defining feature in the organization of living systems" (Maturana and Varela 1973, p. 92 my translation).

In developing this framework, Maturana and Varela (1973, 1984) emphasized that the production of similar but topologically distinct systems depends on causes that derive from the internal self-organization of the unit that reproduces. They adopted the notion of "self-reproduction", which they reinterpreted and adapted within their theory of autopoiesis. Prior to their work, the notion of self-reproduction had already been discussed in various fields, such as theoretical biology, cybernetics, and molecular biology, particularly in relation to self-replicating systems (see below). In the theory of autonomy, self-reproduction is defined as the process through which an autopoietic unit produces another unit with a similar organization. Importantly, the process of self-reproduction is coupled to the process of self-production, so that self-reproduction is an extension or a particular form of self-production and thus exclusive of autopoietic systems. Self-reproduction is contrasted with replication and copy fundamentally in that the mechanism for reproduction is not external to the system that is reproducing, but identical to it (Maturana and Varela 1973). Hence, reproduction remains entirely internal for the logic of autonomy: it presupposes an already constituted individual, and the causal elements involved in its realization are intrinsic to the system itself.

Further developments of the idea of autonomous self-reproduction emphasize the continuity of the self-produced organization beyond the lifespan of the individual system. Following the reasoning proposed by Maturana and Varela, reproduction is conceptualized in functional terms as a process through which the autonomous system produces similar units, thereby succeeding in maintaining its organization beyond the limits imposed by the decay of the precarious autonomous system (Ruiz-Mirazo et al. 2000, 2004). This view faces the challenge that reproductive traits, such as gametes, mating behaviors or reproductive organs, do not appear to contribute to the self-maintenance of the individual organism. In this sense reproductive functions seem to fall outside the organizational regime that define autonomy in its classical formulation. Two strategies have been proposed to resolve this tension. One appeals to higher-order entities, such as populations, species or ecosystems, as the relevant units whose autonomy is supported by reproduction (Mossio et al. 2009). The other refrains from invoking supra-organismic individuality and instead proposes that reproduction contributes to the continuity of organizational structures across generations. On this view, the autonomous system is not defined by the persistent identity of a single unit, but by the maintenance of a self-producing organization that transcends individual life cycles: "self-maintaining organization [...] maintains itself also through reproduction" (Saborido et al. 2011, p. 16). In both cases, reproduction remains framed as a means to preserve organizational identity, either at a higher organizational level or over time.

Importantly, organizational approaches to *autonomous self-reproduction* differ significantly from previous and contemporary views on self-reproduction which center on the possession of a particular hereditary determinant that is theorized to ensure parent–offspring similarity and thus ground faithful inheritance. Examples include the program in von Newmann's automaton theory, the germ plasm in Weismannism, the genetic program in Jacob and Monod's view on molecular biology, and the replicator in Dawkins' gene-eye view. These models conceive reproduction as the transmission of a pre-existing set of instructions, containing all the information necessary to produce similar entities, often overlooking the material and dynamic processes that drive development and reproduction. Thus, reproduction is reduced to the mere production of copies, overlooking the material and dynamic processes that drive development and reproduction. In brief, within these theories, self-reproduction is "self" in the sense that the reproducing individual is assumed to contain all the information necessary to produce a similar entity. The focus lies on the content of the set of instructions, rather than on the processes through which those instructions are interpreted and realized.

In contrast to these informational models, organizational theories conceive self-reproduction in fundamentally different terms. Rather than depending on the transmission of a pre-existing set of instructions, reproduction is understood as the result of an operational continuity between the reproducing and the reproduced systems. What is preserved across generations is not a code, but a mode of organization sustained through material and developmental processes.

A closely aligned view can be found in James Griesemer's notion of material overlap, which emphasizes the physical contribution of the parent organism to the formation of the offspring (Griesemer 2000). For Griesemer, reproduction entails the transmission not of symbolic content, but of developmental capacities grounded in material structures, such as cytoplasmic components, organelles, and even ecological elements that scaffold the ontogeny of the new individual (Griesemer 2014). This view reinforces the material and relational dimension of reproduction, shifting attention from copying to development. As noted by Saborido and colleagues (2011), the key distinction between Griesemer's view and autonomous self-reproduction lies in the level of abstraction: whereas material overlap highlights the intergenerational transmission of developmental potential, autonomous self-reproduction focuses on the preservation of a specific organization. Both, however, depart from reducing reproduction to replication and contribute to expanding the theoretical framework in which reproduction can be understood.

In short, the concept of autonomous self-reproduction encompasses the idea that the main causal factors involved in the production of offspring rely on the internal or endogenous properties, materials and processes of the autonomous self-maintaining individual. The theory of autonomous self-reproduction acknowledges the role of external interactions, but it tends to subordinate them to the internal, self-maintaining organization of the individual. The next section reviews how reproduction needs to be understood beyond the individual.

6.3 Interorganismal Relations in Reproduction

Reproductive processes often involve structural dependencies, mutual regulation, and causal entanglements between organisms, such that the reproduction of one system depends constitutively on its relation to others. These cases provide a basis for re-evaluating the adequacy of classical models of biological autonomy, and for advancing towards a form of *outonomous* reproduction.

Sexual reproduction is one of the most paradigmatic cases of relational dependence in biology. Despite significant differences between phylogenetic groups, all cases of sexual reproduction require the entanglement of materials originating from two different organisms (except for the rare cases of self-fertilization). The degree of physical interaction between organisms during reproduction varies widely, including nucleic, cytoplasmic and/or morphological structures. While this fact is widely recognized, its conceptual consequences for theories of autonomy are often overlooked. It suggests that, in some occasions, reproduction involves the integration of two operationally distinct systems, whose coordinated interaction gives rise to a new system with emergent interorganismal properties (Cortés-García et al. 2024).

Singularly, viviparous modes of reproduction involve an extended period of internal incubation and therefore a closer relationship between the gestating individual and the offspring. A particularly well-studied example is eutherian pregnancy, which a dynamic interplay between maternal and embryonic systems, mediated by the placenta. Far from acting as a passive container, the gestating organism engages in a co-regulated physiological process in which both systems influence each other's development, metabolism, and immune function (Wagner et al. 2014; Erkenbrack et al. 2018). In these cases, the reproductive event is not a discrete act of generation, but a transient configuration of mutual dependence, where the classical boundaries of individuality are blurred. Recent work suggests that pregnancy exemplifies a form of reproductive entanglement where the developing organism not only relies on but also modifies its maternal environment, creating an interdependent structure that challenges traditional notions of biological individuality (Nuño de la Rosa et al. 2021), agency (Nuño de la Rosa 2023) and autonomy (Etxeberria et al. 2023). This view highlights how processes of self-maintenance and reproduction become entangled within broader ecological and physiological networks.

Such analyses contribute to a reconceptualization of reproduction as an interactive system of physiological and developmental mutual dependencies, rather than as a mere transfer of genetic material between discrete individuals. Kepa Ruiz-Mirazo and colleagues (2000) have acknowledged that sexual reproduction challenges classical models of reproduction, since both parent organisms contribute organizationally, not just genetically, to the formation of the new system. James DiFrisco and Matteo Mossio (2020) go further, conceptualizing these events in terms of fusion and fission of autonomous systems, where individuality can be interpreted as a relational and emergent property. In this light, reproductive processes appear less as operations performed by individuals, and more as transformations of individuality itself, resulting from structured interactions between already organized, but interdependent, living systems. This underscores the need to rethink reproductive dynamics as emergent processes, shaped by interactions between distinct yet relationally intertwined autonomous systems.

While sexual reproduction illustrates how reproduction can require the integration of multiple individuals from the same species, symbiotic systems reveal that such integration often crosses species boundaries. In recent years, research on holobionts (i.e., integrated units composed of a host and its associated microbial communities) has transformed our understanding of biological individuality. Yet their implications for reproduction remain underexplored. In many cases, successful reproduction of the host is not possible without the active participation of its symbionts. These associations are not merely physiological or ecological, but developmentally and reproductively constitutive (Chiu and Gilbert 2015). For instance, in mammals, maternal microbial communities play a crucial role in shaping the immune system of the offspring during and after birth and are also fundamental for key physiological processes such as digestion. Similarly, certain insects, such as aphids, are entirely dependent on bacterial symbionts for the biosynthesis of essential nutrients that enable successful reproduction. Without these symbionts, reproduction and survival would be severely compromised. Development and reproduction are thus dependent on interspecies communication (Gilbert et al. 2012). Such cases suggest that reproduction is not the isolated activity of a single organism, but rather it should be understood as a distributed process involving reciprocal scaffolding between structurally distinct systems. The reproductive unit, in these contexts, is not an autonomous individual in the classical sense, but a relational configuration, dynamically sustained through multispecies cooperation. This challenges accounts of autonomy that assumes the self-contained closure of the reproductive process.

Moreover, this pattern is not limited to metazoans. Symbiosis plays a foundational role across the tree of life, from unicellular eukaryotes to bacteria and viruses. Reproductive processes in many microbial systems rely on cross-species interactions, including horizontal gene transfer, endosymbiotic integration, and transient cooperative associations. These dynamics facilitate adaptation, lineage emergence, and metabolic innovation. For instance, the integration of viral genetic material into bacterial genomes demonstrates how reproductive events can depend on cross-species interactions. In addition, some unicellular eukaryotes reproduce more efficiently or acquire key metabolic capabilities by harboring symbiotic bacteria or by engaging in temporary associations with other microorganisms (Dupré and O'Malley 2013).

In addition to this, Lynn Margulis and Dorion Sagan (1986) have proposed a scenario where the emergence of sexual reproduction is deeply linked to ancient symbiotic events that shaped early eukaryotic life. They suggest that the process of endosymbiosis that led to the evolution of the eukaryotic cellular structure not only originated mitochondria and plastids but also laid the groundwork for sexual processes, as the exchange and recombination of genetic material became central to maintaining the stability and adaptability of these newly integrated systems. Sexual reproduction is thus understood as an evolutionary innovation rooted in relationality and cooperation, where genetic recombination, whether through horizontal gene transfer, symbiosis, or sexual fusion, emerges from processes of interaction, fusion, and exchange that challenge traditional views of individuality and autonomy.

The organismal interactions and co-dependencies portrayed here illustrate how the reproductive unit does not necessarily align with the self-maintained biological individual, posing important challenges to existing notions of autonomous self-reproduction.

6.4 Outonomous Reproduction?

I have sought to illustrate some limitations of the notion of autonomous self-reproduction, minimally conceived as a natural result of the endogenous metabolic activity of a living cell, which grows and produces another topologically distinct but organizationally equivalent individual. As shown in the previous section, in many cases, the causes of reproduction are not solely endogenous but also dependent on exogenous interactions, which can take various forms, such as the necessity of sexual partners for mating, parent–offspring dynamics during care and development, host-microbiome relationality, and also broader symbiotic associations.

To adequately account for these phenomena, we need an organizational notion of reproduction that broadens the focus beyond the self-maintaining individual, incorporating inter-organismal relations, while still remaining sensitive to internal organizational constraints. Such an approach would recognize that reproduction is not merely the outcome of an autonomous system's internal processes but often emerges from the interaction between internal and external organizational dynamics in heterogeneous and interdependent systems (Bich and Bechtel 2025, this volume). By integrating these interorganismal and environmental factors, this perspective can provide a more comprehensive understanding of reproduction as a process embedded within both ecological and social networks, where the viability and continuity of life depend on interconnected systems rather than isolated individuals. The concept of outonomous reproduction has the potential to capture those reproductive processes that arise from mutual scaffolding, material entanglements, and coordinated interaction.

This reconceptualization finds important precedents in earlier work within the organizational tradition. Almost two decades ago, Moreno and colleagues (2008) argued, in more general terms, that autonomy cannot be reduced to internal self-organization alone. They distinguished between constitutive and interactive processes, emphasizing that the latter, often dismissed as secondary, are in fact essential for the maintenance of a system's identity. In their words, "autonomy requires more than self-organization or self-maintenance" (Moreno et al. 2008, p. 312). The present proposal extends this insight by showing how, in the case of reproduction, such interactive processes are not merely supportive of autonomy but constitutive of the very possibility of its transmission and transformation.

This project of elaborating a theory of autonomous reproduction finds promising conceptual tools in the formulations of the continuity of material organization discussed earlier (see Saborido et al. 2011; DiFrisco & Mossio 2020). Although often underexplored, this notion offers a potential starting point for integrating the metabolic and physiological dimensions of self-production with the ecological, diachronic and evolutionary aspects of reproduction. To achieve this, the concept of organizational continuity must adopt an interactive and distributed view that can encompass scaffolded reproduction, multispecies consortia and relations of interdependency in reproduction. This implies that the concept of organizational closure might not be a universal criterion for defining the limits of continuous organization. In this view, what persists is not a self-constructed organization, but a network of functional relations sustained and transformed across bodies, environments, and temporal scales. This perspective would preserve the organizational account's emphasis on functional integration, while overcoming some of its internalist assumptions. This idea opens the possibility of understanding different reproductive phenomena as constitutively influenced by environmental and social interactions (Martínez-Quintero and Rodriguez-Muguruza 2025, this volume).

The extended and distributed proposal for an outonomous view of reproduction sketched here aligns with a view of life that shifts away from focusing solely on individual organisms and instead emphasizes global processes. In this perspective, reproduction is understood as a collective and community-wide property where reproductive agency is distributed (Etxeberria 2023). Outonomous reproduction is not solely the re-production of form, but also the maintenance of relational continuity across generations, where what is reproduced is not identity but a network of historically stabilized dependencies. In this sense, outonomous reproduction is not a departure from the theory of autonomy, but a step toward its relational reformulation.

6.5 Conclusions

In this chapter I have tried to summarize some of the problems that our current knowledge about biological reproduction poses for the notion of autonomous self-reproduction. I have outlined different possible responses to these challenges, aiming to foster further discussions on the role of reproduction in biological theories and how the notion of self-produced autonomy might be expanded or reformulated to reflect the interactive and relational nature of living phenomena and reproductive processes. The perspective sketched here questions certain aspects of the theory of autonomy and invites us to consider an extended or distributed view of life and reproduction.

Acknowledgements I acknowledge funding from IAS-Research group funding IT1668-22 (Basque Government); grant PID2023-147251NB-I00 "Outagencies", funded by MCIU/AEI/ https://doi.org/10.13039/501100011033 and FEDER/UE; a predoctoral contract granted by the University of the Basque Country [PIF-2020]; and grant PID2021-127184NB-I00 "Metaphysics of Biology", funded by MICINN.

References

Aguilera M, A Di Paolo E (2019) Integrated information in the thermodynamic limit. Neural Networks 114: 136–146. https://doi.org/10.1016/j.neunet.2019.03.001

Bich L, Bechtel W (2025) Autonomy and heterarchy: organizing control in biological organisms. In: Barandiaran XE, Etxeberria A (eds) Outonomy: fleshing out autonomy beyond the individual. Springer.

Chiu L, Gilbert SF (2015) The birth of the holobiont: multi-species birthing through mutual scaffolding and niche construction. Biosemiotics 8(2):191–210. https://doi.org/10.1007/s12304-015-9232-5

Cortés-García D, Etxeberria A, Nuño de la Rosa L (2024) The evolution of reproductive characters: an organismal-relational approach. Biol Philos 39(5):26. https://doi.org/10.1007/s10539-024-09961-1

DiFrisco J, Mossio M (2020) Diachronic identity in complex life cycles: An organisational perspective. In: Meincke AS, Dupré J (eds) Biological identity: perspectives from metaphysics and the philosophy of biology, (history and philosophy of biology). Routledge, pp 177–199

Dupré J, O'Malley MA (2013) Varieties of living things: life at the intersection of lineage and metabolism. In: Normandin S, Wolfe CT (eds) Vitalism and the scientific image in post-enlightenment life science, 1800–2010, pp 311–343. Springer Netherlands. https://doi.org/10.1007/978-94-007-2445-7_13

Erkenbrack EM, Maziarz JD, Griffith OW, Liang C, Chavan AR, Nnamani MC, Wagner GP (2018) The mammalian decidual cell evolved from a cellular stress response. PLoS Biol 16(8):e2005594. https://doi.org/10.1371/journal.pbio.2005594

Etxeberria A (2023) Jacob's understanding of reproduction: challenges from an organismic collaborative framework. HOPOS: The Journal of the International Society for the History of Philosophy of Science 13(2): 535–553. https://doi.org/10.1086/726256

Etxeberria A (2026) Environment(s), autonomy and (a)symmetries. In: Barandiaran XE, Etxeberria A (eds) Outonomy: fleshing out autonomy beyond the individual. Springer.

Etxeberria A, Cortés-García D, Torres M (2023) Organisms, Life Relations, and Evolution: Inter-Dependencies after Kropotkin's Mutual Aid. ArtefaCToS. Journal of Science and Technology Studies 12(1). https://doi.org/10.14201/art2023121179204

Gilbert SF, Sapp J, Tauber AI (2012) A symbiotic view of life: We have never been individuals. Q Rev Biol 87(4):325–341. https://doi.org/10.1086/668166

Griesemer J (2000) The units of evolutionary transition. Selection 1(1–3):67–80. https://doi.org/10.1556/Select.1.2000.1-3.7

Griesemer J (2014) Reproduction and Scaffolded developmental processes: An integrated evolutionary perspective. In: Minelli A, Pradeu T (Eds) Towards a theory of development, pp 183–202. Oxford University Press. https://doi.org/10.1093/acprof:oso/9780199671427.003.0012

Margulis L, Sagan D (1986) Origins of sex. Yale University Press, Three Billion Years of Genetic Recombination

Martínez-Quintero A, Rodríguez Muguruza A (2025) Autonomy and alienation in menstrual health. In: Barandiaran XE, Etxeberria A (eds.) Outonomy: Fleshing out autonomy beyond the individual. Springer.

Maturana H, Varela F (1973) De máquinas y seres vivos: Autopoiesis, la organización de lo vivo (Sixth Edition 2004). Editorial Universitaria, Grupo Editorial Lumen

Maturana H, Varela, F (1984) El árbol del conocimiento. Editorial Universitaria.

Moreno A, Etxeberria A, Umerez J (2008) The autonomy of biological individuals and artificial models. Biosystems 91(2):309–319. https://doi.org/10.1016/j.biosystems.2007.05.009

Mossio M, Saborido C, Moreno A (2009) An organizational account of biological functions. Br J Philos Sci 60(4):813–841. https://doi.org/10.1093/bjps/axp036

Nuño de la Rosa L (2023) Agency in reproduction. Evol Dev 25(6):418–429. https://doi.org/10.1111/ede.12440

Nuño de la Rosa L, Pavličev M, Etxeberria A (2021) Pregnant females as historical individuals: an insight from the philosophy of Evo-Devo. Front Psychol 11. https://doi.org/10.3389/fpsyg.2020.572106

Pontarotti G (2015) Extended inheritance from an organizational point of view. Hist Philos Life Sci 37:430–448. https://doi.org/10.1007/s40656-015-0088-4

Ruiz-Mirazo K, Etxeberria A, Moreno A, Ibáñez J (2000) Organisms and their place in biology. Theory Biosci 119(3–4):209–233. https://doi.org/10.1007/s12064-000-0017-1

Ruiz-Mirazo K, Peretó J, Moreno A (2004) A universal definition of life: autonomy and open-ended evolution. Orig Life Evol Biosph 34(3):323–346. https://doi.org/10.1023/B:ORIG.0000016440.53346.dc

Saborido C, Mossio M, Moreno A (2011) Biological organization and cross-generation functions. Br J Philos Sci 62(3):583–606. https://doi.org/10.1093/bjps/axq034

Wagner GP, Kin K, Muglia L, Pavličev M (2014) Evolution of mammalian pregnancy and the origin of the decidual stromal cell. The International Journal of Developmental Biology 58(2–4): 117–126. https://doi.org/10.1387/ijdb.130335gw

Chapter 7
Autonomy and Alienation in Menstrual Health

Alejandra Martínez-Quintero and Ainhoa Rodríguez Muguruza

Abstract This chapter redefines autonomy in bioethics by foregrounding menstrual agency as a relational and embodied capacity, rather than an isolated expression of individual choice. It argues that menstrual health has been reduced to reproductive function, excluding the psychological, emotional, and social dimensions of menstruators' lived experience. Despite being reduced and overlooked, the way menstrual health intersects with emotional, social, and cultural dimensions reveals that even in health, autonomy can be experienced as both vulnerability and agency. Drawing on a triadic approach to ailments and the enactive concepts of autonomy, agency, and precariousness, the chapter reconceptualises menstrual well-being as a shared ethical and social concern. In doing so, it challenges dominant notions of autonomy and calls for structural transformations that support menstruators in reclaiming agency over their menstrual lives.

Keywords Menstrual health · Autonomy in bioethics · Enactive agency · Feminist phenomenology

7.1 Introduction

In 2022, the World Health Organisation redefined menstrual health beyond hygiene, recognising it as a physical, emotional, and psychological process integral to overall well-being. Despite this progress, menstrual health has often been narrowly framed around reproduction. While the cycle prepares the body for pregnancy, it also

Both authors contributed equally to the development of this article. The order of authorship reflects internal decisions within the collaboration and does not imply a hierarchy of contribution.

A. Martínez-Quintero · A. R. Muguruza (✉)
IAS Research Centre for Life, Mind and Society, Department of Philosophy, University of the Basque Country (UPV/EHU), Donostia-San Sebastián, Spain
e-mail: arodriguez974@ikasle.ehu.eus

A. Martínez-Quintero
e-mail: alejandra.martinez@ehu.eus

X. E. Barandiaran and A. Etxeberria (eds.), *Outonomy*,
SpringerBriefs in Philosophy, https://doi.org/10.1007/978-3-032-05501-9_7

regulates immune function (Howes 2010), metabolises fats and carbohydrates, and supports muscular, skeletal, gastrointestinal, hepatic, and neural systems (Plant and Zelesnik 2015). Defining menstrual health solely through fertility oversimplifies its systemic complexity (Jasienska 2013).

This paper explores how autonomy can be conceptualised and exercised by menstruators within medical contexts, where menstrual health is often pathologised or dismissed. The principle of autonomy in bioethics was created to protect patients from medical practices that ignore their agency. However, it frequently assumes autonomy as rational, individual, and disembodied (Paul et al. 2003), assumptions that do not reflect the lived experiences of autonomy. We argue that autonomy is not undermined by bodily vulnerability, but constituted through it. Drawing on the triadic approach and enactive theory, we conceptualise autonomy as inherently precarious: it is sustained through ongoing bodily and environmental negotiation. This framework allows us to reconceive the menstrual cycle not as a disruption to autonomy but as an active, ongoing process through which agency is enacted.

7.2 Rethinking Autonomy in Bioethics

Autonomy is foundational in bioethics, but often framed as rational, individual, and context-free (Casado da Rocha and Etxeberria 2012). This narrow view fails to capture how real-life decision-making in health is shaped by bodily states, lived experience and social conditions. Health decisions are not made from a disembodied ideal, but from concrete bodies, with specific vulnerabilities. This is particularly relevant when autonomy in health decision-making seems more challenging, like during illness or physiological conditions like pregnancy, breastfeeding, or the hormonal fluctuations of the menstrual cycle.

Addressing concrete vulnerable bodies sheds light on how the traditional view of autonomy misses that every human life is autonomous and at the same time precarious. Recognising this shifts the analysis from idealised independence to enactive, embodied agency. This section draws on Casado da Rocha and Etxeberria's (2012) triadic model of health, combined with insights from enactive and organisational theories, to argue for understanding autonomy as inherently precarious, socially embedded, and continuously enacted by the agent. This approach offers a nuanced account of agency in clinical contexts, attending to the material, affective, and normative dimensions of lived experience. Integrating the sense of agency with this model will help to explain why menstrual embodiments are often seen as pathological rather than integral to menstruators' agency.

7.2.1 Idealised Autonomy and the Triadic Approach

Bioethics is commonly guided by four principles: respect for autonomy, beneficence, non-maleficence, and justice (Casado da Rocha and Etxeberria 2012). Respect for autonomy affirms a patient's right to make informed decisions about their health. However, Casado da Rocha and Etxeberria argue that treating autonomy as a formal, context-free right, something a patient either has or lacks, fails to reflect the realities of illness. Instead, they propose understanding autonomy not as a fixed right to be granted, but as a capacity, to make decisions, consent to treatment, and act meaningfully, that can be eroded by bodily vulnerability.

They argue that both autonomy and health must be understood across three interrelated dimensions: physiological, subjective, and social. Hence, they propose a triadic model to understand health conditions by distinguishing between disease, illness and sickness as the physiological, subjective and social aspects of ailments. For example, diabetes as a *disease* is defined by the objective measures that signal insulin resistance, such as elevated blood glucose levels. As subjectively lived, *illness* captures the individual's experience of diabetes, such as shivering during hypoglycemia. Finally, as socially lived, *sickness* describes how diabetes is recognised and responded to by others, such as when peers acknowledge the patient's impaired functioning.

The triadic approach shows that autonomy cannot be taken for granted within illness, as each dimension, biological, experiential, or social, can compromise the capacity to act autonomously. This critique suggests that even when bioethical protocols are followed, such as providing adequate information, patients may still experience vulnerability rather than the capacity to act autonomously. This layered view challenges the idealised image of the independent, rational patient and instead presents autonomy as inherently interdependent. Recognising this interdependence shifts the focus from autonomy as an individual possession to a collective responsibility, sustained across medical, social, and relational contexts (Urdangarin and Umerez 2026, this volume).

7.2.2 Using Enactive Concepts: Autonomy, Precariousness and Sense of Agency

Building on the triadic model, enactive and organisational theories can deepen our understanding of the vulnerability of autonomy by framing it as a core property of living systems. Here, *autonomy* refers to a living system's capacity to self-maintain and self-organise (Moreno and Mossio 2015; Di Paolo et al. 2017). Living beings are operationally closed and yet thermodynamically open to material and energetic exchanges. This balance between defining an identity while remaining open illustrates the enactive notion of *precariousness.* Within enactive theory, the concept of *precariousness* carries three related meanings (Di Paolo and Beer 2023): the fragility of the processes that realise operational closure, the intrinsic fragility of the system as a whole, and the vulnerability associated with thermodynamic openness. Here, precariousness refers to a broader sense of *embodied vulnerability*.

Unlike idealised or abstract models of autonomy, an account rooted in embodied vulnerability portrays living beings as constantly navigating this tension, neither fully independent nor fully determined by their environments. This understanding of precarious autonomy has specific implications for how we approach menstrual health, an area where bodily vulnerability is often interpreted as incapacity rather than a dimension of agency. From an enactive view, it is precisely the embodied vulnerability that has the potential for *agency*. The intrinsic tension to sustain life under precarious conditions, gives rise to meaning and action (Di Paolo 2018). Even when regulation falters, the potential for agency remains, as long as autonomy endures. In this sense, precarious conditions, understood as constraints for agency are not always limiting; they can also enable action. When agents interpret precariousness as navigable rather than paralysing, their scope for agency expands. This interpretive stance, what enactivists metaphorically call "surfing" precariousness, allows vulnerability to become a source of agential depth rather than a barrier to autonomy.

Embodied vulnerability, applied to the triadic approach, can manifest across metabolic, sensorimotor, and social levels: from maintaining biological processes (metabolic), to the fragility of habits and skills (sensorimotor), to the breakdown of social coordination, such as disrupted conversations (De Jaegher and Di Paolo 2007). These layers illustrate how autonomy is not a stable trait but a dynamic, precarious process shaped by bodily, cognitive, and relational factors. This view aligns with the triadic model of autonomy in illness, which frames agency as emerging through the interaction of embodiment, social embeddedness, and subjective interpretation. It also resonates with enactive and organisational accounts that distinguish between autonomy as a capacity and agency as enactment (Rubel et al. 2021). Because agency, in this framework, operates across normative domains, biological, sensorimotor, and social, conflict often follows. Yet even when these tensions arise, the underlying capacity for autonomy endures. Agents continue to act within and through these constraints, sometimes in ways that contradict long-term well-being. Autonomy, therefore, remains precarious and subject to limitation, but so long as it persists, the potential for agency remains.

7.3 The Alienation of the Menstrual Cycle

Understanding autonomy through enactive and triadic frameworks deepens what it means to respect autonomy in contexts of illness and reveals the particular challenges faced by non-normative bodies, including menstrual bodies. These are bodies that diverge from dominant biomedical or social norms, whether through gender, reproductive variation, or other physiological differences (Lugones 2007). Menstrual health exemplifies how physiological symptoms, subjective experience, and social stigma intersect to shape agency. Pain, irregularity, and taboo can distort self-understanding and foster alienation.

If illness compromises autonomy by weakening agential capacity, then alienation from one's body has similar effects. Reclaiming agency in menstrual health begins with acknowledging and reintegrating those embodied experiences that have long been marginalised or medicalised.

7.3.1 Alienation and Reclamation: The Menstrual Cycle and the Lived Body

Despite being a natural process, menstruation has long been alienated, framed as disordered, uncontrollable, or pathological. This framing undermines agency by treating menstrual experience as something to manage or conceal rather than as an integral aspect of embodied life. Feminist phenomenologists like Iris Marion Young (2005) argue that scientific objectivity reinforces this alienation by reducing menstruation to biological facts and separating it from lived experience. Medical discourse often limits menstruation to reproduction, ignoring its broader connections to health, well-being, and autonomy.

Even when biological facts are known, such as hormonal fluctuations before menstruation, menstruators are rarely supported in managing the emotional, energetic, or social challenges that follow. Menstrual experience remains largely unacknowledged, while expectations of composure persist despite limited access to affordable products, private facilities, and comprehensive education. The inability to rinse a menstrual cup at work or to sit through an exam while in pain exemplifies how public systems fail to accommodate menstrual needs. These conditions reflect a medical model that treats menstruation as a problem of biology rather than a meaningful, lived experience.

Simone de Beauvoir's existential feminism deepens this critique by showing how agency is shaped through reclaiming subjectivity in the face of bodily objectification. Social forces, such as the male gaze or early sexualisation during puberty, position menstruators as passive objects of attention (Young 2005; Bergoffen 2000), distancing them from bodily ownership. For Beauvoir (1949), reclaiming agency requires owning the lived body and its transitions, including menarche.

Integrating menstrual experience into one's sense of self challenges the dominant view of the body as merely biological. It is a process of reclaiming meaning, resisting objectification, and navigating conflicting norms. Agency, in this light, emerges not by denying bodily experience but by actively incorporating it, through cycles, discomforts, and cultural tensions, into one's autonomous self.

7.3.2 Menstrual Health as a Shared Responsibility

While reclaiming one's body is personal, Beauvoir's existential ethics reminds us that agency is also a shared responsibility. In *The Ethics of Ambiguity*, she argues that true freedom requires working to liberate others from oppression (Bergoffen 2000). This is especially relevant for non-normative bodies, those that deviate from dominant medical, social, or cultural norms, such as menstruators with chronic conditions, disabilities, neurodivergence, or cyclical variability. These individuals often occupy the margins of care and social recognition, requiring both ethical and epistemic attention.

Beauvoir's view challenges the bioethical tendency to treat autonomy as an individual right. Instead, autonomy should be seen as fragile, embodied, and relational, shaped by social, institutional, and medical systems. Respecting autonomy, particularly in the context of menstrual health, means more than avoiding coercion; it demands actively enabling meaningful agency. Stigma, under-researched conditions, and fragmented care often constrain menstruators' ability to act as full agents of their health.

Approaching menstrual health as a shared responsibility means recognising that autonomy is co-constructed, developed within networks of care, trust, and support. Menstrual health should be central to preventive and primary care, including improved research, broader diagnostic models, and equitable access to resources. Yet medical care alone is insufficient. Agency is not merely the capacity to choose but the ability to act in ways that reflect one's embodied self-understanding. This capacity is vulnerable, especially in the context of menstrual pain, emotional fluctuation, and social stigma, and must be supported when it falters. Respecting autonomy, and hence supporting agency, thus means redistributing responsibility across healthcare systems, institutions, and communities. Framing menstrual health in terms of agency, rather than choice or compliance, allows us to respond to its relational and precarious nature.

Ultimately, integrating these insights into menstrual care reshapes expectations and practices. Together, they foster environments where bodily awareness and agency can flourish. This socially sustained view of autonomy sets the stage for the next section, where we move from ethical framing to practical application, offering a redefinition of menstrual health that centers agency and embodied meaning.

7.4 Reinterpreting Menstrual Health

Building on the earlier reframing of agency as relational and embodied, menstrual health should be seen as an interdependent phenomenon encompassing physiological processes, subjective experience, and sociocultural structures. If agency is a fragile, collectively sustained capacity, menstrual health must be understood not merely in biomedical terms but as a dimension of embodied agency. This challenges the conventional reduction of menstrual health to reproductive function (Clough 2002) and opens space to examine how practices, awareness, and relations support or undermine agency.

Autonomy must be redefined, not as detached self-governance but as a capacity shaped by biological rhythms, social connections, and material realities. Menstrual health, then, is not a fixed state but a dynamic lived condition through which agency is enacted. Rather than an entirely new paradigm, this is a reorientation: menstrual health is a key site where bodily knowledge, social norms, and medical discourses converge. It is deeply tied to the enabling conditions of relational autonomy.

7.4.1 Reframing Knowledge on Menstrual Health

To address menstrual health philosophically is to center the body as shaping and enabling agency. Autonomy is enacted within physiological, relational, and structural contexts. Menstrual health exemplifies this embeddedness, not as biological regularity but as a lived and negotiated state shaped by internal cycles, experiential knowledge, and social validation. Iris Marion Young (2005) highlights how menstrual alienation stems from scientific reductionism that renders bodies measurable but separate from lived experience. This framing casts menstrual bodies as unruly or deficient, interpreting deviations from narrow norms as dysfunction. Such objectification fragments self-understanding, discouraging embodied interpretation.

A phenomenological approach restores the body as a site of meaning and knowledge. Menstrual variability, fluctuations in cycle length, hormones, energy, and emotion, should not be pathologized. Biomedical indicators like regularity or balance cannot serve as absolute norms. Irregularities may reflect adaptive physiological responses to environmental, emotional, or metabolic change. Health here is not deviation's absence, but the ability to negotiate embodied rhythms in context. This reframing aligns with critiques of reductive autonomy. Just as autonomy is more than individual decision-making, menstrual health is more than stable biology (Alvergne et al. 2018). It emerges through physiological dynamics and the social, epistemic structures that shape bodily interpretation. We must resist reducing menstruation to isolated systems and instead recognise it as systemic and co-regulating: affecting cognition, emotion, immunity, and metabolism. Simone de Beauvoir's existential feminist ethics deepen this perspective. Reclaiming the body from objectification is crucial to reclaiming agency (Beauvoir 1949). Menstrual reclamation involves recognising the cycle as a meaningful, patterned embodiment, not a disruption. This requires cultivating awareness that treats fluctuations as informative. Menstruation can thus be a source of insight, revealing changing needs and capacities.

Yet this awareness is not solitary. The triadic model of disease, illness, and sickness reminds us that bodily meaning is both personal and collective. Menstrual cycles are interpreted through experience and cultural scripts, medical norms and institutional frameworks. Recognition, by clinicians, educators, and policymakers, is critical for legitimising menstrual knowledge. Understanding menstrual health as a dynamic capacity thus entails confronting epistemic injustice and structural neglect. This reconceptualisation redefines both health and knowledge. Health becomes the body's capacity for adaptation and meaningful interaction with its cycles, and knowledge arises from lived, reflective engagement (Menatti 2026, this volume). Menstrual health becomes an interpretive, context-sensitive process through which bodies are understood and navigated, supporting a more expansive form of agency.

7.4.2 The Role of Bodily Self-Awareness in Menstrual Health

Recognising menstrual health as a dynamic capacity centers bodily self-awareness in the practice of health and autonomy. Health is not static conformity but ongoing responsiveness to internal and external conditions. Through reflective attention to symptoms, shifts, and patterns, menstruators cultivate embodied knowledge: a situated understanding of their cycles essential for self-care and legitimacy. Biomedical models often dismiss subjective reports as anecdotal, privileging quantifiable data. Yet feminist theorists and health advocates argue that experiential knowledge, built over time, offers vital insights. Menstrual cycles affect cognition, mood, metabolism, and energy in context-sensitive ways. For instance, some feel more resilient during ovulation, while others experience premenstrual irritability or clarity (Pels 2022; McEvoy and Osborne 2019). These variations highlight the complexity of hormonal embodiment and the inadequacy of static clinical norms.

Reproductive endocrinology confirms substantial inter- and intra-individual variation (Jasienska 2013), complicating the search for universal biomarkers. This ambiguity reinforces the epistemic value of self-attunement. Variability fosters insight, not uncertainty. Self-awareness is not indulgence; it is an interpretive skill developed through embodied engagement. Feminist phenomenology insists that the body is a site of meaning-making (Young 2005; Bergoffen 2000). This view elevates menstruators' insights as foundational to autonomy. Menstrual health thus emerges as both biologically mediated and phenomenologically lived. It integrates hormonal rhythm with reflective sense-making (Rodriguez-Muguruza 2023). Attunement allows behaviour and care to align with embodied states. Agency, then, resides not in abstraction but in navigating bodily transformation. Awareness is not just preliminary to action; it sustains it. Menstrual knowledge, built through bodily dialogue, reveals agency as situated and responsive.

7.4.3 Integrating Menstrual Knowledge into Agency

If menstrual health is a dynamic, embodied lived experience, then agency must include the cyclical and contingent. Integrating menstrual knowledge strengthens the relationship to the body, enabling intentional adaptation. This does not imply control or optimisation but learning to live responsively within physiological flux.

The concept of a dynamic menstrual health encompasses both physiological rhythms and the systems through which these are interpreted and supported. Attunement lets menstruators adjust expectations and behaviours, for instance, recognising increased sensitivity in the premenstrual phase may guide care and interaction (Rodriguez-Muguruza 2023). This is not about avoiding symptoms but cultivating adaptive agency attuned to lived bodily conditions. Reclaiming autonomy also requires collective transformation. Menstrual health must be affirmed through education, research, and clinical practice. Healthcare systems should treat the cycle as a dynamic biomarker, using symptoms and patterns as indicators of broader health, as emerging research suggests (Rosen et al. 2024; Prior 2021). This must be done without normative assumptions, respecting variability and individual context.

Policy investment is essential to overcome menstrual marginalisation in medical research and care. This is not a novel framework but a return to what is already lived: menstrual health as intelligible, situated knowledge. Validating menstrual experience fosters autonomy and justice. By reclaiming menstruation as a source of embodied insight, we resist abstraction and embrace agency as a responsive, evolving practice.

7.5 Conclusion

Understanding autonomy as embodied vulnerability, as an inherently precarious yet potentially agentive condition, enables menstruators to assert meaningful agency over their health. This perspective challenges the common reduction of menstrual health to reproductive function alone. Rather than viewing autonomy as isolated self-mastery, it emerges from the dynamic interplay of biology, relationships, and material realities. Scientific reductionism often pathologises menstruating bodies, estranging individuals from their embodied experiences. A phenomenological approach counters this by positioning the body as a site of knowledge, where menstrual variability is natural, not deviant. Health, then, is not static but an ongoing negotiation of bodily rhythms within lived contexts, defying rigid biomedical norms.

Bodily self-awareness is central, emerging from engagement with cyclical patterns and shifts. This awareness empowers adaptive responses and challenges norms that dismiss subjective menstrual experience, making these insights foundational to autonomy. Integrating menstrual knowledge means embracing the cyclical nature of embodied life and adapting care to fluctuating needs. This calls for healthcare and policy changes that affirm menstrual health as central to well-being, requiring personalised and context-sensitive support. Ultimately, menstrual health is a vital site of knowledge and agency, involving ongoing negotiation rather than correction. Embracing menstrual variability as part of autonomy challenges marginalisation and promotes more just, humane care. Living responsively within bodily rhythms reclaims bodily autonomy as relational and deeply human.

Acknowledgements AMQ and ARM acknowledge funding from IAS-Research group funding IT1668-22 (Basque Government) grant PID2019-104576GB-I00 "Outonomy" funded by MCIU/

AEI/10.13039/501100011033. AMQ was also funded by a predoctoral grant from the University of the Basque Country (PIF18/163). ARM also from the 'Metaphysics of Biology' project [PID2021-127184NB-I00].

This research was supported by the Basque Government [IT1668-22], grants PID2019-104576GB-I00 for project Outonomy and PID2023-147251NB-I00 for Outagencies funded by MCIU/AEI/10.13039/501100011033 and FEDER/UE, and the 'Metaphysics of Biology' project [PID2021-127184NB-I00].

References

Alvergne A, Högqvist Tabor V (2018) Is female health cyclical? evolutionary perspectives on menstruation. Trends Ecol Evol 33(6):399–414

Beer RD, Di Paolo EA (2023) The theoretical foundations of enaction: precariousness. Biosystems 223:104823. https://doi.org/10.1016/j.biosystems.2022.104823

Bergoffen DB (2000) From Husserl to Beauvoir: Gendering the perceiving subject. In: Fisher L, Embree L (eds) Feminist phenomenology. Springer, Netherlands, pp 57–70

Casado A, Etxeberria A (2012) Towards autonomy-within-illness: applying the triadic approach to the principles of bioethics. In: Carel H, Cooper R (eds) Health, illness and disease: philosophical essays. Acumen Publishing, pp 57–76

Clough S (2002) What is menstruation for? on the projectibility of functional predicates in menstruation research. Stud Hist Philos Biol Biomed Sci 33(4):719–732

de Beauvoir S (1948) The ethics of ambiguity (B. Frechtman, Trans.). Philosophical Library

de Beauvoir S (1949) The Second Sex (Constance Borde & S. Malovany-Chevallier, Trans.; 2011th ed.). Vintage Books, a division of Random House, Inc.

De Jaegher H, Di Paolo E (2007) Participatory sense-making: an enactive approach to social cognition. Phenomenol Cogn Sci 6(4):485–507. https://doi.org/10.1007/s11097-007-9076-9

Di Paolo E (2018) The enactive conception of life. In: Newen A, Bruin LD, Gallagher S (eds) The Oxford handbook of 4E cognition (4 edition). Oxford University Press.

Di Paolo EA, Buhrmann T, Barandiaran XE (2017) Sensorimotor life: an enactive proposal. Oxford University Press.

Howes M (2010) Menstrual function, menstrual suppression, and the immunology of the human female reproductive tract. Perspect Biol Med 53(1):16–30

Jasienska G (2013) The fragile wisdom: an evolutionary view on women's biology and health. Harvard University Press

Lugones M (2007) Heterosexualism and the colonial/modern gender system. Hypatia 22(1):186–209

McEvoy K, Osborne L (2019) Allopregnanolone and reproductive psychiatry: an overview. Int Rev Psychiatry 31(3):237–244

Moreno BAJ, Mossio M (2015) Biological autonomy: a philosophical and theoretical enquiry. Springer Netherlands

Menatti L (2026) Salutogenesis, adaptivity and the continuum of health, Outonomy, fleshing out the concept of autonomy beyond the individual. In: Barandiaran XE, Etxeberria A (eds) Outonomy: fleshing out autonomy beyond the individual (p. in press). Springer

Paul EF, Miller FD, Jr, Paul J (eds) (2003) Autonomy. Cambridge University Press

Pels M (2022) Fast like a girl: a woman's guide to using the healing power of fasting to burn fat, boost energy, and balance hormones. Penguin Random House

Plant TM, Zelesnik AJ (2015) Knobil and Neill's physiology of reproduction (2 vols). Academic Press

Prior JC (2021) Women's reproductive system as balanced estradiol and progesterone actions: a revolutionary, paradigm-shifting concept in women's health. Drug Discov Today Dis Model 32:31–40

Rodriguez-Muguruza A (2023) Menstrual cycles as key to embodied synchronisation. In: Viejo JM, Sanjuán M (eds) Life and mind (Vol. 8) Springer

Rosen Vollmar AK, Mahalingaiah S, Jukic AM (2024) The menstrual cycle as a vital sign: a comprehensive review. F&S Reviews 6(1)

Rubel A, Castro C, Pham A (2021) Autonomy, agency, and responsibility. In: Algorithms and autonomy: the ethics of automated decision systems, pp 21–42. Cambridge University Press

Urdangarin M, Umerez J, (2026) Rethinking the autonomy of subjects-in-common, Outonomy, fleshing out the concept of autonomy beyond the individual. In: Barandiaran XE, Etxeberria A (eds) Outonomy: fleshing out autonomy beyond the individual, p in press. Springer.

Young IM (2005) On female body experience: "throwing like a girl" and other essays. Oxford University Press

Part III
The Psychic Self and Its Environment

Chapter 8
Process and Relational Ontology in Enactive Psychiatry

Enara García

Abstract This chapter examines mental disorders from an enactive perspective. It explores two key ontological claims—the processual and relational nature of cognition—and their implications for our understanding of mental disorders. Rather than viewing them as isolated brain disorders, mental disorders are presented as developmental sensorimotor trajectories that are shaped by embodied interactions and social contexts. It highlights the dynamic interplay between an individual's autonomy and their social environment in the emergence of mental disorders.

Keywords Mental disorders · Enactive cognition · Intersubjectivity · Process ontology · Relational autonomy

8.1 Introduction

Contemporary understanding of mental health has evolved significantly, moving beyond the notion of the self-sufficient autonomous individual. It now encompasses a more holistic view that recognizes the intricate interplay between personal well-being and the broader social, environmental, and relational contexts in which individuals live. This perspective emphasizes that mental health is not solely a matter of individual resilience or autonomy, but is deeply influenced by the quality of our relations with others, our communities, and the environments we inhabit.

In recent years, enactive cognition theories have garnered growing interest as a relational framework that transcends internalist, individualist, brain-centered and biomedical models of mental health (de Haan 2020; Maiese 2022; Nielsen 2023). One of the main contributions resides in the acknowledgement that mental processes –and therefore mental disorders– are scaffolded by processes that extend to the sociomaterial environment. It challenges prevalent dualisms between mind and body, or physiology and psychology and promotes viewing autonomous individuals as embodied, situated and ecological agents. Accordingly, the enactive approach

E. García (✉)
Department of Psychology, University of Southern Denmark, Donostia-San Sebastián, Spain
e-mail: enaragarcia@health.sdu.dk

X. E. Barandiaran and A. Etxeberria (eds.), *Outonomy*,
SpringerBriefs in Philosophy, https://doi.org/10.1007/978-3-032-05501-9_8

conceptualizes mental disorders as phenomena emerging from the dynamic interplay between the agent and its environment, thereby recognizing the interconnectedness, mutual dependence, and multiscale embeddedness of psychiatric phenomena.

The aim of this chapter is to delve into two ontological principles that ground enactive psychiatry, its processual and relational ontology,[1] and clarify their relevance to better understanding psychiatric conditions.

8.2 Process Ontology

Philosophy of mind and psychiatry has long exhibited a static bias. The cognitivist framework, which was dominant in the 90s, viewed the mind as a series of discrete, static mental states, each generated by decomposable cognitive modules, viewing mental disorders as faulty or malfunctioning mental states (e.g., faulty beliefs in schizophrenic delusions). The same static bias is present in current models, such as the DSM, which classifies disorders based on fixed symptoms, or the biomedical model, which attributes them to specific brain dysfunctions. All these approaches have neglected the temporal course, diachronic character, and inherent dynamics of mental disorders. In contrast, the enactive perspective rejects this static view of the mind and adopts a process-oriented framework, emphasizing the dynamic nature of mental activity as processes that unfold in time, have a particular trajectory, and produce cumulative changes (Vintiadis 2022). Cognition is viewed as emerging from the regulation of organism-environment interactions, constituted by interactive processes that encompass the brain-body-environment system. Change, thus, is considered a fundamental property of cognition rather than a mere accident.

The enactive framework, drawing from organizational approaches in biology, views living organisms as self-producing autonomous entities that maintain their identity under precarious conditions (Varela et al. 1991, 2017). Autonomy extends beyond the biological (metabolic) domain to include sensorimotor and intersubjective dimensions (see Virenque 2026, this volume). Sensorimotor autonomy comes from networks of habits that endow the agent with adaptive behavior (Di Paolo et al. 2017), while intersubjective autonomy arises from social interactions, where individuals co-construct shared meanings, emotions, and collective identities (Di Paolo et al. 2017, 2018). The individual is thus constituted and traversed by normative processes that occur across these multiple domains of autonomy, often in tension with one another (García and Barandiaran 2024; Thompson and Varela 2001). Cognition involves the adaptive management of this plurality of normative tensions across the organic, sensorimotor and intersubjective domains, which are functionally coordinated at different timescales (e.g., the tension between biological hunger, cutlery skills and social manners in a formal dinner). This perspective rejects reductionism, by understanding domains of autonomy not as discrete levels that can be reduced

[1] Here, ontology refers not to metaphysical assumptions about ultimate reality, but to the objects of specific sciences (i.e., cognitive science, psychology, psychiatry).

to their isolated components, but as processes that maintain each other dynamically across different timescales. The dynamic interaction between local processes of a system leads to emergent processes that, in turn, exert a "global-to-local" influence on those elements (Thompson and Varela 2001).

Similarly, mental disorders can be understood as emergent, organized wholes constituted by interacting processes across organic, sensorimotor, and intersubjective domains. This idea is also captured by the concept of "Dynamic Gestalt Patterns"— a set of interrelated factors that, while not individually necessary, collectively define a psychiatric disorder (Gallagher 2024). These complex, multi-layered feedback systems do not follow a linear cause-effect model but operate through organizational non-linear causality (Gallagher 2022; de Haan 2020). Changes in one part of the pattern influence and modify other parts, resulting in a constantly evolving, integrated whole. The apparent stability of mental disorders is, therefore, not a fixed trait of individuals but a temporary outcome of their dynamic self-organization.

One consequence of this view is that mental disorders are closely tied to the historical and developmental processes of individuation of the person. They are not external entities that can simply be removed from the individual; rather, they are ways in which the person is organized. This explains the self-illness ambiguity often seen in mental disorders —the difficulty of distinguishing between an individual's sense of self and the symptoms of the condition (e.g., identifying with negative thoughts in depression or manic states in bipolar disorder). In other words, they involve disturbances in the sense of self. Therefore, by shifting our focus from viewing individuals and selves as fixed and fulfilled to exploring their individuation process and becoming, we can better grasp the temporal asymmetry and path-dependence of mental disorders. Their progression over time—e.g., emergence, recovery, relapse, and chronicity—is not just a feature of traditionally recognized developmental disorders but is integral to all mental conditions. Plaintly said, I suggest that not only those traditionally classified as developmental disorders are indeed developmental.

One way of making sense of this path-dependence is through Piagetian mechanisms of sensorimotor equilibration (Di Paolo et al. 2017). The development of new skills and habits occurs through a dynamic equilibration between integrating new experiences into existing cognitive and sensorimotor schemas and adapting these schemas to accommodate new experiences. While developmental trajectories remain flexible, they also exhibit a diachronic channelling of possibilities within the broader space of behavioral possibilities. As habits and sensorimotor structures stabilize, they constrain future developmental paths by making some coping mechanisms more accessible while rendering others less likely. This form of habit stabilization can be viewed as the *character* of the person, that is an idiosyncratic cognitive, affective and behavioral style that marks a distinct personal identity. A crucial point here is that habitual interaction styles imply unique vulnerabilities, which predispose individuals to specific conditions over others (Hovhannisyan and Vervaeke 2022). The reason is that if sensorimotor individuation constitutes a person's character, then all characters involve a reduction of potential behaviors, limiting the individual's developmental field and predisposing them to specific rigidities and maladaptations. These rigidities endow the person with differential vulnerabilities, which draw idiosyncratic patterns of onset, relapse, and recovery in a person's history of mental health. All living systems are precarious, and thus, vulnerable. However, given the idiosyncratic nature of developmental individuation processes, not all persons are vulnerable in the same way and to the same extent.

In this regard, non-linear dynamical models offer both the mathematical and conceptual tools necessary to model mental conditions in a processual fashion and to understand developmental rigidities (Nelson et al. 2017; Olthof et al. 2023). Mental disorders are represented as dynamical networks of collective variables (Borsboom 2017), whose evolution over time is explained by general principles of pattern formation in complex adaptive systems. Psychopathological states, such as persistent sadness or fluctuating moods, are interpreted as attractors—stable states that the system naturally gravitates towards. Mental disorders are thus understood as "stuck states". For instance, a person may be drawn into a state of depression, or cycle between depressive and manic episodes, forming what is called a fixed-point or limit-cycle attractor. Certain psychopathological dynamics unfold slowly, such as episodes of depression or psychosis, which can remain stable for extended periods, often lasting for months. In contrast, other dynamics evolve rapidly, like panic attacks, which represent attractors that persist for only a few minutes. And most of them present a combination of attractors at different timescales that influence each other. The persistence of such habitual states over time, especially when an individual cannot escape them and overrule the performance of other situationally relevant habits and behaviors, is a common feature of psychopathology (Ramírez-Vizcaya and Froese 2019).

In mental disorders the brain-body-environment dynamics can be either too flexible (e.g., psychotic and dissociative conditions) or too rigid (e.g., neurotic conditions), but in either cases, they imply a diminishment of metastability and meta-flexibility in the behavior of the system. A healthy system, in order to cope with changes in the environment, must keep a relative degree of metastability, that is, a state of mixture between stable and unstable patterns, not being trapped into rigid attractors, but not being disintegrated either. This requires meta-flexibility —the ability to dynamically adjust its level of flexibility in response to a stressor while maintaining a degree of robustness in the system. This second-order flexibility allows resilient systems to balance change and preservation and to maintain an adequate range of degrees of freedom, while ensuring their integrity under varying conditions. Note that meta-flexibility and metastability define mental disorders in a continuous-dimensional manner, rather than establishing a categorical and binary health-disease demarcation. Yet, the explanatory relevance of dynamical models is that although they describe phenomena at a particular level of analysis, their dynamics can be linked to higher-scale processes. This allows us to describe and explain mental disorders in a processual, multiscale and multidimensional manner.

8.3 Relational Ontology

The relational ontology underpinning the enactive approach posits that cognition is inherently situated within the continuous, dynamic interaction between an individual and its sociomaterial environment. This framework rejects the traditional view of cognition as an isolated, brain-bound process, instead framing it as emergent from embodied engagement with the world. Cognition is thus not a matter of passively representing the world, but an active engagement with it, where the individual exercises autonomy in shaping and being shaped by its sociomaterial environment.

Ontologically, the relational nature of cognitive agents can be understood in two complementary ways (Dengsø and Kirchhoff 2023): On the one hand, the agent and its environment can be viewed as autonomous and individualized systems that interact and form relationships with each other, that is, constitutive processes precede interactive ones, with the relata being a priori separated entities that interact externally. On the other hand, both systems can be understood as differentiated through distributed, metastable relations, where the entities (relata) do not precede the relations but rather co-exist with and are shaped by them. I shall focus on this latter view, where agent and environment are not pre-existing, independent entities placed into relation, but instead, it is the broader relational dynamics that co-constitute and individuate them. Here, autonomy is understood, not as a property of individuals, but as emerging from distributed entangled processes along the individual-environment system that establish significant local asymmetries between them (McGann 2024). This relational perspective is present in the Simondonian turn in enactivism (Di Paolo 2021; García 2023; García and Arandia 2022; James 2020), where individuals are said to emerge from matrices of relational forces, and also in Hans Jonas's concept of "mediation", which refers to the human "inwardness" or self-referentiality as a form of dialectical achievement of encounters with others (Benevides et al. 2023). This shift proposes to look at sympoiesis (co-organization) rather than autopoiesis (self-organization) as fundamental biological structures that support mindedness (Dengsø and Kirchhoff 2023). As McGann puts it, "we become individuals, therefore, not by separation, but by differential entanglement" (2024, p. 8).

The enactive approach to social cognition as participatory sense-making (De Jaegher and Di Paolo 2007), can indeed be read from these two perspectives. Participatory sense-making explains how two autonomous agents come to create shared meanings within an autonomous relational domain that is, to some extent, independent from individual intentions. The autonomy of the relational domain allows for subtle or transformative modulations of individual meaning-making processes, enabling the co-creation of new meanings that would not be accessible to individuals in isolation. In its original formulation, social cognition is viewed as the process by which individual and autonomous agents come together to engage in shared meanings, highlighting the need to maintain individual autonomy for a social interaction to be genuinely social. However, from this latter relational perspective, participatory sense-making may also be seen as the process by which individuals engage with and shape each other's potential for growth and development, that is, the way by which we influence in the individuation of the other. Indeed, taking a diachronic perspective, there is a sense in which the interactants are individuated by the wider relational system they are elements of, via "global to local" or "top down" constitution. Rather than assuming that individuals exist independently before any interaction, we can view interaction itself as the force for individuation (James and Loaiza 2020). Humans are inherently relational beings, assemblies of historically developed interpersonal interactions and affective entanglements that define and individuate their embodied being-in-the-world.

Following this perspective shift, a recent relational turn has taken place calling for a figure/ground inversion between social and non-social cognition (e.g., Dingemanse et al. 2023; Trasmundi and Steffensen 2024). The point is to challenge the prevailing belief in cognitive science that by understanding basic, non-social cognition (e.g., perception of objects, navigation, etc.) we will be better equipped to understand social cognition as its complex derivative. However, this individualistic approach may be misleading, as the human brain has evolved in response to social demands and is largely shaped by our need to monitor and navigate complex social contexts (Dunbar 1998). Human cognitive flexibility arises from neoteny, as much of our cognitive development takes place postnatally through social interactions. This social embedding fosters remarkable plasticity, enabling learning, habit formation, and emotional attachment, which in turn enhance our ability to adapt to diverse socio-ecological niches through enculturation. This is not trivial, as many of the autonomous processes that constitute our sensorimotor identity extend to our coordination with others. Even the most fundamental sensorimotor schemes, like the Piagetian breastfeeding scheme, require coordination between the child and caregiver. Indeed, developmental psychologists have long noted the innate "readiness to interact", coordinate and imitate present in human infants (Meltzoff 2002; Reddy 2008).

The key point here is that human openness to interaction and underdeveloped potential are not only essential for growth but also create the conditions for mental disorders to emerge (Brüne 2000). This cognitive flexibility allows for diverse, socially shaped developmental paths to become maladaptive. Indeed, a widespread symptom in diverse mental disorders involves interpersonal misattunement, a sense of disconnectedness from a shared world and altered forms of interpersonal coordination (Gallagher 2013). Examples in adulthood can be found in personality disorders, where the core issue often lies in the individual's impaired ability to skillfully and adaptively engage with others and conform to socially accepted norms (Roche and Ansell 2020; Wright et al. 2022) or in schizophrenia –which has been traditionally understood as disturbances of the individual self in phenomenological psychopathology, but which also involves altered patterns of self- and other-centeredness perspective taking (Kyselo 2016; Nelson et al. 2009). Moreover, human developmental openness and freedom often manifest as existential anxiety and fear, underlying many disorders (Fuchs 2013). In other words, dysfunction arises when one fails to fulfill an evolutionarily fixed function, whereas disorder stems from maladaptive coping mechanisms arising in social development.

Consequently, mental disorders should not be conceptualized merely as isolated individual conditions but rather as interactively organized processes. Enactivism supports a systemic approach, emphasizing how social values and norms are embodied through interactions, shaping character, habits, and social repertoires. Rather than being strictly individual or social, mental disorders arise as (mal)adaptive responses relative to particular social contexts (e.g., adaptive preferences, Maiese 2026, this volume). This is evident in concepts like the "double empathy problem" in autism (Milton et al. 2018) and relational models of disability. While neural correlates of disorders may exist, they reflect circular causal processes involving social interactions rather than a fixed underlying dysfunction. In other words, there is no singular brain-based cause behind interpersonal difficulties—rather, these difficulties both constitute and express the disorder over time. The issue is not just "in the head" but in our ability to coordinate and engage with others, which are interpersonally developed skills. Mental disorders emerge thus as relational phenomena—impairments in the ability to engage in successful social interactions, meet others' expectations, coordinate behaviors, and maintain standards of predictability in interpersonal relationships.

In conclusion, although individual autonomy and its impairments have often been the focus of describing mental disorders, autonomy should be viewed as a regulatory process that extends diachronically to the history of interactions with the sociomaterial environment. The relational and processual view of cognition presented in this chapter redefines autonomy as a distributed phenomenon, sustained and transformed within the web of interpersonal entanglements and contextual relations in which the subject is embedded. Within this framework, psychiatric conditions cannot be understood merely as internal failures of the individual but as dynamic configurations that emerge from interaction patterns across multiple levels of organization and constitute forms of the individual's relational patterns. Mental disorders are seen as processes evolving along the developmental history of the person and compromise their metaflexibility and metastability in their relational habit repertoire. Mental disorders, therefore, are no longer seen as isolated dysfunctions but as specific modes of regulation and dysregulation within a broader relational system. This shift in perspective not only challenges traditional reductionist approaches but also opens new pathways for understanding and addressing mental health, fostering interventions that consider both the individual's organization and the interpersonal and collective dynamics that sustain it (e.g., promoting salutogenic environments, Menatti 2026, this volume).

Acknowledgements EG acknowledges funding from IAS-Research group funding IT1668-22 (Basque Government); grants PID2019-104576GB-I00 "Outonomy" and PID2023-147251NB-I00 "Outagencies", funded by MCIU/AEI/10.13039/501100011033 and FEDER/UE. This work has also received funding from the European Union's Horizon Europe Marie Skłodowska-Curie postdoctoral grant agreement No. 101205668.

References

Benevides R, Feiten TE, Chemero A (2023) Life after 'life after Kant' other minds with Jonas and Merleau-Ponty. J Conscious Stud 30(11–12):104–130

Borsboom D (2017) A network theory of mental disorders. World Psychiatry: off J World Psychiatr Assoc 16(1):5–13

Brüne M (2000) Neoteny, psychiatric disorders and the social brain: hypotheses on heterochrony and the modularity of the mind. Anthropol Med 7(3):301–318

de Haan S (2020) Enactive psychiatry. Cambridge University Press

De Jaegher H, Di Paolo E (2007) Participatory sense-making. Phenomenol Cogn Sci. https://doi.org/10.1007/s11097-007-9076-9

Dengsø MJ, Kirchhoff MD (2023) Beyond individual-centred 4e cognition: systems biology and sympoiesis. Constructivist Foundations 18(3):351–364

Dingemanse M, Liesenfeld A, Rasenberg M, Albert S, Ameka FK, Birhane A, Wiltschko M (2023) Beyond single-mindedness: a figure-ground reversal for the cognitive sciences. Cogn Sci 47(1):e13230

Di Paolo EA (2021) Enactive becoming. Phenomenol Cogn Sci 20(5):783–809

Di Paolo EA, Cuffari EC, De Jaegher H (2018) Linguistic bodies: the continuity between life and language. MIT Press

Di Paolo E, Buhrmann T, Barandiaran X (2017) Sensorimotor life: an enactive proposal. Oxford University Press

Dunbar RI (1998) The social brain hypothesis. Evol Anthropol: Issues, News, Rev: Issues, News, Rev 6(5):178–190

Fuchs T (2013) Existential vulnerability: toward a psychopathology of limit situations. Psychopathology 46(5):301–308

Gallagher S (2013) Intersubjectivity and psychopathology. International perspectives in philosophy and psychiatry. Oxford handbook of philosophy and psychiatry 258–274.

Gallagher S (2022) Integration and causality in enactive approaches to psychiatry. Front Psych 13:870122

Gallagher S (2024) The self and its disorders. Oxford University Press, London, England

García E (2023) Affectivity in mental disorders: an enactive-simondonian approach. Phenomenol Cogn Sci. https://doi.org/10.1007/s11097-023-09929-8

García E, Arandia IR (2022) Enactive and simondonian reflections on mental disorders. Front Psychol 13:938105

García E, Barandiaran XE (2024) Varieties of normativity and mental health. An enactive approach. Synthese.

Hovhannisyan G, Vervaeke J (2022) Enactivist Big Five Theory. Phenomenol Cogn Sci 21(2):341–375

James MM (2020) Bringing forth within: enhabiting at the intersection between enaction and ecological psychology. Front Psychol 11. https://doi.org/10.3389/fpsyg.2020.01348

James MM, Loaiza JM (2020) Coenhabiting interpersonal inter-identities in recurrent social interaction. Front Psychol 11:577

Kyselo M (2016) The enactive approach and disorders of the self - the case of schizophrenia. Phenomenol Cogn Sci 15(4):591–616

Maiese M (2026) Mindshaping and adaptive preferences. In: Barandiaran XE, Etxeberria A (eds) Outonomy: fleshing out autonomy beyond the individual. Springer

Maiese M (2022) Autonomy, enactivism, and mental disorder: a philosophical account. Taylor & Francis

McGann M (2024) Facing life: the messy bodies of enactive cognitive science. Phenomenology and the Cognitive Sciences, 1–18

Meltzoff AN (2002) Imitation as a mechanism of social cognition: origins of empathy, theory of mind, and the representation of action. Blackwell Handbook of Childhood Cognitive Development, 6–25

Menatti L (2026) Salutogenesis, adaptivity and the continuum of health. In: Barandiaran XE, Etxeberria A (eds) Outonomy: fleshing out autonomy beyond the individual. Springer
Milton D, Heasman B, Sheppard E (2018) Double empathy. Encyclopedia of autism spectrum disorders
Nelson B, McGorry PD, Wichers M, Wigman JTW, Hartmann JA (2017) Moving from static to dynamic models of the onset of mental disorder: a review. JAMA Psychiat 74(5):528–534
Nelson B, Sass LA, Thompson A, Yung AR, Francey SM, Amminger GP, McGorry PD (2009) Does disturbance of self underlie social cognition deficits in schizophrenia and other psychotic disorders? Early Interv Psychiatry 3(2):83–93
Nielsen K (2023) Embodied, embedded, and enactive psychopathology: reimagining mental disorder. Springer Nature
Olthof M, Hasselman F, Oude Maatman F, Bosman AMT, Lichtwarck-Aschoff A (2023) Complexity theory of psychopathology. J Psychopathol Clin Sci 132(3):314–323
Ramírez-Vizcaya S, Froese T (2019) The enactive approach to habits: new concepts for the cognitive science of bad habits and addiction. Front Psychol 10:301
Reddy V (2008) How infants know minds. Harvard University Press
Roche MJ, Ansell EB (2020) Interpersonal models of personality pathology. The Cambridge handbook of personality disorders, 171–184
Thompson E, Varela FJ (2001) Radical embodiment: neural dynamics and consciousness. Trends Cogn Sci 5(10):418–425
Trasmundi SB, Steffensen SV (2024) Dialogical cognition. Lang Sci 103:101615
Varela FJ, Thompson E, Rosch E (1991/2017) The embodied mind, revised edition: cognitive science and human experience. MIT Press
Vintiadis E (2022) Mental disorders as processes: a more suited metaphysics for psychiatry. Philosophical Psychology, 1–18
Virenque L (2026) Intrinsic purposiveness and autonomy in interaction. In: Barandiaran XE, Etxeberria A (eds) Outonomy: fleshing out autonomy beyond the individual. Springer
Wright AGC, Ringwald WR, Hopwood CJ, Pincus AL (2022) It's time to replace the personality disorders with the interpersonal disorders. https://doi.org/10.31234/osf.io/7syvf

Chapter 9
Salutogenesis, Adaptivity and the Continuum of Health

Laura Menatti

Abstract Salutogenesis is a theory of health and disease that emphasises the promotion of beneficial measures besides the prevention of risk factors and counteracting pathogens. This paper reframes salutogenesis by situating it within the account of biological autonomy and adaptivity, drawing on recent developments in organisational accounts of living systems. By doing so, the paper provides new insights into the relational, situated and continuous nature of health, and it introduces the importance of supportive 'salutogenic environments' to foster adaptivity as the individual and collective capacity to change ourselves, including our environments, to promote health.

Keywords Adaptivity · Biological autonomy · Salutogenic environments · Health continuum · Organism-environment interaction

9.1 Introduction

The salutogenic approach represents a paradigm shift in how we conceptualise health and well-being. Salutogenesis emphasises the promotion of beneficial measures rather than solely focusing on the prevention of risk factors, in contrast to medical approaches centred on pathogenesis. Furthermore, medicine has been criticised for employing a compartmentalised view that overlooks broader ecological contexts. There is growing recognition that public health and biomedical frameworks need to integrate ecological considerations, as evidenced by approaches like *OneHealth* and *planetary health*, which acknowledge the fundamental connections between human well-being and environmental factors.

This chapter examines the foundations of salutogenesis, relating them to the notion of autonomy in biological systems and its significant contribution to contemporary healthcare practices. The analysis of the *Sense of Coherence* and the concept of

L. Menatti (✉)
IHPST, Institut d'Histoire et de Philosophie des Sciences et des Techniques, Université Paris 1 Panthéon-Sorbonne & CNRS, Paris, France
e-mail: laura.menatti@gmail.com

X. E. Barandiaran and A. Etxeberria (eds.), *Outonomy*,
SpringerBriefs in Philosophy, https://doi.org/10.1007/978-3-032-05501-9_9

health as a *continuum* shows how salutogenesis can provide a more comprehensive perspective on human health. Importantly, the paper introduces the novel concept of 'salutogenic environments', which, when examined through the lens of autonomy and adaptation, reveals how health is related to how organisms actively engage with and adapt to their surroundings rather than merely reacting to environmental pressures. This perspective offers a significant advancement in our understanding of the dynamic relationship between health, autonomy, and environmental interactions.

9.2 What Is Salutogenesis? A Short History and Its Pillars

The term salutogenesis is derived from the Latin words *salus* (health) and *genesis* (production, generation), signifying 'carrier of health'. Salutogenesis is a theory of health and disease that emphasises the promotion of beneficial measures besides the prevention of risk factors and counteracting pathogens.

A defining characteristic of salutogenesis is its proactive approach to health that focuses on enhancing factors that can improve individuals' health and their adaptive capacities with respect to the social and natural environment. To illustrate the foundational concept of salutogenesis compared to pathogenesis, scholars have employed the metaphor of the 'river of life' (Antonovsky 1979; Eriksson and Lindström 2008). According to this metaphor, solely promoting health by avoiding stressors or building bridges across the river to save people from drowning remains within a pathogenic approach. Instead, medicine should empower individuals to navigate these waters independently through health promotion, education, and preventive strategies that foster well-being without paternalism.

The salutogenic framework was developed by Aaron Antonovsky (1979, 1987), a medical sociologist whose research primarily examined stress, particularly the interplay between physiological and social stressors and their impact on health and disease across various social groups. These groups, based mainly in the United States and Israel, included menopausal women, Holocaust survivors, minorities, marginal populations, as well as diverse patient categories. Antonovsky dedicated his efforts to implementing and applying the salutogenic framework until his passing in 1994.

Antonovsky was a sociologist of health, yet his work was influenced by endocrinology, microbiology, psychiatry, and psychology to create a conceptualisation of the complexity of health, disease, and illness (Vinje et al. 2016). His model has gained importance in medicine and the social sciences, with applications across various fields (Mittelmark and Bauer 2017; Mittelmark and Bauer 2022). It is also utilised in decision-making processes, patient-centred medicine, and integrative care practices (Grover et al. 2022; Gartner et al. 2022; Menatti et al. 2022). Salutogenesis provides a specific framework and tools, such as the Sense of Coherence scale, to assess patient needs and manage stressors (Grover et al. 2022; Gartner et al. 2022; Menatti et al. 2022; Pelikan 2022; see also Dietscher et al. 2022).

In this chapter, I explore the salutogenic approach to health, its relationship with the environment and its connection to the notion of autonomy. Two main elements will be discussed: the concept of a *continuum* of health and the relationship between the organism and its environment, particularly the capacity to adapt and change.

A first pillar of the salutogenic approach developed by Antonovsky is *The Sense of Coherence*. It describes individual and collective capabilities to adapt to diverse life stressors. It reflects how individuals perceive and respond to their social surrounding, encompassing three key aspects: understanding (comprehensibility), resourcefulness (manageability), and purpose (meaningfulness). Understanding represents the capacity to make sense of and comprehend what is occurring around oneself, grasping the nature of challenges faced. Resourcefulness is the belief that one has access to sufficient resources, both personal and social, to address and manage situations that arise. Purpose involves the ability to find meaning and motivation within circumstances (Antonovsky 1996, 15). These aspects are measured through the Sense of Coherence Scale (see Eriksson and Contu 2022) to assess the collective and individual coping mechanisms that enable people to adjust to various situations and develop the necessary resources to handle changes and challenges. This idea closely aligns with biological autonomy, particularly with self-regulation and self-maintenance. They both address how organisms (or individuals) perceive, manage, and find meaning in their environment, offering a wider perspective on adaptation and well-being. Section 9.4 will analyse this adaptive capacity as an improved conceptualisation of health.

The other pillar of the salutogenic approach is the idea of health as a *continuum.* This idea, further discussed in Sect. 9.3, helps update current conceptualisations of health. Salutogenesis posits that health exists on a continuum between the two poles of complete wellness and illness. It encourages healthcare professionals to consider not only the treatment of diseases but also the strengthening of patients' resources and coping abilities. It fosters a more balanced, comprehensive understanding of human health and resilience.

In summary, salutogenesis advocates for a more systemic understanding of health that incorporates both preventive measures and proactive strategies while complementing pathogenic approaches with salutogenic initiatives (Becker et al. 2010).

9.3 Differences Between Salutogenesis, Health Promotion and Preventive Health

I argue that while providing innovative concepts on health, salutogenesis differs from traditional medical frameworks by focusing on adaptation and autonomy, extending beyond conventional preventive medicine and health promotion.

Preventive medicine typically refers to efforts aimed at disease prevention, both at the individual and community levels. It encompasses activities that reduce the risk of disease, disability, and death (Britannica 2022; see also Nikku and Eriksson 2012). Historical practices in preventive medicine included dietary prescriptions and the isolation of sick individuals (Becker 1988), as well as interventions in living and healthcare environments (Ward Thompson 2011). Measures such as quarantines and environmental management to avoid disease have been documented (Meloni 2021; Martini and Lippi 2021). Yet, contemporary medicine has focused on pathogenic risks following the development of germ theory and the discoveries of L. Pasteur and R. Koch (Snowden 2020; Bingham et al. 2004; Gaynes 2019; Gradmann 2009; Porte 1998).

Health promotion (for a history see Bingenheimer et al. 2003; Raingruber 2012; Tulchinsky and Varavikova 2015), instead, has been defined as the process of 'enabling people to increase control over their health determinants in order to improve their health and thereby be able to live an active and productive life', as stated in the Ottawa Charter (WHO 1986). In 2009, the *American Journal of Health Promotion* provided a comprehensive definition of health promotion aimed at the achievement of the *optimal state of health.* It conceived health promotion as the art and science of helping individuals align their passions with *optimal* health, enhancing motivation for lifestyle changes that achieve a balanced state of physical, emotional, social, spiritual, and intellectual well-being (O'Donnell 2009, iv).

The salutogenic approach acknowledges both prevention and health promotion at the individual and community levels. Antonovsky's commentators note that salutogenesis aligns with the Ottawa Charter, in recognising social determinants, setting objectives for an active life, and promoting dynamic processes toward health (Lindröm and Eriksson 2005). However, salutogenesis adds significant theoretical dimensions to health promotion by shifting focus from individual risks to population health and communities not necessarily at risk, advocating for a broader understanding of health that encompasses all aspects of life (Antonovsky 1996). While preventive medicine concentrates on pathogenic aspects and risk factors, salutogenesis avoids idealised notions of 'optimal health', addressing concerns in line with the critics of the WHO's 1948 definition being overly idealised (Saracci 1997; Bircher 2005). Rather than merely maintaining wellness, salutogenesis focuses on understanding the complexities of human health systems (Antonovsky 1996).

Salutogenesis emphasises health as a *continuum* rather than an ideal state opposed to illness. Individual life encompasses variation across different states between pure health and death. Compared to preventive medicine and health promotion, salutogenesis adopts a proactive stance by focusing on creating supportive social contexts and highlighting *adaptive capacities* within health dynamics (Becker et al. 2010; Antonovsky 1996).

Having established these distinctions, we can examine how the salutogenic approach contributes to our understanding of health through the health continuum and adaptivity. These concepts are particularly relevant when seen through the lens of biological autonomy, to emphasise how organisms actively engage with their environment rather than merely respond to external pressures.

9.4 Health as a *Continuum* and Health as Adaptivity

Salutogenesis, as I reframe it by including environmental interactions, offers valuable insights for updating our theoretical and practical understanding of health and well-being. The first general lesson derived from it is the need for a proactive stance that prioritises enabling factors and environments supporting people's adaptive capabilities. This perspective shifts our attention beyond treating illness and identifying pathogenic risks to actively promoting health and well-being, by building frameworks, strategies and actions to improve and empower people's capabilities (see Becker et al. 2010).

Two key notions from the salutogenic account may help update our idea of health: *continuum* and *adaptivity*. Both concepts are already in *nuce* in the salutogenic account, and can be further developed through the philosophy of medicine and of biology. Antonovsky's cognisance of the coeval debates on adaptation and homeostasis in biological systems (Vinje et al. 2016) facilitates the integration of his analysis into contemporary philosophical discourses on health, biology, and medicine.

The *continuum* of health concept, introduced by Antonovsky (1979), challenges the rigid healthy/sick dichotomy by introducing an 'ease/dis-ease continuum'. This model views health as a multifaceted, dynamic process where individuals constantly navigate between states of health and illness throughout their lives. Physical and social stressors influence an individual's position on this continuum, pushing them toward either pathogenic or salutogenic ends. Health is characterised by this continuous movement between intertwined pathogenic and salutogenic states. This perspective aligns with positive definitions of health, including the WHO's 1948 view, and it is especially relevant to chronic conditions. On this view, the emergence of a disease does not necessarily equate to a complete loss of health but rather represents a shift along the continuum (for a different characterisation of life as a trajectory rather than a continuum, see Etxeberria 2020).

Building on the continuum model, Rose (1992) introduced the 'continuum of risks and severity' concept, advocating for population-wide health strategies rather than focusing solely on high-risk individuals. Similarly, Valles (2018) proposed viewing health as a lifelong phenomenon, emphasising the dynamic interaction between individual and population health within social contexts. These perspectives highlight the importance of considering health as a continuous, complex process influenced by various factors over time, rather than a series of discrete states.

Strictly related to the idea of continuum is the concept of adaptation. Antonovsky discusses adaptation in several essays, framing health as a problem of disequilibrium concerning the "active adaptation to an environment in which stressors are omnipresent and inevitable" (Vinje et al. 2017). He argues that salutogenesis paves the way for rehabilitating stressors in human life through a continuous process of adaptation. In this context, Antonovsky highlights the potential of variability and disequilibrium for health by adopting the term "negative entropy" or "negentropy"

(Antonovsky 1987, pp. 8–9), which underscores that salutogenesis focuses on stressors that are inevitably present in the environment. These terms refer to the process of creating structure in the face of life's inherent chaos, emphasising the human capacity to generate health and meaning despite omnipresent stressors.

In philosophy of biology, the notion of adaptation employed by Antonovsky is related to adaptivity. Adaptivity has been recently developed in the organisational account of regulatory control (Bich et al. 2016). Di Paolo (2005) defines adaptivity as the ability of a system, like an organism, to sustain its viability in its environment through self-regulation. It refers to how well a system can manage changes in its surroundings. This concept has been developed into a theoretical framework in philosophy of biology about controlling the constraints responsible for a system's internal processes and behaviours (Bich and Bechtel 2026, this volume). This control involves adjusting constraints and realising new physiological and behavioural regimes based on changes in both internal and external conditions. Special constraints or mechanisms carry out this adjustment by assessing disturbances and responding appropriately.

Starting from these conceptual developments, recent work in the philosophy of biology and philosophy of medicine can help reframe health as a movement along a continuum defined by the adaptive capacities of human beings to the everyday environmental stressors encountered in their environments.

9.5 The Salutogenic Approach and the Environments for Health

To complement the salutogenic approach, I propose in this final section an additional key concept: the interconnection between health, adaptive capabilities, and the environments or what I could define as 'salutogenic environments'. By considering the environmental aspect, we recognise that health is not just about internal processes, but also about how well an individual can adapt to and interact with her surroundings. Understanding this relationship can provide a more comprehensive view of health, acknowledging the dynamic interplay between an organism's well-being, its ability to adapt, and the environmental context in which it exists.

As related to health, the external environment is often complex. It encompasses non-genetic influences, including physical, social, and cultural factors. It can be categorised as natural, altered, or built, each presenting unique health risks. This classification aids in analysing environmental diseases and developing targeted public health policies to address both human and ecosystem risks (Riegelman and Kirkwood 2019).

Yet the environment in medicine is still often considered as pathogenic; it is depicted as a source of hazards that need to be blocked, counteracted, or eliminated. The pathogenic view of the environment tends to overlook the positive or preventive interactions aimed at fostering, rather than just re-establishing health (Menatti et al. 2022; see also Garcia 2025, this volume). Environmental psychology, cognitive science and architecture have been investigating the positive role of the environment for health and well-being. Mostly natural spaces are considered to promote stress reduction and restore attention in diverse contexts (Ulrich 1984; Menatti and Casado da Rocha 2016; see also *Evidence Based Design*). In medicine, this poses various concerns for evidence-based studies, even though medical sciences are increasingly recognising the role of the environment in prevention, care and also for the well-being of healthcare professionals (Ulrich et al. 2020; Whall et al. 1997).

An important theoretical and philosophical step in this direction should imply the introduction and analysis of the idea of *salutogenic environments*, which are aspects of our surroundings that can positively impact health and well-being. These environments encompass physical, social, and cultural elements that promote health by fostering adaptivity for individuals, groups, or entire populations, for their different capabilities and needs.

On this view, environments are considered salutogenic when they promote health by emphasising active adaptation and engagement with the surroundings. The basic idea is to consider individuals and groups not simply as subjected to the effect of the environment and trying to counteract it, but as capable of adaptivity, that is, of modifying themselves and the environment to promote their viability. Accordingly, this approach views the environment's impact on health as relational, dependent on people's adaptive capabilities. It supports individuals along the health continuum, seeing environmental variability as an opportunity for growth and viable change rather than just a risk. Salutogenic environments, therefore, are those spaces that facilitate a dynamic, health-enhancing relationship between people and their surroundings. Taking these points into consideration can be particularly valuable for designing and managing both public and private spaces, starting from, but not limited to, healthcare facilities.

Acknowledgements LM acknowledges funding from grants PID2019-104576GB-I00 "Outonomy" and PID2023-147251NB-I00 "Outagencies", funded by MCIU/AEI/10.13039/501100011033 https://doi.org/10.13039/501100011033 and FEDER/UE.

References

Antonovsky A (1979) Health, stress and coping. Jossey-Bass

Antonovsky A (1987) Unraveling the mystery of health. How people manage stress and stay well. Jossey-Bass

Antonovsky A (1996) The salutogenic model as a theory to guide health promotion. Health Promot Int 11(1):11–18. https://doi.org/10.1093/heapro/11.1.11

Becker DM (1988) History of preventive medicine. In Becker DM, Gardner LB (eds) Prevention in clinical practice. Springer, pp 13–21. https://doi.org/10.1007/978-1-4684-5356-0_2

Becker CM, Glascoff MA, Felts MW (2010) Salutogenesis 30 years later: where do we go from here? Int Electron J Health Educ 13:25–32

Bich L, Mossio M, Ruiz-Mirazo K, Moreno A (2016) Biological regulation: controlling the system from within. Biol Philos 31(2):237–265. https://doi.org/10.1007/s10539-015-9497-8
Bingham P, Verlander NQ, Cheal MJ (2004) John Snow, William Farr and the 1849 outbreak of cholera that affected London: a reworking of the data highlights the importance of the water supply. Public Health 118(6):387–394. https://doi.org/10.1016/j.puhe.2004.05.007
Bingenheimer JB, Repetto PB, Zimmerman MA, Kelly JG (2003) A brief history and analysis of health promotion. In: Gullotta TP et al (eds) Encyclopedia of primary prevention and health promotion. Springer, Boston, MA. https://doi.org/10.1007/978-1-4615-0195-4_3
Bich L, Bechtel W (2026) Autonomy and heterarchy: organizing control in biological organisms. In: Barandiaran XE, Etxeberria A (eds) Outonomy: fleshing out autonomy beyond the individual. Springer.
Bircher J (2005) Towards a dynamic definition of health and disease. Med Health Care Philos 8(3):335–341. https://doi.org/10.1007/s11019-005-0538-y
Di Paolo EA (2005) Autopoiesis, adaptivity, teleology, agency. Phenomenol Cogn Sci 4(4):429–452. https://doi.org/10.1007/s11097-005-9002-y
Dietscher C, Winter U, Pelikan JM (2022) The application of salutogenesis in hospitals. In: Mittelmark MB et al (eds.) The handbook of salutogenesis, 2nd ed. Springer, pp 397–418.
Eriksson M, Contu P (2022) The sense of coherence: measurement issues. In: Mittelmark MB (ed) The handbook of salutogenesis. Springer, pp 79–91. https://doi.org/10.1007/978-3-030-79515-3_11
Eriksson M, Lindström B (2008) A salutogenic interpretation of the Ottawa Charter. Health Promot Int 23(2):190–199. https://doi.org/10.1093/heapro/dan014
Etxeberria A (2020) Regulation, milieu, and norms: Georges Canguilhem's individual organisms as relations. In: Methot P-O, Sholl J (eds) Vital norms. Canguilhem's the normal and the pathological in the twenty-first century. Hermann Ed., pp 295–332
Garcia E (2025) Process and relational ontology in enactive psychiatry. In: Barandiaran XE, Etxeberria A (eds) Outonomy: fleshing out autonomy beyond the individual. Springer
Gartner JB, Abasse KS, Bergeron F, Landa P, Lemaire C, Côté A (2022) Definition and conceptualization of the patient-centered care pathway, a proposed integrative framework for consensus: a concept analysis and systematic review. BMC Health Serv Res 22(1):558. https://doi.org/10.1186/s12913-022-07960-0
Gaynes RP (2019) Germ theory: medical pioneers in infectious diseases. Wiley
Gradmann C (2009) Laboratory disease: Robert Koch's medical bacteriology. John Hopkins University Press
Grover S, Fitzpatrick A, Azim FT, Ariza-Vega P, Bellwood P, Burns J, Burton E, Fleig L, Clemson L, Hoppmann CA, Madden KM, Price M, Langford D, Ashe MC (2022) Defining and implementing patient-centered care: an umbrella review. Patient Educ Couns 105(7):1679–1688. https://doi.org/10.1016/j.pec.2021.11.004
Lindström B, Eriksson M (2005) Salutogenesis. J Epidemiol Community Health 59(6):440–442. https://doi.org/10.1136/jech.2005.034777
Martini M, Lippi D (2021) SARS-CoV-2 (COVID-19) and the teaching of Ignaz Semmelweis and Florence Nightingale: a lesson of public health from history, after the "Introduction of Handwashing" (1847). J Pre Med Hyg 62(3): E621–E624. https://doi.org/10.15167/2421-4248/jpmh2021.62.3.2161
Meloni M (2021) The politics of environments before the environment: biopolitics in the longue durée. Stud Hist Philos Sci 88:334–344
Menatti L, Bich L, Saborido C (2022) Health and environment from adaptation to adaptivity: a situated relational account. Hist Philos Life Sci 44(3):38. https://doi.org/10.1007/s40656-022-00515-w
Menatti L, Casado da Rocha A (2016) Landscape and health. Connecting psychology, aesthetics and philosophy through the concept of affordance. Front Psychol 7:571. https://doi.org/10.3389/fpsyg.2016.00571

Mittelmark MB, Bauer GF (2017) The meanings of salutogenesis. In Mittelmark et al M (eds) The handbook of salutogenesis. Springer, New York, pp 7–15

Mittelmark MB, Bauer GF (2022) Salutogenesis as a theory, as an orientation and as the sense of coherence. In: The handbook of salutogenesis. Springer, pp 11–18. https://doi.org/10.1007/978-3-030-79515-3_3

Nikku NB, Eriksson E (2012) Preventive medicine. In Chadwick R (ed) Encyclopedia of applied ethics, 2nd ed. Academic Press, pp 584–589

O'Donnell MP (2009) Definition of health promotion 2.0: embracing passion, enhancing motivation, recognizing dynamic balance, and creating opportunities. Am J Health Promot: AJHP 24(1):iv. https://doi.org/10.4278/ajhp.24.1.iv

Pelikan JM (2022) Applying salutogenesis in healthcare settings. In: Mittelmark MB et al (eds) The handbook of salutogenesis, 2nd ed. Springer, pp 389–395. https://doi.org/10.1007/978-3-030-79515-3_36

Porter R (1998) The greatest benefit to mankind: a medical history of humanity from antiquity to present. Norton and Company

Raingruber B (2012) Contemporary health promotion in nursing practice. Jones & Bartlett Learning

Rose G (1992) The strategy of preventive medicine. Oxford University Press

Riegelman R, Kirkwood B (2019) Public Health 101: improving community health. Jones & Bartlett Learning

Saracci R (1997) The World Health Organisation needs to reconsider its definition of health. BMJ (Clin Res Ed.) 314(7091):1409–1410. https://doi.org/10.1136/bmj.314.7091.1409

Snowden FM (2020) Epidemics and society. From the black death to the present. Yale University Press

The Editors of Encyclopaedia Britannica (2022) Preventive medicine. Encyclopedia Britannica, https://www.britannica.com/science/preventive-medicine.

Tulchinsky TH, Varavikova EA (2015) The new public health, 3rd ed. Elsevier

Ulrich RS (1984) View through a window may influence recovery from surgery. Science (New York, NY) 224(4647):420–421. https://doi.org/10.1126/science.6143402

Ulrich RS, Cordoza M, Gardiner SK, Manulik BJ, Fitzpatrick PS, Hazen TM, Perkins RS (2020) ICU patient family stress recovery during breaks in a hospital garden and indoor environments. HERD 13(2):83–102. https://doi.org/10.1177/1937586719867157

Valles S (2018) A philosophy of population health science: philosophy for a new public health era. Routledge

Vinje HF, Langeland E, Bull T (2017) Aaron Antonovsky's development of salutogenesis, 1979 to 1994. In: Mittelmark MB (eds.) et. al., The handbook of salutogenesis, pp 25–40. Springer.

Whall AL, Black ME, Groh CJ, Yankou DJ, Kupferschmid BJ, Foster NL (1997) The effect of natural environments upon agitation and aggression in late stage dementia patients. Am J Alzheimers Dis 12(5):216–220. https://doi.org/10.1177/153331759701200506

Vinje HF, Langeland E, Bull T. (2016) Aaron Antonovsky's development of salutogenesis, 1979 to 1994. 2016 Sep 3. In: Mittelmark MB, Sagy S, Eriksson M et al (eds) The handbook of salutogenesis [Internet]. Springer, Cham (CH)

Ward Thompson C (2011) Linking landscape and health: the recurring theme. Landsc Urban Plan 99:187–195. https://doi.org/10.1016/j.landurbplan.2010.10.006

World Health Organization (1986) The Ottawa charter for health promotion. WHO

Chapter 10
Pain Beyond Nociception: A Biological Autonomy Perspective

Alberto Monterde-Fuertes

Abstract Pain science and management have long grappled with significant conceptual challenges, particularly the differentiation of pain from nociception. This chapter addresses this challenge by adopting the framework of biological autonomy, which conceptualizes living systems as self-regulating entities dynamically interacting with their environments. From this perspective, pain emerges as a context-sensitive phenomenon that protects autonomy by guiding adaptive behavior and anticipating future threats. In contrast, nociception is a mechanistic process that transduces and transmits noxious stimuli to elicit protective reflexes. By integrating insights from pain research, medicine, and philosophy, the chapter advances a relational and functional understanding of pain while outlining its practical implications.

Keywords Pain · Nociception · Biological autonomy · Biopsychosocial model · Reductionism · Adaptive behaviors · Organism-environment interaction

10.1 Introduction

The study of pain has posed conceptual and empirical challenges in scientific research and medicine. The Cartesian approach, dominant in the twentieth-century, conceptualized pain as a mechanical response to tissue damage. Pain was thus viewed as a physiological process directly linked to noxious stimuli, conflating it with nociception—defined as the neural encoding of harmful stimuli (Melzack and Wall 1996). However, reductionist accounts failed to capture pain's complexity and subjectivity. These limitations prompted a paradigm shift, recognizing pain as a multidimensional, emergent phenomenon shaped by psychological, social, and environmental factors (Casey and Melzack 1968; Melzack and Wall 1996).The biopsychosocial model further expanded this view, integrating cognitive, emotional, and sociocultural dimensions (Adams and Turk 2018).

A. Monterde-Fuertes (✉)
IAS-Research Centre for Life, Mind and Society, Department of Philosophy, University of the Basque Country (UPV/EHU), Donostia-San Sebastián, Spain
e-mail: alberto.monterde@ehu.eus

X. E. Barandiaran and A. Etxeberria (eds.), *Outonomy*,
SpringerBriefs in Philosophy, https://doi.org/10.1007/978-3-032-05501-9_10

Despite these advances, challenges remain in conceptualizing pain and nociception as distinct phenomena (Butler and Moseley 2017; Lee et al. 2020). This chapter addresses these challenges through the biological autonomy framework, emphasizing pain's relational and functional roles in preserving autonomy. By situating both pain and nociception within this framework, I argue for a more substatian distinction between their respective organizational functions. Pain is a subjective and integrative phenomenon mediating an organism's interaction with its environment. At the same time, nociception is a mechanistic process confined to detecting and transmitting noxious stimuli to elicit withdrawal responses. This distinction has practical implications, underscoring the need for interdisciplinary, patient-centered approaches to pain management that integrate biological, psychological, and social dimensions.

This chapter proceeds in four sections. First, I examine the conceptual challenges in distinguishing pain from nociception. Next, I introduce the biological autonomy framework, highlighting its potential to clarify the distinct roles of pain and nociception. In the third section, I apply this framework to demonstrate how pain emerges as a relational, adaptive phenomenon that integrates sensory, emotional, and contextual dimensions to promote self-maintenance. Finally, I explore the practical implications of this approach, advocating for evidence-based interdisciplinary strategies in pain research and management.

10.2 The Challenge of Distinguishing Pain from Nociception

Distinguishing pain from nociception has been a longstanding challenge in pain science (Lee et al. 2020; Melzack and Wall 1996). Nociception is the neural encoding of potentially harmful stimuli (Woolf and Ma 2007), while pain is a subjective, integrative experience shaped by internal and external contexts (Butler and Moseley 2017; Melzack and Wall 1996). This distinction has often been oversimplified, reducing pain explanations to nociceptive mechanisms (e.g., Sweet 1959). However, this reductionist stance overlooks pain's complexity and variability, which extends far beyond nociceptive input (Butler and Moseley 2017; Melzack and Wall 1996). It also conflates two different questions: explaining what causes a painful event versus what causes pain to be subjective. Although knowledge of the mechanisms that cause a painful event has increased over time, it cannot account for what causes pain to be subjective (Melzack 1996). Addressing that requires evidence on how pain perception is modulated beyond purely physiological mechanisms (Adams and Turk 2018).

Pain scientists have long argued that pain and nociception are distinct yet related phenomena. Earlier accounts justified this distinction by emphasizing pain's complexity, which resisted its identification with nociceptive mechanisms (Casey and Melzack 1968; Melzack and Wall 1996). However, these arguments lacked conceptual precision, relying on hypothesized mechanisms. Contemporary perspectives describe pain as a complex emergent phenomenon, related to nociception but not limited to it. Most accounts now hold that pain arises when an organism perceives a threat and cannot be deduced from physiology alone (Butler and Moseley 2017; Gifford 2014). Yet this view, often grounded in the biopsychosocial (BPS) model, has its own limits. The model is frequently criticized for failing to clearly define the relationships among biological, psychological, and social factors, raising concerns about its clinical and conceptual utility (Quintner et al. 2007).

Addressing these conceptual and practical challenges requires examining the distinct biological roles of pain and nociception. Historically, pain's function has been framed through two perspectives: exteroception and interoception. Exteroception refers to the sensory detection of stimuli originating from outside the body, such as touch, temperature, and potential injury. In this view, pain functions as an alarm system, responding to nociceptive signals to protect the organism from harm (Sherrington 1906). Interoception, by contrast, involves sensing internal body states, such as hunger, thirst, or visceral discomfort. From this perspective, pain guides an organism's behaviour to avoid further harm or promote (Craig 2003). While often seen as mutually exclusive, these views can be complementary (Price 2017), with pain informing the organism about both external threats and internal states vital to survival.

Yet, this combined view relies on the assumption that pain's main role is to convey information about damage. Laurenz Casser (2021) challenges this assumption, arguing that empirical findings undermine pain's role as an informational signal. For example, modulation mechanisms within the nervous system can inhibit or amplify pain perception independent of tissue damage, revealing a dissociation between pain and nociceptive input. Casser also notes little evidence that pain was evolutionarily selected to inform organisms about harm. These points question the informational model and highlight the need for a clearer functional distinction between and nociception.

These challenges call for a framework that accommodates both the relational and functional aspects of pain and nociception. Biological autonomy is well-positioned to fulfill this role, offering a conceptual basis for biological functions and organism-environment interactions. Situating pain and nociception within the biological autonomy framework elucidates their distinct organizational roles and resolves these conceptual challenges.

10.3 Biological Autonomy: A Theoretical Framework for Understanding Pain

The biological autonomy framework offers a compelling lens for understanding the differentiation of pain from nociception. Biological autonomy conceptualizes living systems as capable of producing components to maintain themselves despite external changes, ensuring survival and reproduction (Moreno and Mossio 2015). This capability is grounded in organizational closure, a self-maintaining network of processes where components sustain one another and regulate their activities (Bich 2024). Closure enables a system to maintain its organization and functional integrity while providing a basis for understanding its relative autonomy from the environment.

A key concept within the biological autonomy framework is the notion of organizational functions (Mossio et al. 2009). Functions are understood as the contributions of a system's components to maintaining and reproducing the system's organization. This account emphasizes that biological functions are inherently tied to the system's capacity for self-maintenance. By contributing to the system's ongoing integrity, functions acquire normative and teleological significance: they are "good" for the system insofar as they preserve its autonomy. This idea offers a robust theoretical basis for distinguishing the roles of pain and nociception within a self-maintaining organism.

It is important to note that biological autonomy extends beyond internal regulatory mechanisms to encompass an organism's dynamic interactions with its environment. Thus, conceptualizing how organisms actively engage with and modify themselves to adapt to their surroundings, maintain organization, and ensure survival (Bechtel and Bich 2024; Menatti et al. 2022; Saborido and Heras-Escribano 2023). This perspective emphasizes the reciprocal relationships between organisms and their environments: by interacting with and shaping their environments, organisms sustain the conditions necessary for preserving their structural and functional integrity (Menatti 2026, this volume).

Several scholars have recently applied the biological autonomy framework to pain, emphasizing pain's interactive and relational aspects when differentiating it from physiological processes. For instance, John Quintner, Milton Cohen, and collaborators have argued that pain is a subjective experience irreducible to biological substrates while accepting the principles of biological autonomy. For them, pain plays a crucial role in the survival of living beings, which they understand as "integral, autonomous systems" (Cohen et al. 2018, p. 5). If this is true, they contend, "pain is a threat to the autonomy and thus to the existential integrity of a living system" (Cohen et al. 2018, p. 5). Consequently, they defined pain as "a mutually recognizable somatic experience that reflects a person's apprehension of threat to their bodily or existential integrity" (Cohen et al. 2018, p. 6).

According to this view, the self-referential nature of living systems (engaged in continuous interaction with their environments) means that pain emerges in ways that resist reduction to biological, psychological, or social factors alone (Quintner et al. 2007). Their theoretical proposal, influenced by the work of Maturana and Varela (e.g., 1980) conception of autonomy as autopoiesis, highlights the brain's self-referential role within an autopoietic system. This role serves as a foundation for rethinking clinical practice. In this view, the clinical encounter is a meeting of two autopoietic systems, each with its own norms, beliefs, actions, and interpretations of the shared experience called pain (Quintner et al. 2007). When interpreted through the lens of interactive biological autonomy, the clinical encounter becomes a "third space": a moral and epistemic space that requires mutual understanding necessary to foster effective treatment and prevent the stigmatization of suffering. Quintner et al. approach aligns with the enactive concept of participatory sense-making (De Jaegher and Di Paolo 2007), which emphasizes how meaning emerges through social interaction. This enriches the concept of the third space as a site of transformative relational engagement.

Moreover, Keith Farnsworth and Robert Elwood (2023) have explored the evolutionary basis of pain through the lens of biological autonomy. They argue that pain is essential for organisms capable of anticipatory behavioral autonomy (ABA), as it enables context-sensitive action selection grounded in internal predictive models. These models allow organisms to evaluate potential outcomes and flexibly prioritize their responses. On this view, pain is not merely a reflexive reaction to harmful stimuli but a motivational force that drives threat avoidance while supporting the pursuit of higher-order goals. This account aligns with the concept of organizational functions in biological autonomy (Mossio et al. 2009; Saborido and Heras-Escribano 2023), highlighting pain's contribution to self-maintenance by guiding adaptive interactions with the environment. By integrating internal predictive models and responses to external stimuli, organisms can anticipate and evaluate the consequences of their actions (Farnsworth and Elwood 2023), reinforcing the dynamic interplay between internal regulation and environmental engagement (Bechtel and Bich 2024; Menatti et al. 2022). In this light, pain facilitates survival-oriented decision-making within a self-organizing system, extending the phenomena beyond a mechanistic withdrawal response and reflecting both the heterarchical control model (Bich and Bechtel 2026, this volume) and the purposive agency central to autonomy theory (Virenque 2026, this volume).

10.4 Distinguishing Pain from Nociception: A Biological Autonomy Approach

The biological autonomy framework provides a foundation for differentiating pain and nociception, addressing conceptual challenges in scientific discussions on pain. Within this framework, pain is understood as an interactive phenomenon that enables adaptive responses to environmental disturbances (Farnsworth and Elwood 2023). It integrates past experiences, contextual cues, and cultural norms, helping organisms navigate their environments, safeguard survival, and promote self-maintenance (Butler and Moseley 2017; Craig 2003). This dynamic coupling of the organism with its environment underscores pain's organizational role in supporting immediate survival and long-term adaptive capacity.

Therefore, pain, as an emergent phenomenon, operates at a broader organizational level than nociception. While nociception is a mechanistic process confined to detecting and transmitting noxious stimuli to elicit protective reflexes (Baliki and Apkarian 2015; Woolf and Ma 2007), pain encompasses a broader range of sensory, emotional, and contextual dimensions. It guides adaptive behaviors by shaping responses to perceived environmental threats, fostering adequate response (Farnsworth and Elwood 2023; Price 2017). In humans, social, psychological, and cultural influences shape the interactional nature of pain. For example, cultural norms significantly affect how pain is perceived and expressed, shaping coping strategies and treatment outcomes (Orhan et al. 2018). Social contexts also modulate pain experiences, as research shows that social rejection activates brain regions associated with physical pain, such as the anterior cingulate cortex (Eisenberger 2012). Conversely, social bonding can reduce pain perception through the release of endogenous opioids, emphasizing the role of supportive relationships in mitigating pain (Inagaki et al. 2016).

Moreover, clinicians and societal attitudes shape pain narratives, profoundly influencing patients' beliefs and behaviors. For instance, advice such as "lift with your knees, not your back," may lead to overprotection of injured areas, delaying recovery and reinforcing maladaptive beliefs about pain (Darlow et al. 2013). Similarly, patients' expectations regarding recovery or damage can shape their pain perception, with those anticipating severe pain more likely to experience prolonged episodes (Carrière et al. 2023). These examples illustrate how pain emerges as a relational phenomenon, modulated by immediate and broader environmental contexts alongside individual expectations and experiences.

From the perspective of biological autonomy, pain and nociception serve distinct organizational functions. Pain involves organism-environment interactions that guide behaviors to protect autonomy and promote recovery (Butler and Moseley 2017; Craig 2003; Farnsworth and Elwood 2023). Nociception, by contrast, is a mechanistic process that transduces and transmits noxious stimuli to trigger immediate protective reflexes. This distinction clarifies their defining roles: pain engages the whole organism in its ongoing relationship with the environment, whereas nociception operates within neural circuits to support rapid, localized responses (Baliki and Apkarian 2015; Woolf and Ma 2007). By adopting this framework, pain and nociception emerge as complementary yet distinct phenomena, separated by their organizational functions. Pain restrains the organism from harm and promotes healing by modulating behaviour, while nociception triggers withdrawal responses to harmful stimuli. These differentiated roles highlight their unique but complementary contribution to maintaining the organism's autonomy.

10.5 Practical Implications for Pain Research and Pain Management

Clinically, biological autonomy reinforces the need to integrate biological, psychological, and social dimensions in pain management. Because meaning and trust are central to patient-clinician relationships (De Jaegher and Di Paolo 2007; Quintner et al. 2007), empathetic care that empowers patients becomes essential. Addressing psychosocial factors, such as beliefs, fear-avoidance behaviors, and language that foster resilience, is crucial in this process, as these factors shape decision-making, pain perception, and recovery (Butler and Moseley 2017; Gifford 2014). Incorporating patient narratives strengthens trust, validates individual experiences, and ensures care is tailored to the patient's context; aligning with evidence-based biopsychosocial approaches (Gatchel et al. 2014; Staudt 2022).

Key policy recommendations include updating medical curricula to reflect the biopsychosocial complexity of pain, promoting education in evidence-based practice, expanding access to multidisciplinary pain management services in underserved areas, and fostering research on pain's relational and emergent dimensions. The demonstrated effectiveness of interdisciplinary approaches supports these reforms and highlights the urgent need for accessible, patient-centered care to replace outdated treatment practices (Gatchel et al. 2014; Meghani et al. 2012). Embedding these principles bridges conceptual and practical gaps, promoting equitable, evidence-based care that reflects pain's multidimensional reality.

10.6 Conclusion

This chapter has argued that the biological autonomy framework offers a robust foundation for distinguishing pain from nociception (Cohen et al. 2018; Farnsworth and Elwood 2023; Quintner et al. 2007). From this perspective, pain serves an adaptive function by mediating organism–environment interactions and guiding behaviors that promote recovery and protect both existential and physical integrity (Cohen et al. 2018; Farnsworth and Elwood 2023; Price 2017). In contrast, nociception functions as a mechanistic process, limited to detecting and transmitting noxious stimuli to elicit withdrawal protective responses (Baliki and Apkarian 2015; Woolf and Ma 2007). This perspective not only situates pain within the systemic dynamics of biological autonomy but also highlights its extended dimensions, including the relational interplay with environmental factors (Bechtel and Bich 2024; Menatti et al. 2022) and social contexts (De Jaegher and Di Paolo 2007), which jointly contribute to the organism's capacity for self-maintenance.

This distinction highlights the need to move beyond reductionist and overly simplistic pain models that conflate pain with nociception (Quintner et al. 2007). The biological autonomy framework emphasizes pain's relational and organizational roles, accounting for the cultural, social, and psychological factors that modulate pain (Eisenberger 2012; Orhan et al. 2018). It thus provides a comprehensive conceptual basis that bridges scientific, philosophical, and clinical perspectives on pain. In doing so, it reinforces and deepens theoretical models such as the biopsychosocial approach (Adams and Turk 2018) and understanding of pain as an emergent phenomenon (Butler and Moseley 2017).

Viewing pain through the lens of biological autonomy reinforces the need for interdisciplinary, patient-centered approaches that integrate biological, psychological, and social dimensions. This perspective fosters resilience and autonomy through participatory sense-making and culturally sensitive care (Butler and Moseley 2017;

De Jaegher and Di Paolo 2007; Gifford 2014). It also advocates incorporating patient narratives into clinical practice, attending to the relational dynamics of therapeutic encounters, and promoting interventions tailored to individual and contextual factors (Butler and Moseley 2017; Gifford 2014). At a systemic level, supports reforms in medical education to reflect pain's complexity, the expansion of access to multidisciplinary care (Gatchel et al. 2014; Meghani et al. 2012), and ongoing research into pain's emergent and relational dimensions. By adopting these principles, the biological autonomy framework bridges conceptual and clinical gaps, advancing pain science and medical practice. Ultimately, it offers a pathway toward equitable, evidence-based care that respects the multidimensional reality of pain, promoting recovery, autonomy, and well-being for individuals and communities alike.

Acknowledgements I thank the editors for their diligent work and helpful comments. I'm also grateful to my supervisors, Leonardo Bich and Cristian Saborido, for their guidance on various drafts. A.M.F acknowledges funding from IAS-Research group funding IT1668-22 (Basque Government); grants PID2019-104576GB-I00 "Outonomy" and PID2023-147251NB-I00 "Outagencies", funded by MCIU/AEI/10.13039/501100011033 and FEDER/UE. This work was also supported by grant PID2021-128835NB-I00 "NORMABioMed" and the Basque Government predoctoral grant PRE_2022_2_0148.

References

Adams LM, Turk DC (2018) Central sensitization and the biopsychosocial approach to understanding pain. J Appl Biobehav Res 23(2):e12125. https://doi.org/10.1111/jabr.12125

Baliki MN, Apkarian AV (2015) Nociception, pain, negative moods, and behavior selection. Neuron 87(3):474–491. https://doi.org/10.1016/j.neuron.2015.06.005

Bechtel W, Bich L (2024) Situating homeostasis in organisms: maintaining organization through time. J Physiol 602(22):6003–6020. https://doi.org/10.1113/JP286883

Bich L (2024) Biological organization. In: Elements in the philosophy of biology. https://doi.org/10.1017/9781009393959

Bich L, Bechtel W (2026) Autonomy and heterarchy: organizing control in biological organisms. In: Barandiaran XE, Etxeberria A (eds) OUTONOMY: fleshing out the concept of autonomy beyond the individual. Springer, p. in press

Butler DS, Moseley GL (2017) Explain pain supercharged.

Carrière JS, Donayre Pimentel S, Bou Saba S, Boehme B, Berbiche D, Coutu M-F, Durand M-J (2023) Recovery expectations can be assessed with single-item measures: Findings of a systematic review and meta-analysis on the role of recovery expectations on return-to-work outcomes after musculoskeletal pain conditions. Pain 164(4):e190–e206. https://doi.org/10.1097/j.pain.0000000000002789

Casey K, Melzack R (1968) Sensory, motivational, and central control determinants of pain. In: The skin senses, pp 423–439

Casser LC (2021) The function of pain. Australas J Philos 99(2):364–378

Cohen M, Quintner J, van Rysewyk S (2018) Reconsidering the international association for the study of pain definition of pain. Pain Rep 3(2):e634. https://doi.org/10.1097/PR9.0000000000000634

Craig AD (2003) A new view of pain as a homeostatic emotion. Trends Neurosci 26(6):303–307. https://doi.org/10.1016/s0166-2236(03)00123-1

Darlow B, Dowell A, Baxter GD, Mathieson F, Perry M, Dean S (2013) The enduring impact of what clinicians say to people with low back pain. Ann Fam Med 11(6):527–534. https://doi.org/10.1370/afm.1518

De Jaegher H, Di Paolo E (2007) Participatory sense-making. Phenomenol Cogn Sci 6(4):485–507. https://doi.org/10.1007/s11097-007-9076-9

Eisenberger NI (2012) The neural bases of social pain: Evidence for shared representations with physical pain. Psychosom Med 74(2):126–135. https://doi.org/10.1097/PSY.0b013e3182464dd1

Farnsworth KD, Elwood RW (2023) Why it hurts: with freedom comes the biological need for pain. Anim Cogn 26(4):1259–1275. https://doi.org/10.1007/s10071-023-01773-2

Gatchel RJ, McGeary DD, McGeary CA, Lippe B (2014) Interdisciplinary chronic pain management: past, present, and future. Am Psychol 69(2):119–130. https://doi.org/10.1037/a0035514

Gifford L (2014) Aches and pains. CNS Press.

Inagaki TK, Ray LA, Irwin MR, Way BM, Eisenberger NI (2016) Opioids and social bonding: Naltrexone reduces feelings of social connection. Soc Cogn Affect Neurosci 11(5):728–735. https://doi.org/10.1093/scan/nsw006

Lee I-S, Necka EA, Atlas LY (2020) Distinguishing pain from nociception, salience, and arousal: how autonomic nervous system activity can improve neuroimaging tests of specificity. NeuroImage 204:116254. https://doi.org/10.1016/j.neuroimage.2019.116254

Maturana HR, Varela FJ (1980) Autopoiesis and cognition: the realization of the living. Reidel Publishing Co. https://doi.org/10.1007/978-94-009-8947-4

Meghani SH, Polomano RC, Tait RC, Vallerand AH, Anderson KO, Gallagher RM (2012) Advancing a national agenda to eliminate disparities in pain care: Directions for health policy, education, practice, and research. Pain Med (Malden, MA) 13(1):5–28. https://doi.org/10.1111/j.1526-4637.2011.01289.x

Melzack R (1996) Gate control theory: on the evolution of pain concepts. Pain Forum 5(2):128–138

Melzack R, Wall PD (1996) The challenge of pain: A modern medical classic, updated 2nd ed. Penguin Books

Menatti L (2026) Salutogenesis, adaptivity and the continuum of health. In Barandiaran XE, Etxeberria A (eds) OUTONOMY: fleshing out the concept of autonomy beyond the individual. Springer, p. in press

Menatti L, Bich L, Saborido C (2022) Health and environment from adaptation to adaptivity: a situated relational account. Hist Philos Life Sci 44(3):38. https://doi.org/10.1007/s40656-022-00515-w

Moreno A, Mossio M (2015) Biological autonomy: a philosophical and theoretical enquiry. Springer.

Mossio M, Saborido C, Moreno A (2009) An organizational account of biological functions. Br J Philos Sci 60(4):813–841. https://doi.org/10.1093/bjps/axp036

Orhan C, Van Looveren E, Cagnie B, Mukhtar NB, Lenoir D, Meeus M (2018) Are pain beliefs, cognitions, and behaviors influenced by race, ethnicity, and culture in patients with chronic musculoskeletal pain: a systematic review. Pain Physician 21(6):541–558

Price DD (2017) A view of pain based on sensations, meanings, and emotions. In: Corns J (ed) The Routledge handbook of philosophy of pain. Routledge Handbooks Online, pp 113–123. https://doi.org/10.4324/9781315742205.ch9

Quintner J, Cohen MJ, Williamson O (2007) Pain medicine and its models: helping or hindering? Pain Med 9(7):824–834. https://doi.org/10.1111/j.1526-4637.2007.00391.x

Saborido C, Heras-Escribano M (2023) Affordances and organizational functions. Biol Philos 38(1):6. https://doi.org/10.1007/s10539-023-09891-4

Sherrington CS (1906) The integrative action of the nervous system. Yale University Press.

Staudt MD (2022) The multidisciplinary team in pain management. Neurosurg Clin North Am 33(3):241–249. https://doi.org/10.1016/j.nec.2022.02.002

Sweet WH (1959) Pain. In: Field J, Magoun H, Hall V (eds) Handbook of physiology: Section I. Neurophysiology. American Physiology Society, vol 1, pp 459–506

Virenque L (2026) Intrinsic purposiveness and autonomy in interaction. In Barandiaran XE, Etxeberria A (eds) Outonomy: Fleshing out the concept of autonomy beyond the individual. Springer, p. in press

Woolf CJ, Ma Q (2007) Nociceptors—Noxious stimulus detectors. Neuron 55(3):353–364. https://doi.org/10.1016/j.neuron.2007.07.016

Part IV
Technology, Ecology & Politics

Chapter 11
Autonomy and Technology: From Instrumentalism to Technocomplexity

Antonio Calleja-López, Marta Pérez-Verdugo, and Xabier E. Barandiaran

Abstract In this chapter, we briefly present different visions of the relationships between technology and autonomy. We accomplish this by a historical and (partly) dialectical exploration of three positions. We start with the modern thesis by which autonomous humans instrumentalize tools and techniques for their own benefit and self-determination. Next, we address the antithesis: the notion that technological systems have become autonomous, subordinating people to their own self-maintenance. Finally, we explore a synthetic position, which underlines that the only space for autonomy in a technologically mediated world is a technopolitical autonomy that takes the individual beyond itself, back to the ontotechnical constitution of its being, and forward into a personal and collective, ethical and political, participation in its becoming.

Keywords Instrumentalism · Autonomy of Technology · Technopolitical Autonomy · Technocomplexity

11.1 Thesis. Technoinstrumentalism: Politics and Morality Subordinate Technique

Although the condition, practice and experience of autonomy may be traced back to early human societies, its western conceptualization derives from the ancient greek notion of αὐτονομία, composed of "*autos*" (self) and "*nomos*" (norm, rule). Etymologically, its meaning points to the capacity of creating, having or living by

A. Calleja-López (✉)
Open University of Catalonia (UOC), Barcelona, Spain
e-mail: acallejalo@uoc.edu

M. Pérez-Verdugo · X. E. Barandiaran
University of the Basque Country (UPV/EHU), Donostia—San Sebastián, Spain
e-mail: perezverdugo.marta@gmail.com

X. E. Barandiaran
e-mail: xabier.barandiaran@ehu.eus

X. E. Barandiaran and A. Etxeberria (eds.), *Outonomy*,
SpringerBriefs in Philosophy, https://doi.org/10.1007/978-3-032-05501-9_11

"one's own norm or law". Contrary to much contemporary understanding, in its original sense autonomy had a predominantly collective and political character because the self (*autos*) it primarily referred to was the city (*polis*), which valued its self-determination against external powers. Meanwhile, technique (*tekne*) was a form of know-how, art, craft, or skill, perceived as a questionable complement to nature (*physis*) (Mitcham 1994, Epilogue). According to the Platonic version of the myth of Prometheus, fire and techniques were given to humanity to complement a human body lacking key survival capacities. But techniques had to be complemented, in turn, with justice (*dike*) and other virtues to ensure collective flourishing. More broadly, in Ancient Greece, techniques and technical work were symbolically and materially subordinated to philosophical and political life.

The concept of autonomy revived in the sixteenth century still with a political meaning. But during the seventeenth, the concept of sovereignty came to occupy its place on the political field, and autonomy shifted towards a moral and personal understanding, associated with debates concerning freedom of conscience (Rosich 2020). This process culminated in the eighteenth century in the work of Immanuel Kant. For Kant, human freedom and morality are grounded in the subject's ability to discover a categorical imperative and align its will with it, not as a vassal adhering to an extrinsic rule (heteronomy), but as a rational, universal legislator capable of identifying, sanctioning, and following an endogenous, universal norm (Kant 1998).

These transformations correlated with social, cultural and technical changes. The late medieval and early modern rise in relevance of mechanical arts had convinced Francis Bacon that science and arts were key instruments for salvation, commanded by God to be deployed to control nature, rather than to complement it occasionally as suggested by the ancient greeks. The scientific revolution (associated to a centuries long accumulation of new artifacts such as mechanic clocks, the printing press, microscopes, or telescopes) saw the world itself as a machine regulated by universal laws, a clockwork built by a clockmaker God that could be measured and controlled by a science that correctly read, and increasingly tinkered with, the mathematical book of nature.

This vision culminated in the Enlightenment and utilitarianism, and bequeathed a position that is part of our common sense nowadays: technological instrumentalism (or technoinstrumentalism). From this perspective, techniques and artifacts (progressively tied to science, which would ultimately bring about modern technology[1]) are instruments, axiologically neutral and controlled means to achieve predefined ends. In the early days of the industrial revolution, the modern narrative went beyond Bacon and suggested that the "God hypothesis" was no more necessary (as stated by Laplace), humanity had reached its majority of age (according to Kant), and humans were tool-making animals (as claimed by Benjamin Franklin) ready to save themselves. Humans were becoming autonomous moral subjects able to control and transform a mechanic, axiologically neutral world by means of increasingly powerful and axiologically neutral knowledge, artifacts, and techniques.

---

[1] Etimologically, the term "technology" emerged from a combination of *tekne* and *logos*, understood as systematic discourse or rationality.

Etymology is revealing: *instrumentum* comes from *in*, "inside", *struere*, "to gather together", and *mentum*, a "means" for something. What grants instruments their ontological status is human intentionality in designing and producing them (Baker 2004). The designer is thereby central. But the focus of modern instrumentalism is even more on the side of the user and its relation to technology. Technological instrumentalism enshrines de vision of "the master" and "the tool": a powerful and amoral human holding a basic type of artifact (Winner 1978). An *instrumentum* is then understood as a means that can be set inside a course of action to contribute to control and ensure the achievement of its ends (i.e.: the transformation of goals into results) without altering its orientation. That orientation depends primarily on factors such as foresight, interpretation, and evaluation. So, instruments are supposed to affect the subject's capacity to perceive and act (usually, to increase it) but not warp its thought, its will or its identity. Humans must become more autonomous thanks to technology. As a corollary, when morality (and politics) are considered, good and evil, power and responsibility, lie exclusively with the autonomous subject, its decisions and uses. These are some of the key tenets of technological instrumentalism, a "common sense view" in contemporary societies.

11.2 Antithesis. Technoautonomism: Technology Subordinates Morality and Politics

An antithetic conception of technology, technological autonomism (or technoautonomism) emerged at the end of the 18th century, rose during the 19th, and peaked between the 50s and 70s of the 20th. It can be traced from the foundational myth of Frankenstein (a modern and careless Prometheus) to Chaplin's Modern Days or the unstoppable war systems of Dr. Strangelove. A milestone within this trajectory is the work of Karl Marx, who, at the peak of the industrial revolution, reconceived the relations between technology and autonomy, be it moral or political. Marx considered techniques and artifacts as forces of production (along factors such as human labour or raw materials) that operate as key drivers in the production and reproduction of society. In correspondence with those forces emerge specific relations of production, such as property relations, which constitute the "economic base" of society. In turn, a social superstructure, including the political and the moral realms, is constituted and acts back upon such a foundation. "The hand-mill gives you a society with the feudal lord; the steam-mill a society with the industrial capitalist" (Marx 1976, p. 166), he sentenced. For Marx, political and moral autonomy are socioeconomically grounded in material conditions defined by labour and technology, as well as the struggles around them. In capitalism, technologies are a means for and a chrystallization of the accumulation of capital. Under the control of the capitalist class, technologies are incorporated (as fixed capital, dead labour) into a system of exploitation that alienates workers, who in the factory become "a living appendix" of a "lifeless mechanism" which they themselves have created (Marx 1906, pp. 461–462). Capital and the capitalist class become autonomous (although surely not independent nor separate), labour and workers become heteronomous, while alienating technologies codify such situation, since they are subordinated to the former to subordinate the latter.

A century later, Jacques Ellul went beyond Marx in prioritising technology as a key sociohistorical factor and conceiving it as autonomous and value laden,[2] definitely turning the instrumentalist vision upside down. A long tradition had addressed the momentum, as well as the unanticipated, unintended or undesired consequences of technological systems, which defy instrumentalist optimism concerning both technology and human capacities for foresight, choice, or control (Winner 1978). But Ellul (1964) went beyond that in suggesting we live in a "technological society" where all rationalities, including the economic, are subordinated to a technical rationality defined by a drive for "absolute efficiency". Such technical rationality turns everything into a means and is unable to ponder ends. It subverts Kant's moral rationality, which sanctioned the role of human beings as autonomous, universal legislators. The Enlightenment's dream of instrumental reason (in Horkheimer and Adorno's terms) generated a modern monster, *la Technique* (no more the ancient *tekne*), a mass of methods, techniques, artifacts, forms of organization (e.g. bureaucracies, corporations), megasystems (e.g. chemistry, electricity, automotion, nuclear energy…) and their conditions (the means of the means) which, from 18th century onwards, have slowly become both material and normative conditions for modern society.

For Ellul, modern humans have willingly developed, and come to love and rely on, technological innovations and their benefits. However, the increasing number, scale, opacity, interdependency, interconnection and interpotentiation of those technologies has not only entrenched and made the total ensemble difficult to change, but has increasingly made it self-generating, self-determining and self-augmenting; ultimately, the key force defining the evolution of society. Only selected social groups (technicians, scientists, etc.) know and understand parts of such an ensemble, but not even them can do much to redefine it. For Ellul, technology has become anthropomorphic (e.g. self-determining) because humans have become technomorphic, externally enframed by the whole ensemble and internally reconfigured by its drive for rational efficiency and optimization. In what Winner (1978) calls a "reverse adaptation", those forms and ends of human life that fit within the ensemble, succeed, and those that do not, wither away. With Ellul, the unbridled development of the arts and sciences, which Bacon saw as a way to overcome the original sin, becomes itself the original sin of modernity.

[2] Feenberg (1999) distinguished four key theories of technology: technological determinism (e.g. "traditional Marxism"), that conceives technology as autonomous (non-humanly controlled) and neutral (a means differentiated from ends); technological substantivism (e.g. Ellul), that conceives technology as autonomous and value-laden (a way of life that includes ends); instrumentalism, that conceives technology as humanly controlled and neutral; and, finally, critical theory of technology, which conceives technology as humanly controlled and value laden. This last position, which Feenberg defends, is connectable to our proposals in the synthesis section of this chapter. Meanwhile, technodeterminism and technosubstantivism are forms of what, in the current section, we are calling "technoautonomism".

Ellul stressed the autonomy of the technological ensemble at the macro-level, but others have attended to the micro-level of technical objects. Simondon (2017) provided arguments that allow to characterize technical objects as autonomous, as they develop through a process of concretization (functional and structural material integration), generating "evolutionary" lineages and essences that humans discover rather than create. In more Darwinian views, technical objects have been seen as units of evolution and humans as environments that select among them (Basalla 1988). Ironically, when technical objects become a systemic condition of society, there emerges the so-called "technological imperative", which demands not only to use them (as its most common understanding suggests) but also to adapt their environment (society and nature) to them to ensure their operation (Winner 1978). Against the Kantian categorical imperative, this new imperative seems to enshrine the growing autonomy of the technological and the heteronomy of the human. More recently, evolutionist leitmotivs can be found among authors such as Kurzweil (2005), who has crafted a history of the universe from the perspective of technical objects (specially, general artificial intelligence), culminating in a Technological Singularity where the human first recombines and then dissolves into an AI complex that grows and recrafts the whole cosmos. Less hyperbolic narratives also consider lower forms of AI and other technical objects (e.g. self-driving cars) as autonomous, mixing reality and myth in visions of humans either guided or substituted by machines (Bradshaw et al. 2013), in ways that sometimes recall debates on automation of the previous two centuries.

Finally, other analyses have attended to technological influence in psychological terms. Discussions about behavior-shaping technological environments have surfaced in contemporary behavioural economics and digital design, as in Eyal's (2014) guidelines for creating engagement or Thaler and Sunstein's (2008) concept of nudging as a design of the user's choice environment oriented to bring about a predictable change in behaviour. In this line, Zuboff (2019) denounced the rise of a surveillance capitalism where big digital corporations surveil and *surwill* (as labelled in Barandiaran et al. 2024; Calleja-López et al. 2018), that is, try to predict and shape users' behaviours to make a profit from it, thereby threatening moral and political autonomy. Ultimately, the "societies of control" heralded by Deleuze are defined by technologies oriented to shape the minds and habits of *dividuals* (the result of the datafication and decomposition of the modern individual) and their swarms (de la Torre et al. 2025).

All these philosophical views and historical processes have stressed the ascendancy and rule of technology (at various levels and in various forms, driven autonomously or by factors such as capital) over moral and political autonomy.

11.3 Synthesis. Technocomplexity: Reconstructing the Relations Between Technology, Morality, and Politics

Since the mid-twentieth century, different brands of cybernetics and their technologies, from servomechanisms to artificial life and intelligence, have focused on the integration of humanity and technology into increasingly complex and digitalized systems. Soon, the postmodern myth of the cyborg was born. Simultaneously, developments in paleoanthropology and philosophy went beyond Franklin's idea of the human as toolmaker and explored the relations of the human species and technology in terms of co-evolution and co-constitution: silex with cortex and hand (Leroi-Gourhan 1993), tools with language and sociopolitical norms (Birch 2021). Similarly, the extended mind thesis (Clark and Chalmers 1998) has gone beyond individualism and bio-centrism to highlight the role of technology in the constitution of the human mind, through dynamical relations that go from the sensorimotor (Pérez-Verdugo and Barandiaran 2023) to the institutional domain (Maiese 2026, this volume). Technologies are no more conceived as neutral instruments nor autonomous realities but as mediators in human-technology-world relations. These relations take a variety of forms –e.g. embodiment, hermeneutic, alterity, background (Ihde 1995), cyborg, composite (Verbeek 2008)– depending on which elements of the triad occupy the foreground or the background, resulting in different configurations of human interpretation, intentionality, action, and responsibility. Latour (2002, 2005) has suggested exploring the net-works of actants that, as quasi-subjects and quasi-objects, enter in a variety of associations to generate any form of self (*autos*), other (*allos*), and normativity (*nomos*). Going towards the spatial macroscale, Katheryne Hayles (2017) has examined global cognitive ecologies that entangle human and non-human actors in new collective forms of intelligence, decision, and action. Earlier, and still with modern undertones, Hans Jonas's (1985) "imperative of responsibility" to maintain genuine human life on Earth had widened the temporal and ecological horizons of analyses of technology. Together, these views contribute to a multiscalar ontological rethinking of autonomy (specially, of the *autos*) in the context of human-technology-world relations and human-and-non-human complexes and ecosystems; a third historical position that we may label "technocomplexity".

Bringing some of these insights into the field of morality, the ethics of design has mapped the variegated shaping of user behaviour –through coercion, decision, seduction or persuasion, depending on the strength and overtness of the influence– (Tromp et al. 2011). In the same line, it has questioned linear understandings of the influence of design intentions upon artefact utilisation by stressing the relevance of emergent and potentially unforeseen contexts of use (Albrechtslund 2007). Finally, as a complement, it has attended and proposed changes to the structural conditions of responsibility in design practice (Swierstra and Jelsma 2006).

But of more interest to us are political takes on technocomplexity. Langdon Winner convincingly argued that "artifacts have politics" and thereby connect to "ways of life". He showed that technologies are "politeia", "institutions in the making" that bring about a "second constitution" of society beyond the political-legal one (Winner 1986, pp. 54–55). For this reason, he stressed the potential of experiments in participatory design, and reclaimed new political virtues for this purpose (Winner 1992). Shared critical reflection by designers and users has been demanded (Sengers et al. 2005) as a way to unearth, analyse, choose and operate upon hidden or unconscious factors (e.g. cultural values or biases) shaping technology and its relation to human life. Meanwhile, recent calls for community-centred and intersectional approaches to technological design (attentive to discriminations based on ethnicity, gender, class, ability or other factors, and inclusive of affected groups and their interests) look to ensure more socially just technological artifacts and systems (Costanza-Chock 2020). Complementarily, the reflections of Donna Haraway (2016) and others (Driessen 2014; Cabello et al. 2026, this volume) suggest that such interventions should be careful, response-able and inclusive of non-human living beings, opening to a more diverse *autos*. Along these newly included actors, a diversity of values and virtues may be incorporated into design and use, a widening of *nomos* opposed to the absolutism of technical neutrality, efficiency, and proficiency. This may also challenge capitalism as a regime of universal heteronomy where, as Marx diagnosed, any principle, practice, or value is tendentially subordinated to exchange value.

Against Bacon's technoinstrumentalist dream and Ellul's technoautonomist nightmare, this third position suggests that technology should not dominate or serve to dominate humans and non-humans (old modern society and nature). Instead, new democratic technopolitical forms may appropriately involve those humans and non-humans (and their interests, values…) in the detection and framing of problems, the formulation of potential responses and the choice between those responses (which may or may not call for technologies as the way to advance), moving to the moments of technological design, development, and deployment, as well as the monitoring and evaluation of impacts, iteratively. This implies to recognize and productively incorporate the various scales of *autos* and *tekne* mentioned above, from the nano to the megascale, in both spatial terms (from *dividuals* to human-and-non-human orders, from the local to the global) and temporal terms (past, present and future, from the fleeting instant to deep time). This position critically builds upon earlier ones also by exploring the shapes, possibilities, and limits of technical knowledge (foresight and transparency but also uncertainty and opacity), control (flexibility and participation but also technological momentum and breakdown), intentionality (planning and assessment but also unintendedness and reverse adaptation), and value (fairness and justice but also biases and power contexts).

Building upon ontological, moral and political technocomplexity, this third position points towards a descriptive and prescriptive, empirical and normative, transformation of the modern *logos* around *tekne*. As an example, this may imply reducing technological complexity by opting for various forms of small, appropriate, low or slow tech in specific situations, and opting for big, high, fast and still appropriate technologies in others. In both cases, such technological options should incorporate autonomy (in the expanded sense –moral, political, ecological…– that we are outlining) as an ongoing precondition and as an ongoing result, as a central element in the complexes of principles and practices defining technological becomings. In digital societies built on top of multilayered stacks (of hardware, software, data, AI systems, etc.), to achieve this may require different cycles and forms of technopolitical democratization (Calleja-López 2021).

To sum up, the crucial form of autonomy in our technologically hypermediated world may be a recursive *technopolitical autonomy* that reflexively incorporates technocomplexity, taking the individual beyond itself, back to the ontotechnical and ecological constitution of its being, and forward into a personal and collective, ethical and political (careful, intersectional and mutispecific) participation in sociotechnical becomings. This is all to be considered at various scales, from concrete artifacts and people to wide megasystems and collectivities, with an orientation towards free, diverse and common forms of flourishing in the short, mid, and long term (Barandiaran et al. 2024; Chapter 5; Calleja-López et al. 2022, Sect. 5). New myths and makings will be necessary for such a struggle.

Acknowledgements XEB and MPV acknowledge IAS-Research group funding IT1668-22 from Basque Government, XEB, MPV and AC acknowledge grants PID2019-104576GB-I00 for project Outonomy and XEB and MPV PID2023-147251NB-I00 for Outagencies both funded by MCIU/AEI/10.13039/501100011033 and FEDER/UE. MPV is developing her PhD thanks to the Grant PRE2020-096494 of the Spanish National Research Agency (AEI) and cofunded by the European Social Fund.

References

Albrechtslund A (2007) Ethics and technology design. Ethics Inf Technol 9(1):63–72. https://doi.org/10.1007/s10676-006-9129-8

Baker LR (2004) The ontology of artifacts. Philos Explor 7(2):99–111. https://doi.org/10.1080/13869790410001694462

Barandiaran XE, Calleja-López A, Monterde A, Romero C (2024) Decidim, a technopolitical network for participatory democracy. philosophy, practice and autonomy of a collective platform in the age of digital intelligence. Springer

Basalla G (1988) The evolution of technology. Cambridge University Press

Birch J (2021) The skilful origins of human normative cognition. Analyse & Kritik 43(1):191–202. https://doi.org/10.1515/auk-2021-0010

Bradshaw JM, Hoffman RR, Johnson M, Woods DD (2013) The seven deadly myths of 'autonomous systems.' IEEE Intell Syst 28(3):54–61. https://doi.org/10.1109/MIS.2013.70

Cabello V, Merlo A, Mancilla M, Siqueiros J, Barandiaran XE (2026) Autonomy and its limits in social-ecological systems. In: Barandiaran XE, Etxeberria A (eds) Outonomy: fleshing out the concept of autonomy beyond the individual (p. in press). Springer

Calleja-López A (2021, September 29). Democratización tecnológica: Reimaginando la sociedad digital de abajo arriba. Anuario Internacional CIDOB, 57

Calleja-López A, Barandiaran XE, Monterde A (2018) Dalle reti sociali alle reti (tecno)politiche. In: Gambetta D (ed) Datacrazia. Politica, cultura algoritmica e conflitti al tempo dei big data (d Editore)

Calleja-López A, Cancela E, Cambronero M (2022) Desplazar los ejes: Alternativas tecnológicas, derechos humanos y sociedad civil a principios del siglo XXI. (Working Paper No. 1;

Tecnopolítica Working Papers). UOC. https://tecnopolitica.net/content/desplazar-los-ejes-alternativas-tecnologicas-derechos-humanos-y-sociedad-civil-principios
Clark A, Chalmers DJ (1998) The extended mind. Analysis 58(1):7–19
Costanza-Chock S (2020) Design Justice: community-led practices to build the worlds we need. MIT Press
de la Torre PG, Pérez-Verdugo M, Barandiaran XE (2025) Attention is all they need: cognitive science and the (techno)political economy of attention in humans and machines. AI & Soc. https://doi.org/10.1007/s00146-025-02400-z
Driessen C (2014) Animal deliberation, pp. 90–104. https://doi.org/10.1007/978-1-349-68308-6_7
Ellul J (1964) The technological society. Vintage Books
Eyal N (2014) Hooked: How to build habit-forming products. Portfolio
Feenberg A (1999) Questioning technology. Routledge
Haraway DJ (2016) Staying with the trouble: making Kin in the Chthulucene. Duke University Press
Hayles NK (2017) Unthought: the power of the cognitive nonconscious. University of Chicago Press
Ihde D (1995) Postphenomenology: essays in the postmodern context. Northwestern University Press
Jonas H (1985) The imperative of responsibility. University of Chicago Press, In search of an ethics for the technological age
Kant I (1998) Groundwork of the metaphysics of morals. Cambridge University Press
Kurzweil R (2005) The singularity is near: when humans transcend Biology. Penguin
Latour B (2002) Morality and technology (trans: C. Venn). Theory, Cult & Soc, 19(5–6), 247–260 https://doi.org/10.1177/026327602761899246
Latour B (2005) Reassembling the social: an introduction to actor-network-theory. Oxford University Press
Leroi-Gourhan A (1993) Gesture and speech. MIT Press
Maiese M (2026) Mindshaping and adaptive preferences. In: Barandiaran XE, Etxeberria A (eds) Outonomy: fleshing out the concept of autonomy beyond the individual (p. in press). Springer
Marx K (1906) Capital, vol I, 3rd Ed (tans: Moore S, Aveling E). The Modern Library
Marx K (1976) The poverty of philosophy. In: Marx K, Engels, F (eds) Marx/Engels Collected Works, vol. VI. Progress Publishers
Mitcham C (1994) Thinking through technology: the path between engineering and philosophy. Chicago University Press
Pérez-Verdugo M, Barandiaran X (2023) Personal autonomy and (digital) technology: an enactive sensorimotor framework. Philosophy & Technology, 36(4). https://doi.org/10.1007/s13347-023-00683-y
Rosich G (2020) The contested history of autonomy: interpreting European modernity. Bloomsbury Academic
Sengers P, Boehner K, David S, Kaye J 'Jofish' (2005) Reflective design. In: Proceedings of the 4th decennial conference on critical computing: between sense and sensibility, 49–58. https://doi.org/10.1145/1094562.1094569
Simondon G (2017) On the mode of existence of technical objects. University of Minnesota Press
Swierstra T, Jelsma J (2006) Responsibility without moralism in technoscientific design practice. Sci Technol Human Values 31(3): 309–332. https://doi.org/10.1177/0162243905285844
Thaler RH, Sunstein CR (2008) Nudge: improving decisions about health, wealth, and happiness. Yale University Press
Tromp N, Hekkert P, Verbeek P-P (2011) Design for socially responsible behavior: a classification of influence based on intended user experience. Des Issues 27(3):3–19. https://doi.org/10.1162/DESI_a_00087
Verbeek P-P (2008) Cyborg intentionality: rethinking the phenomenology of human–technology relations. Phenomenol Cogn Sci 7(3):387–395

Winner L (1978) Autonomous technology: technics-out-of-control as a theme in political thought. MIT Press
Winner L (1986) The whale and the reactor: a search for limits in an age of high technology. University of Chicago Press
Winner L (1992) Citizen virtues in a technological order. Inquiry. https://doi.org/10.1080/00201749208602298
Zuboff S (2019) The age of surveillance capitalism: the fight for a human future at the new frontier of power,1st Edition. Public Affairs

Chapter 12
Autonomy and Its Limits in Social-Ecological Systems

Violeta Cabello, Alejandro Merlo, María Mancilla, Jesús M. Siqueiros, and Xabier E. Barandiaran

Abstract Traditionally, autonomy has been perceived through the lens of individualism and internalism, a view increasingly challenged by contemporary philosophical approaches, as well as by the context of global sustainability. Environmental challenges underline the need to shift from Earth-imposed limits to social-ecological limitations to achieve autonomy, democracy, and sustainability. In the realm of sustainability sciences, the concept of social-ecological systems has been developed to explore the interdependencies between humans and their environments. Despite the significance of autonomy in discussions around sustainability, its exploration within this field remains limited. This chapter aims to discuss the potential contribution of the concept of outonomy for social-ecological systems and the planetary scale and, conversely, to open up the concept of autonomy to planetary-ecological dependencies.

Keywords Social-ecological systems · Earth limits · Gaia · Social-ecological outonomy

---

V. Cabello (✉)
Basque Centre for Climate Change, Bilbao, Spain
e-mail: Violeta.Cabello@bc3research.org

A. Merlo · X. E. Barandiaran
IAS-Research Center for Life, Mind, and Society, Department of Philosophy, University of the Basque Country (UPV/EHU), Donostia-San Sebastián, Spain
e-mail: Alejandro.merlo@ehu.eus

X. E. Barandiaran
e-mail: xabier.barandiaran@ehu.eus

M. Mancilla
Stockholm Resilience Centre, University of Stockholm, Stockholm, Sweden
e-mail: maria.mgarcia@su.se

J. M. Siqueiros
Instituto de Investigaciones en Matemáticas Aplicadas y en Sistemas, UAEY-IIMAS, UNAM, Mexico City, México
e-mail: jmario.siqueiros@iimas.unam.mx

X. E. Barandiaran and A. Etxeberria (eds.), *Outonomy*,
SpringerBriefs in Philosophy, https://doi.org/10.1007/978-3-032-05501-9_12

> The need to "stay with the trouble," (...) Such concern is what enables me to discern, and cast my lot with, a new understanding of autonomy as the invention of ways of living, not just surviving, in the ruins—whatever the final outcome.
>
> STENGERS, 2017

12.1 The Modern Notion of Autonomy and Social-Ecological Thinking

The concept of autonomy, defined as a system's capacity to govern itself through self-generated norms, is central to Western modernity. Its use spans biology (Varela 1979; Moreno and Mossio 2015), psychology (Legault and Inzlicht 2013), moral philosophy (Mele 1995), and social and political theory (Castoriadis 1991; Hardt and Negri 2005; Zibechi 2007). However, autonomy has traditionally been seen as confined within the boundaries of the individual or social system in an abstract, rationalistic, self-sufficient manner (see Barandiaran and Etxeberria 2026, this volume). The received notion of autonomy has been questioned across disciplines, from individual agency to societal scales (Armstrong et al. 2019). Still, nothing seems to challenge its core precepts more than crossing the boundaries of environmental sustainability on a planetary scale (Rockström et al. 2009).

While Earth's conditions set material boundaries for the material expansion of human societies, capitalist economies seem to defy external limits. The issue then is how to transit from limits determined by Earth's life-sustaining dynamics to self-imposed limits as a condition necessary for autonomy, democracy (Castoriadis 1991; Kallis 2019), and sustainability. Feminist scholars—including those in new materialisms or posthumanisms—critique the view of autonomy as the self-production of a self-sufficient individual (Haraway 2016; De La Bellacasa 2017; see also Urdangarin & Umerez 2025). They call for recognizing interdependencies and caring relations as the foundation for existence and social-ecological thriving. While we agree with this call, these criticisms address only a narrow view of autonomy—one that has been enriched by relational and enactivist perspectives, as discussed in the next section.

With Stengers (2017, p. 398), in this text, we seek to *reclaim* a new understanding of autonomy that enables "the invention of ways of living, not just surviving, in the ruins". We argue that an updated notion of autonomy that applies to the Earth system is critical at both descriptive and prescriptive levels: the former to better conceptualize the complex adaptive potential of beyond-the-individual social-ecological assemblages (Spies and Alff 2020); the latter to improve the promotion of the ensuing response-ability (Haraway 2016) that such a conceptualization brings forth.

12.2 Autonomy and Interdependence in Life and Mind

The concept of autonomy has been developed in biological and cognitive sciences through the legacy of Maturana and Varela's notion of autopoiesis (Maturana and Varela 1980). The original focus on operational closure has progressively led to a thermodynamically open (Ruiz-Mirazo and Moreno 2004), adaptively agential (Barandiaran et al. 2009), interactively constituted (Gallagher 2020) and social-ecologically interdependent conception (Escobar 2018). At its root, the autonomy of life is the capacity of living organisation to sustain itself (far-from-equilibrium in the face of a continuous flow of matter and energy) as a network of production and repair processes (metabolism) while differentiating such a network from an environment it, nevertheless, depends upon. The paradigmatic example is the cell: absorbing molecules from the environment to feed its metabolic reaction network, while producing a membrane that encapsulates the network and mediates with the environment. In doing so, the cell defines a set of viability *norms* (requirements to keep itself alive: temperature, nutrient input rate, etc.) and a *self*: an individual produced and kept distinct from its environment. Yet, as Hans Jonas put it, the relationship with the environment is not an opposing or purely self-differentiating one but one of "needful freedom" (Jonas 1966).

Enactivism has extended this concept of biological autonomy to the cognitive domain (Di Paolo et al. 2017; Varela et al. 1991). Far from the Kantian self-sufficiency of encapsulated reason to guide behaviour, sensorimotor autonomy implies a radical openness to the environment to constitute mental processes as interactive structures (sensorimotor coordinations, habits, activities, etc.). A fundamental dimension of this openness is linguistic sociality. It is constitutive of human autonomy, leaving it open to a world participated by and with others (Di Paolo et al. 2018). In fact, many worlds, some from an indigenous and decolonial stand, reclaim a deep sense of autonomy rooted in earthly social-ecological communal forms of life (Escobar 2018). In human life, as we know it, that kind of autonomy can only be realized through a deep understanding of the concept that includes political participation in radical democracy and the material limits of the Earth system (Asara et al. 2013; Castoriadis 1991; Maiese and Hanna 2019).

The notion of autonomy is therefore understood as (re)emerging in different domains or scales: the molecular-metabolic, the multicellular, the neurobehavioural, the sociolinguistic, the political and the social-ecological. However, this last one has, surprisingly, attracted little attention from the complex systems approach to autonomy and ecology. Some notable exceptions build a concept of function in ecosystems in analogy with that of organismic function (Nunes-Neto et al. 2014) or, by drawing inspiration from (Clarke 2020) or in conflict with (Haraway 2016), the autopoietic or autonomous concept of organism at ecological and planetary scales. And yet, the study of social-ecological systems is constituted by some of the ingredients essential to the bio-enactivist concept of autonomy.

12.3 Autonomy and Social-Ecological Systems

The concept of social-ecological systems (SES) emerged in the field of sustainability sciences to study human–environment interdependencies (Berkes and Folke 1998; Berkes et al. 2003; Anderies et al. 2004). Rooted in complex systems theory and theoretical ecology, SES are defined as complex adaptive systems (Folke et al. 2016) comprised of intertwined social and ecological constituents (Schlüter et al. 2020). SES self-organize, producing emergent rules and patterns (Ostrom 1992; Aggarwal and Anderies 2023; Schlüter et al. 2019), and are viewed as open networks linking local and global scales (Laroche et al. 2020). Although autonomy is not explicitly studied in SES, we identify features that support an expanded, relational understanding of the concept, with the goal of conceptually integrating and enriching these different research traditions.

The field of SES research has evolved over time along with the development of theoretical perspectives and through their variegated applications (Colding and Barthel 2019). Early definitions viewed social and ecological systems as separate entities, with the social constituent self-organizing according to its own institutions aimed at governing the environmental constituent (Berkes and Folke 1998). The idea of *adaptability* was central to these early conceptions, together with that of resilience, formulated as the capacity of a SES to navigate change without substantially compromising its functions (Berkes et al. 2003). Following this, Gunderson and Hooling (2003) defined the *adaptive cycle* as periodic shifts from stability to transformation driven by non-linear interactions, implying that SES both persist and adapt through time.

One of the most significant evolutions in the study of SES is the concept of *intertwinedness,* which shifts the conception of the social and the ecological as separated elements to a co-constituted view of SES through continuous processes of intra-action (Schlüter et al. 2020). Social–ecological phenomena—such as a fishery collapse or a forest's spiritual value—emerge from multi-level, evolving relations among humans and other entities (Schlüter et al. 2019). This view resonates with the process interdependence view in organizational and enactive accounts of autonomy.

Normativity and *viability* are fundamental notions in both the autonomy and SES fields. However, these two traditions hold different understandings of these terms. As outlined in the previous section, norms in autonomy are conceived as behavioural or physiological preferences, constraints or regulations over multiple available possibilities that emerge from the activity of the system, directed to maintain itself within viability limits or to expand those limits (e.g. to regulate the temperature within survival ranges in an animal or pump ions at a given rate to avoid an osmotic crisis on a cell). This conceptualisation resonates with research on the ecological side of SES, where, for example, diversity in the trophic networks has been shown to be fundamental for the viability of ecosystems. Nevertheless, the most common understanding of norms within sustainability sciences is inherited from social scientists' contributions to the field, that is, as social-institutional norms: formal or informal rules created by social actors to regulate and act upon social-ecological dynamics.

Various schools have studied how norms are socially created and enacted, from Elinor Ostrom's studies on local common pool resource management to more ample studies on environmental policy and adaptive, collaborative or multi-level governance (Ostrom 1992; Emerson et al. 2012; Newig and Koontz 2014). Contrary to norms in autonomous agents, regulatory aspects in SES permeate different organizational scales and levels of abstraction and concretization: from policies and laws dictated by external regulatory institutions (e.g. the EU) to the practical application and integration of such norms in the different contexts, or the concrete "needs" and practices of forms of life in SES.

The challenge lies in moving from norms conceived as purely socially contingent to norms as social-ecologically intertwined. The SES literature is only recently addressing this integration of social and ecological norms. For instance, Schlüter et al. (2019) distinguish between social norms and biophysical rules and structures (such as food webs or climatic conditions) in determining social-ecological phenomena. Another example is how Aggarwal and Anderies (2023) link cultural theory and SES analysis to advance a conceptualization of governance as emergent social-ecological feedback structures that enable a fine-tuning of SES relations. If we adopt the definition of norms put forward in enactive accounts of autonomy, we could further argue that a social-ecological norm establishes the viability limits of SES as an autonomous system and ensures its ecological and social long-term sustainability.

The enactment of such a norm requires defining viability limits for social-ecological intra-actions within the boundaries of each SES, which leads to the problem of many SES not having clearly delineated frontiers. For example, where to set the border of a fishery or a natural protected area is a difficult governance and analytical question. This type of decision is not trivial, as illustrated by the ample literature discussing how to 'fit' social and ecological boundaries (Moss 2012) and whether these boundaries are 'real' or 'constructed' according to particular analytical goals, scales, and methods (Wu 2013).

Another key point is that SES are open systems and thus their metabolic relations (such as food production, fishing, transport, mining, fuel extraction or consumption of technologies) are always open and integrated across multiscale production chains that partially determine local practices and regulations (Giampietro et al. 2011; Laroche et al. 2020). For this reason, it would be particularly hard to define their limits in the form of an organizational or operational closure. As IPBES (2024) has bluntly put, in global capitalist economies, the capacity of the multitude of SES on Earth to redefine what is good, viable and sustainable for (and by) themselves, create their own response-able norms and care for their intra-actions is nowadays hampered.

This last problem of establishing the boundaries of SES brings us to the level of the whole earth as the ultimate SES and anchor of autonomy.

12.4 Gaia: Social-Ecological Autonomy at the Planetary Scale

The concept of Gaia—viewing the Earth system as a living entity (Kleidon 2023; Lenton et al. 2020; Lovelock and Margulis 1974)—represents a convergence point between theories of biological autonomy and socio-ecological systems (SES). This perspective challenges the conventional dichotomy between living organisms and their environments (Etxeberria 2026, this volume), proposing instead that they form integrated, self-regulating entities. In this expanded framework, life is not confined to individual organisms but emerges from the collective activities of living systems and their interactions with their surroundings, including atmospheric and geological processes over long timescales.

James Lovelock and Lynn Margulis initially articulated Gaia theory by suggesting that Earth's atmospheric composition is regulated by living processes, akin to how an organism maintains homeostasis (Lovelock and Margulis 1974). Margulis, in particular, emphasized the self-creative nature of life through her engagement with autopoiesis, influenced by Francisco Varela. Her work argued for biology's independence from reductionist paradigms in physical and molecular sciences, asserting that the simplest autopoietic entity is the bacterial cell and the largest is Gaia itself (Lovelock and Margulis 1974; Clarke 2020). This view situates Gaia within a continuum from cells to ecosystems, emphasizing cooperative and symbiotic processes as foundational.

Two main challenges have been raised against a conception of Gaia rooted in biological autonomy. Building on Margulis's insights, Haraway and others have advocated for shifting from autopoiesis to sympoiesis, emphasizing symbiotic collaboration (Dempster 1998; Haraway 2016). While the term sympoiesis highlights the central role of symbiosis in life, we argue that it complements rather than replaces autopoiesis. Biological autonomy continues to provide a critical framework for understanding the integrity of individual cells and the organized, systemic nature of Earth as an 'ecosystem of ecosystems'. Latour, on the other hand, critiques Gaia theory's cybernetic roots, suggesting that such frameworks impose reductive, top-down, and engineering-centric perspectives (2015: 78, 81–83). However, this critique overlooks advances in second-order cybernetics that challenge the separation of observer and system, emphasizing their co-dependence (Clarke 2020). These developments align with contemporary theories of biological autonomy, offering a non-reductive, bottom-up approach that recognizes Gaia not only as self-organizing and inherently resistant to external control but also precarious and vulnerable to malfunctioning and "disease".

The climate crisis is a manifestation of this autonomy being challenged. It brings to the surface that there are some "norms" at a planetary level that have been broken, that something is "malfunctioning" (Rockström et al. 2009). Any discussion about SES sustainability and autonomy is thus necessarily enmeshed with that of global sustainability. Moreover, the possibility of autonomy of local SES, at the scale of certain human-cultural-ecosystemic life-forms (like those of indigenous social-ecological systems), might be about to get irreversibly lost in the capitalocenic acceleration. This acceleration is bringing planetary scale autonomy (Gaia) down to the human scale of SES, rapidly merging the pace of local SES with that of the planetary scale.

Ultimately, here is the paradox: the modern category of autonomy, encompassing biological, moral and political spheres, as that of an independent self-governing individual, cannot find any satisfying member other than the Earth system itself. This is the only form of living existence that, floating in the void, only depends on the energy of nuclear reactions of the sun and the planetary nucleus. Below this, we are deemed to live outonomously, that is, acknowledging and bringing forth our deep mutual interdependence with the environment we produce, and we are part of, together with other living and non-living entities.

12.5 Conclusion

Global warming, the loss of biodiversity or the acidification of the oceans call into question the individualistic vision of self-regulation and self-sufficiency that the modern conception of autonomy brought with it. It forces us to think that if the concept of autonomy has an ontological, epistemic and normative value, it is because it is necessarily relational, non-anthropocentric, and increasingly open to include larger scales of caring. We have argued that an updated notion of autonomy, as developed in organization and enactive traditions to the philosophy of biology and mind, can meet contemporary trends and can contribute to identifying limits, norms and regulatory capacities in SES research. Furthermore, we posit that it is even crucial in order to enhance our capacity to design for (Escobar 2018), to commit to and to inhabit more sustainable shared forms of life, ultimately encompassing the whole earth as an autonomous form of life.

Acknowledgements XEB and AM acknowledge IAS-Research group funding IT1668-22 from Basque Government, grants PID2019-104576GB-I00 for project Outonomy and, together with VC PID2023-147251NB-I00 for Outagencies funded by MCIU/AEI/10.13039/501100011033 and FEDER/UE. VC has been funded by the Spanish Ministry of Science and Innovation Ramón y Cajal (RYC2021- 031626-I) and María de Maeztu (CEX2021- 001201-M) programs, and by the Basque Government BERC 2022-2025. MMG acknowledges the Swedish Research Council (VR) under grant number 2018-05792.

References

Aggarwal RM, Anderies JM (2023) Understanding how governance emerges in social-ecological systems: Insights from archetype analysis. Ecol Soc 28(2) https://doi.org/10.5751/ES-14061-280202

Anderies JM, Hanssen MA, Ostrom E (2004) A framework to analyze the robustness of social-ecological systems from an institutional perspective. Ecol Soc 9(1:18)

Armstrong A, Green K, Sangiacomo A (2019) Spinoza and relational autonomy: being with others. Edinburgh University Press

Asara V, Profumi E, Kallis G (2013) Degrowth, democracy and autonomy. Environ Values 22(2):217–239. https://doi.org/10.3197/096327113X13581561725239

Barandiaran XE, Etxeberria A (2025) Outonomy, the very idea. In: Barandiaran XE, Etxeberria A (eds) Outonomy: fleshing out the concept of autonomy beyond the individual. Springer

Barandiaran XE, Di Paolo E, Rohde M (2009) Defining agency: individuality, normativity, asymmetry, and spatio-temporality in action. Adapt Behav 17(5):367–386. https://doi.org/10.1177/1059712309343819

Berkes F, Folke C (1998) Linking sociological and ecological systems: management practices and social mechanisms for building resilience. Cambridge University Press

Berkes F, Colding J, Folke C (2003) Introduction. In: Navigating social-ecological systems: building resilience for complexity and change, Cambridge University Press, pp. 1–30

Castoriadis C (1991) Philosophy, politics, autonomy. Oxford University Press

Clarke B (2020) Gaian systems: Lynn Margulis, Neocybernetics, and the end of the Anthropocene. University of Minnesota Press. https://doi.org/10.5749/j.ctv16f6d9c

Colding J, Barthel S (2019) Exploring the social-ecological systems discourse 20 years later. Ecol Soc 24(1). https://doi.org/10.5751/ES-10598-240102

Di Paolo EA, Buhrmann T, Barandiaran XE (2017) Sensorimotor life: An enactive proposal, 1st edn. Oxford University Press

Di Paolo EA, Cuffari EC, De Jaegher H (2018) Linguistic bodies: the continuity between life and language. MIT press

Emerson K, Nabatchi, T, Balogh, S (2012) An Integrated framework for collaborative governance. J Public Adm Res Theory 22. https://doi.org/10.4324/9780203635926

Escobar A (2018) Designs for the Pluriverse: radical interdependence, autonomy, and the making of worlds. Duke University Press

Etxeberria A (2026) Environment(s), autonomy and (a)symmetries. In: Barandiaran XE, Etxeberria A (eds) Outonomy: fleshing out the concept of autonomy beyond the individual. Springer

Folke C, Biggs R, Norström A, Reyers B, Rockström J (2016) Social-ecological resilience and biosphere-based sustainability science. Ecol Soc 21(3). https://doi.org/10.5751/ES-08748-210341

Gallagher S (2020) Action and interaction. Oxford University Press

Giampietro M, Mayumi K, Sorman A (2011) The Metabolic Pattern of Societies (0 ed.). Routledge. https://doi.org/10.4324/9780203635926

Gunderson LH, Holling CS (eds) (2002) Panarchy: understanding transformations in human and natural systems. Island Press, Washington, D.C., USA

Gunderson L, Holling C (2003) Panarchy: understanding transformations in human and natural systems. Bibliovault OAI Repository, the University of Chicago Press, 114. https://doi.org/10.1016/S0006-3207(03)00041-7

Haraway DJ (2016) Staying with the Trouble. Duke University Press.

Hardt M, Negri A (2005) Multitude: war and democracy in the age of empire. Penguin

IPBES (2024) Summary for policymakers of the thematic assessment report on the underlying causes of biodiversity loss and the determinants of transformative change and options for achieving the 2050 vision for biodiversity of the intergovernmental science-policy platform on biodiversity and ecosystem service*s*. O'Brien, K., Garibaldi, L., ... (eds.). IPBES secretariat, Bonn, Germany

Jonas H (1966) The phenomenon of life: toward a philosophical Biology, vol 64. Northwestern University Press

Kallis G (2019) Limits: why Malthus was wrong and why environmentalists should care. Stanford briefs

Kleidon A (2023) Understanding the earth as a whole system: from the Gaia hypothesis to thermodynamic optimality and human societies. Heidelberg University Publishing. https://doi.org/10.17885/heiup.857

Laroche PCSJ, Schulp CJE, Kastner T, Verburg PH (2020) Telecoupled environmental impacts of current and alternative Western diets. Glob Environ Chang 62:102066. https://doi.org/10.1016/j.gloenvcha.2020.102066
Legault L, Inzlicht M (2013) Self-determination, self-regulation, and the brain: autonomy improves performance by enhancing neuroaffective responsiveness to self-regulation failure. J Pers Soc Psychol 105(1):123–138. https://doi.org/10.1037/a0030426
Lenton TM, Dutreuil S, Latour B (2020) Life on Earth is hard to spot. Anthr Rev 7(3):248–272. https://doi.org/10.1177/2053019620918939
Lovelock JE, Margulis L (1974) Atmospheric homeostasis by and for the biosphere: The Gaia hypothesis. Tellus 26(1–2):2–10
Maiese M, Hanna R (2019) The mind-body politic, 1st edn. Palgrave Macmillan
Maturana HR, Varela FJ (1980) Autopoiesis and cognition. D. Reidel Publishing Company
Mele AR (1995) Autonomous agents: from self-control to autonomy. Oxford University Press, USA. http://gen.lib.rus.ec/book/index.php?md5=af29b834ad96c44388b21df15684313c
Moreno A, Mossio M (2015) Biological autonomy: a philosophical and theoretical enquiry. Springer
Moss T (2012) Spatial fit, from panacea to practice: implementing the EU water framework directive. Ecol Soc 17(3), art2. https://doi.org/10.5751/ES-04821-170302
Newig J, Koontz TM (2014) Multi-level governance, policy implementation and participation: the EU's mandated participatory planning approach to implementing environmental policy. J Eur Publ Policy 21(2):248–267. https://doi.org/10.1080/13501763.2013.834070
Nunes-Neto N, Moreno A, El-Hani CN (2014) Function in ecology: an organizational approach. Biol Philos 29(1):123–141. https://doi.org/10.1007/s10539-013-9398-7
Ostrom E (1992) Crafting institutions for self-governing irrigation systems. ICS Press, Distributed to the trade by national book network
Puig de La Bellacasa M (2017) Matters of care: speculative ethics in more than human worlds. University of Minnesota Press. https://www.jstor.org/stable/https://doi.org/10.5749/j.ctt1mmfspt
Rockström J, Steffen W, Noone K, Persson Å, Chapin FSI, Lambin E, Lenton T, Scheffer M, Folke C, Schellnhuber HJ, Nykvist B, de Wit C, Hughes T, van der Leeuw S, Rodhe H, Sörlin S, Snyder P, Costanza R, Svedin U, Falkenmark, M, Karlberg L, Corell RW, Fabry VJ, Hansen J, Walker B, Liverman D, Richardson K, Crutzen P, Foley J (2009) Planetary boundaries: exploring the safe operating space for humanity. Ecol Soc 14(2). https://doi.org/10.5751/ES-03180-140232
Ruiz-Mirazo K, Moreno A (2004) Basic autonomy as a fundamental step in the synthesis of life. Artif Life 10(3):235–259. https://doi.org/10.1162/1064546041255584
Schlüter M, Haider L, Lade S, Lindkvist E, Martin R, Orach K, Wijermans N, Folke C (2019) Capturing emergent phenomena in social-ecological systems: An analytical framework. Ecology and Society 24(3). https://doi.org/10.5751/ES-11012-240311
Schlüter M, Hertz T, Mancilla García M (2020) Social-ecological intertwinedness: an attempt at a clarification. SSRN Electron J. https://doi.org/10.2139/ssrn.3727968
Spies M, Alff H (2020) Assemblages and complex adaptive systems: a conceptual crossroads for integrative research? Geogr Compass 14(10):e12534
Stengers I (2017) Autonomy and the intrusion of Gaia. South Atlantic Quarterly 116(2):381–400. https://doi.org/10.1215/00382876-3829467
Urdangarin M, Umerez J (2025) Autonomy in the making: From self-sufficiency to subjects-in-common. In: Barandiaran XE, Etxeberria A (eds) Outonomy: fleshing out the concept of autonomy beyond the individual. Springer
Varela FJ (1979) Principles of biological autonomy. North Holland
Varela FJ, Thompson E, Rosch E (1991) The embodied mind: cognitive science and human experience. MIT Press
Wu J (2013) Hierarchy theory: an overview. In Rozzi R, Pickett STA, Palmer C, Armesto JJ, Callicott JB (eds) Linking ecology and ethics for a changing world. Springer Netherlands, pp. 281–301. https://doi.org/10.1007/978-94-007-7470-4_24

Zibechi R (2007) *Autonomías y emancipaciones. América Latina en movimiento*. Fondo Editorial de la Facultad de Ciencias Sociales, Unidad de Post Grado, UNMSM

Chapter 13
From Self-Sufficient Individuals to Subjects-In-Common

Mikel Urdangarin and Jon Umerez

Abstract The aim of this chapter is to review the criticism of the self-sufficient individual and to consider how autonomy can be thought from the subjects-in-common. As Goikoetxea affirms, "one is not born a subject, it is made". Subjects are not autonomous owners of themselves. Instead, they are constantly overcome and dispossessed by the relationships that constitute them. If the subject is made and determined, how can autonomy be thought of? Our hypothesis is that being determined, done and dispossessed, is a precondition for autonomy instead of an external limit to it, although it is not a guarantee. The question is how to determine it. The question is not, therefore, whether one has or does not have links, but about what kind of links one has. In conclusion, against the model of autonomy understood as a pre-social property of a self-sufficient individual, we propose an alternative model of autonomy: a situated and plural capacity for self-governance developed within, through, and against social relationships.

Keywords Subject · Autonomy · Self-sufficiency · Interdependence · Common

13.1 Introduction

Adapting De Beauvoir's famous dictum, and synthesizing decades of philosophy from Foucault to Butler, Jule Goikoetxea states that "(o)ne is not born a subject, it is made" (2017). She summarizes this way the thesis that the subject is not the autonomous owner of itself, but is constantly overcome and dispossessed by the relationships that constitute it.

But, if the subject is made and, accordingly, determined, how can autonomy be thought of? Does being produced deny us the possibility to act? Is autonomy

---

M. Urdangarin (✉) · J. Umerez
IAS-Research Centre for Life, Mind, and Society, Department of Philosophy, University of the Basque Country (UPV/EHU), Donostia-San Sebastián, Spain
e-mail: mikel.urdangarin.irastorza@gmail.com

J. Umerez
e-mail: jon.umerez@ehu.eus

X. E. Barandiaran and A. Etxeberria (eds.), *Outonomy*,
SpringerBriefs in Philosophy, https://doi.org/10.1007/978-3-032-05501-9_13

possible in this dispossession? Our hypothesis is that *being determined, done and dispossessed, instead of being an external limit to autonomy is a precondition for it, even if not a guarantee.* The question is, then, how the subject is determined and made. The question is not as much whether to have links or not, as the debate is frequently introduced, but what kind of links they are.

In order to explain this, we will divide the chapter into three sections: first, we will review the criticism of possessive individualism (Macpherson, 1962); second, we will introduce the notion of subjects-in-common; third, we will consider how autonomy can be understood under this form of subjectivity.

13.2 Critique of Possessive Individualism

Advocates of the notion of *subjects-in-common* have based their model of subject on a straightforward criticism of possessive individualism. According to the theorists of the social contract, i.e. Hobbes, Locke or Mill, every 'man' was free and equal by birth and nature. The free choice of the individual was the main specificity of the modern world and, therefore, the subject could no longer be definitely predetermined from birth in a situation and place. The authors and the axes of the social contract had to be the autonomous individuals. As Pateman characterizes it:

> [The contractarian individual] is seen as naturally complete himself. That is to say, the boundaries that separate one individual from another are so tightly drawn that an individual is pictured as existing without any relationships with others. The individual's capacities and attributes owe nothing to any other individual or to any social relationship; they are his alone. The contractarian individual necessarily is the proprietor of his person and his attributes, or, in C. B. Macpherson's famous description, he is a possessive (Pateman 1988: 55).

In this sense, the contractarian individual was *self-sufficient*, such that he was sufficient to exist by himself; *pre-social*, as constituted before any social relation; and *possessive*, developing the relations and contracts in order to protect his property from the perspective of his self-interest. In short, as a proprietor of his property, his conscience, and his relationships, he was sovereign of himself or, as Locke put it, "every individual man has a property in his own person; this is something that nobody else has any right to" (Locke [1690] 2017: 11) And also, for instance, Mill states that "In the part which merely concerns himself, his independence is, of right, absolute. Over himself, over his own body and mind, the individual is sovereign" (Mill [1859] 2004: 37). The autonomy, therefore, was pre-social and the social contract was the instrument to secure it: "The great purpose for which men enter into society is to be safe and at peace in their use of their property; and the great instrument by which this is to be achieved is the laws established in that society" (Locke 2017: 43).

But, according to Gil, this ideal of autonomy is built on the three fallacies (2014: 298–299). Firstly, it is based on the denial of the collective dimension of existence, privatizing the sense and intentions of life. Secondly, it is based on the idea that consciousness is sufficient for itself to be, as if knowing oneself were possible without the interpellation and mediations of others. In this sense, and lastly, it affirms self-sufficiency, denying physical, corporal and social bonds and concealing the care work they demand within the sexual contract.

As a preliminary conclusion, then, we claim that the possessive and self-sufficient individual is not sustainable (see also Cabello et al. 2026, this issue). It is based on the invisibility and exploitation of the works and relationships that make life possible. That supposed universal subject is very particular: a heterosexual, white, bourgeois man who speaks the hegemonic language. Subjects need to be thought differently.

13.3 Subjects-In-Common

Diverse feminisms have drawn a different kind of subject built from the previously outlined criticism. As Goikoetxea says, we are not born subjects, but mammals. Men, women, basques, whites, workers, or bourgeois… the subject is done a posteriori (Goikoetxea 2017: 275). How to understand that "doing"? Since we cannot deal with an exhaustive analysis of every author that has attempted to answer this question, we will focus here on some contributions by Butler and Haraway.

In Butler's opinion the sovereign subject is dangerous, and it must be displaced. To do so, she proposes, as an alternative, the notion of dispossessed and precarious subjects. This concept moves, not only beyond standard approaches to autonomy, but also beyond simple relational ones: "Despite my affinity for the term relationality, we may need other language to approach the issue that concerns us, a way of thinking about how we are not only constituted by our relations but also dispossessed by them as well" (Butler 2004a: 24).

She underlines three characteristics: First the subject is made in common, under certain material and symbolic conditions, responding to the interventions and interpellations of others. The subject is not foundational, because in order to be able to do, it has to be done before, socially. Others touch us, feed us, take care of us, place us in a discourse and a language, establish specific social norms for recognition, etc. This object of care, languaging, and normalization only emerges later as a subject, always in a limited way: "we are, from the start, given over to the other, one in which we are, even prior to individuation itself and, by virtue of bodily requirements, given over to some set of primary others" (Butler 2004a: 31). In this sense, it is not self-sufficient, it is conditioned and mediated by norms, discourses and social supports. Consequently, the "I" is not a presocial entity or a substance. On the contrary, the "I" is a set of relations and processes immersed in a world that goes beyond the individual. We cannot escape from that shared condition. These relations make us.

Secondly, these relationships not only shape us, they dispossess us too. The relations and processes that cross the subject make it partially opaque to itself. The subject is limited and not transparent, because the narrative "I" cannot fully explain and control its formation, even less in first person: "I may try to tell the story of myself, but another story is already at work in me, and there is no way to distinguish between the 'I' who has emerged from this infantile condition and the 'you'—the set of 'you's'— who inhabits and dispossesses my desire from the outset" (Butler 2005: 74). This inscrutable condition cannot be fully explained, though it cannot be avoided. That opacity must be constant before it is cleared up. In this sense, the subject is not entirely coherent either, because while they make us, they decentre and disorient us. Instead of possessive individuals, we are dispossessed subjects, because the links that form us partially are the same ones that prevent the self from being totally mine. In that sense, the subject is incomplete and open-ended.

Thirdly, the subject is permeable and vulnerable. This close dependence on previous and cross-sectional links makes us not only dependent but vulnerable: we are not in our hands, we are dependent and vulnerable to what is not ours. These primary relationships not only shape and support us, but also limit us, threaten us and exclude us, making us vulnerable to the recognition, contact, intervention and violence of others: "our being socially constituted bodies, attached to others, at risk of losing those attachments, exposed to others, at risk of violence by virtue of that exposure" (Butler 2004a: 20). Accordingly, she makes a difference between precariousness and precarity. Precariousness is an inevitable and common dimension of bodily life. However, precarity is an evitable and differential redistribution of that shared precariousness according to political and social conditions.

Butler, therefore, calls into question the self-sufficient, sovereign, coherent, transparent and pre-social subject. The subject is, in her view, the articulation of a set of relationships and processes. It is vulnerable, incomplete, contradictory, profoundly implicated in the lives of others. In short, it is a precarious and dispossessed subject.

Going deeper, Haraway also invites us to think of the subject in another way: "refigure the kind of persons we might be. These persons can no longer be, if they ever were, master subjects, nor alienated subjects, but—just possibly—multiply heterogeneous, inhomogeneous, accountable, and connected human agents" (Haraway 1991: 3). To elaborate this, she has proposed some interesting metaphors. On the one hand, in the face of *autopoiesis* she proposes *sympoiesis* and "become-with" (Cabello et al. 2026, this volume). We become who and what we are with others, in those sympoietic relations. Without a prior essence, the subjects form themselves in these relationships in a continuous process: they are "coconstitutive relationships in which no partner will preexist the relationship, and the relationship is never done once and for all" (Haraway 2003:12). Following Barad (2007), Haraway suggests in a more recent book (2016) the category of intra-action to explain this. It's not an interaction between complete units. On the contrary, the units are completed and constituted in those relations.

In turn, Haraway extends the scope of dependence and intra-action. By linking "humanus" with "humus" (earth), she expands this intra-action into *humusities*. That is, in complex, continuous and dynamic assemblages, associated with non-human subjects. In this sense, she emphasizes that human beings and other beings exist in a shared compost, underlining the ecodependencies in her idiosyncratic style: "human beings are not in a separate compost pile. We are humus, not Homo, not anthropos; we are compost, not posthuman" (Haraway 2016: 55). Immersed in humusities, the subjects became-with in these multiple sympoietic and intra-active relationships. Using her metaphor, the subjects are *companion species*.

However, this common compost is not a holistic, benign and harmonious Mother Earth. It's not the idyllic Other that needs to be rebalanced. In Haraway's words, nature is a "coding trickster with whom we must learn to converse" (1991: 201). Since the world is "a knot in motion" (2003: 6), it is a complex, heterogeneous, contradictory, contingent and often unpredictable assemblage, which is made through social, cultural and ecological interactions. Besides, among these non-linear connections, these socioecological interconnections are necessarily partial and situated: "nobody lives everywhere; everybody lives somewhere. Nothing is connected to everything; everything is connected to something" (Haraway 2016: 31). In this sense, the subject is situated.

Therefore, different authors have profoundly revolutionized the idea of a presocial individual. The following conclusions can be drawn from these criticisms and their alternative approaches. On the one hand, the subject and autonomy, more than the foundational starting point, is rather the incomplete product of many works and processes. On the other hand, interdependence/ecodependence is not a network of relations that is tied up later by the presocial subject, but a primary and permanent condition that configures us as a subject. Finally, these dependencies not only make us, they also dispossess us. Consequently, the subject can no longer be represented as self-sufficient, transparent and complete. It is a concrete articulation of a set of relationships and processes, incomplete, contradictory and heterogeneous. We will use "subjects-in-common" (Llaguno 2018: 72) to express that kind of subject.

13.4 Autonomy in Terms of Relationality

Given the common and precarious dimensions of our lives, how can we rethink autonomy? We do not have to choose in terms of the classic alternatives, between the liberation from ties or the conformity to ties. Whether they propose the union or the separation, both of the approaches presuppose a presocial subject. Garcés revolutionizes this starting point asking: "What if the bodies are not united or separated? Beyond the duality union / separation, the bodies continue each other' (Garcés 2013: 30). Immersed in humusities, the question again is not whether to have links or not, but what kind of links exist in such a continuity. Here is the tension: in the face of the fantasy of breaking off the links, the subject will have to be liberated within the links, by making the links more liberating. Garcés expresses this creative tension thus: "this life, which is not mine, is mine" (2013: 150). Also this is the space where the notion of *outonomy* explored in this book is situated (Barandiaran & Etxeberria 2025, this volume).

But how do we do it? In this respect, the next question emerges. If the subject is made and determined, how should one think and exercise autonomy? Does having been done deny us the possibility of doing? It doesn't have to be that way. To have the capacity to act, the subject must be capacitated to act. In other words, in order to act ourselves, others have to act on us. Although it may seem paradoxical, we can only individualize ourselves in sociality: "The self must, in this way, be dispossessed in sociality in order to take possession of itself" (Butler 2004b: 7).

Therefore, the fact that they have done us does not exclude the possibility of doing. But it doesn't even guarantee it because those relations also undo and disable us. So, what to do? "What can I do with the conditions that form me? What do they constrain me to do? What can I do to transform them?" (Butler 2004a:16).

To make mine what is not mine, we will have to get involved in what is not mine or, in other words, in what is common. More specifically: within, through and against those links. *Within*, because there is not a 'pure' body outside the relational assemblage and power relations that cross it. *Through*, because through the same disciplinary and biopolitical mechanisms that modulate us and condition us, the subject is made and enabled to act. For example, we have to go through a process of domestication to learn how to read and write, which is essential for democratization. Finally, *against*, because those links not only capacitate and sustain us, but they also subdue us and threaten us by redistributing vulnerability in a differential way. The politicization and transformation of these links is therefore also fundamental. The maintenance of this tension is essential, as we are subjects in the ambivalence between the affirmation and problematization of those relationships. In other words, in the tension between subjection and subjectivity.

This forces us to understand autonomy differently. Firstly, autonomy must be understood as a capacity rather than as a property. Autonomy is no longer the originative property of the possessive individual, who must be the object of negotiation, guarantee, or delimitation a posteriori. It cannot be a pre-social property because we are dispossessed from the very beginning. In the face of this, in Goikoetxea's approach, it is the sociopolitical capacity for self-governance that matters, one that can only develop in concrete socioecological conditions. Precisely, it is the territorialized and institutionalized capacity of self-governing according to one's own decision (Goikoetxea 2017). In other words, the capacity to be equally free: that is, to be capable (free) and as capable as the most capable (equal) to self-govern our lives. Or, rather, a constant social process to capacitate, since it is a relation and not a thing.

Besides, it must be understood in plural rather than in singular. If the autonomy is relational, that autonomy must be extended to all relations that cross life. On the road to democratisation, Olariaga proposes the representation of autonomy as a polyhedron (Olariaga 2020: 83). In this sense, more and more authors speak about autonomies, in plural form. Bodies, lands, energy, communities, data, livelihoods… In short, it is claimed that autonomy is about all the dimensions of life(s). In turn, as those shared lives are situated in concrete ties, autonomy will also have to materialize in these situated interrelations, according to its limits: "A common livable world must be composed, bit by bit, or not at all" (Haraway 2016: 40).

Hence, de-democratization occurs when that socio-political capacity of self-governance is privatized and disabled. On the contrary, democratization may consist in the expansion and equalisation of that capacity.

In the Basque Country we have many examples of vindications of plural and situated autonomies. This is evidenced, for example, by the autonomy ("burujabetza", in Basque) model claimed by the movement *Bizi!*. On the one hand, it is plural, because every dimension that goes through life is taken into account: energy, care, nutrition, body, housing, language, economy, culture… In a polyhedral way, the intention is to articulate and strengthen each other: "We will regain possession of the conditions of our lives according to models adapted to each area of life, which will inspire and reinforce each other" (Bizi 2018: 7). On the other hand, it is territorial, because it is located in the (Northern) Basque Country, and they claim to return to the territories: "It is time to put our feet back on the ground, in the territories of which we are a part, to make them live up to the challenges of this very crucial period, by regenerating the links which have been damaged" (Bizi 2018: 9). Thus, within, through and against these links, the goal is to build a sovereign, sustainable and solidary territory and "to take possession of living conditions again" (Bizi 2018: 1).

13.5 Conclusions

We can therefore draw three main conclusions.

1. The subject and autonomy are, rather than foundational premises, open-ended and differential productions of many works and processes. Immersed in social and ecological assemblages, the subject should be understood "in common".
2. As subjects-in-common, the question is not to have links or not, but what kind of links, as we have repeatedly defended. We will have to liberate ourselves within the links, by making those links more liberating. This is a creative tension.
3. This requires redefining autonomy. It is no longer a pre-social property. On the contrary, it must be understood as a process of capacitation developed within, through, and against social relationships. Specifically, understood in these terms, in the socio-political sense, autonomy is the situated and plural capacity to self-govern our lives.

That is the challenge: the expansion and equalisation of that capacity. That is, to take possession of oneself in the dispossession. To make our lives, which are shared and not ours, ours.

Acknowledgements The authors acknowledge IAS-Research group funding IT1668-22, from Basque Government, and grants PID2023-147251NB-I00 and PID2019-104576GB-I00 for projects Outonomy and OUTAGENCIES, funded by MCIN/AEI/10.13039/501100011033. Mikel Urdangarin acknowledges the grant and funding by the Joxe Azurmendi Katedra, EHU.

References

Barad K (2007) 'Getting real: techno scientific practices and the materialization of reality. In: Karen barad: meeting the universe halfway: quantum physics and the entanglement of matter and meaning. Duke University Press, London, pp 189–222

Barandiaran XE, Etxeberria A (2025) Outonomy, the very idea. In: Barandiaran XE, Etxeberria A (eds) Outonomy: fleshing out the concept of autonomy beyond the individual. Springer.

BIZI (2018) Burujabe: Gure bizi baldintzak berreskuratuz (https://bizimugi.eu/wp-content/uploads/2018/10/WEBburujabeEU.pdf)

Butler J (2004a) Precarious life: the powers of mourning and violence. Verso Books, Londres

Butler J (2004b) Undoing gender. Routledge, London and New York

Butler J (2005) Giving an account of oneself. Fordham University Press, New York

Cabello V, Merlo A, Mancilla M, Siqueiros J, Barandiaran XE (2026) Autonomy and its limits in social-ecological systems. In: Barandiaran XE, Etxeberria A (eds) Outonomy: fleshing out autonomy beyond the individual (p. in press). Springer.

Garcés M (2013) Un mundo común, Bartzelona, Bellaterra

Gil SL (2014) Ontología de la precaridad en Judith Butler. Repensar la vida en común. Éndoxa. Series Filosóficas 34:287–302

Goikoetxea J (2017) Demokraziaren pribatizazioa. Kapitalismo Globala, Europa eta Euskal Lurraldeak, Donostia, Elkar

Goikoetxea J(2020) 'Subiranotasuna ez da gauza bat, erlazio mota bat da', Jakin.eus 2020–03–13 (www.jakin.eus/albisteak/jule-goikoetxea-mentxaka-subiranotasuna-ez-da-gauza-bat-erlazio-mota-bat-da/357)

Haraway DJ (1991) Simians, cyborgs, and women. The reinvention of nature. Routledge, London

Haraway DJ (2003) The companion species manifesto. Dogs, people, and significant otherness. Prickly Paradigm Press, Chicago

Haraway DJ (2016) Staying with the trouble. Making Kin in the Chthulucene. Duke University Press, Durham

Llaguno T (2018) Feminismo del 99%: haciendo política, construyendo subjetividad. In: VV.AA. (2018) Un feminismo del 99%, Madrid: Lengua de Trapo, pp 54–82

Locke J (1690 [1980]) Second treatise of government. Hackett Publishing Company, Indianapolis

Macpherson CB (1962) The political theory of possessive individualism: Hobbes to Locke. Oxford University Press, Oxford

Mill JS (2004): (1859 [2001]) On liberty, Kitchener, Batoche Books. https://socialsciences.mcmaster.ca/econ/ugcm/3ll3/mill/liberty.pdf

Olariaga A (2020) Euskal matxinada. Genealogia eta egungo eztabaidak, Tafalla, Txalaparta

Pateman C (1988) The sexual contract. Stanford University Press, California. http://www.feministes-radicales.org/wp-content/uploads/2012/04/Carole-Pateman-The-Sexual-Contract.pdf

Chapter 14
Mindshaping and Adaptive Preferences

Michelle L. Maiese

Abstract Agents with adaptive preferences participate readily in oppressive social practices, even when doing so is in tension with their broader interests or overall well-being. To make sense of the way in which social influences sometimes undermine agency, I look to enactivist notions of embodied habit and mindshaping. Adaptive preferences should be understood as habit bundles that result from covert social influences, become rigidly engrained, and signify a localized autonomy deficit.

Keywords Adaptivity · Enactivism · Habits · Socialization

14.1 Introduction

By way of socialization and enculturation, agents are deeply molded by their social environment, often without even being self-reflectively aware of it. One phenomenon that reveals the potentially pernicious impact of socially-inculcated values and attitudes is adaptive preferences (AP's) (Elster 1982); social and political philosophers have used this term to highlight instances in which members of marginalized groups come to desire "that which is oppressive to them" (Cudd 2006, 181) because satisfying such desires confers social advantages. To make sense of how social influences can undermine autonomous agency, I look to enactivist notions of embodied habit and mindshaping. By way of social coordination, habit formation, and the embodied internalization of norms and expectations, agents are mindshaped by their environment. Such mindshaping can be primarily enabling or destructive, depending on the nature of the habits it cultivates. Because agents are embedded in a social environment, they are vulnerable to being molded in pernicious ways. AP's can be understood as habit bundles that form in response to dominant practices, help agents adapt to their social surroundings, and yet also prove to be harmful. To make sense of such harms, I propose that AP's encompass embodied habits that (1) result from necessarily covert social influences, (2) are in tension with an agent's broader network of

M. L. Maiese (✉)
Emmanuel College, Boston, MA, USA
e-mail: maiesemi@emmanuel.edu

X. E. Barandiaran and A. Etxeberria (eds.), *Outonomy*,
SpringerBriefs in Philosophy, https://doi.org/10.1007/978-3-032-05501-9_14

interests, intentions, and values, and (3) have become rigidly engrained. Conceptualizing APs in enactivist terms helps to naturalize these disruptions to agency and also reveals autonomy's important relational dimension.

14.2 Adaptive Preferences as Localized Autonomy Deficits

Feminist philosophers have argued that in a world where some expectations and norms support unjust and inegalitarian social systems, someone's social surroundings "can effectively socialize [them] to prefer conditions or options that are bad for [them]" (Terlazzo 2016 206). Consider, for example, a woman who wants to undergo breast augmentation to make herself more attractive, or a man who refuses to seek treatment for depression because he takes this to be in tension with masculinity. The concept of adaptive preference (AP) has value because it does "political work": it allows philosophers to oppose the claim that "women's enjoyment of sexist practices makes such practices morally and politically unproblematic" (Khader 2012, 303).

While theorists tend to agree that people's preferences can be molded in pernicious ways, they disagree about (a) whether these preferences signify an autonomy deficit, and (b) whether use of the concept of 'adaptive preference' will result in disrespectful modes of treatment. If those who perpetuate their own oppression are viewed as irrational or cast as "dupes of patriarchy" (Khader 2012, 302), will this legitimize paternalistic intervention or coercion? Terlazzo (2016) proposes that "rather than choosing between using the concept of adaptive preferences and showing persons respect, we should aim to do both" (210). Although the concept can function as a valuable tool for combatting marginalization, by explaining which preferences deserve to be scrutinized, it also is important to exhibit appropriate consideration for people's agency.

An adequate account of AP's needs to explain what makes them simultaneously both "adaptive" and detrimental to a person's well-being. Feminist philosophers have noted that on the one hand, these preferences are beneficial in the sense that they help people to survive, whether emotionally or physically, in circumstances that are beyond their control (Bruckner 2009). On the other hand, they often involve disruptions to autonomous agency and result in behavior that is in tension with an agent's broader interests. However, because it is doubtful whether any human agent can exercise this capacity fully in every domain of their lives and at every moment, it would be a mistake to view autonomy as an "all-or-nothing property" of a person's whole life (Christman 1991, 3). Instead, we should distinguish between (i) possessing a general capacity for autonomy, and (ii) being able to exercise it fully at a particular time. AP's signify a *local* disruption to agency rather than a *global* disruption in the capacity to exercise autonomy.

Casting AP's as localized autonomy deficits "allows that people can perpetuate their oppression and retain critical attitudes toward some norms" (Khader 2012, 308). Because individuals in oppressive contexts often retain a normative perspective and find ways to actively bargain with their situation, it is problematic to view them simply as "victims" of oppression. To show "recognition respect" to such agents requires that we give proper weight to the fact that they are *persons*, i.e., that they are capable of some degree of self-governance (Darwall 1977, 45). Paternalistic modes of intervention (for example, forbidding women from acting on their desire to veil in public or bind their feet) would constitute a failure to respect their autonomy. Can concepts drawn from enactivism shed light on APs?

14.3 Enactivism, Habits, and Mindshaping

Enactivism emphasizes that cognition is fundamentally relational, environmentally situated, and bound up with the dynamics of living systems (Weber & Varela 2002). To regulate themselves and respond selectively to their surroundings, living organisms do not passively form an internal representation of things in a pre-given world, but instead actively "bring forth" (i.e., enact) a unique cognitive domain. By way of "sense-making" (Thompson 2007), they gauge what counts as a useful resource (or a threat), depending on their bodily structure, needs, and where and how they are situated. Among humans, worldly engagements take on an especially sophisticated form; agents pursue goals, execute coordinated movement sequences, and display selective attunement to their surroundings. Over the course of continuous engagement with their environment, they begin to exhibit recurring patterns of bodily expressivity and response (Di Paolo et al. 2017).

Although a focus on computations and information processing has become central to much contemporary research in philosophy of mind and cognitive science, Egbert and Barandiaran (2014) turn our attention to the way in which the mind is "made out of *habits*, and by *habit*" (2). Continuous interaction with the environment allows for the formation of autonomous sensorimotor structures that allow agents to navigate their world and act intelligently. As more and more sets of coordinated movement patterns develop and become part of an agent's repertoire, habits begin to overlap and become integrated, so that they mutually stabilize and form a bundle. Habit bundles that an agent reliably enacts to perform various tasks include customary ways of moving, speaking, handling artifacts, and interacting with others. Some habit bundles are enacted explicitly and repeatedly, for the sake of achieving various goals, and then refined via practice and feedback. Everyday examples of highly coordinated, skillful activity include dancing, playing a sport, and using tools and technology. These habitual modes of engagement are self-sustaining, yet also *precarious*. Repeated enactments of a movement sequence reinforce a particular configuration of brain and bodily dynamics: "the more frequently a pattern of behavior… is performed, the more likely it will be repeated in the future" (Egbert and Barandiaran 2014, 3). Conversely, the muscular dispositions and neural connectivity patterns that support habits bundles destabilize if not exercised frequently enough.

In addition to habitual movement patterns, human agents develop coordinated patterns of attention. Just as sensorimotor patterns are reinforced through repetition, what subjects focus on is modulated by what they have paid attention to in the past. Habits of mind encompass schemas for interacting with and interpreting one's surroundings, and include, for example, a tendency to notice some considerations while ignoring others. These habits arise in conjunction with habitual movement patterns, via the development and self-maintenance of neurobiological configurations and built-up patterns of bodily attunement. Some habit bundles usually are followed temporally by others, other sets can be enacted in parallel, and some interfere with or are in tension with one another. The exercise of one set of habits reinforces or inhibits other patterns of behavior and attention, and this interdependence makes them richer in potentiality. Habits also undergird an agent's enduring concerns and reflect *what they care about*. For example, if an agent has developed habits of wearing makeup, reading beauty magazines, and monitoring their weight, this indicates that they care about their physical appearance.

The notion of habit serves as a possible bridge between an enactivist conception of biological autonomy and discussions of autonomous agency found in moral philosophy. First, living organisms are autonomous in a basic biological sense: they regulate their coupling with their environment according to norms of adaptivity, to ensure their continued existence and well-being (Di Paolo 2005, 443). Second, at a higher level of organization, *sensorimotor autonomy* involves the formation of dynamic neurobiological and sensorimotor patterns. These dynamically configured stable patterns simultaneously allow for both stability and control, as well as flexibility and *reasons-responsiveness*. On the one hand, habits constitute built-up patterns of engagement that are readily available for use. Because they integrate past experiences, they give agents the skillful know-how to carry out a wide range of tasks. On the other hand, the flexibility of habit allows agents to adjust their behavior in response to changing circumstances. Rather than being a mere triggered response to stimuli, action is *guided* and *selectively targeted*. Thus, adaptive habits are *metastable* and involve a kind of "plastic equilibrium" (Barandiaran & Di Paolo 2014, 5) that prevents them from operating as "unchangeable automatisms" (Di Paolo et al. 2017, 102).

For human agents, adaptive self-regulation goes beyond mere survival and biological self-maintenance and involves *adapting* and *faring well* in a specific sociocultural context. Enactivists rightly emphasize that habit formation is socially embedded and guided by shared normative practices. Just as biological processes of self-maintenance depend on energetic resources, the formation and maintenance of habits depends on social resources. As children engage with specific aspects of their sociocultural environment, their performance is subject to normative assessment as better or worse, and as more or less correct, given situational demands and sociocultural norms. As a child attempts to name various colors, for example, she receives feedback and thereby acquires a "feel" for which uses are acceptable. As she plays with toys, she learns what sort of play, with which sorts of toys, is appropriate in her specific society.

Shared cultural practices continue to shape meaning-making throughout adulthood, by "prescribing and normalizing certain modes of experience and action while proscribing (and perhaps pathologizing) certain others" (Kirmayer and Ramstead 2017). Rather than relying on explicit rules to tell them what to do, agents adapt continuously to the people around them and let situational and contextual demands constrain their behavior. Along these lines, Haslanger (2019) maintains that "those who have internalized the cultural techne of their context develop dispositions to participate in the practices fluently and to correct those who don't" (19). Dominant practices encompass a set of prevailing attitudes and beliefs that function as tools for social regulation. Related social norms and expectations modulate how agents behave at parties, how they speak to their colleagues, and even how they walk down the street. As agents learn how to use tools and other resources, neurobiological configurations and behavioral patterns form and take root. This allows them to display a rich and recognizable array of mental states that are "suitably tailored to the kind of agency [they] are expected or permitted to develop in [their] given cultural milieu" (McGeer 2019, 52).

The notion of habit helps to make sense of the way in which sociocultural influences are internalized and anchored in patterns of engagement, so that agents' living bodies become "socially saturated." Insofar as these influences mold agents' habits of behavior and attention and coordinate their shared activity with others, they become part of their lives in a quite literal sense, by modifying their neurobiological dynamics and patterns of bodily attunement. Human agents are thereby *mindshaped:* their sense-making processes and embodied habits are *partially determined*, or *shaped*, by the social world.

How does this occur? Enactivists emphasize that bodily coordination is central to human sociality. De Jaegher and Di Paolo (2007) characterize "coordination" as the non-accidental correlation between two or more coupled systems, so that their behavior matches to a degree far beyond what is expected given what those systems can do. Once two or more interactors are part of a coupled system, their expressions, behaviors, and bodily dynamics modulate those of the other person(s); their habits and expressions begin to resonate. Instances of mutual coordination include synchronization, mirroring, and anticipation. This reciprocal bodily attunement begins in infancy and grows more complex over time as agents develop a range of projects that require them to communicate and cooperate with others. Because humans are essentially social creatures who yearn for acceptance and connection, it's inevitable that social norms and cultural expectations will have a significant impact on their ongoing habit formation.

14.4 An Enactivist Account of Adaptive Preferences

Mindshaping often is constructive and enabling insofar as it helps individuals to develop the habits and skills associated with various socially defined activities. Because they can reliably expect that others will respond to, complement, or complete their own actions in particular ways, agents can engage in various forms of joint activity. Social settings such as families and workplaces, for example, offer forms of social coordination that agents are highly motivated to engage in and which prove to be highly valuable (Haslanger 2019, 6). The fact that agents are mindshaped by various socio-normative practices enables them to be part of a community and develop various skills. Thus, the notion of mindshaping helps to make sense of autonomy's integral relational dimension: we are not self-made, self-sufficient beings who exist separately from others, nor should we aspire to such independence (See Urdangarin & Umerez, this volume). Social relations frequently provide crucial scaffolding for autonomous agency. Acknowledging the potential benefits of mindshaping helps us to conceptualize, in enactive terms, the sense in which AP's are *adaptive.* At a basic biological level, adaptivity concerns survival and self-maintenance. But at a higher level of organization, adaptivity is defined partly in relation to normative constraints that are underdetermined by biology, and which derive from the sociocultural environment (See Virenque, this volume). People comply with dominant practices because there is a sense in which it contributes to their human flourishing, as members of a culture. Some modes of engagement are adaptive insofar as they enable the individual to gain status and social recognition, and some are maladaptive insofar as they involve heavy penalties or social disapproval. Thus, one central reason why AP's are "adaptive" is that they allow an agent to behave in ways that others understand, approve of, and find meaningful.

However, habits formed in the context of oppressive social practices also can cause significant harm. In cases of destructive mindshaping, harmful social influences modulate cognition, affectivity, and agency in ways that run counter to a person's broader interests. Once associated habits become internalized and anchored in the body, they may go unquestioned. Consider, for example, how "women are induced to wear high heels by a system that defines high heels as attractive and that prompts women themselves to find these shoes attractive" (Walsh 2015, 834). AP's then can be understood as habit bundles that encompass customary behavioral patterns and a particular orientation toward the surrounding world. The habits that comprise harmful APs form largely due to overdetermining social influences, ones which (a) necessarily operate covertly, and (b) significantly undermine plasticity and flexible agency.

First, social influences are over-determining in the sense that they operate covertly, without the agent being self-reflectively aware of their impact. Following Colburn (2011), I understand covert social influences to be ones whose impact on an agent's behavior or attention is *necessarily hidden* from her. That is, the social influence must remain hidden, outside of an agent's conscious awareness, for it to exert its effect. If someone is brainwashed into following the rules of a cult, for example, there is something about which they cannot know that explains their behavior. It is precisely because this agent remains unaware of the impact of these social influences, and unable to critique them, that resulting habits have such as strong grip on their behavior. In cases of AP, the "brainwashing" typically is subtler; the agent may be vaguely aware that their preferences have been molded by social forces yet remain unaware of the extent to which associated habits have been shaped by dominant norms. This lack of insight increases their tendency to comply with, or even become invested in, oppressive practices.

However, since agents often are unaware of the full extent to which they have been molded by social forces, covert influence is not yet sufficient. In addition, to qualify as overdetermining, social influences must contribute to the formation of habits that are overly rigid. Such habits undermine autonomous agency insofar as they pose a threat to flexibility: agents may become "stuck" in patterns of behavior and attention and inadequately responsive to relevant considerations and situational contingencies. Rigidly engrained behavior patterns may very well overrule or inhibit other situationally relevant actions; likewise, ossified habits of mind may render subjects oblivious to relevant considerations and closed off to alternative ways of viewing things. For example, suppose that socially-inculcated habits associated with conforming to prevailing beauty norms begin to operate somewhat mechanically, outside of reflective awareness. In such cases, the feedback loops between the individual and the social world are quite lopsided, and there is little in the way of active contribution or experimentation. "Scripts" and their associated habits are enacted unthinkingly, and socialization functions more like indoctrination.

These rigid habits pose a threat to well-being partly because they interfere with the enactment of other habit bundles and goal-oriented pursuits that are important to the agent. Consider, for example, a woman who feels they "must" wear high-heeled shoes, even when this interferes with other important goals and interests (e.g., playing with their toddler). Likewise, someone who "prefers" to comply with dominant beauty practices may devote lots of time, energy, and money to this project, leaving them with less resources to enact more fulfilling habits. And a man who "prefers" to exhibit stoicism and habitually suppresses their emotional experiences may find it difficult to enact habit bundles associated with a caretaking role (e.g., being an attentive father). Furthermore, because the habits of behavior and attention that comprise AP's have become "second nature" and begun to operate as a matter of common sense, agents may enact them even in cases where it is evidently inappropriate or harmful to do so.

However, my proposed account also can acknowledge that even when agents exhibit these localized disruptions to autonomy, their general capacity for autonomous agency remains intact. Embodied-enactive principles emphasize that human agents are not passive subjects; although they are shaped by the social world, they also can influence their social environment via their contributions and responses. As autonomous agents, they have some power to resist dominant social practices and develop counter-cultural habits. And when individuals succeed in altering their habits of behavior and attention, this can have a salient rippling effect on other agents and potentially pave the way for the formation of new cultural practices. Consider how belonging to a feminist consciousness-raising group can strengthen agents' ability to reflect on social norms and develop skills for resisting harmful social practices. Such group activity can be understood as an instance of socially scaffolded engagement that strengthens participants' ability to exercise autonomy. Conversely, when an agent enacts habits associated with oppressive social practices, this increases the likelihood that other people in their social world will behave in similar ways. Thus, the notion of mindshaping helps to conceptualize how oppressed people sometimes perpetuate oppressive practices, by way of compliance with dominant norms.

It's worth noting that some agents enact and maintain the habits associated with AP's more self-reflectively and with a greater degree of autonomy. Indeed, cases in which the agent has scrutinized their preferences but continues to enact associated habits for strategic reasons show that social norms often are not internalized wholesale. Consider, for example, a woman who recognizes that her preference to wear make-up is socially inculcated and problematic in some respects, yet also recognizes that it brings social rewards. Some oppression-complicit behaviors are rational in the sense that they reveal active bargaining with a set of social constraints; given limited options, agents strive to do the best they can to advance their interests, and in some cases, all available options may involve some sort of harm or penalty. Arguably, this agent exercises a greater degree of autonomy than someone who has not even considered the mindshaping impact of dominant social practices.

14.5 Conclusion

Agents who have been molded by oppressive social influences and practices may form adaptive preferences and find it difficult to scrutinize or resist associated habits. These influences are harmful insofar as they operate covertly, undermine plasticity, and potentially contribute to internal instability. As a result, agents sometimes become "stuck" in specific patterns of engagement and their attunement to relevant options and considerations diminishes. The notion of mindshaping helps to conceptualize how dominant social norms are internalized and anchored in the body, in the form of engrained bodily habits. However, the disruptions to autonomous agency associated with AP's occur not because the agent has been influenced by their social surroundings—for this is always the case—but rather because associated behavior patterns interfere with the enactment of other important habits and make it more difficult for them to engage effectively with their surroundings.

In addition, it is important to recognize that members of oppressed social groups are not only victims, but also agents, and that their individual acts of resistance sometimes contribute to a radical modification of the social world. In many cases, this occurs via more constructive mindshaping: working together, agents investigate their habits and endeavor to reshape them. Enactivism thereby lends support to the relational view of autonomy endorsed by many feminist philosophers.

References

Barandiaran XE, Di Paolo EA (2014) A genealogical map of the concept of habit. Front Hum Neurosci 8:522

Bruckner DW (2009) In defense of adaptive preferences. Philos Stud 142:307–324

Christman J (1991) Autonomy and personal history. Can J Philos 21(1):1–24

Colburn B (2011) Autonomy and adaptive preferences. Utilitas 23(1):52–71

Cudd A (2006) Analyzing oppression. Oxford University Press

Darwall S (1977) Two kinds of respect. Ethics 88(1):36–49

De Jaegher H, Di Paolo E (2007) Participatory sense-making: an enactive approach to social cognition. Phenomenol Cogn Sci 6(4):485–507

Di Paolo E (2005) Autopoiesis, adaptivity, teleology, agency. Phenomenol Cogn Sci 4(4):429–452

Di Paolo E, Buhrmann T, Barandiaran X (2017) Sensorimotor life: an enactive proposal. Oxford University Press

Egbert MD, Barandiaran XE (2014) Modeling habits as self-sustaining patterns of sensorimotor behavior. Front Human Neurosci 8:590

Elster J (1982) Sour grapes: utilitarianism and the genesis of wants. In: Sen A, Williams B (eds) Utilitarianism and beyond. Cambridge University Press, pp 219–238

Haslanger S (2019) Cognition as a social skill. Australasian Philos Rev 3(1):5–25

Khader SJ (2012) Must theorising about adaptive preferences deny women's agency? J Appl Philos 29(4):302–317

Kirmayer L, Ramstead M (2017) Embodiment and enactment in cultural psychiatry. In: Durt C, Fuchs T, Tewes C (eds) Embodiment, enaction, and culture: investigating the constitution of a shared world. MIT Press, Cambridge

McGeer V (2019) Mindshaping is inescapable, social injustice is not: reflections on Haslanger's critical social theory. Australasian Philos Rev 3(1):48–59

Terlazzo R (2016) Conceptualizing adaptive preferences respectfully: an indirectly substantive account. J Polit Philos 24(2):206–226

Thompson E (2007) Mind in life: biology, phenomenology, and the sciences of the mind. Belknap Press, Cambridge

Walsh MB (2015) Feminism, adaptive preferences, and social contract theory. Hypatia 30(4):829–845

Weber A, Varela F (2002) Life after Kant: natural purposes and the autopoietic foundations of biological individuality. Phenomenol Cogn Sci 1(2):97–125

Index

X. E. Barandiaran and A. Etxeberria (eds.), *Outonomy*,
SpringerBriefs in Philosophy, https://doi.org/10.1007/978-3-032-05501-9

MIX
Papier aus verantwortungsvollen Quellen
Paper from responsible sources
FSC® C105338

If you have any concerns about our products,
you can contact us on
ProductSafety@springernature.com

In case Publisher is established outside the EU,
the EU authorized representative is:
Springer Nature Customer Service Center GmbH
Europaplatz 3, 69115 Heidelberg, Germany

Printed by Libri Plureos GmbH
in Hamburg, Germany